冨樫義博

I finally got this volume out. Thank you for waiting. I promise to work hard, in many ways.

Yoshihiro Togashi

Yoshihiro Togashi's manga career began in 1986 at the age of 20, when he won the coveted Osamu Tezuka Award for new manga artists. He debuted in the Japanese **Weekly Shonen Jump** magazine in 1989 with the romantic comedy **Tende Shôwaru Cupid**. From 1990 to 1994 he wrote and drew the hit manga **YuYu Hakusho**, which was followed by the dark comedy science-fiction series **Level E**, and finally this adventure series, **Hunter x Hunter**, available from VIZ Media's SHONEN JUMP Advanced imprint. In 1999 he married the manga artist Naoko Takeuchi.

HUNTER X HUNTER Volume 28
SHONEN JUMP ADVANCED Manga Edition

STORY AND ART BY
YOSHIHIRO TOGASHI

English Adaptation & Translation/Lillian Olsen
Touch-up Art & Lettering/Mark McMurray
Design/Matt Hinrichs
Editor/Shaenon K. Garrity

HUNTERxHUNTER © POT (Yoshihiro Togashi) 2010. All rights reserved. First published in Japan in 2010 by SHUEISHA Inc., Tokyo. English translation rights arranged by SHUEISHA Inc.

The stories, characters and incidents mentioned in this publication are entirely fictional.

No portion of this book may be reproduced or transmitted in any form or by any means without written permission from the copyright holders.

Printed in the U.S.A.

Published by VIZ Media, LLC
P.O. Box 77010
San Francisco, CA 94107

10 9 8 7 6 5 4 3 2
First printing, September 2012
Second printing, August 2015

PARENTAL ADVISORY
HUNTER X HUNTER is rated T+ for Older Teen and is recommended for ages 16 and up. Contains realistic violence and mature language.
ratings.viz.com

RATED T+ FOR OLDER TEEN

www.viz.com

THE WORLD'S MOST CUTTING-EDGE MANGA
SHONEN JUMP ADVANCED
www.shonenjump.com

D MANGA

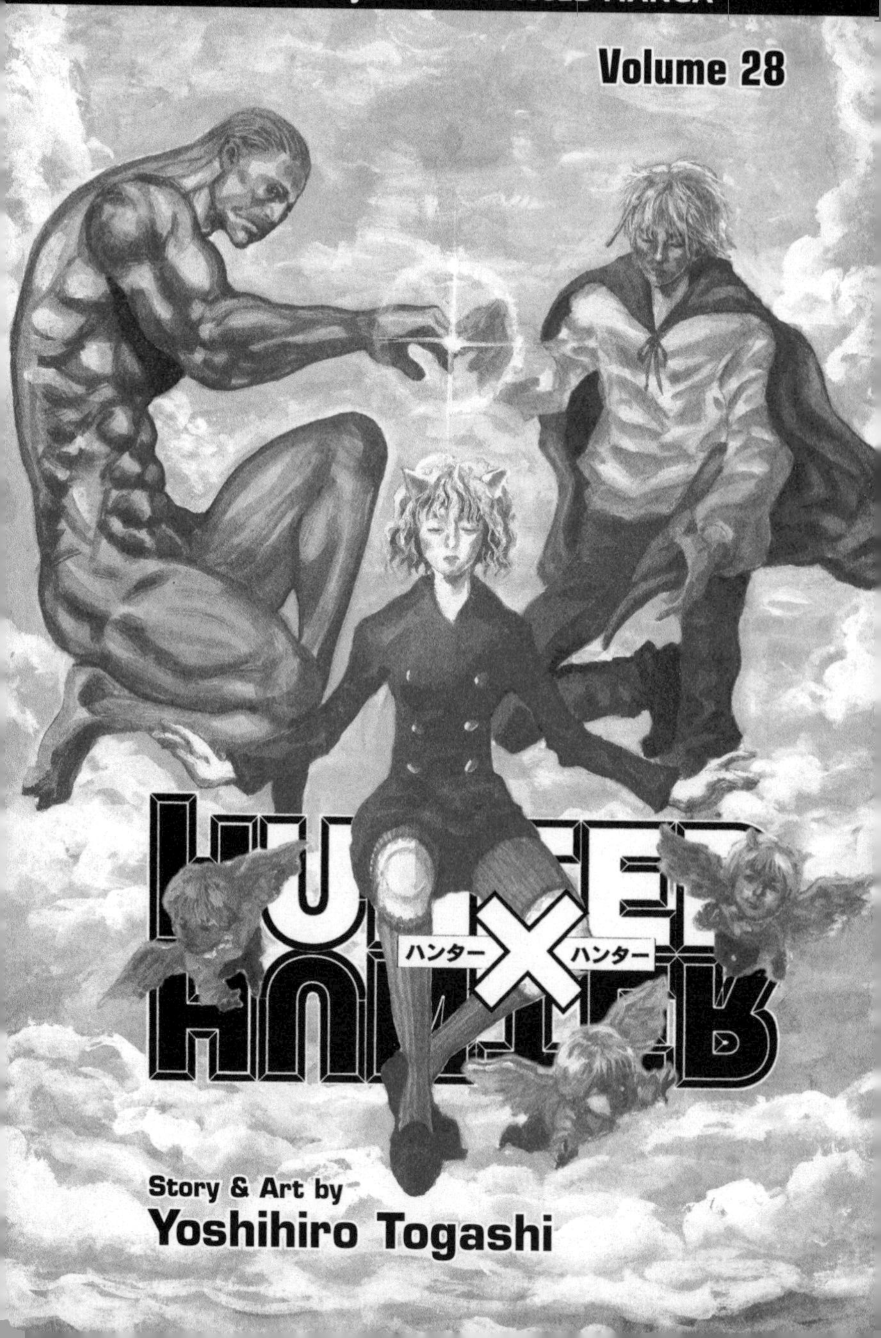

Volume 28
HUNTER ハンター × ハンター HUNTER
Story & Art by
Yoshihiro Togashi

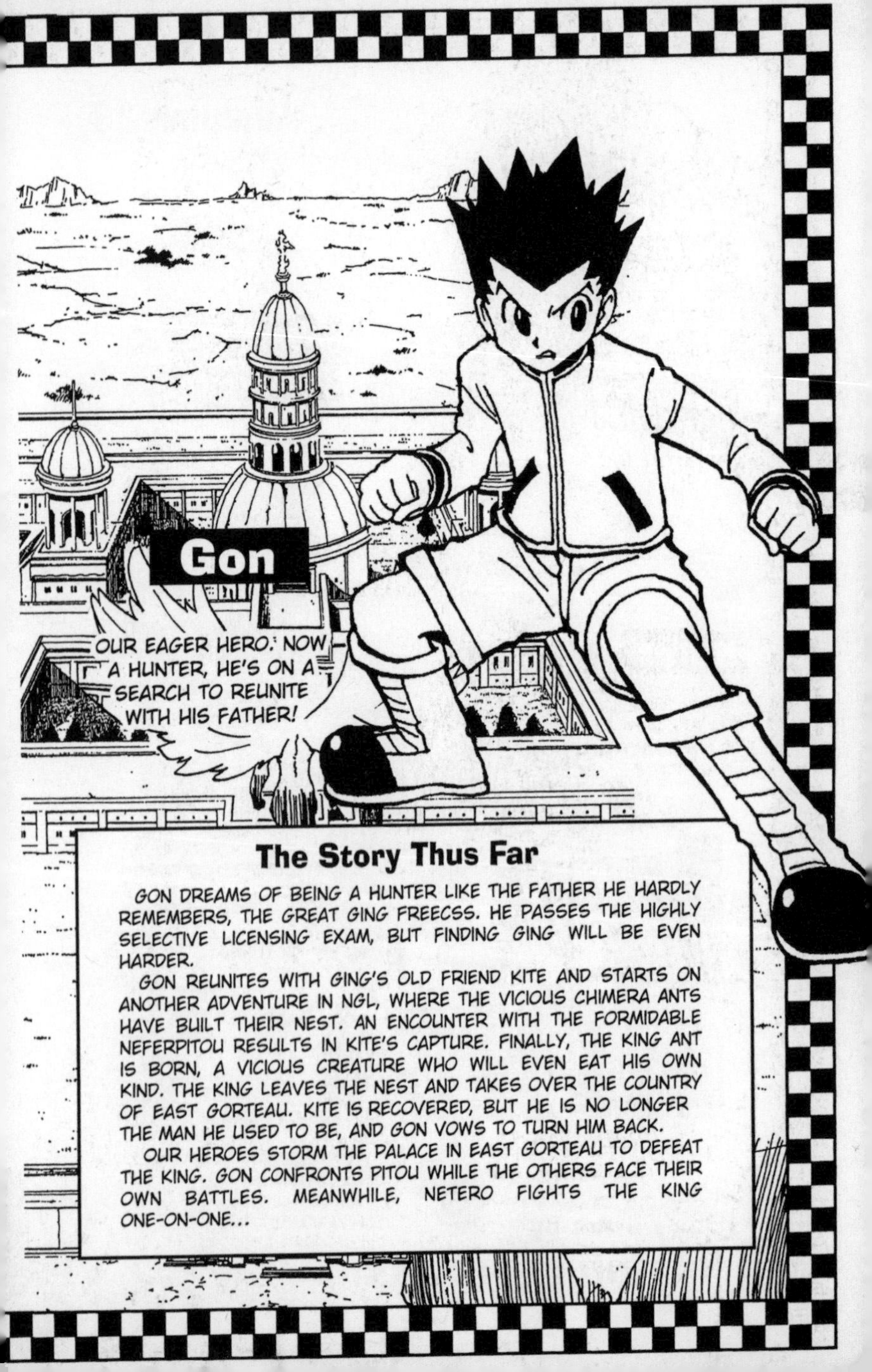
Gon
OUR EAGER HERO: NOW A HUNTER, HE'S ON A SEARCH TO REUNITE WITH HIS FATHER!

The Story Thus Far

GON DREAMS OF BEING A HUNTER LIKE THE FATHER HE HARDLY REMEMBERS, THE GREAT GING FREECSS. HE PASSES THE HIGHLY SELECTIVE LICENSING EXAM, BUT FINDING GING WILL BE EVEN HARDER.

GON REUNITES WITH GING'S OLD FRIEND KITE AND STARTS ON ANOTHER ADVENTURE IN NGL, WHERE THE VICIOUS CHIMERA ANTS HAVE BUILT THEIR NEST. AN ENCOUNTER WITH THE FORMIDABLE NEFERPITOU RESULTS IN KITE'S CAPTURE. FINALLY, THE KING ANT IS BORN, A VICIOUS CREATURE WHO WILL EVEN EAT HIS OWN KIND. THE KING LEAVES THE NEST AND TAKES OVER THE COUNTRY OF EAST GORTEAU. KITE IS RECOVERED, BUT HE IS NO LONGER THE MAN HE USED TO BE, AND GON VOWS TO TURN HIM BACK.

OUR HEROES STORM THE PALACE IN EAST GORTEAU TO DEFEAT THE KING. GON CONFRONTS PITOU WHILE THE OTHERS FACE THEIR OWN BATTLES. MEANWHILE, NETERO FIGHTS THE KING ONE-ON-ONE...

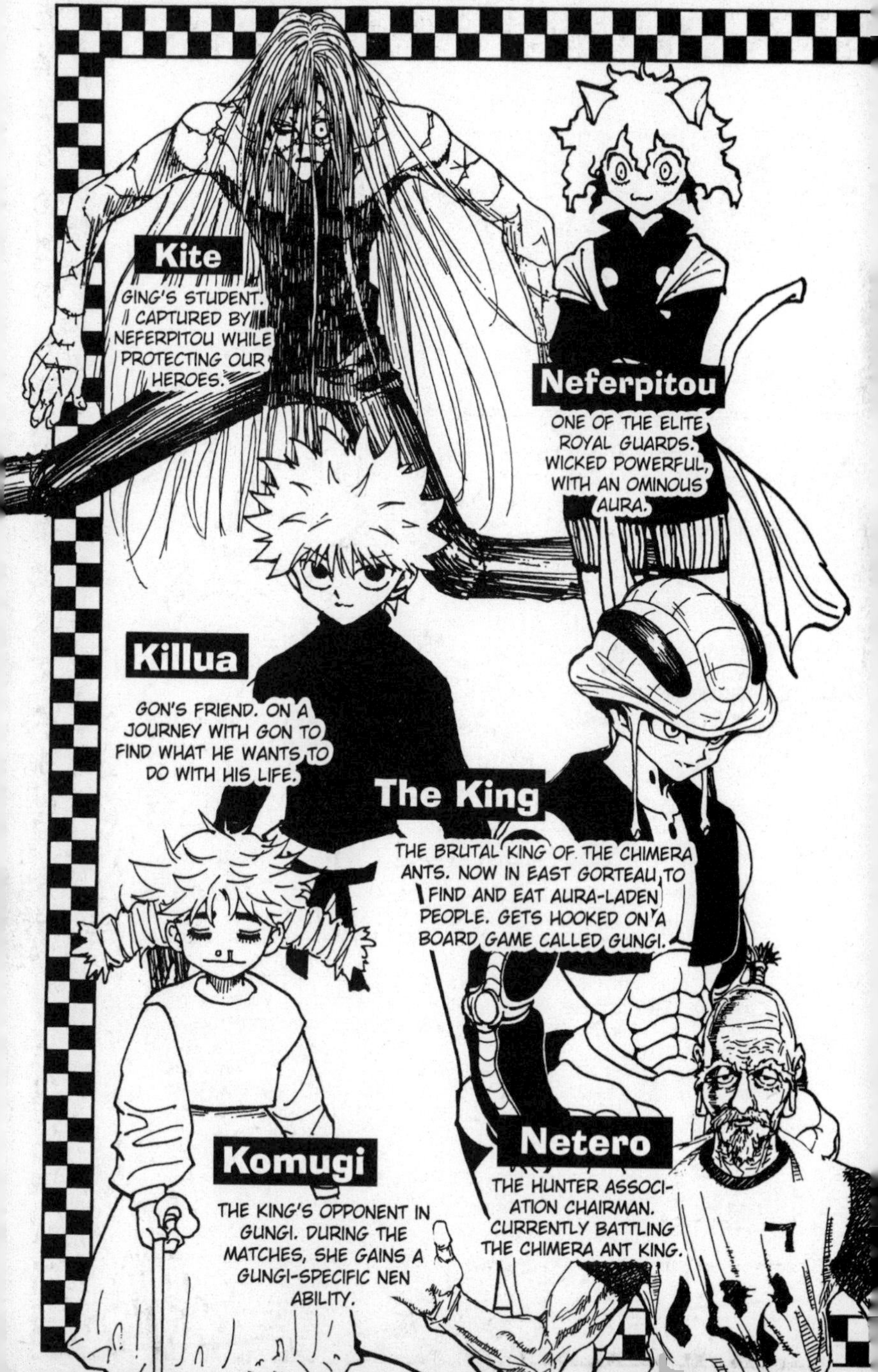
Kite
GING'S STUDENT. CAPTURED BY NEFERPITOU WHILE PROTECTING OUR HEROES.
Neferpitou
ONE OF THE ELITE ROYAL GUARDS. WICKED POWERFUL, WITH AN OMINOUS AURA.
Killua
GON'S FRIEND. ON A JOURNEY WITH GON TO FIND WHAT HE WANTS TO DO WITH HIS LIFE.
The King
THE BRUTAL KING OF THE CHIMERA ANTS. NOW IN EAST GORTEAU TO FIND AND EAT AURA-LADEN PEOPLE. GETS HOOKED ON A BOARD GAME CALLED GUNGI.
Netero
THE HUNTER ASSOCIATION CHAIRMAN. CURRENTLY BATTLING THE CHIMERA ANT KING.
Komugi
THE KING'S OPPONENT IN GUNGI. DURING THE MATCHES, SHE GAINS A GUNGI-SPECIFIC NEN ABILITY.

HUNTER × HUNTER

ハンター ハンター

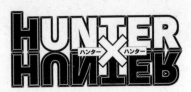

Volume 28

CONTENTS

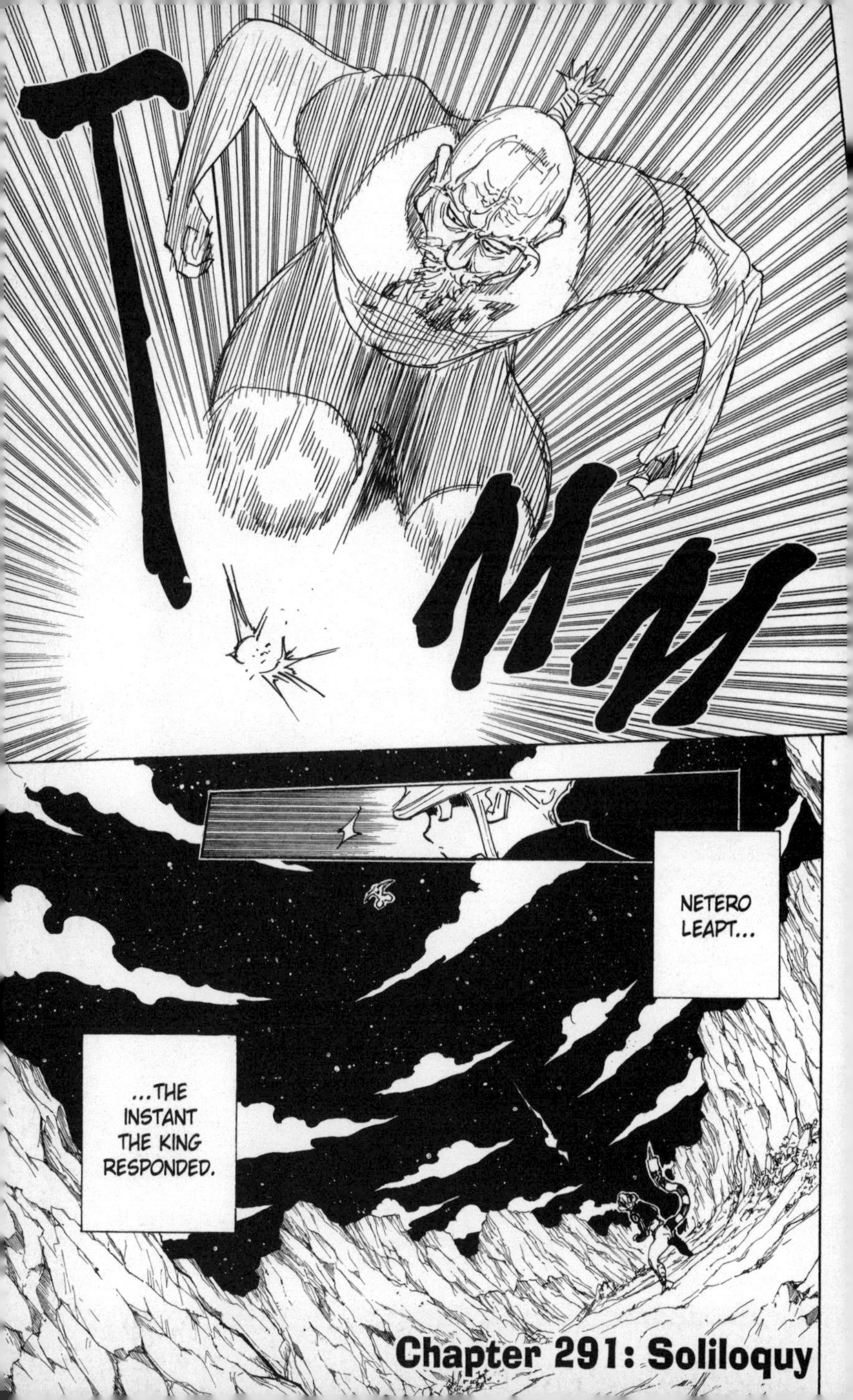
NETERO LEAPT...
...THE INSTANT THE KING RESPONDED.

Chapter 291: Soliloquy

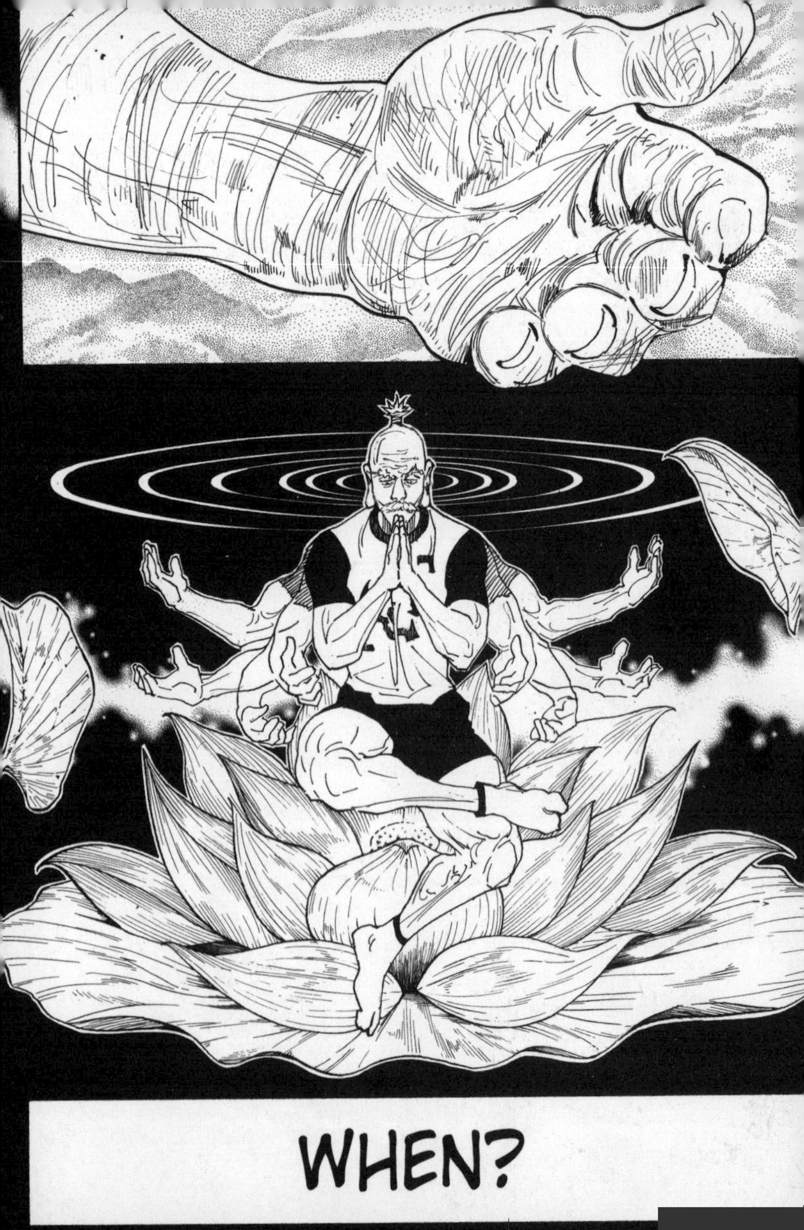
WHEN?

READ THIS WAY

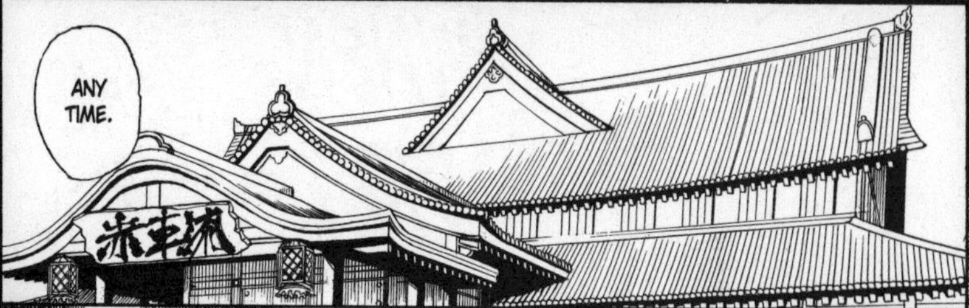
ANY TIME.

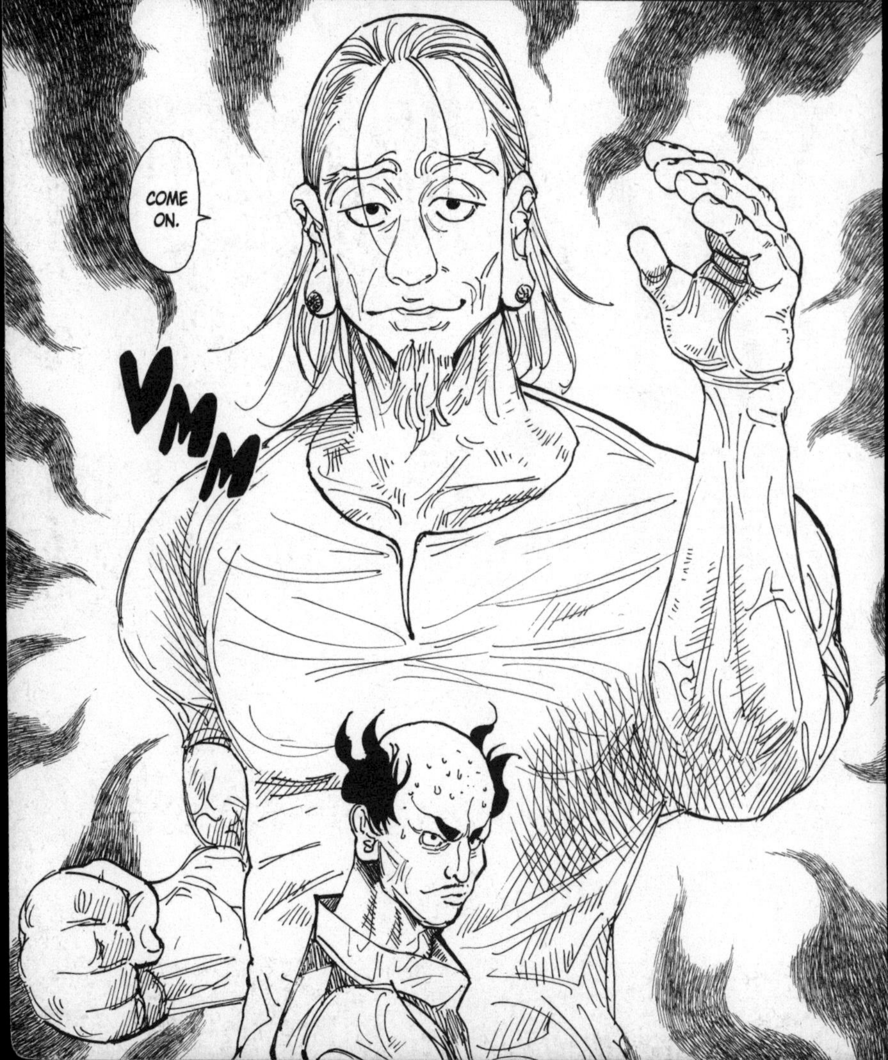
COME ON.
VMM

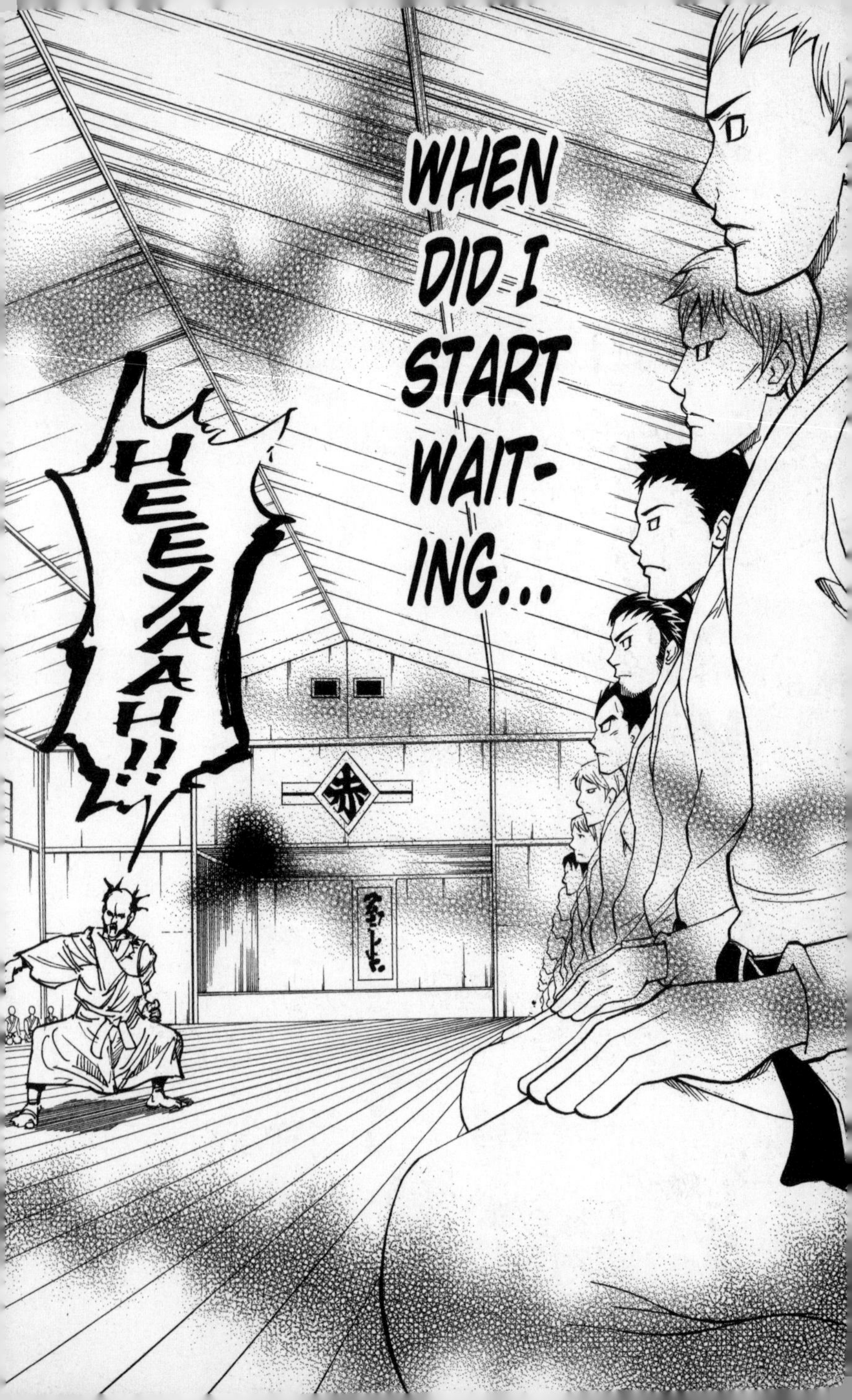
WHEN DID I START WAIT-ING...
HEEYAAH!!

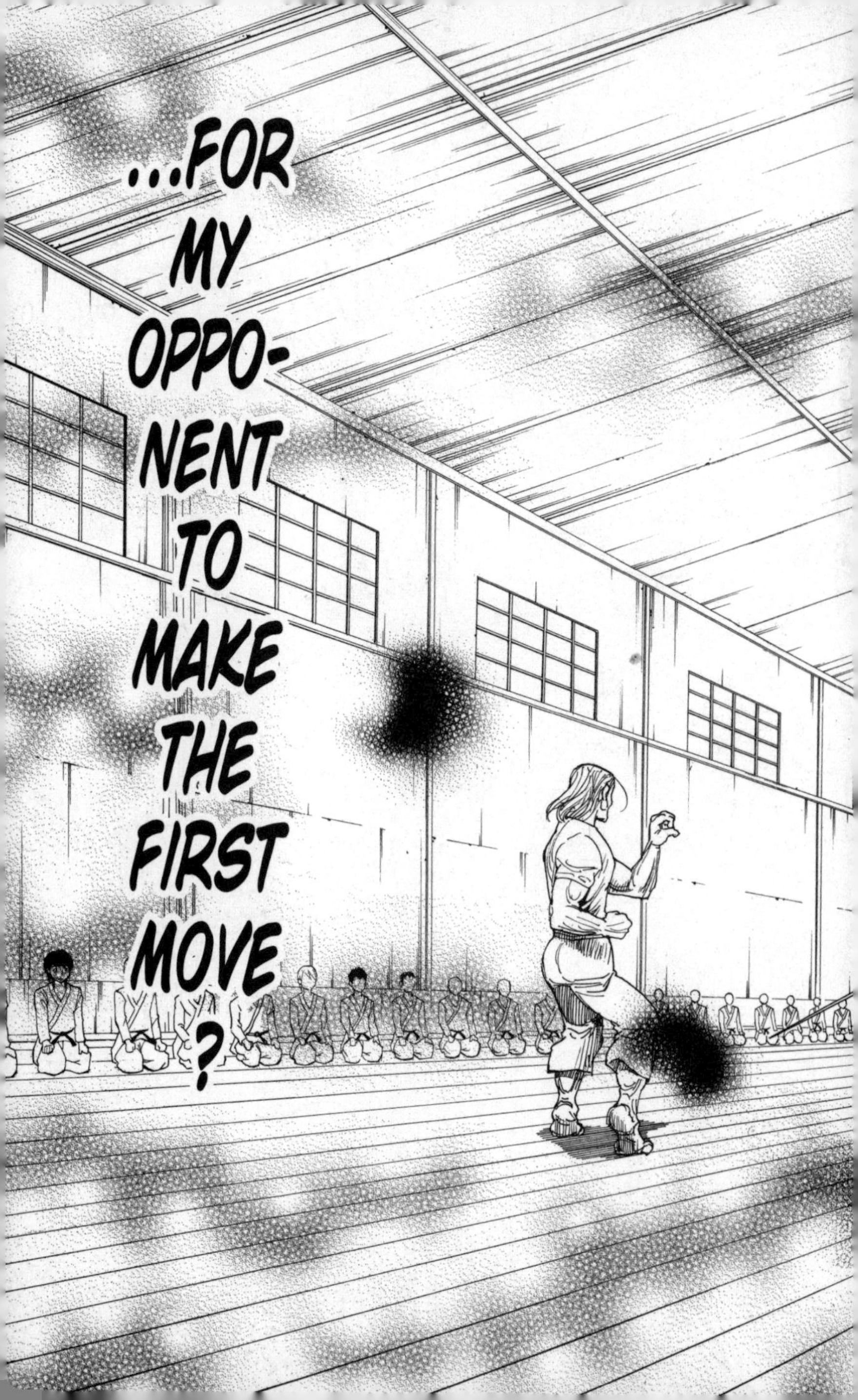
...FOR MY OPPO-NENT TO MAKE THE FIRST MOVE?

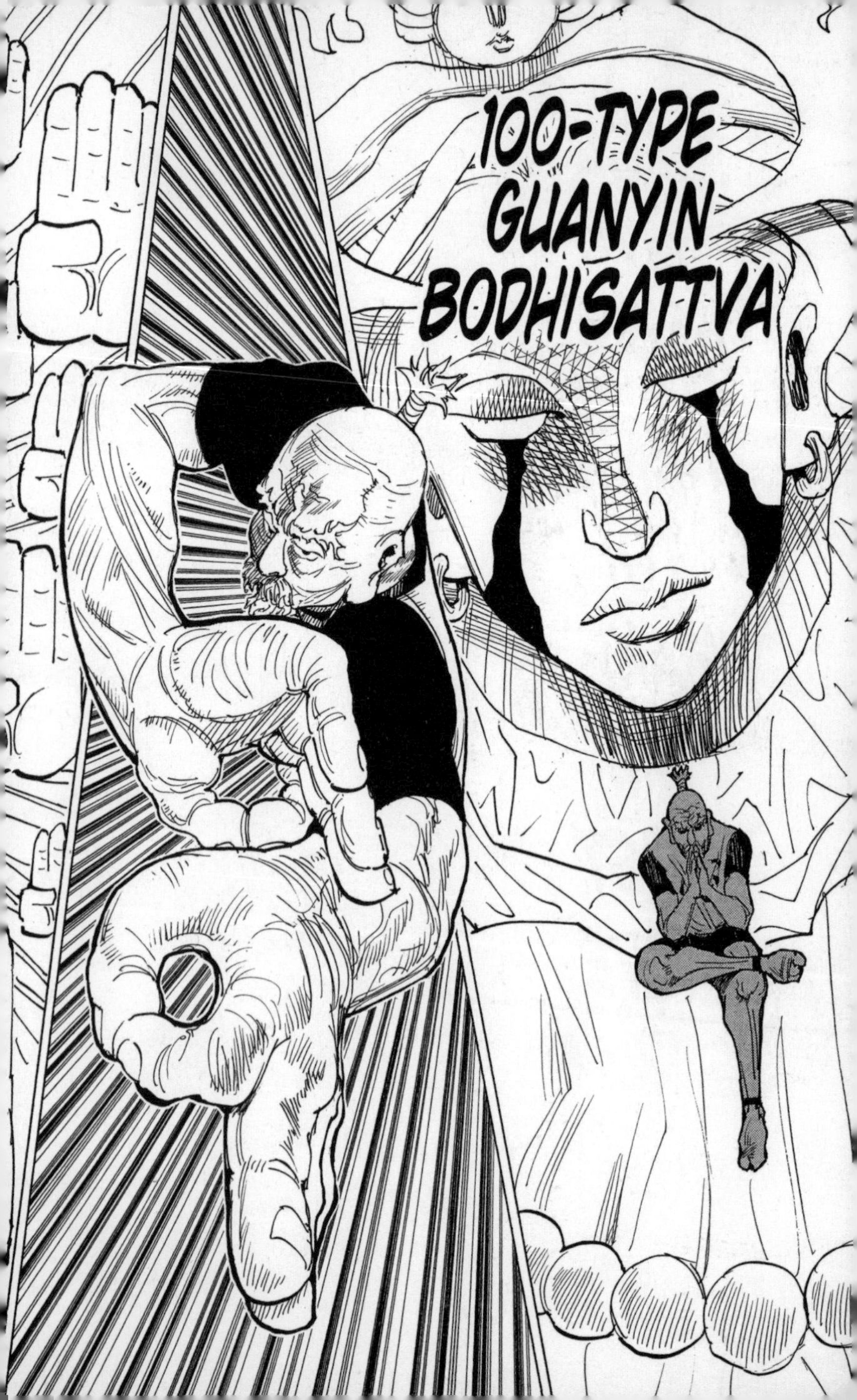
100-TYPE GUANYIN BODHISATTVA

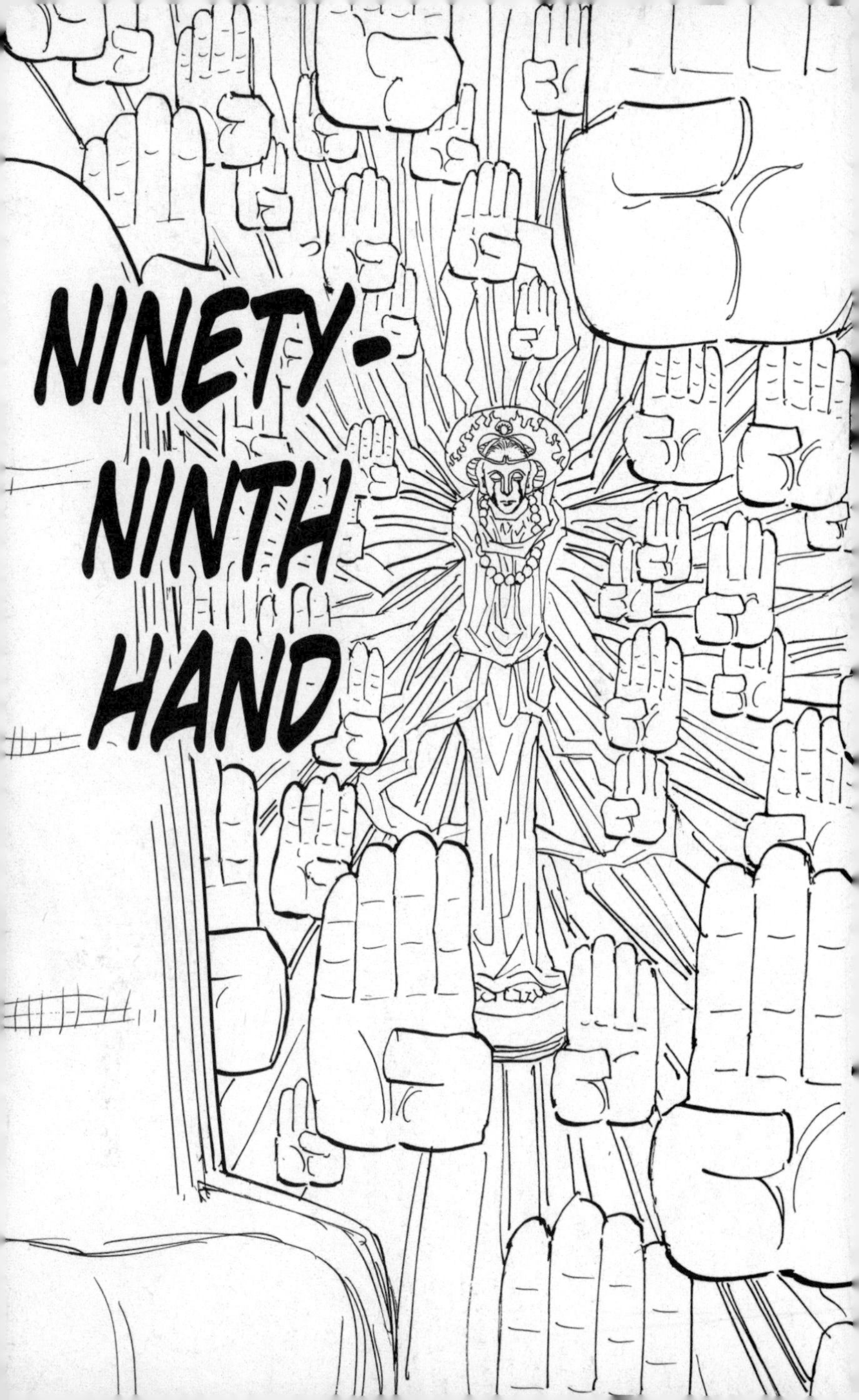
NINETY-
NINTH
HAND

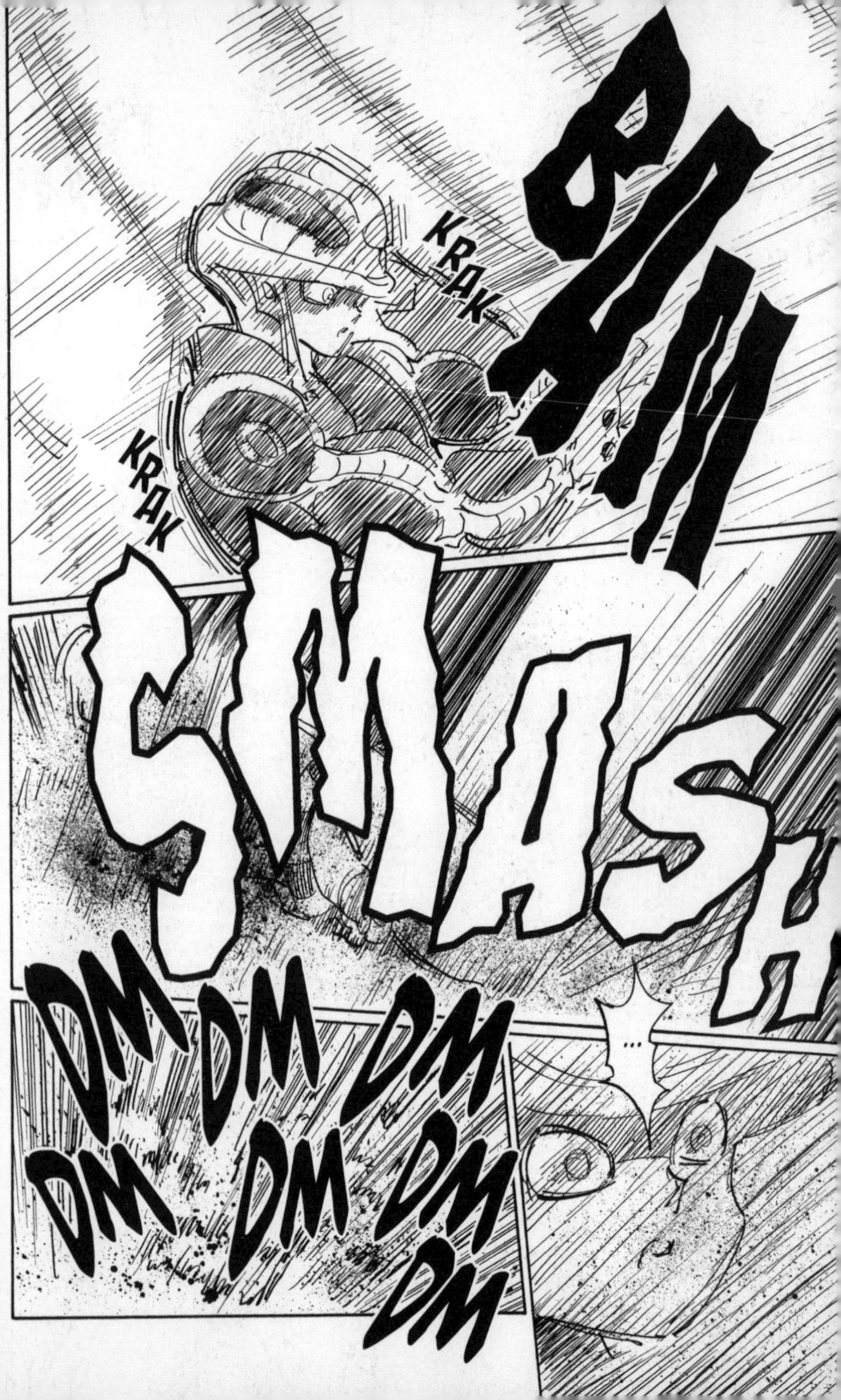
BAM
KRAK
KRAK
SMASH
...
DM DM DM
DM DM DM DM
DM DM DM

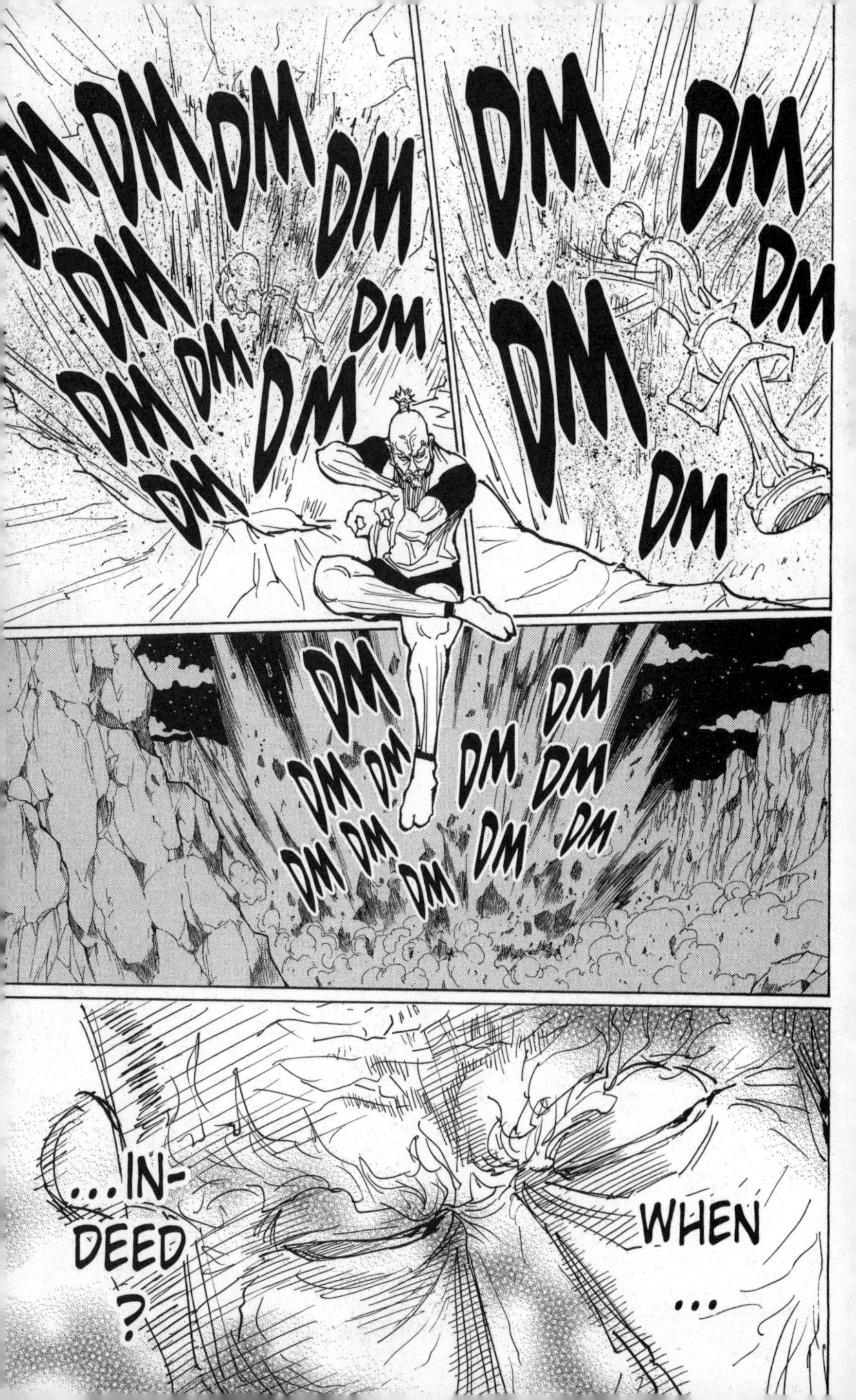
DM DM DM DM DM
DM DM DM DM DM DM DM DM DM DM DM
DM DM DM DM DM DM DM DM DM DM DM DM DM
WHEN...
...IN-DEED?

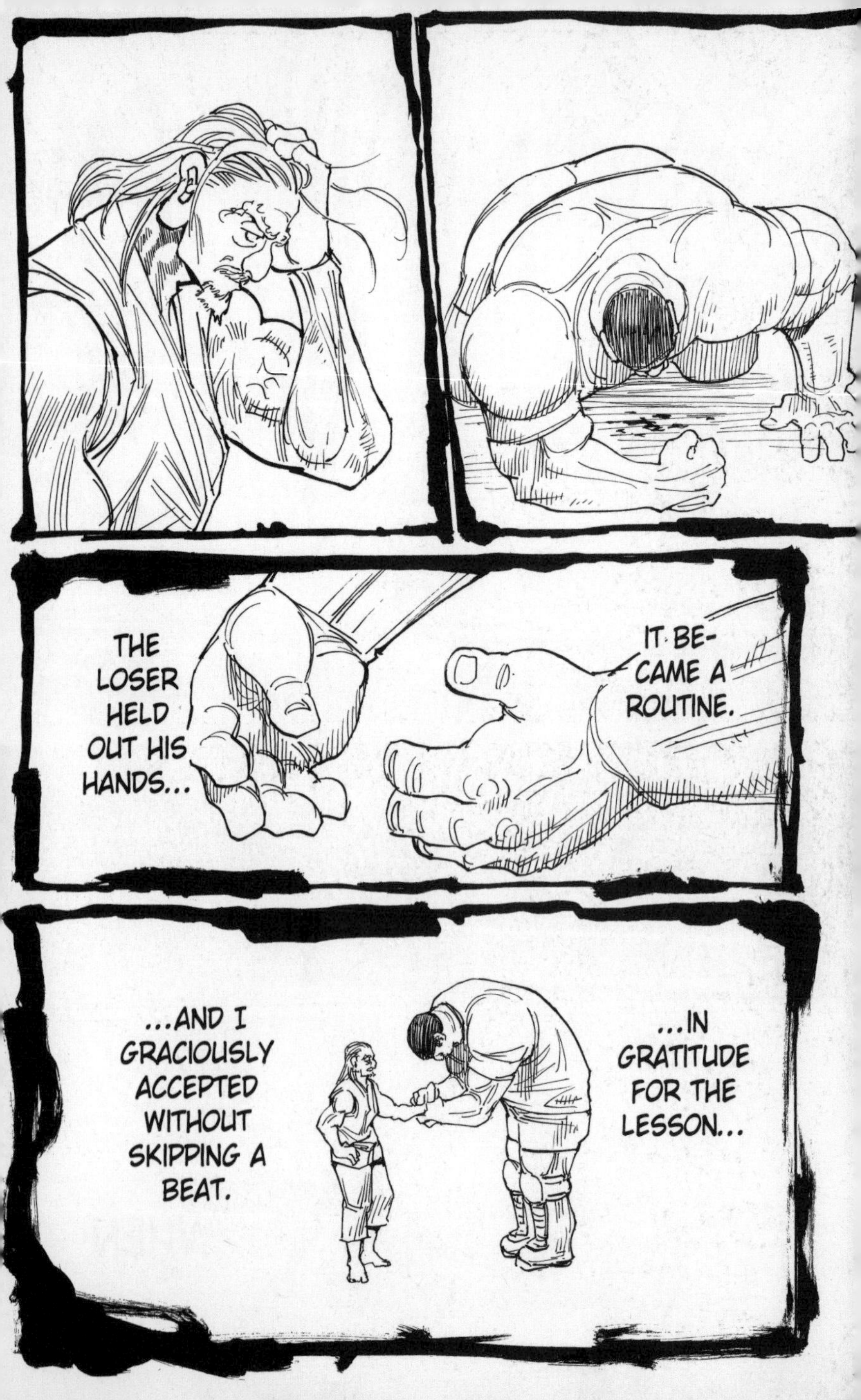
IT BE-CAME A ROUTINE.
THE LOSER HELD OUT HIS HANDS...
...IN GRATITUDE FOR THE LESSON...
...AND I GRACIOUSLY ACCEPTED WITHOUT SKIPPING A BEAT.

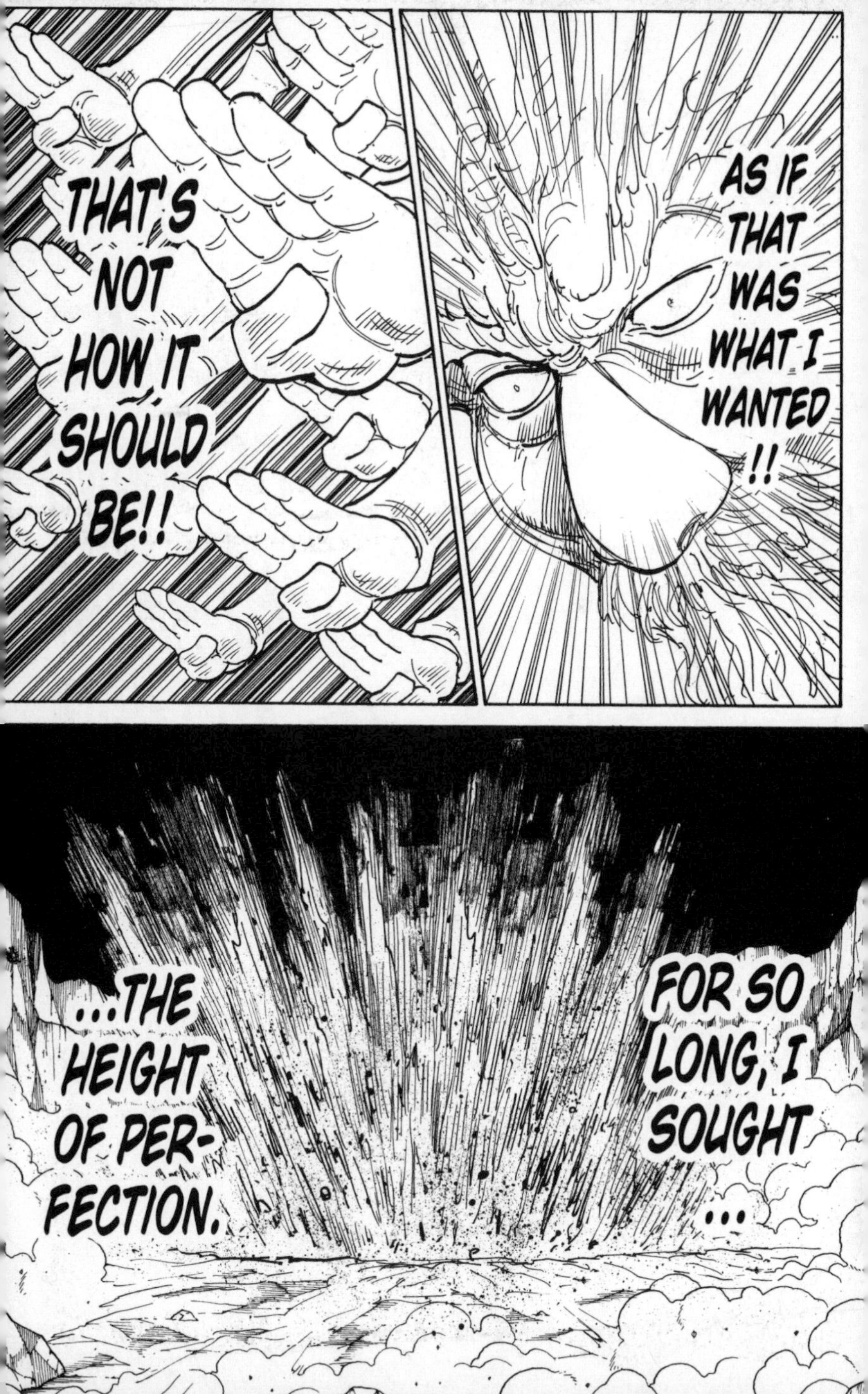
AS IF THAT WAS WHAT I WANTED!!
THAT'S NOT HOW IT SHOULD BE!!
FOR SO LONG, I SOUGHT...
...THE HEIGHT OF PER-FECTION.

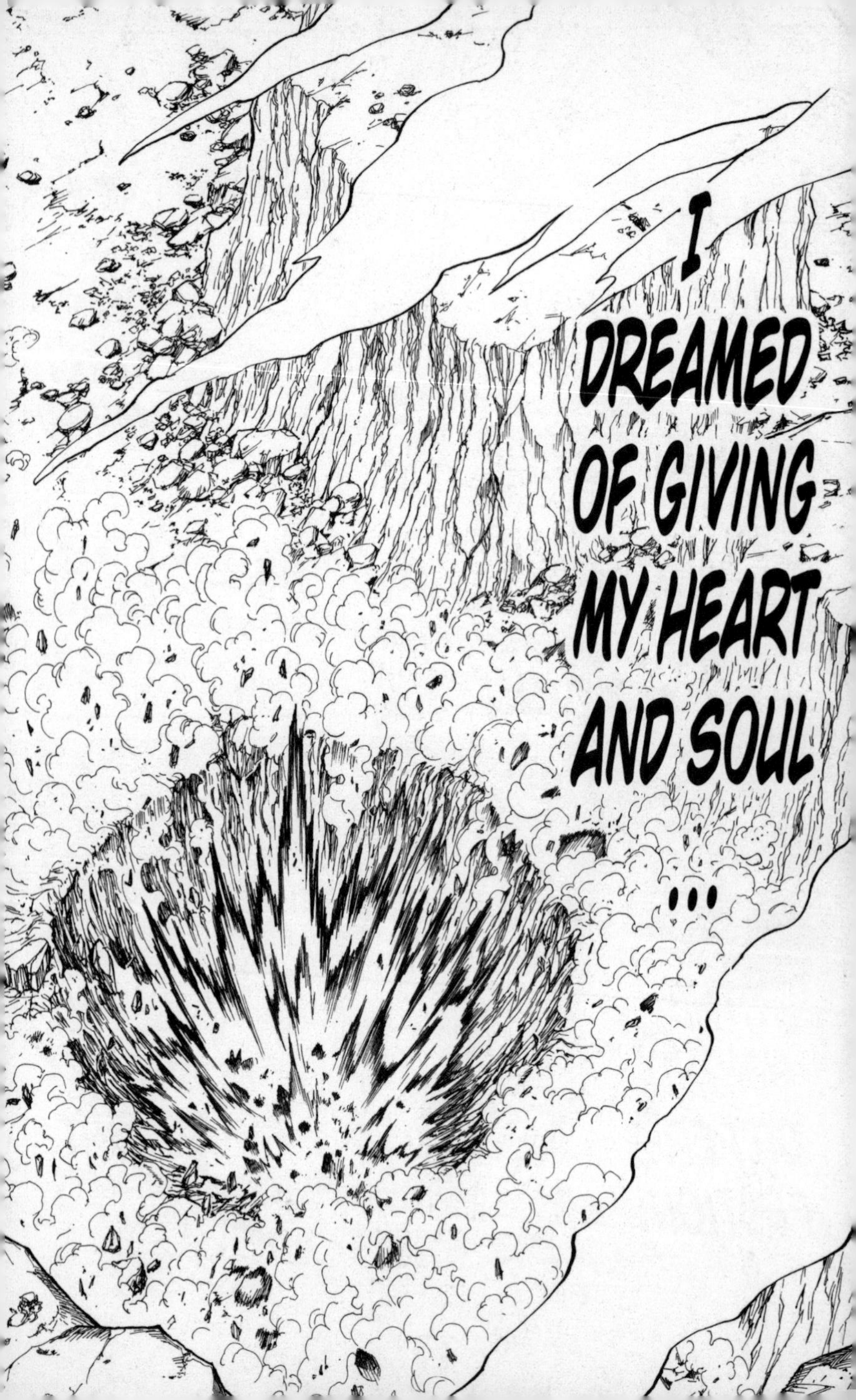
I DREAMED OF GIVING MY HEART AND SOUL ...

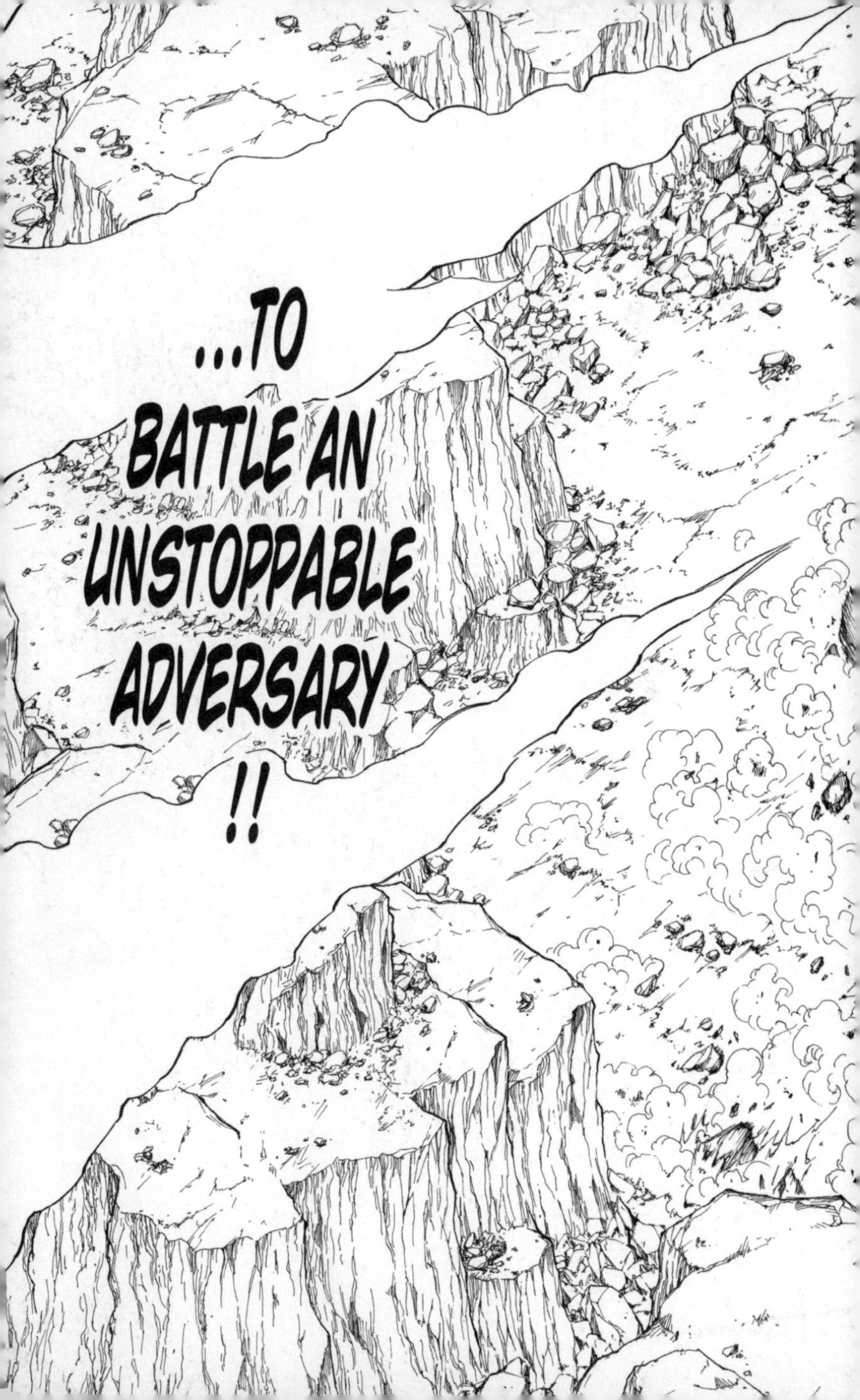
...TO BATTLE AN UNSTOPPABLE ADVERSARY !!

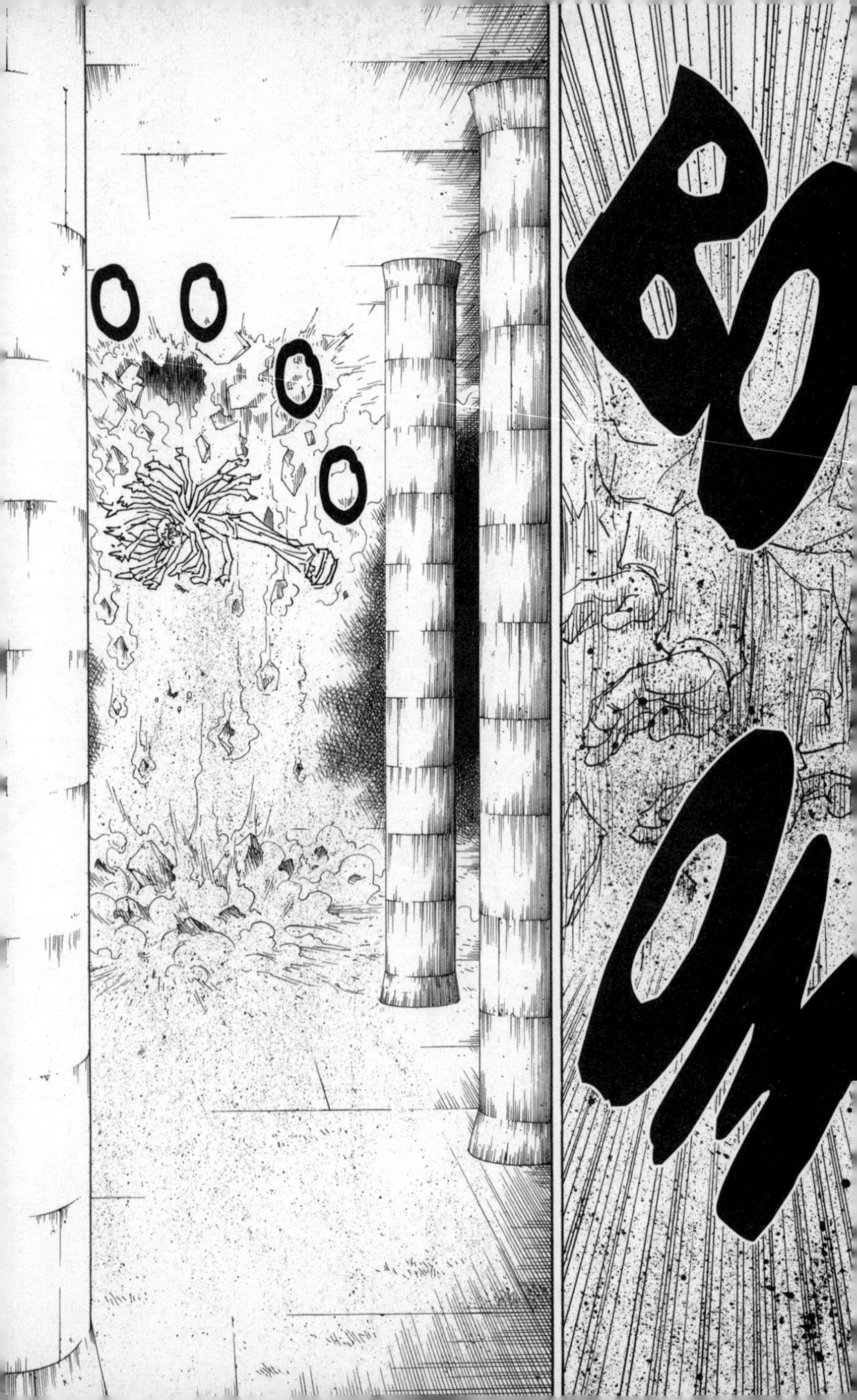
BOOM

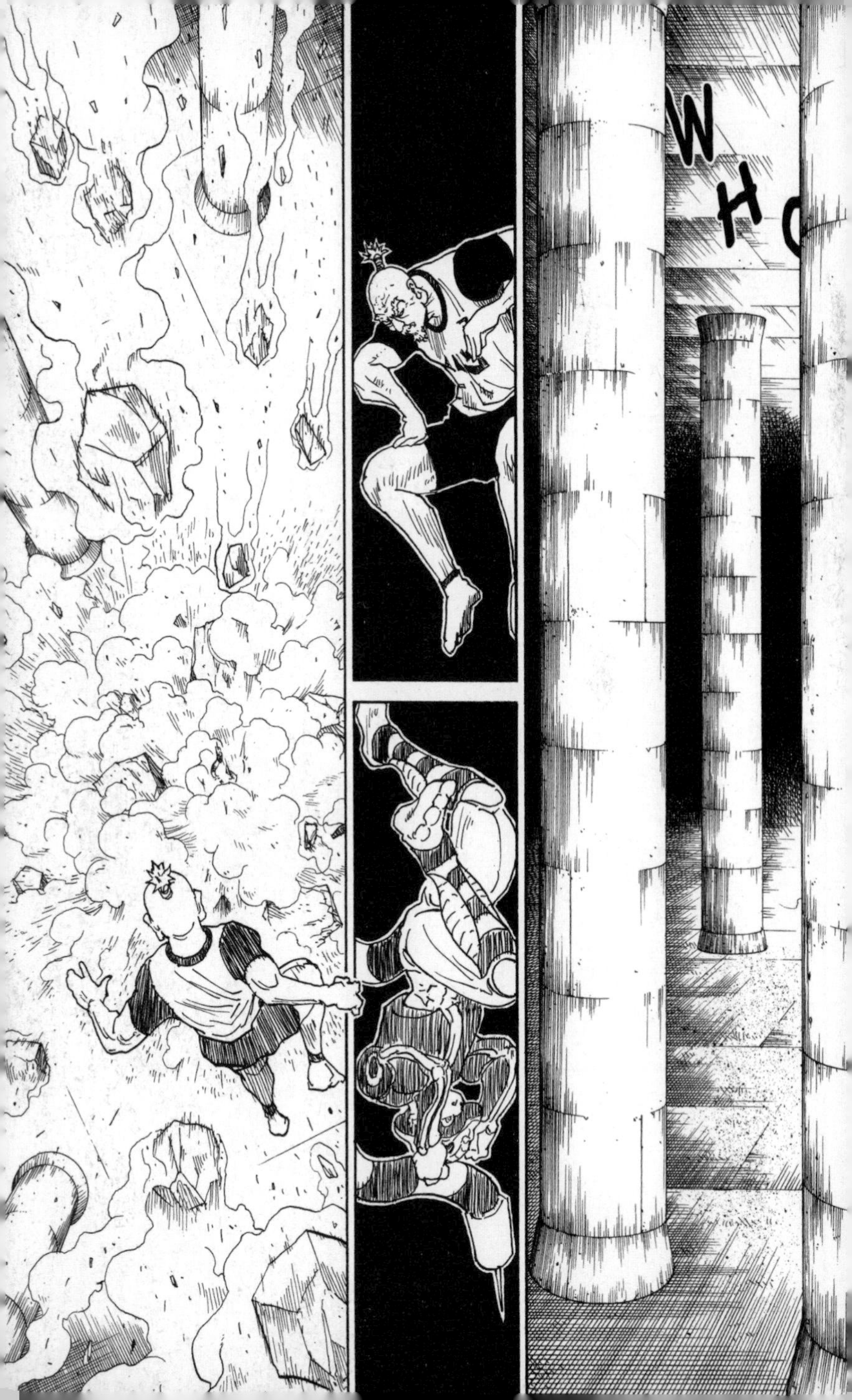
WHO

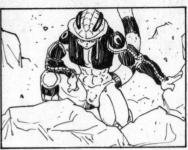

...IS A GRAVE.

THIS...

YOURS.

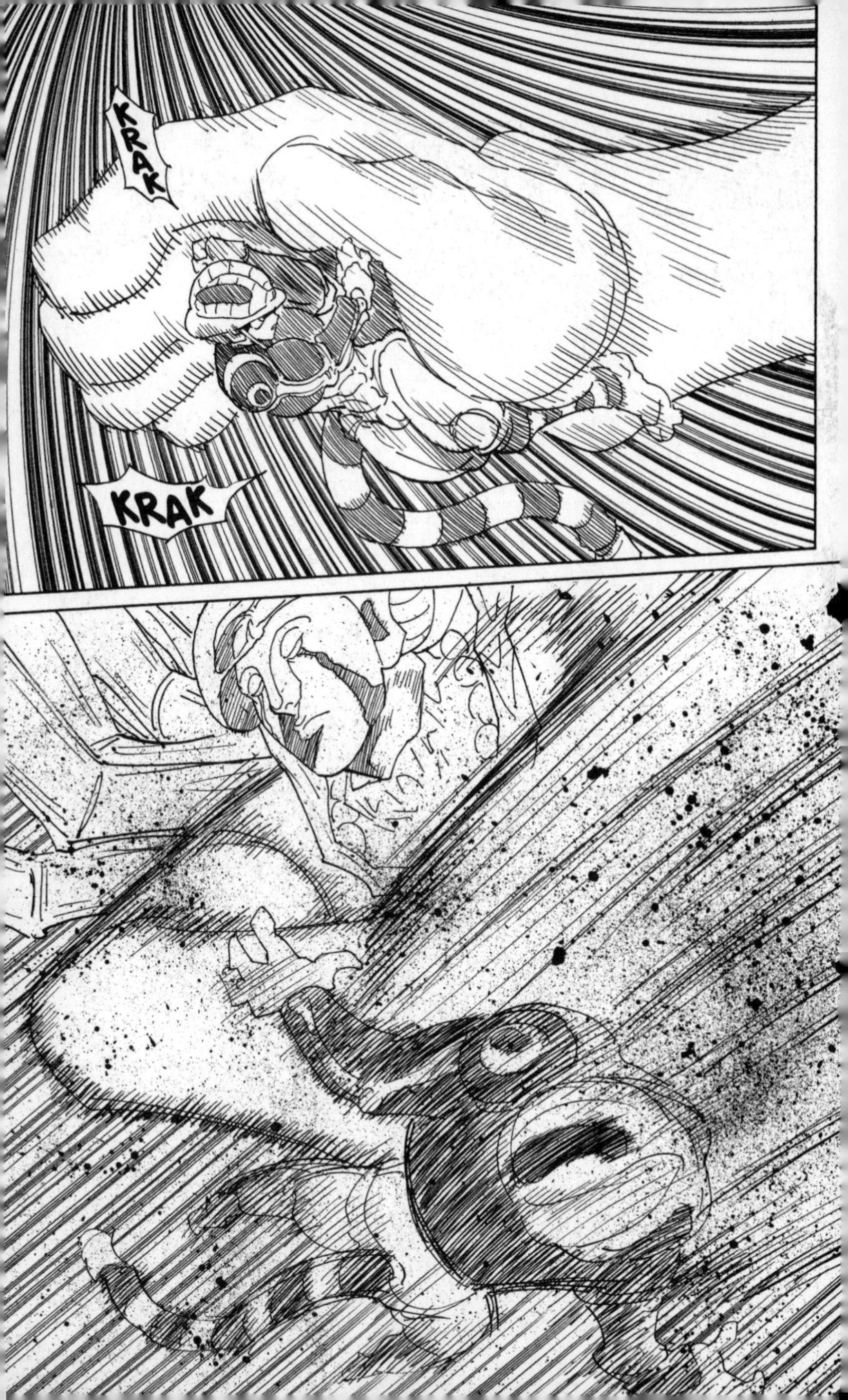
KRAK
KRAK

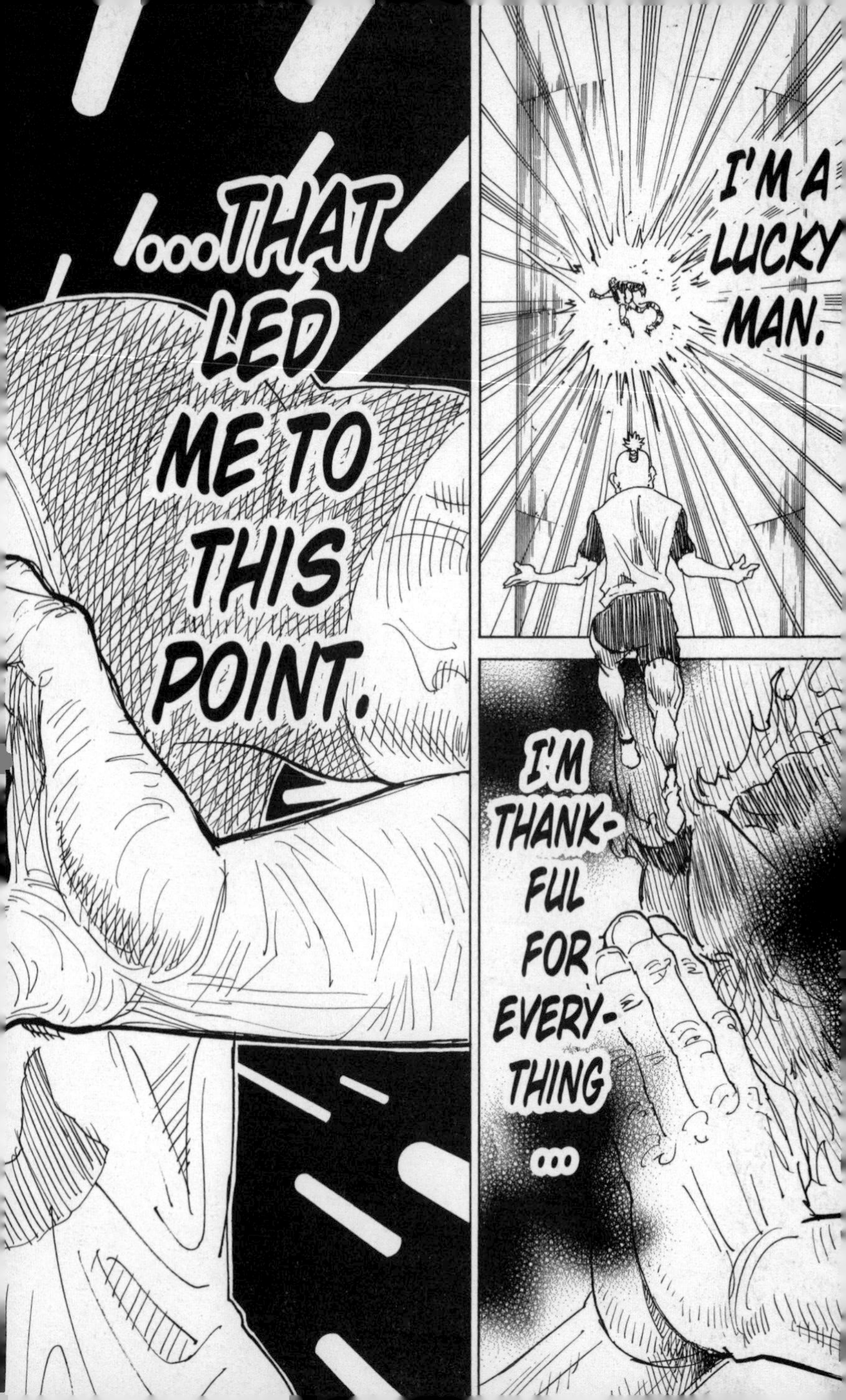
I'M A LUCKY MAN.
I'M THANK-FUL FOR EVERY-THING...
...THAT LED ME TO THIS POINT.

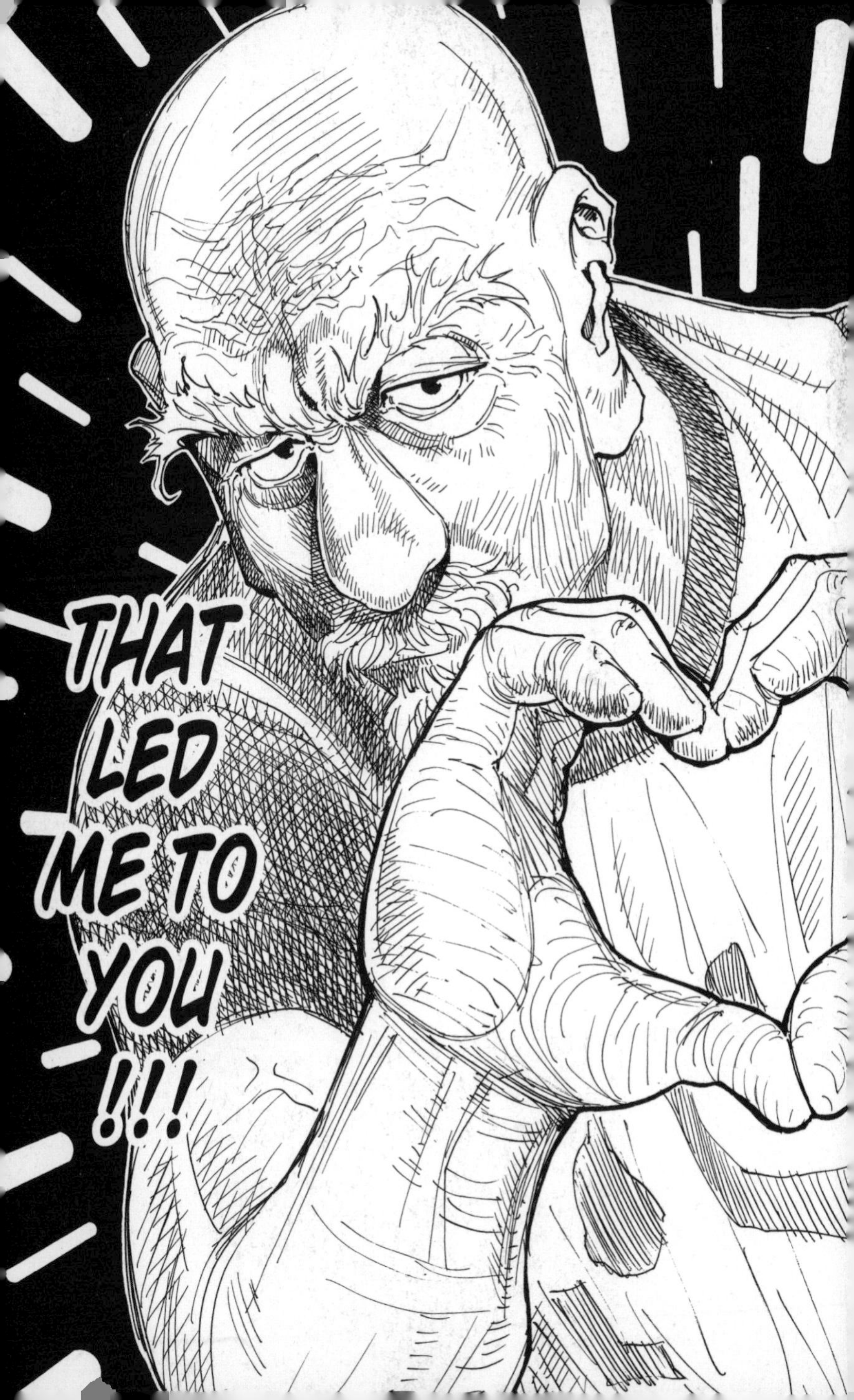
THAT LED ME TO YOU !!!

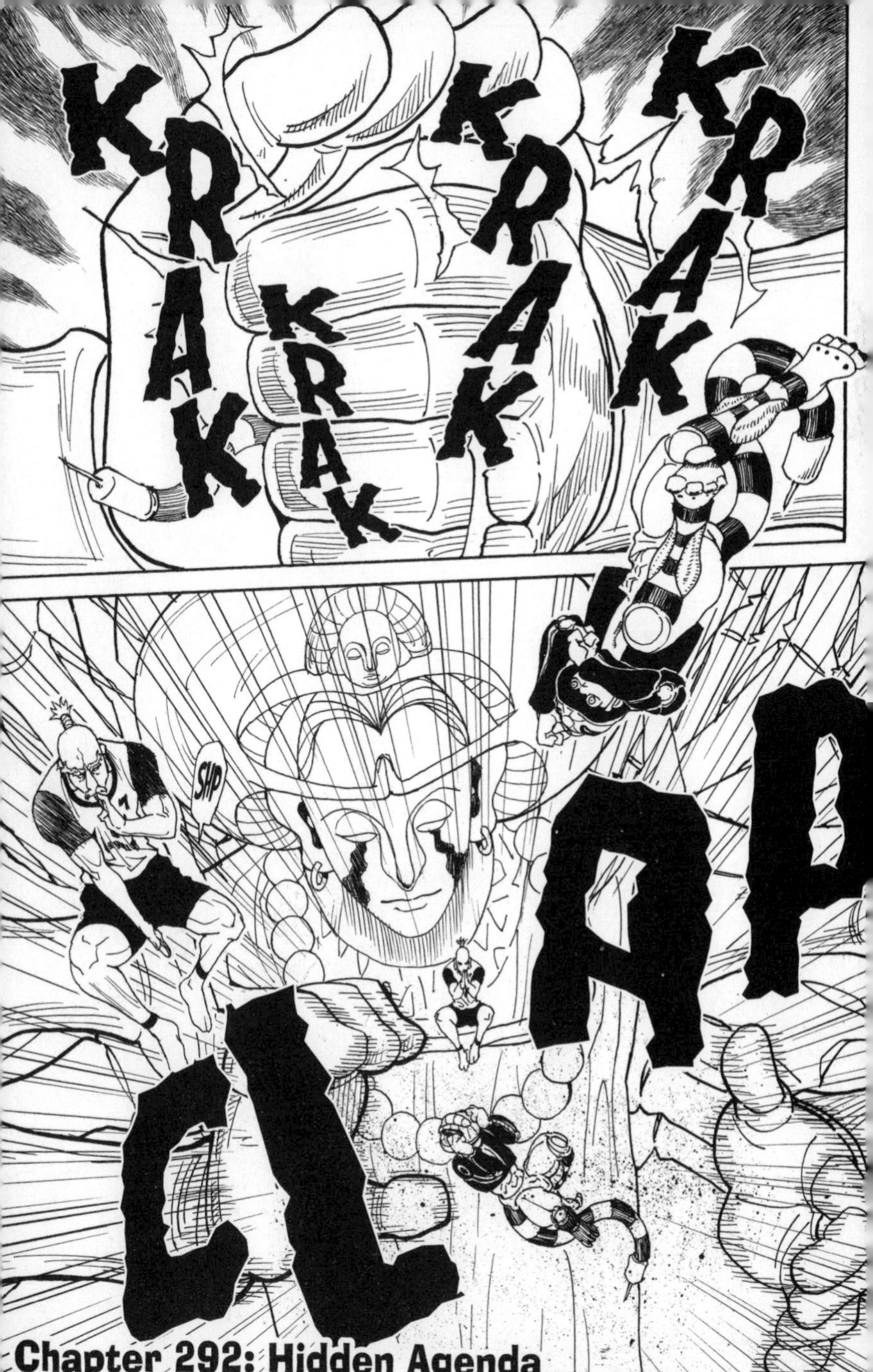
KRAK
KRAK
KRAK
KRAK
CLAP
SHP

Chapter 292: Hidden Agenda

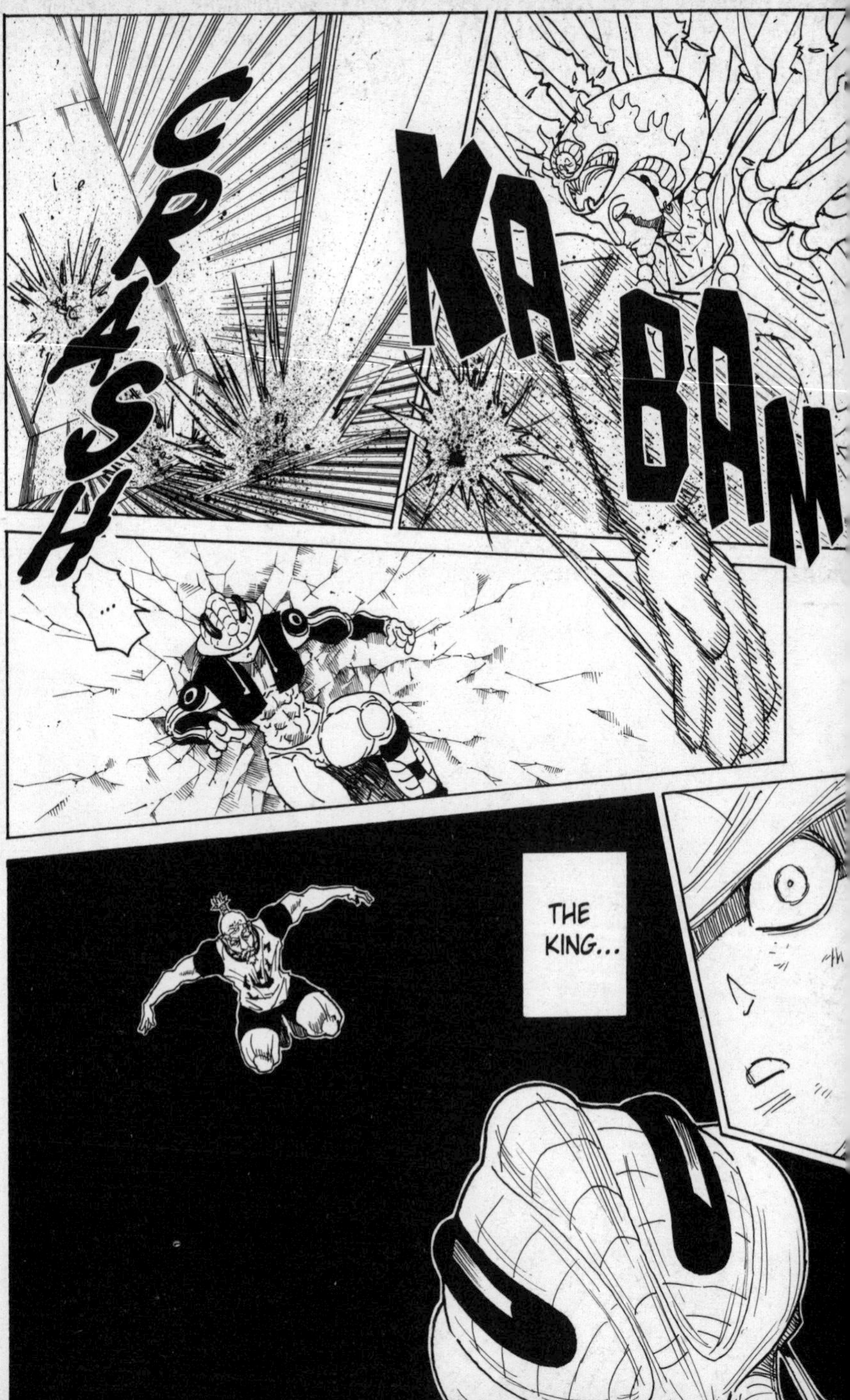
KA BAM
CRASH
...
THE KING...

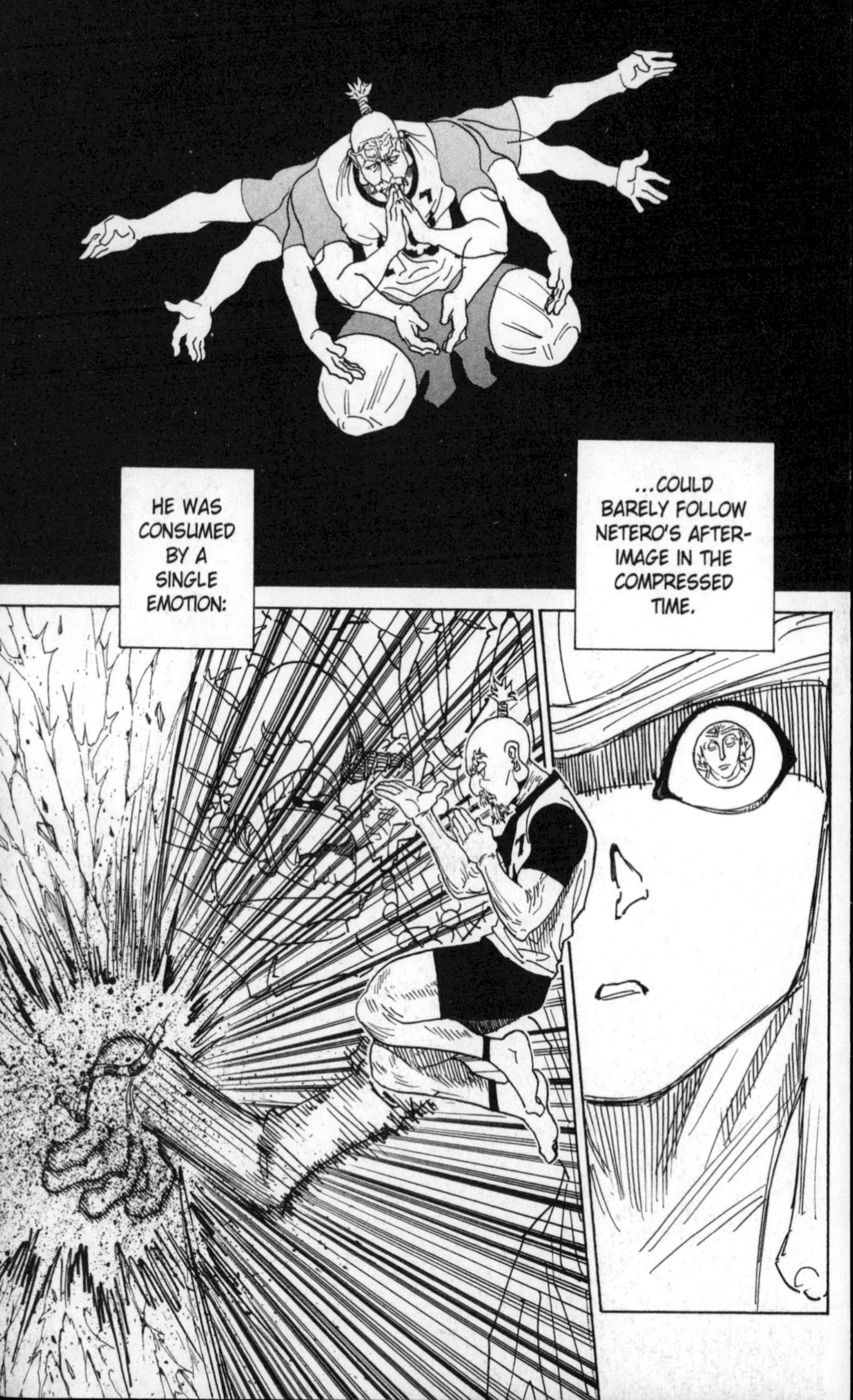
...COULD BARELY FOLLOW NETERO'S AFTER-IMAGE IN THE COMPRESSED TIME.
HE WAS CONSUMED BY A SINGLE EMOTION:

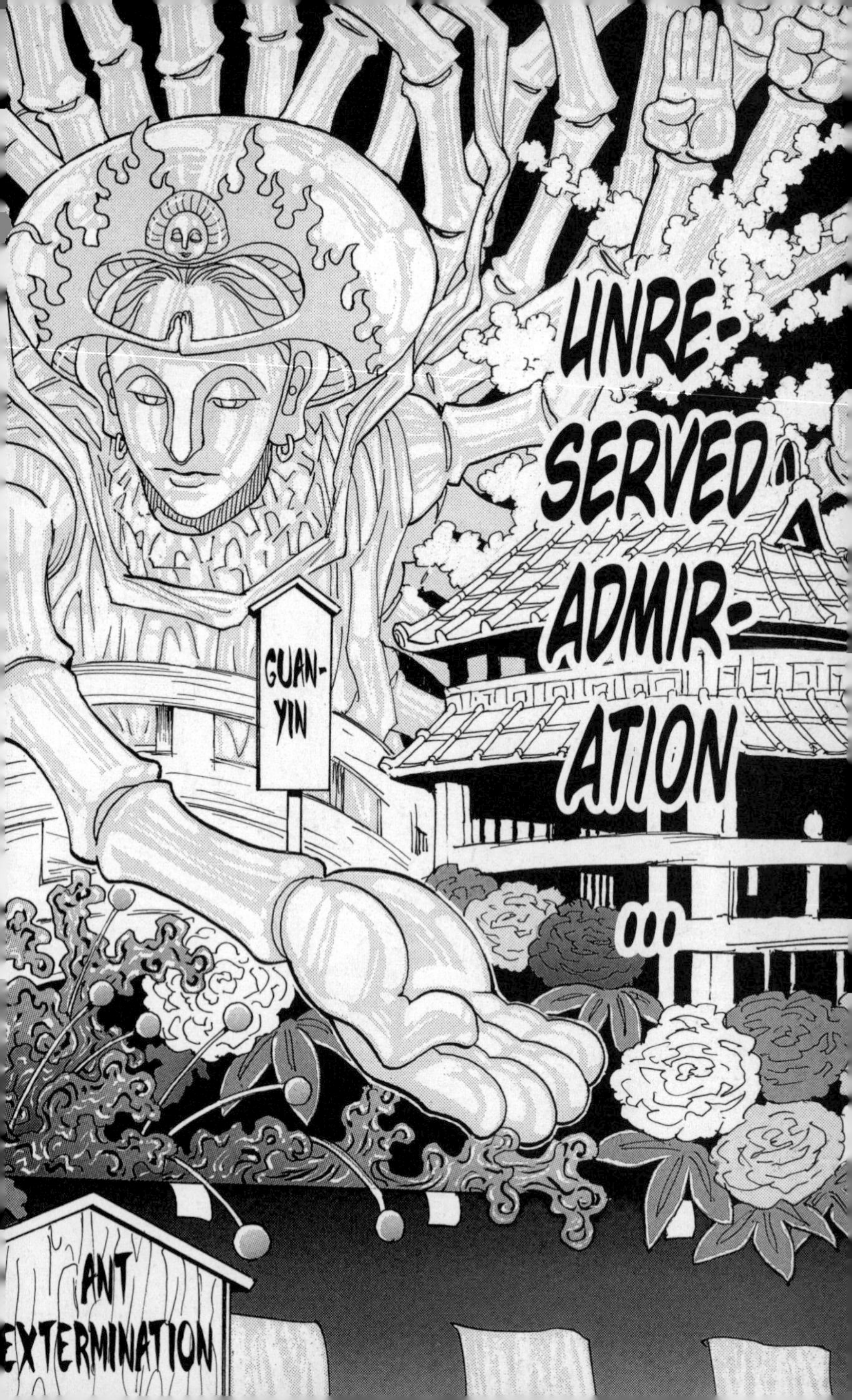
UNRE-SERVED ADMIR-ATION...
GUAN-YIN
ANT EXTERMINATION

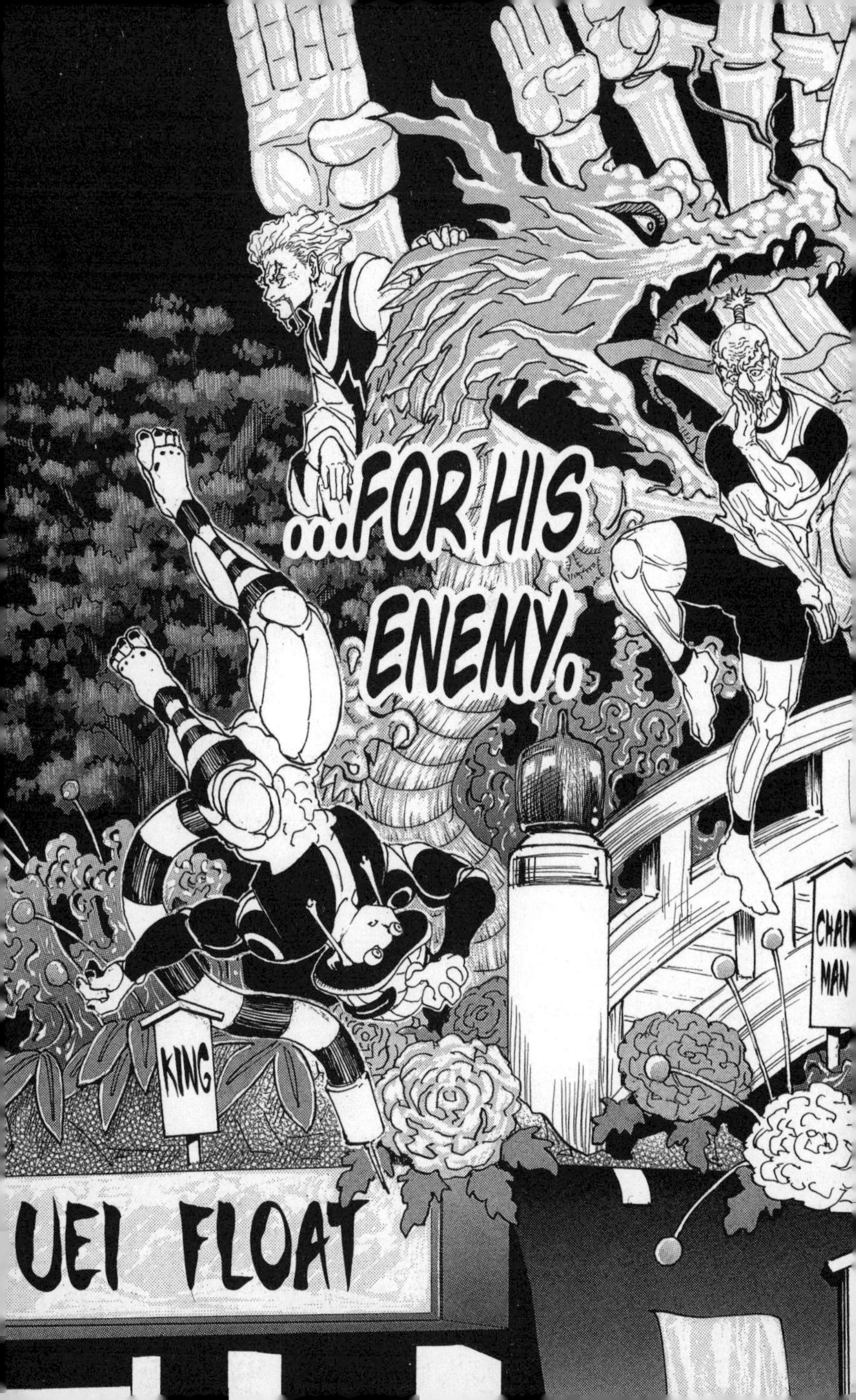

...FOR HIS ENEMY.
CHAIRMAN
KING
UEI FLOAT

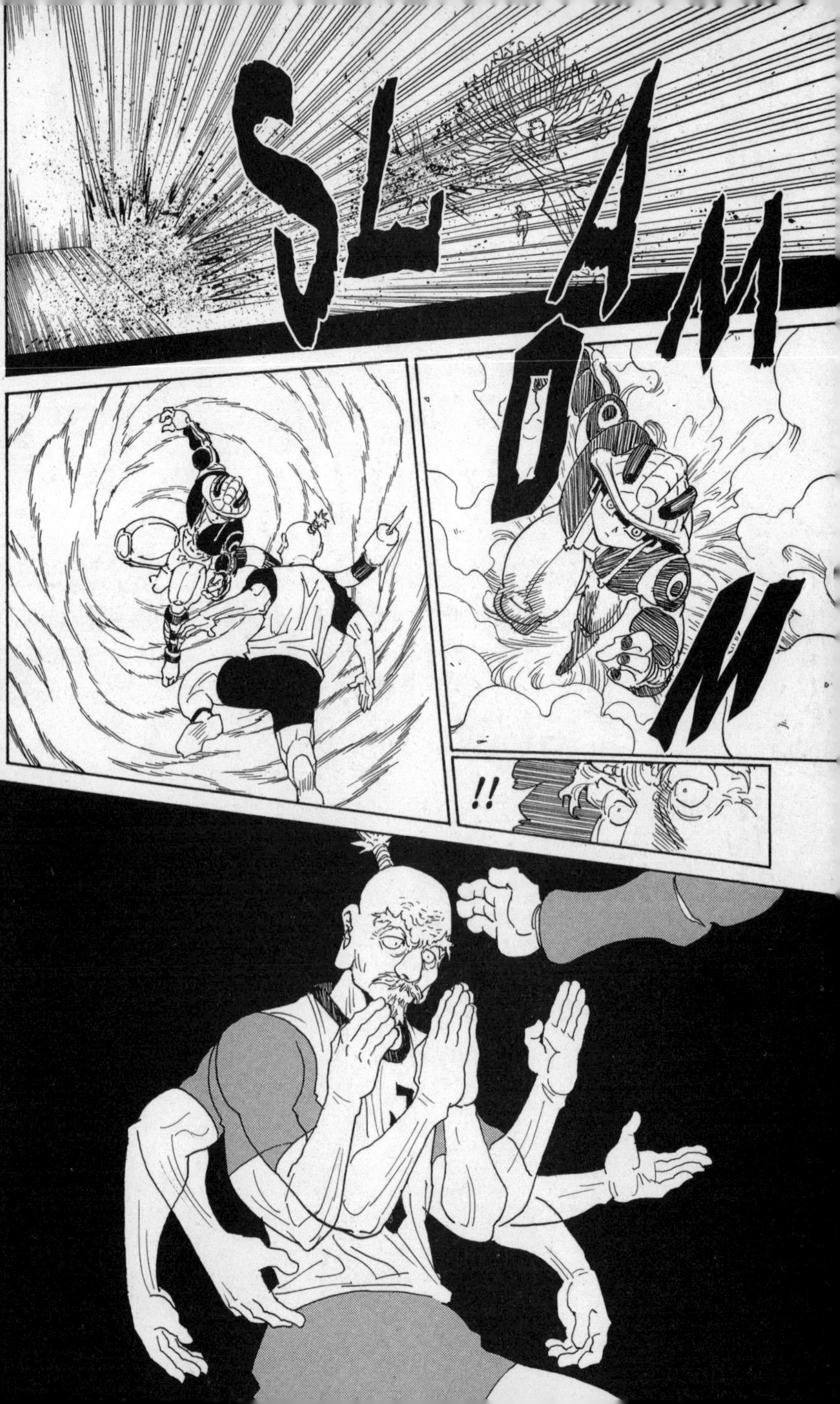
SLAM
DOOM
!!

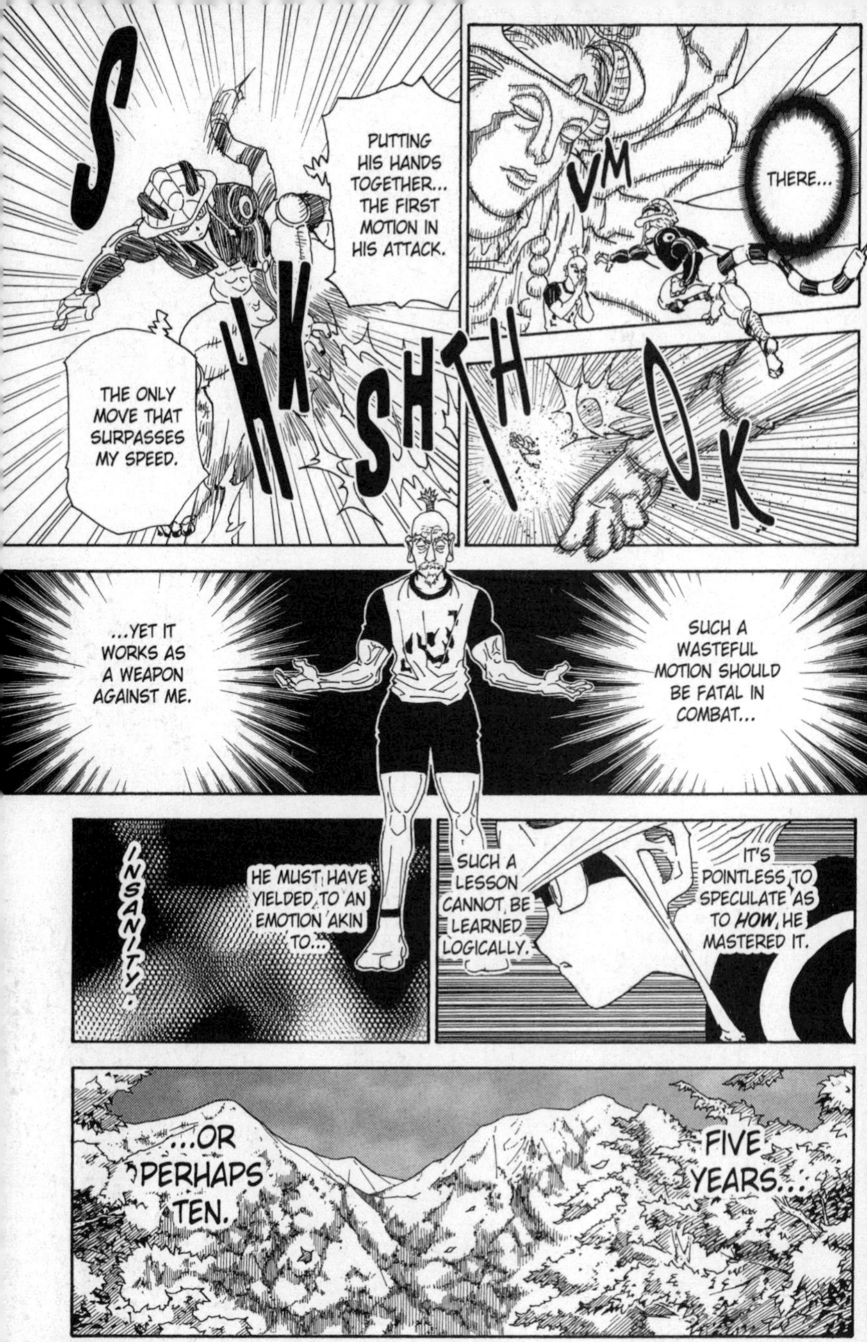
VM
THERE...
S
PUTTING HIS HANDS TOGETHER... THE FIRST MOTION IN HIS ATTACK.
THE ONLY MOVE THAT SURPASSES MY SPEED.
HK
SHTH
OOK
SUCH A WASTEFUL MOTION SHOULD BE FATAL IN COMBAT...
...YET IT WORKS AS A WEAPON AGAINST ME.
IT'S POINTLESS TO SPECULATE AS TO *HOW* HE MASTERED IT.
SUCH A LESSON CANNOT BE LEARNED LOGICALLY.
HE MUST HAVE YIELDED TO AN EMOTION AKIN TO...
INSANITY.
FIVE YEARS...
...OR PERHAPS TEN.

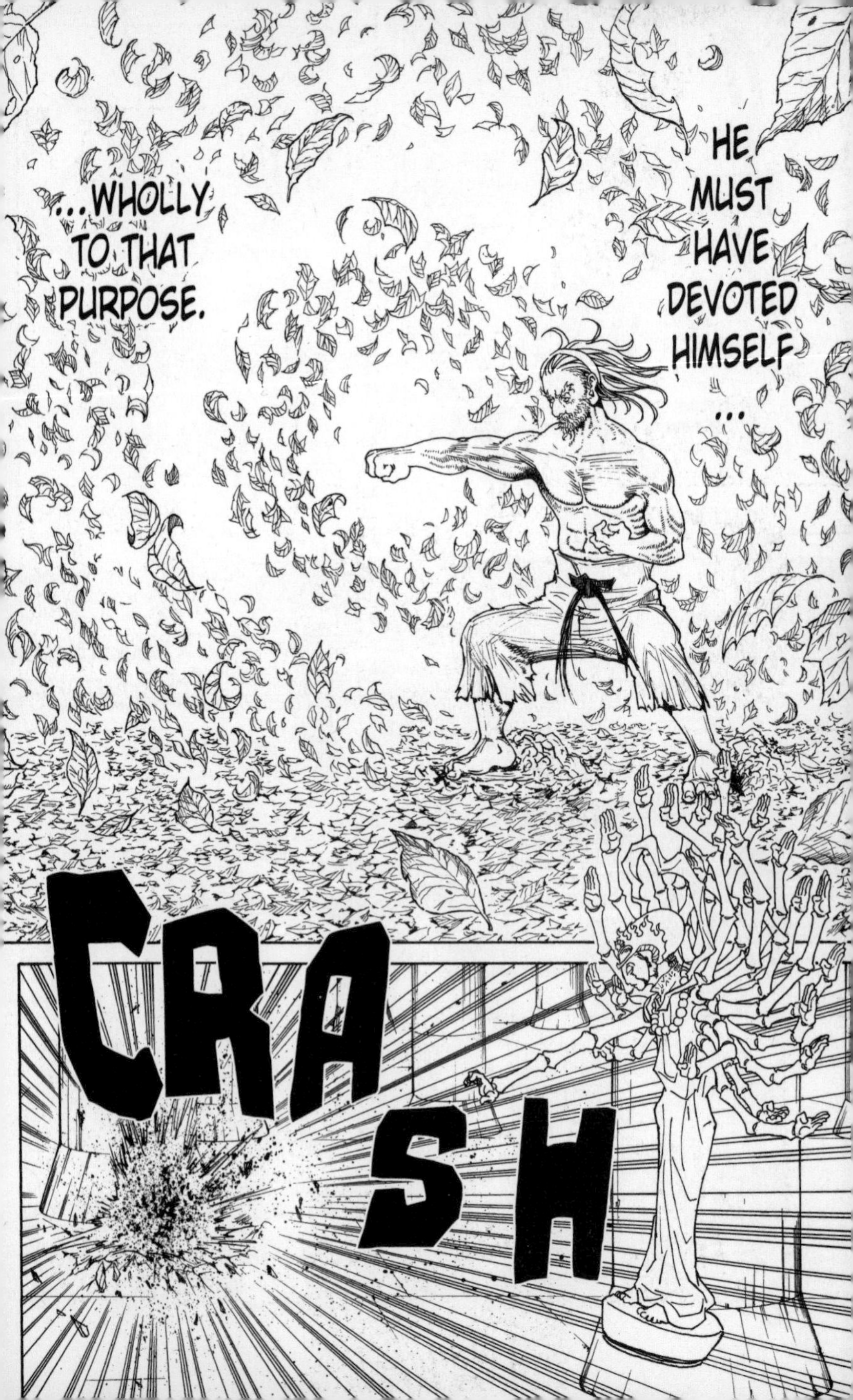
HE MUST HAVE DEVOTED HIMSELF ...
...WHOLLY TO THAT PURPOSE.
CRASH

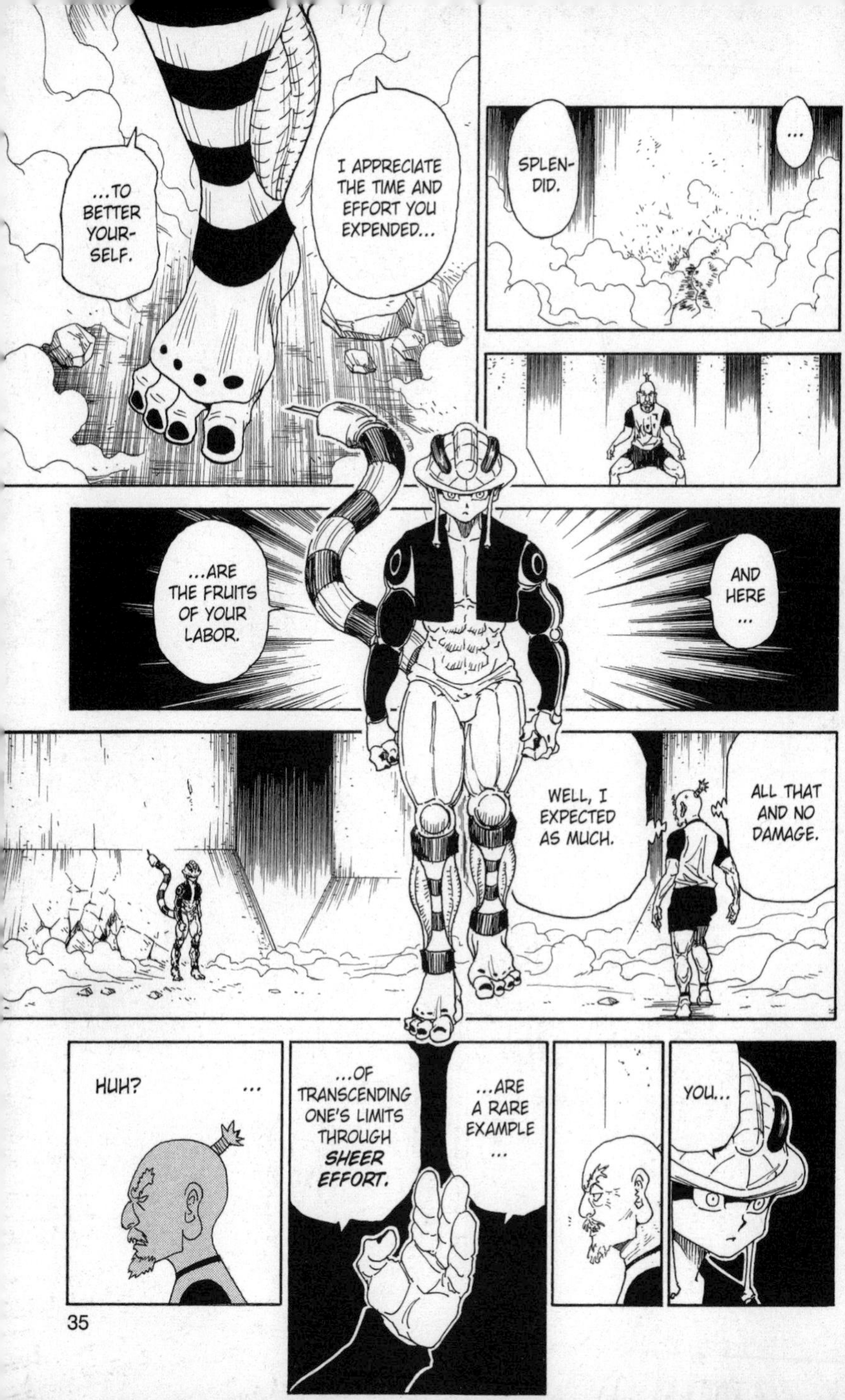
...
SPLEN-DID.
I APPRECIATE THE TIME AND EFFORT YOU EXPENDED...
...TO BETTER YOUR-SELF.
AND HERE ...
...ARE THE FRUITS OF YOUR LABOR.
ALL THAT AND NO DAMAGE.
WELL, I EXPECTED AS MUCH.
YOU...
...ARE A RARE EXAMPLE ...
...OF TRANSCENDING ONE'S LIMITS THROUGH *SHEER EFFORT.*
...
HUH?

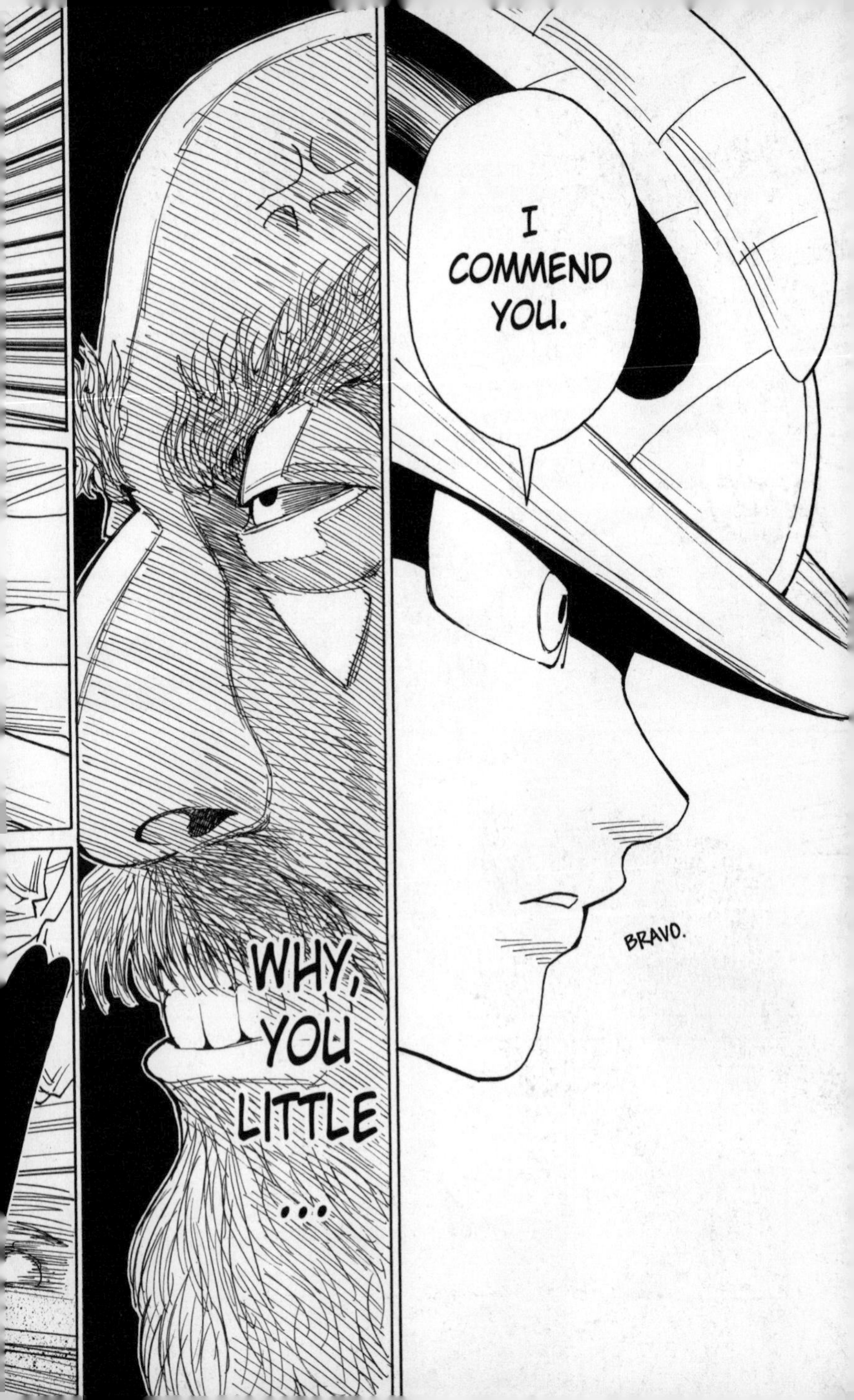
I COMMEND YOU.
BRAVO.
WHY, YOU LITTLE ...

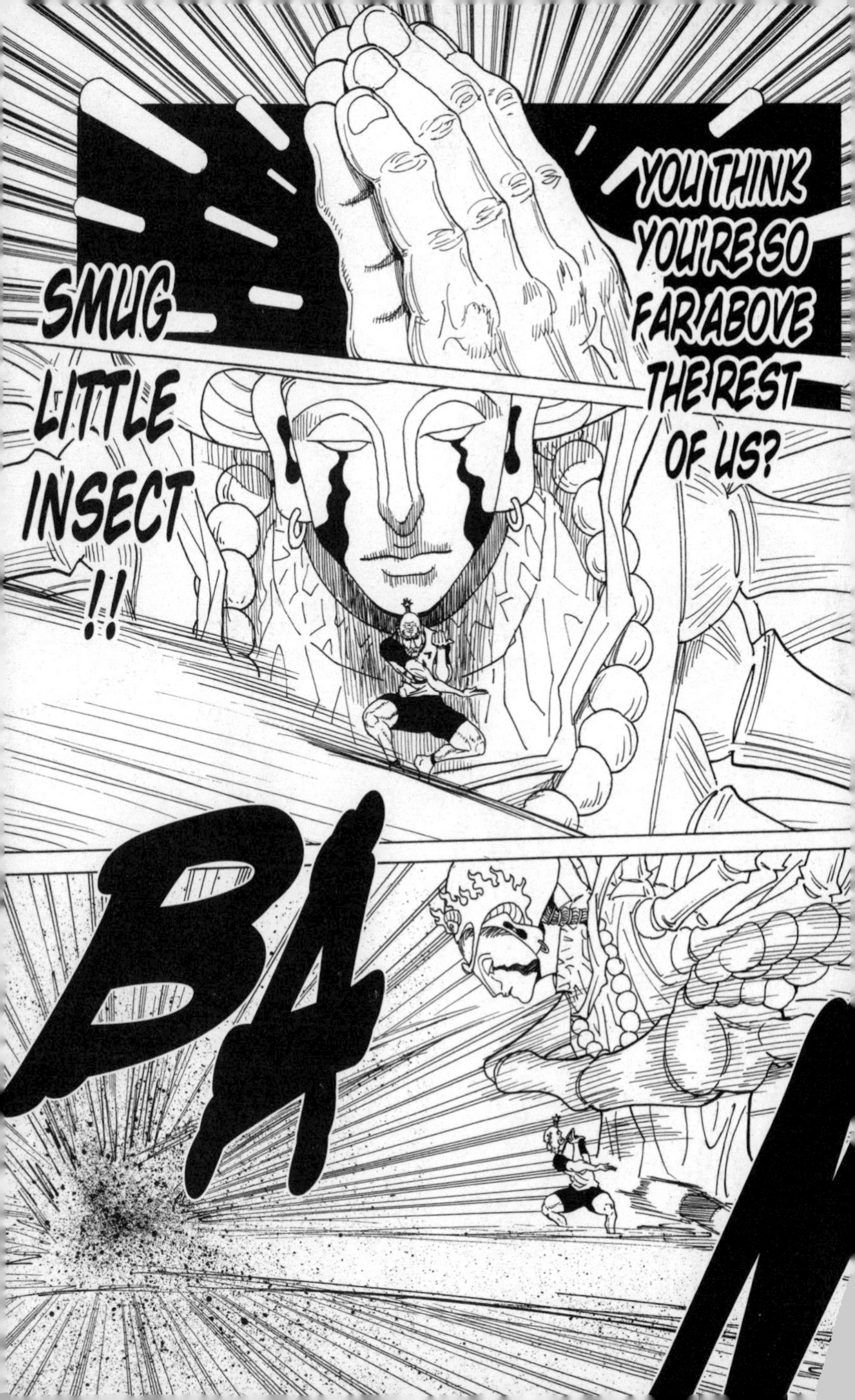
YOU THINK YOU'RE SO FAR ABOVE THE REST OF US?
SMUG LITTLE INSECT !!
BAM

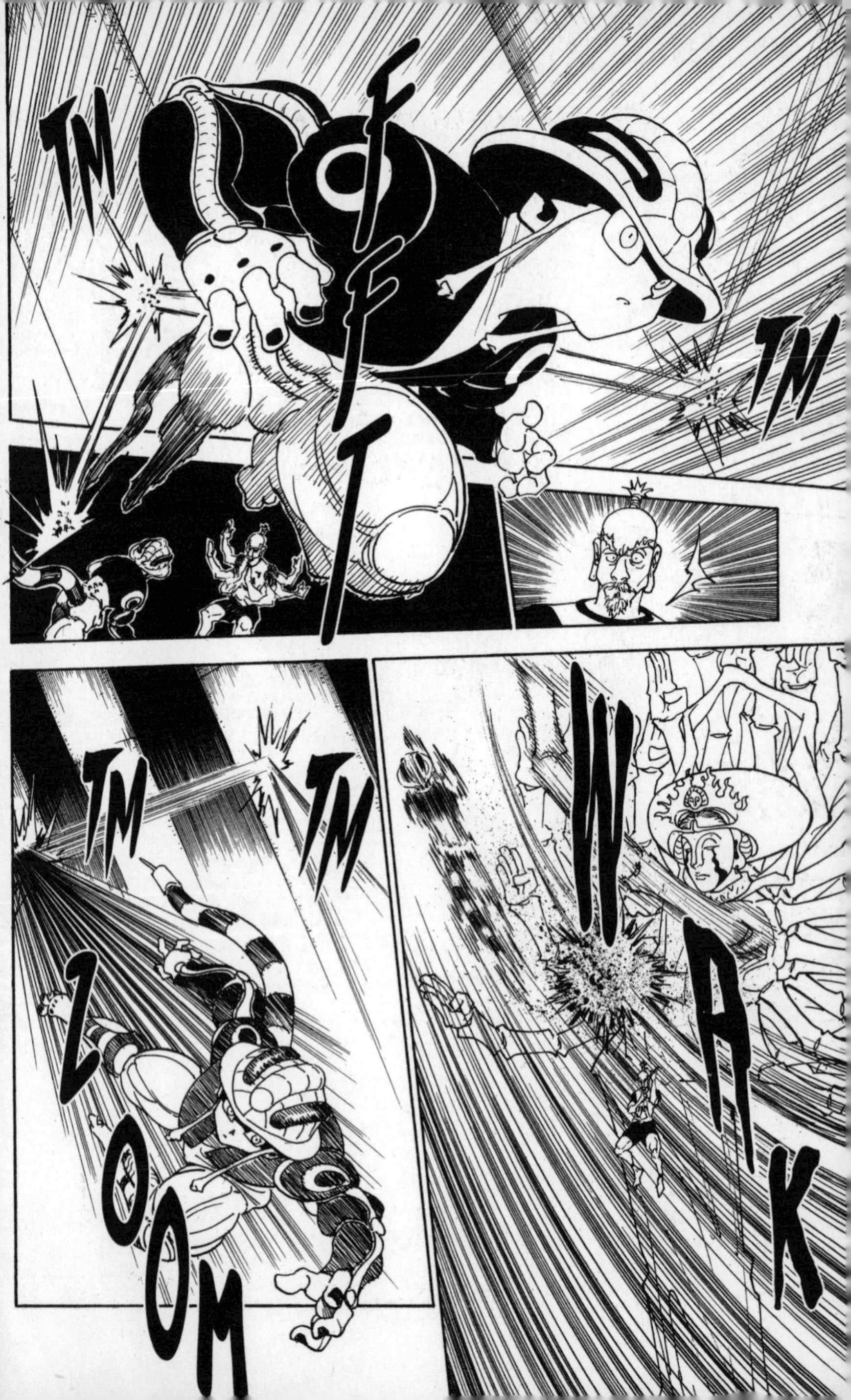

TM
FFT
TM
WAK
TM
TM
ZOOM

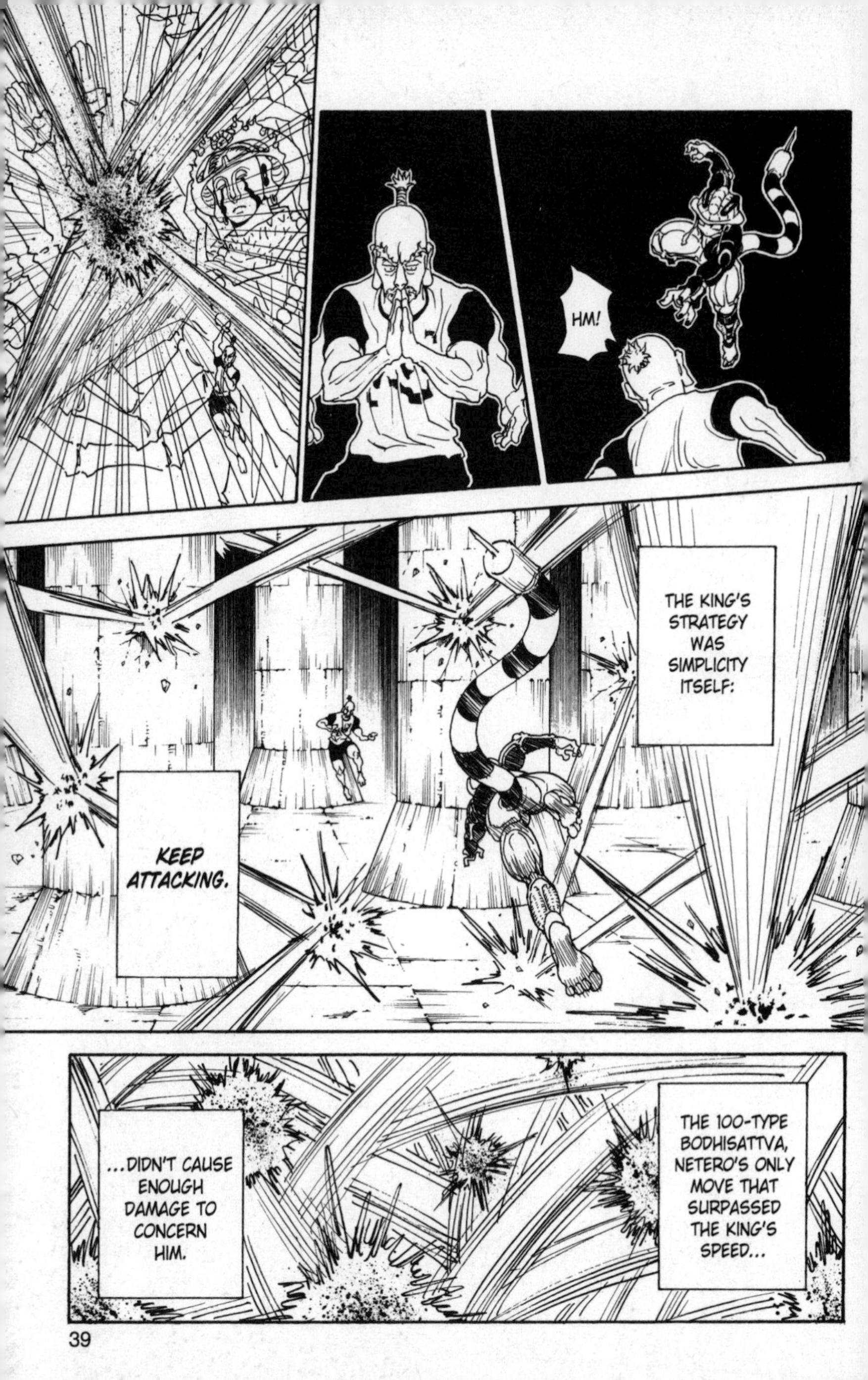
HM!
THE KING'S STRATEGY WAS SIMPLICITY ITSELF:
KEEP ATTACKING.
THE 100-TYPE BODHISATTVA, NETERO'S ONLY MOVE THAT SURPASSED THE KING'S SPEED...
...DIDN'T CAUSE ENOUGH DAMAGE TO CONCERN HIM.

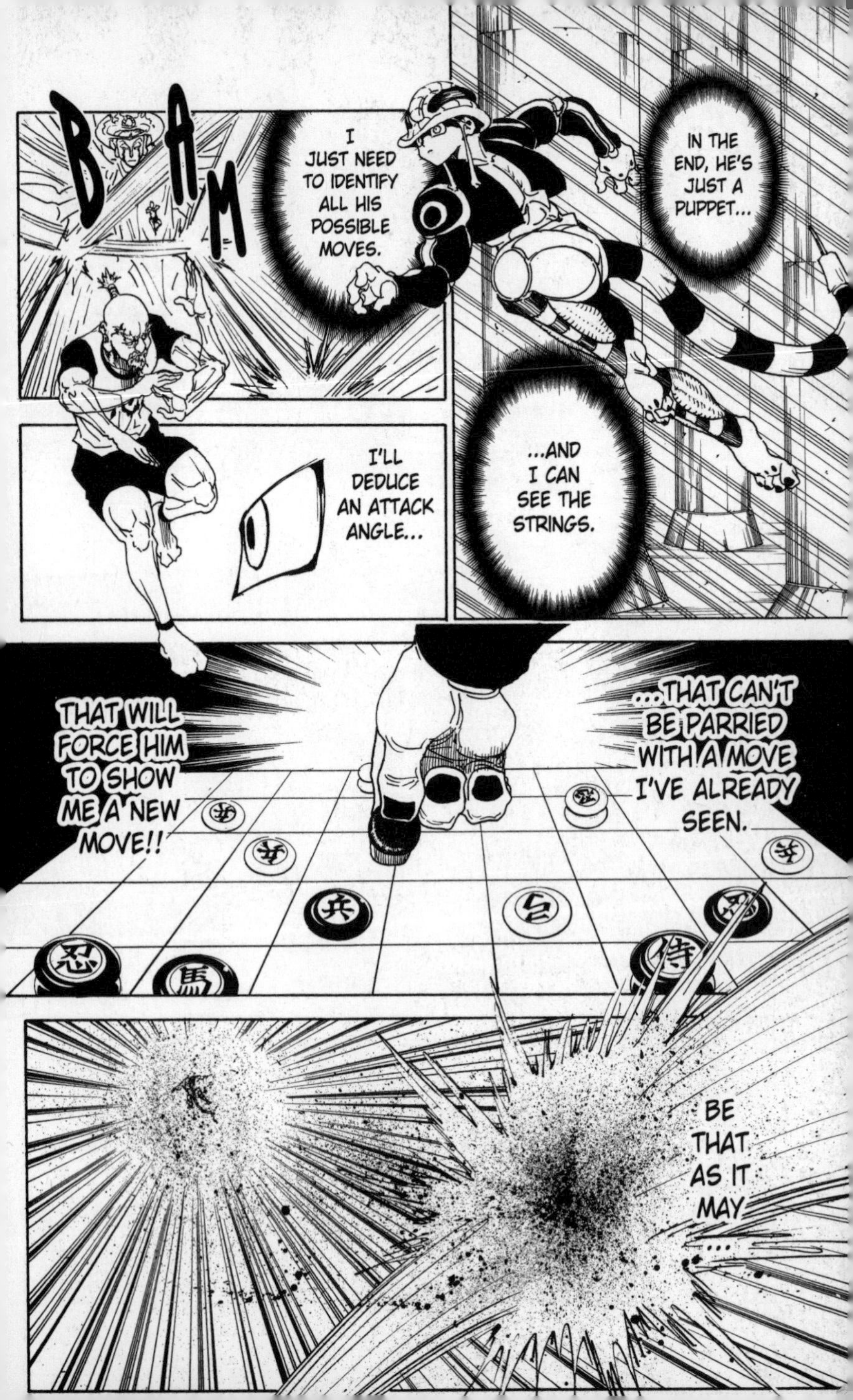
IN THE END, HE'S JUST A PUPPET...
...AND I CAN SEE THE STRINGS.
BAM
I JUST NEED TO IDENTIFY ALL HIS POSSIBLE MOVES.
I'LL DEDUCE AN ATTACK ANGLE...
...THAT CAN'T BE PARRIED WITH A MOVE I'VE ALREADY SEEN.
THAT WILL FORCE HIM TO SHOW ME A NEW MOVE!!
BE THAT AS IT MAY...

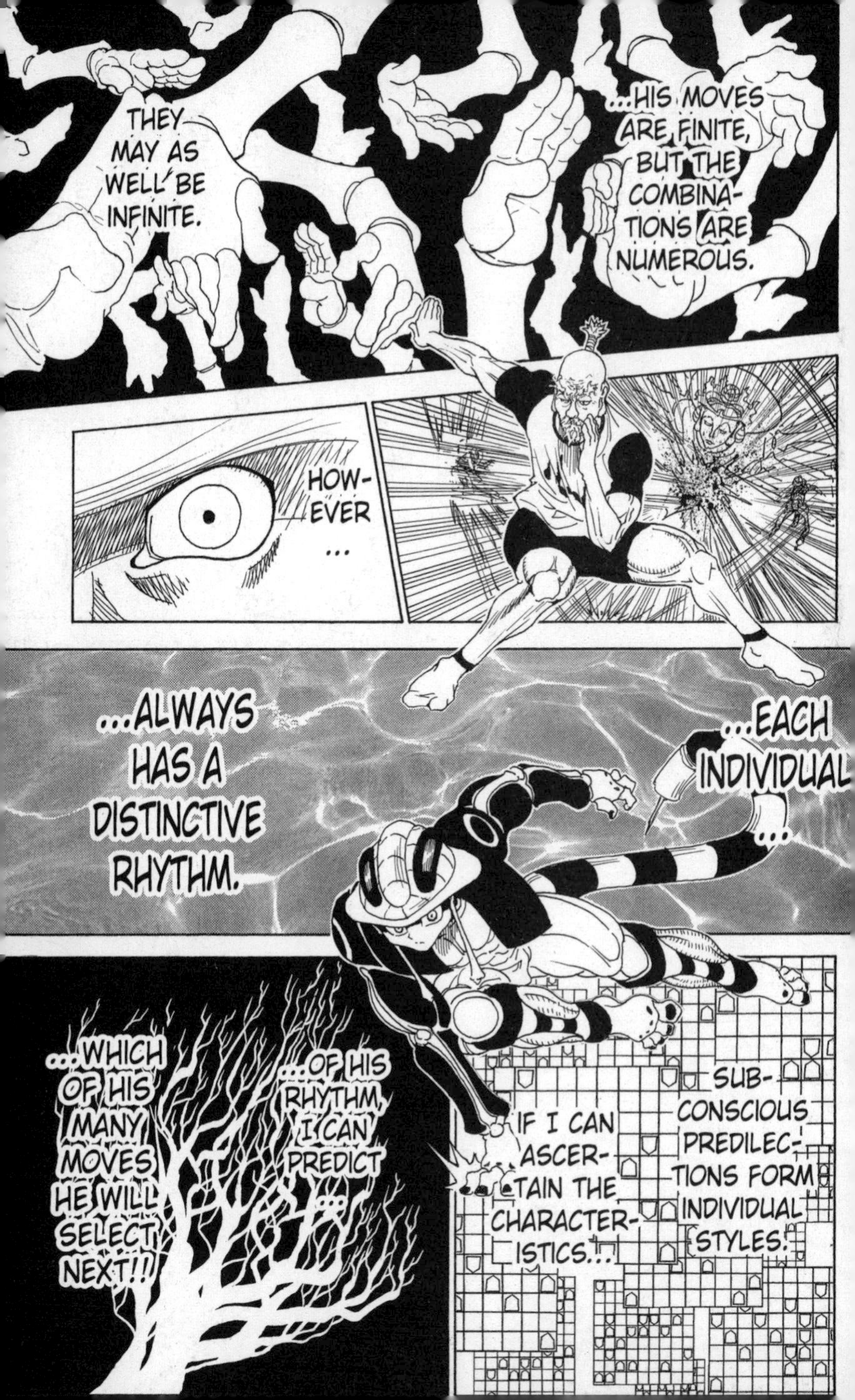
...HIS MOVES ARE FINITE, BUT THE COMBINATIONS ARE NUMEROUS.
THEY MAY AS WELL BE INFINITE.
HOWEVER...
...EACH INDIVIDUAL...
...ALWAYS HAS A DISTINCTIVE RHYTHM.
SUBCONSCIOUS PREDILECTIONS FORM INDIVIDUAL STYLES.
IF I CAN ASCERTAIN THE CHARACTERISTICS...
...OF HIS RHYTHM, I CAN PREDICT...
...WHICH OF HIS MANY MOVES HE WILL SELECT NEXT!!

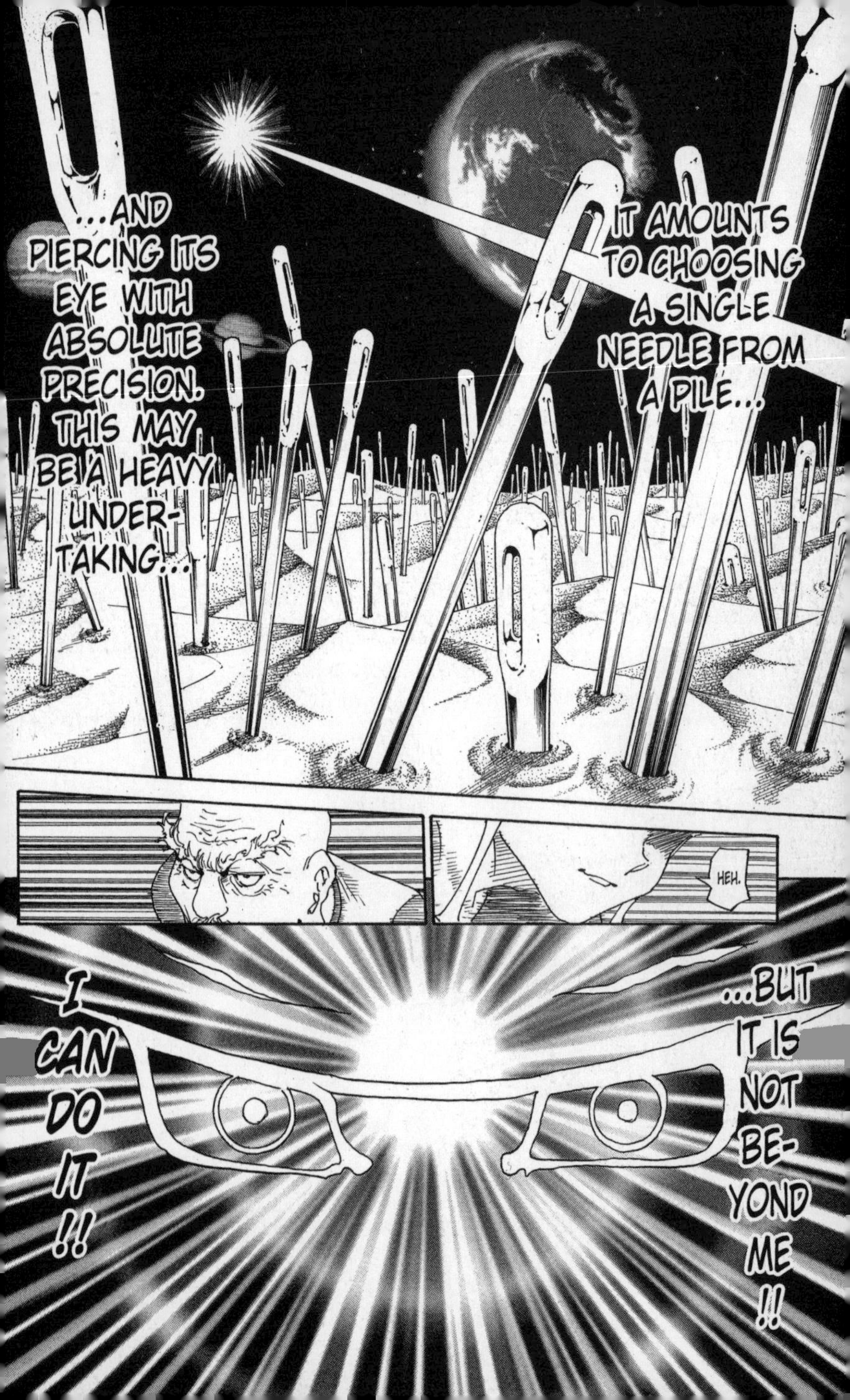
IT AMOUNTS TO CHOOSING A SINGLE NEEDLE FROM A PILE...
...AND PIERCING ITS EYE WITH ABSOLUTE PRECISION. THIS MAY BE A HEAVY UNDER-TAKING...
HEH.
...BUT IT IS NOT BE-YOND ME!!
I CAN DO IT!!

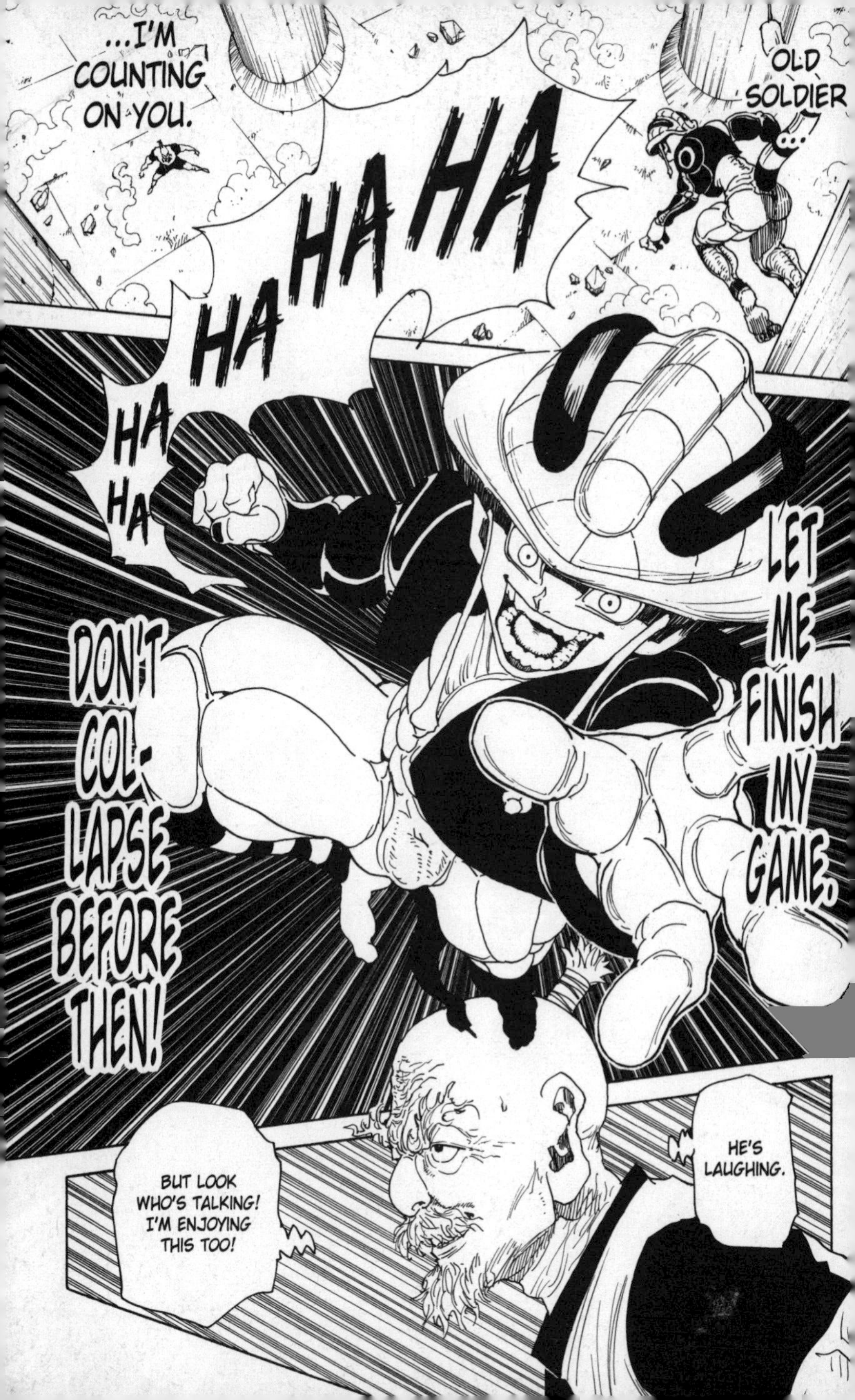
OLD SOLDIER...
...I'M COUNTING ON YOU.
HA HA HA HA
HA HA HA
LET ME FINISH MY GAME.
DON'T COL-LAPSE BEFORE THEN!
HE'S LAUGHING.
BUT LOOK WHO'S TALKING! I'M ENJOYING THIS TOO!

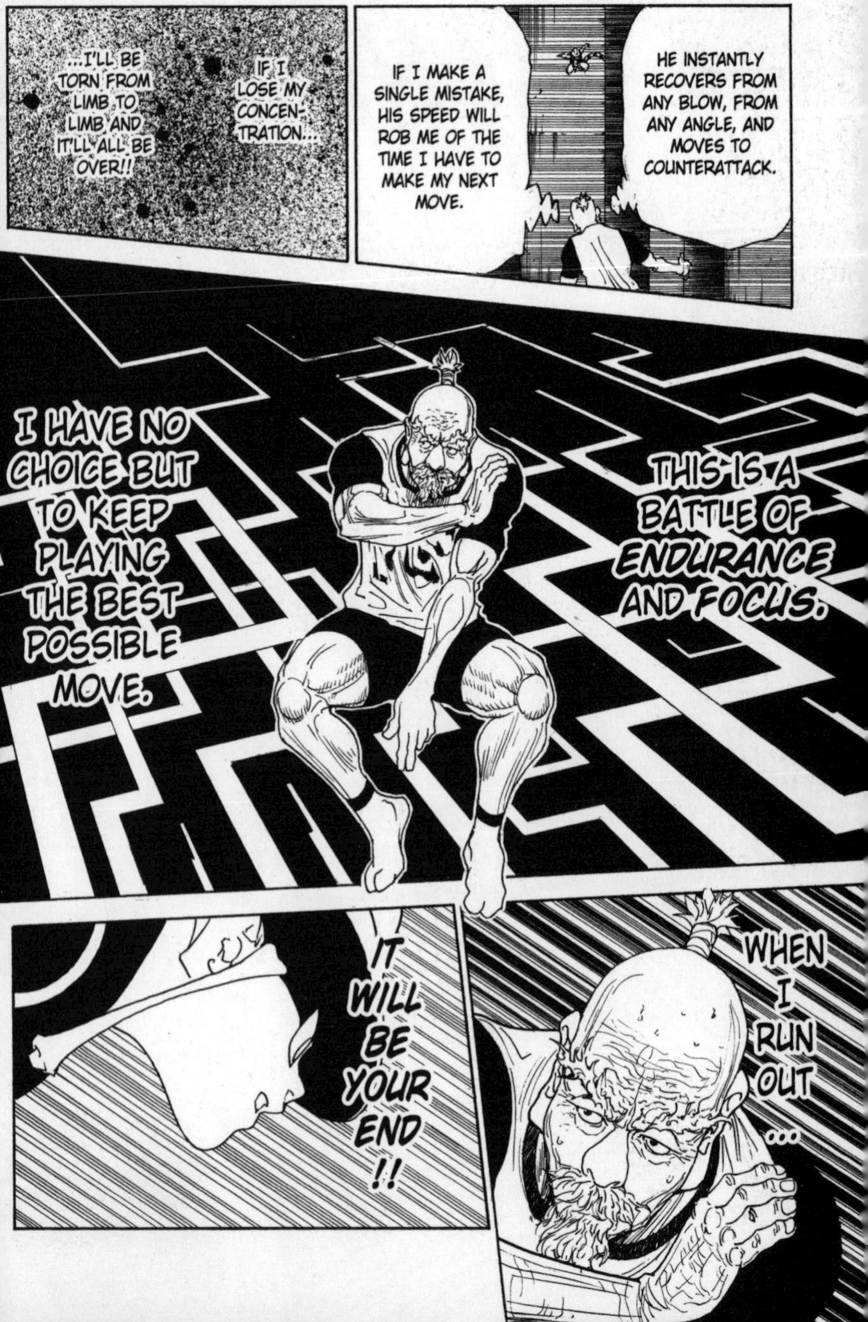
HE INSTANTLY RECOVERS FROM ANY BLOW, FROM ANY ANGLE, AND MOVES TO COUNTERATTACK.
IF I MAKE A SINGLE MISTAKE, HIS SPEED WILL ROB ME OF THE TIME I HAVE TO MAKE MY NEXT MOVE.
IF I LOSE MY CONCEN-TRATION...
...I'LL BE TORN FROM LIMB TO LIMB AND IT'LL ALL BE OVER!!
THIS IS A BATTLE OF ENDURANCE AND FOCUS.
I HAVE NO CHOICE BUT TO KEEP PLAYING THE BEST POSSIBLE MOVE.
WHEN I RUN OUT...
IT WILL BE YOUR END!!

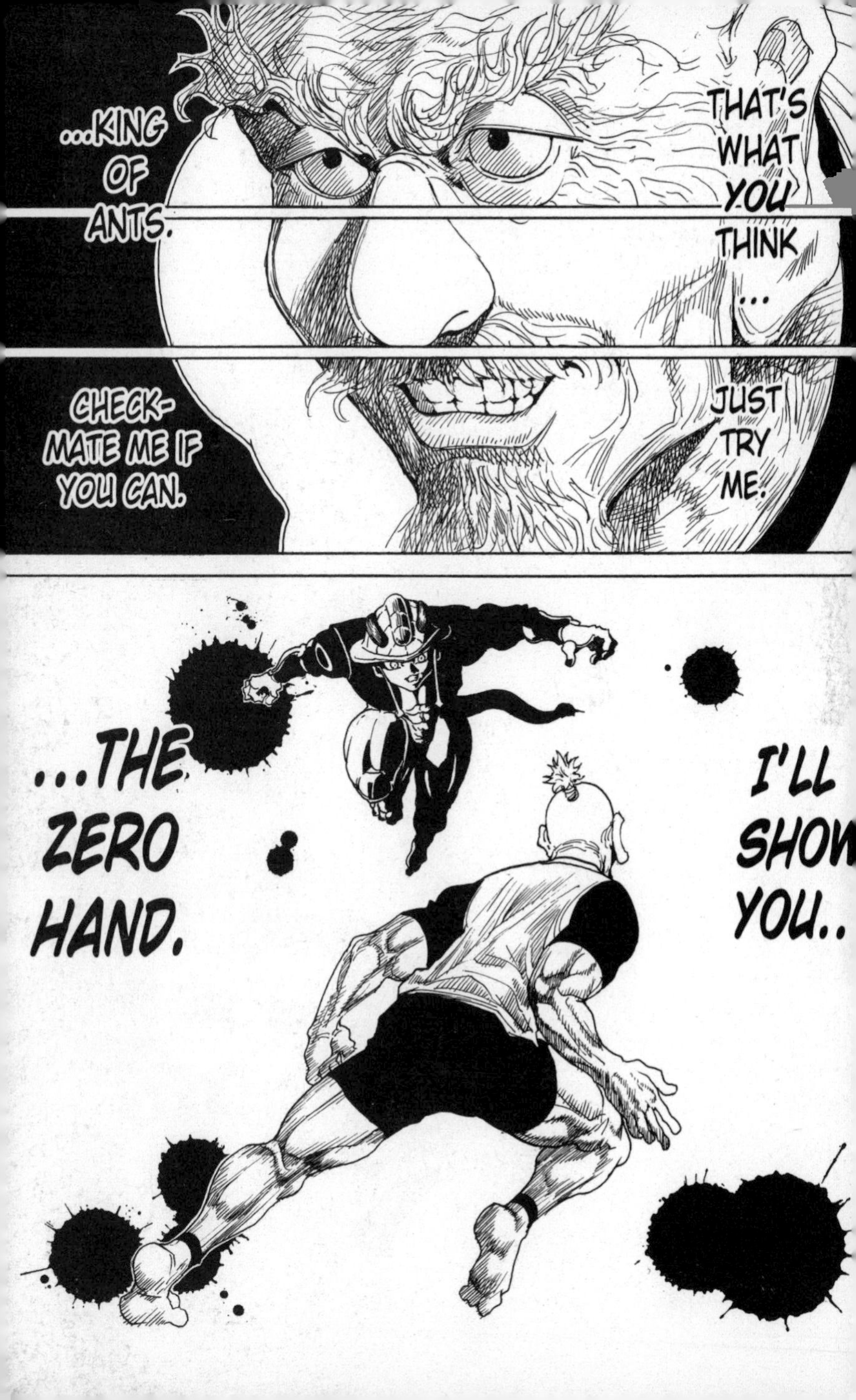
THAT'S WHAT YOU THINK...
...KING OF ANTS.
JUST TRY ME.
CHECK-MATE ME IF YOU CAN.
I'LL SHOW YOU...
...THE ZERO HAND.

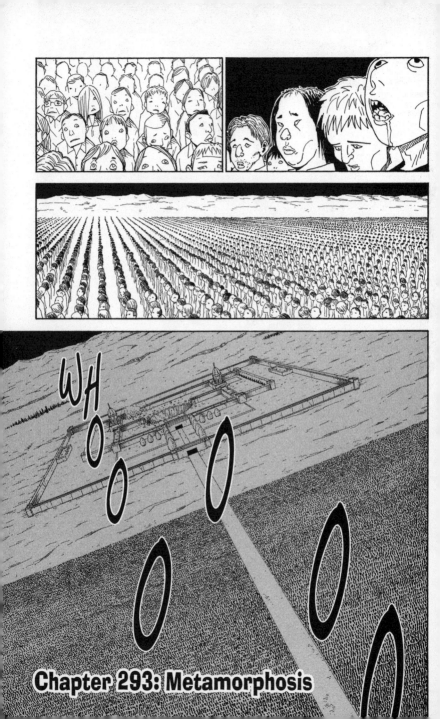

Chapter 293: Metamorphosis

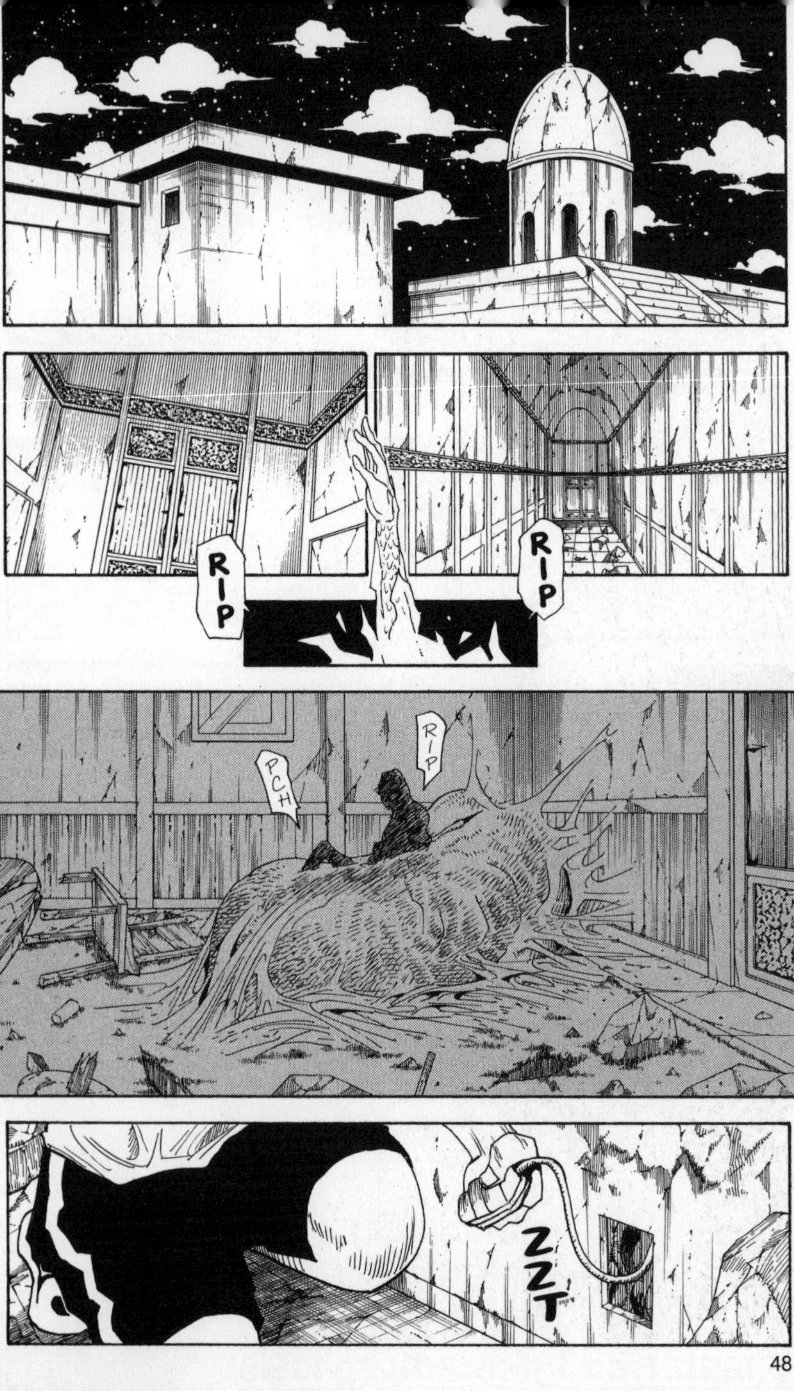
RIP
RIP
RIP
PCH
ZZT

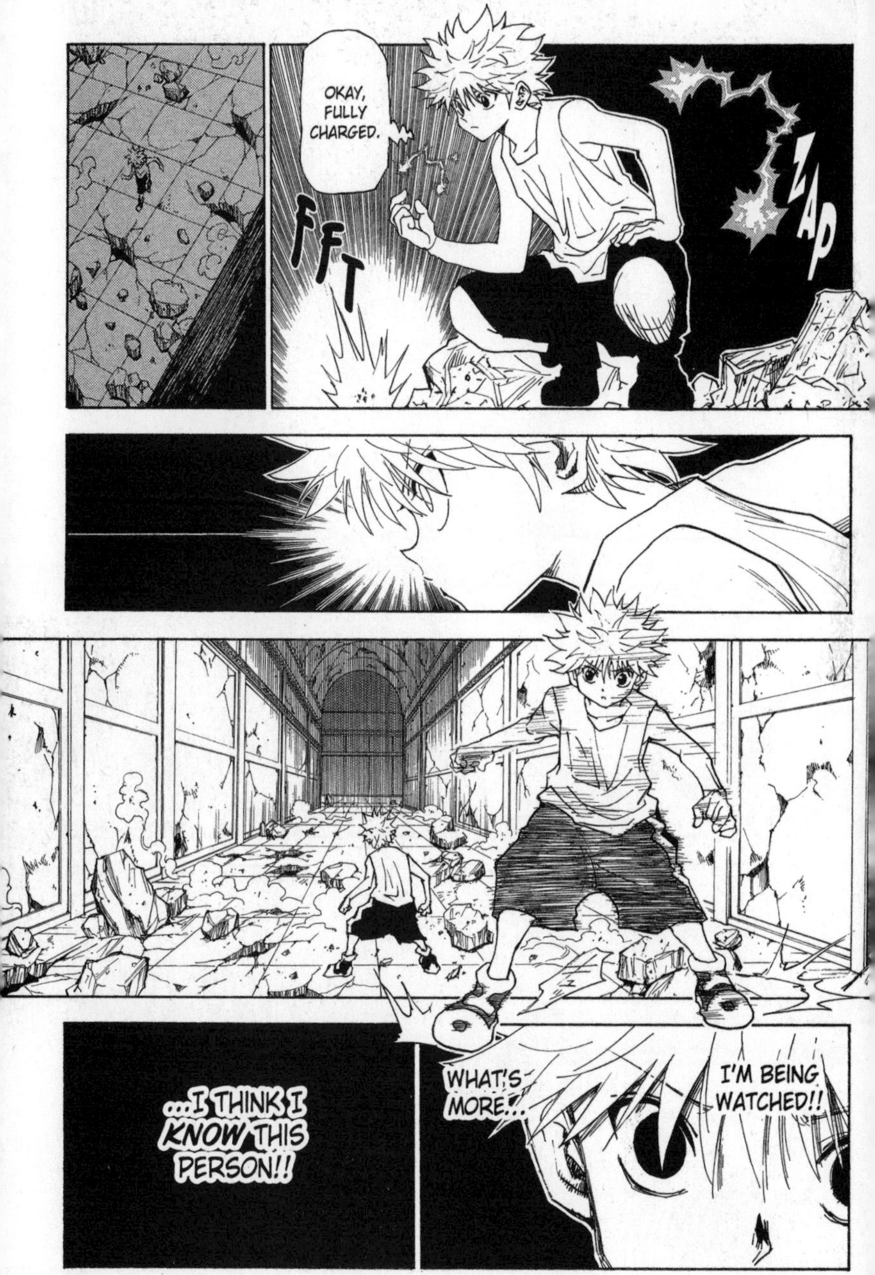
OKAY, FULLY CHARGED.
FFT
ZAP
...I THINK I KNOW THIS PERSON!!
WHAT'S MORE...
I'M BEING WATCHED!!

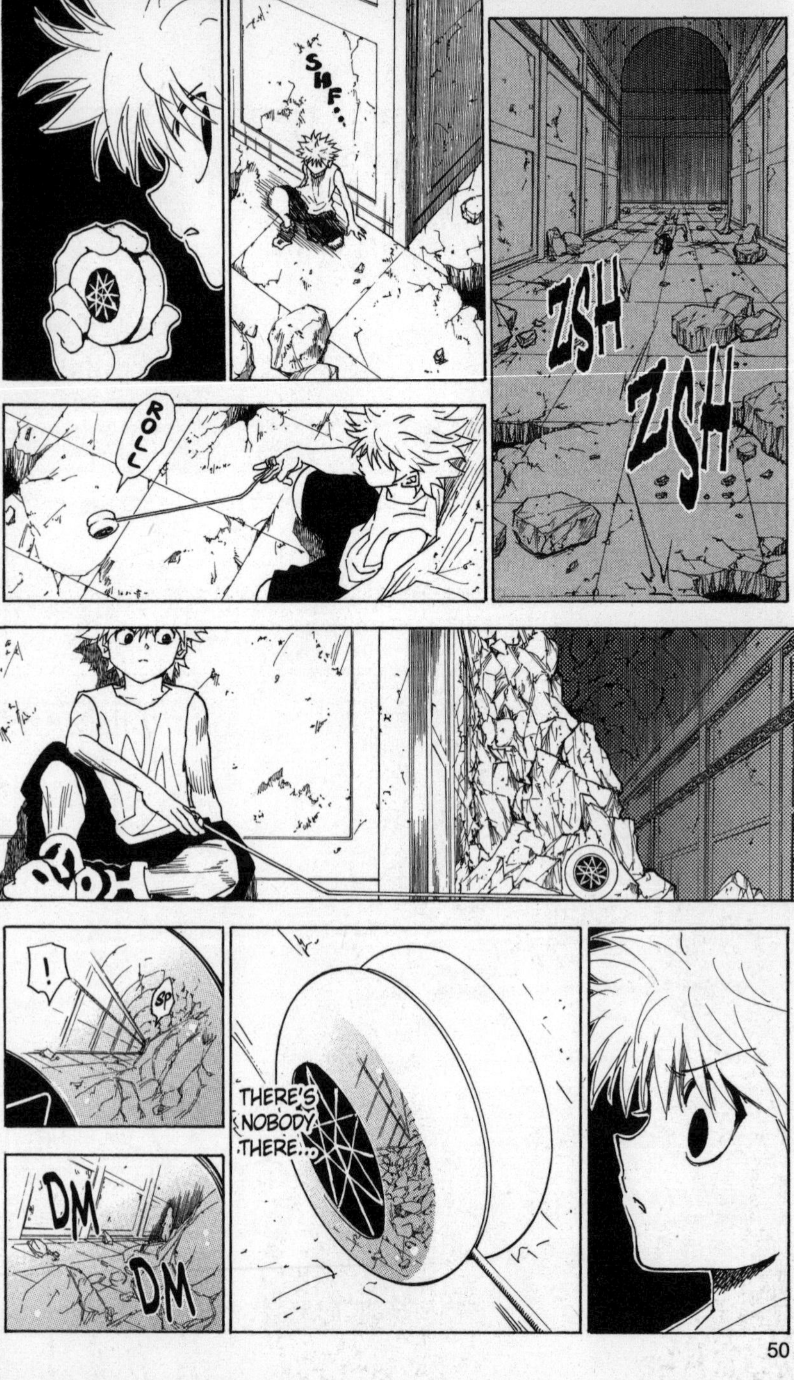
ZSH
ZSH
SHF...
ROLL
THERE'S NOBODY THERE...
!
SP
DM
DM

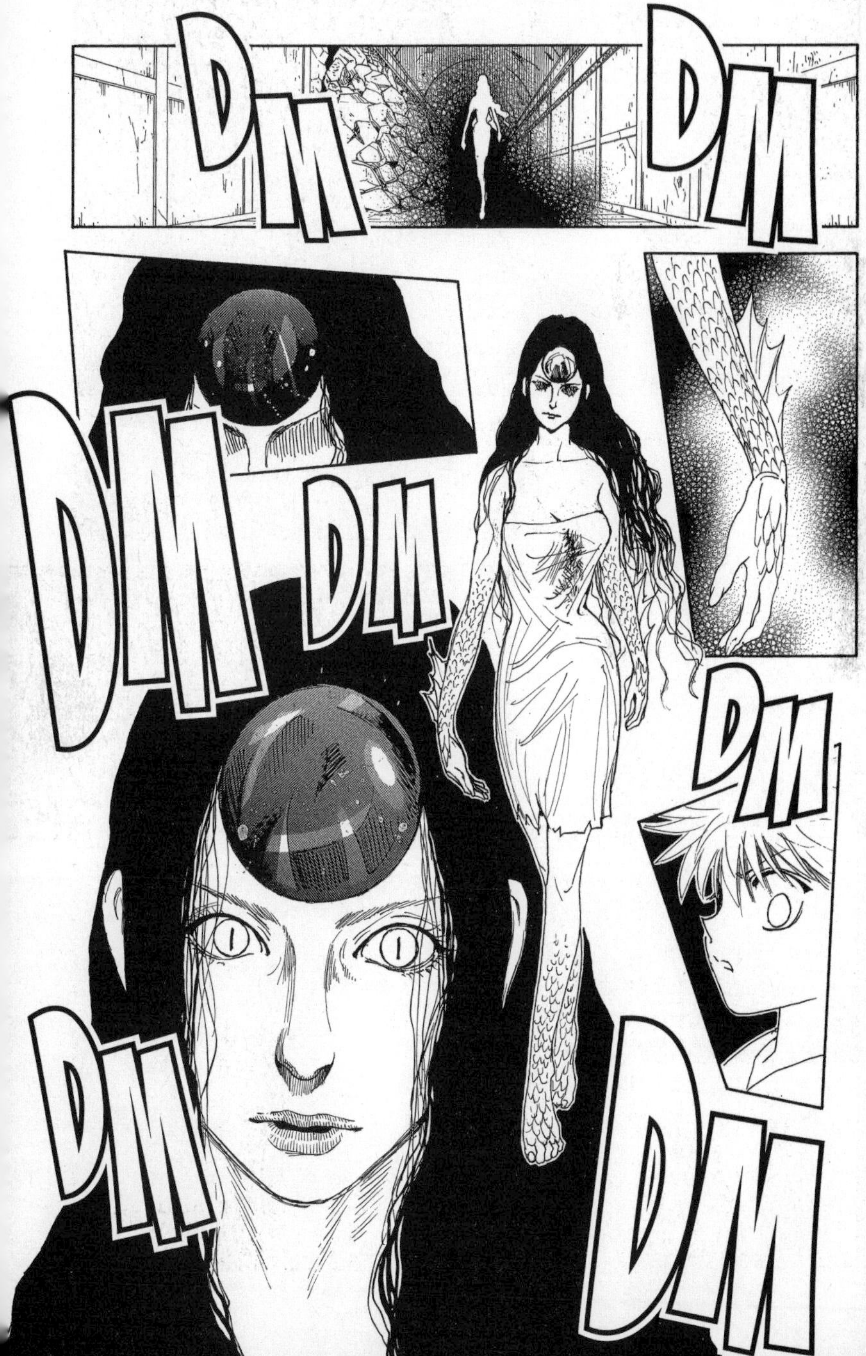
DM
DM
DM
DM
DM
DM
DM

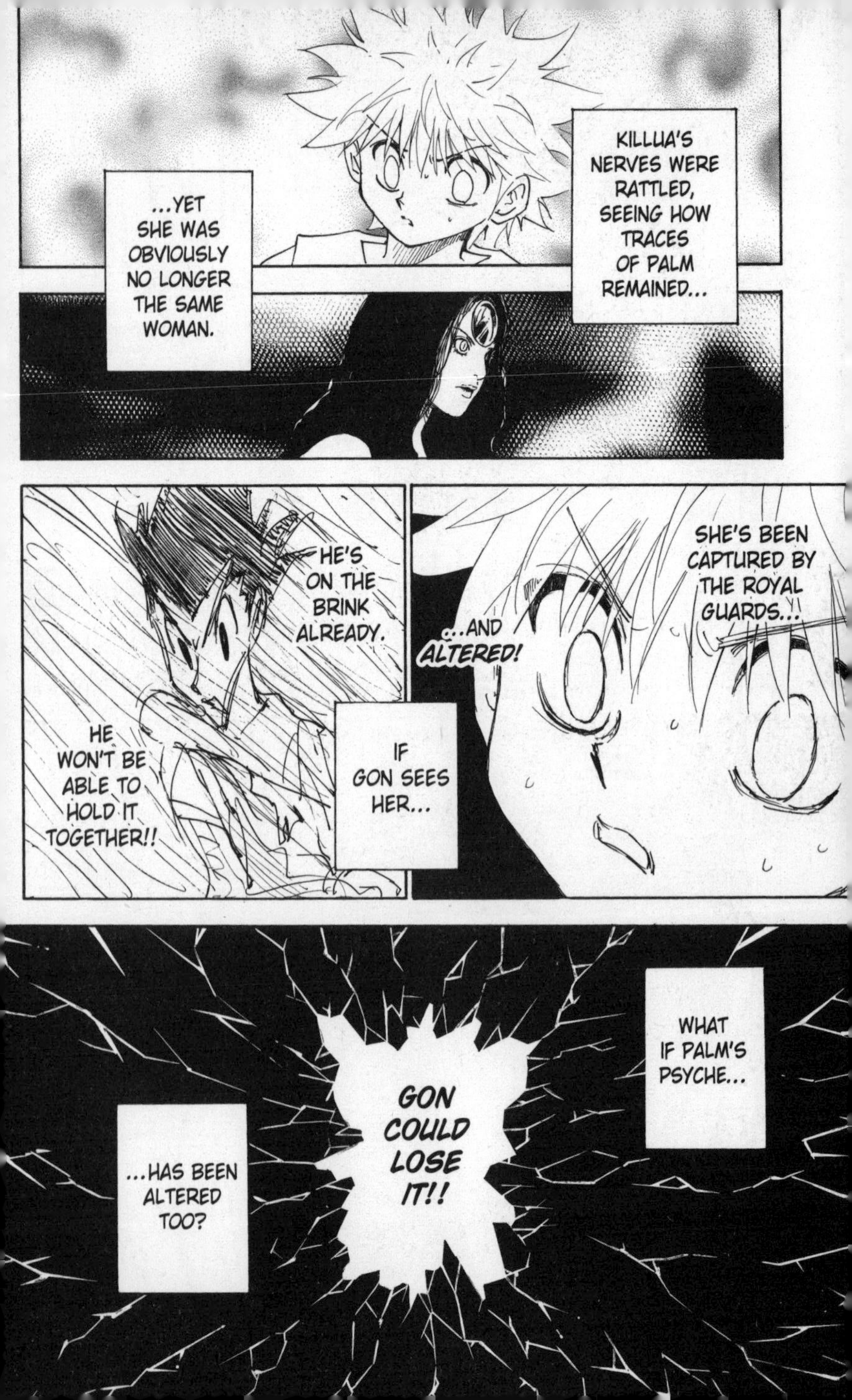
KILLUA'S NERVES WERE RATTLED, SEEING HOW TRACES OF PALM REMAINED...
...YET SHE WAS OBVIOUSLY NO LONGER THE SAME WOMAN.
SHE'S BEEN CAPTURED BY THE ROYAL GUARDS...
...AND ALTERED!
HE'S ON THE BRINK ALREADY.
IF GON SEES HER...
HE WON'T BE ABLE TO HOLD IT TOGETHER!!
WHAT IF PALM'S PSYCHE...
GON COULD LOSE IT!!
...HAS BEEN ALTERED TOO?

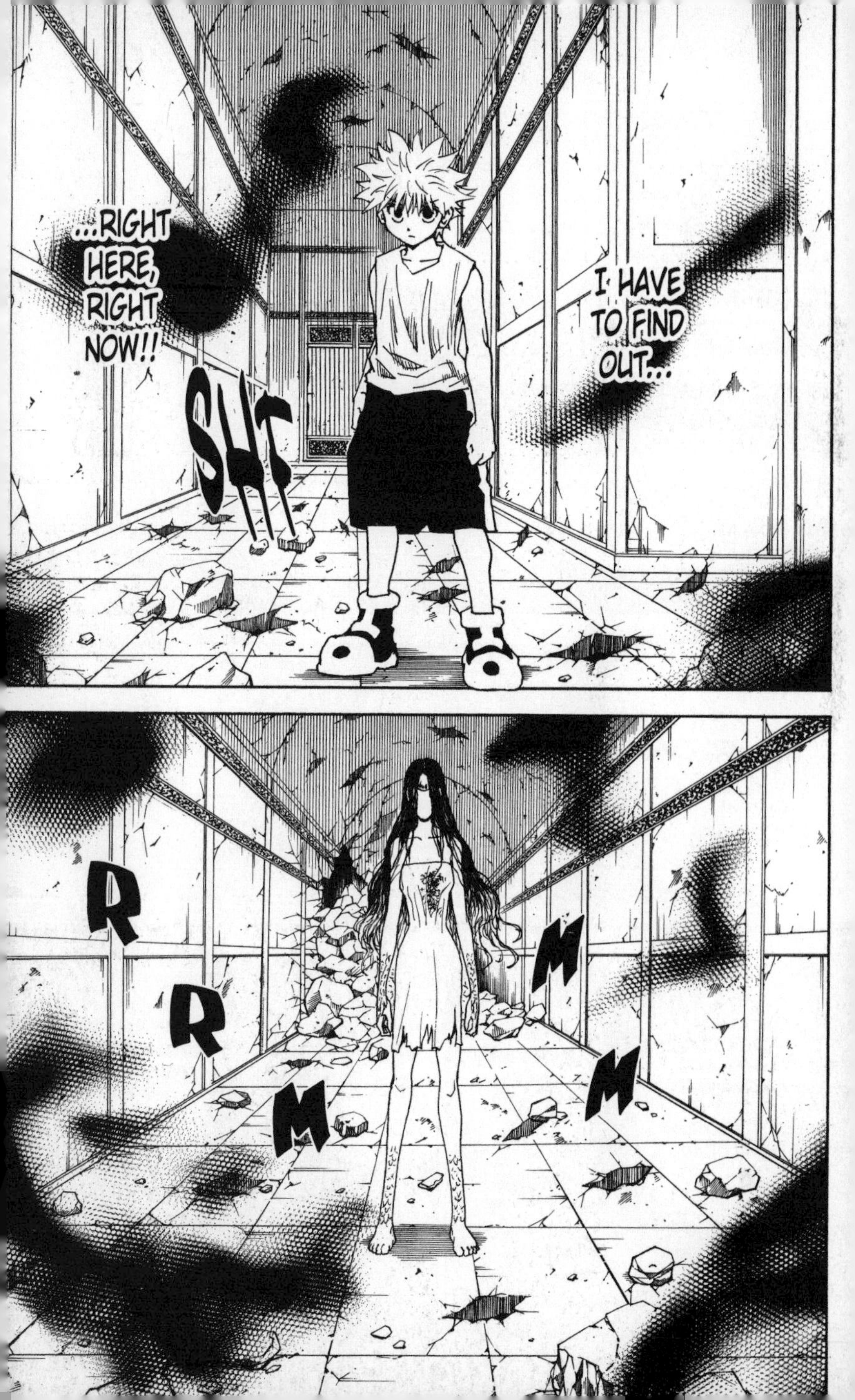
I HAVE TO FIND OUT...
...RIGHT HERE, RIGHT NOW!!
SHF
RRMMM

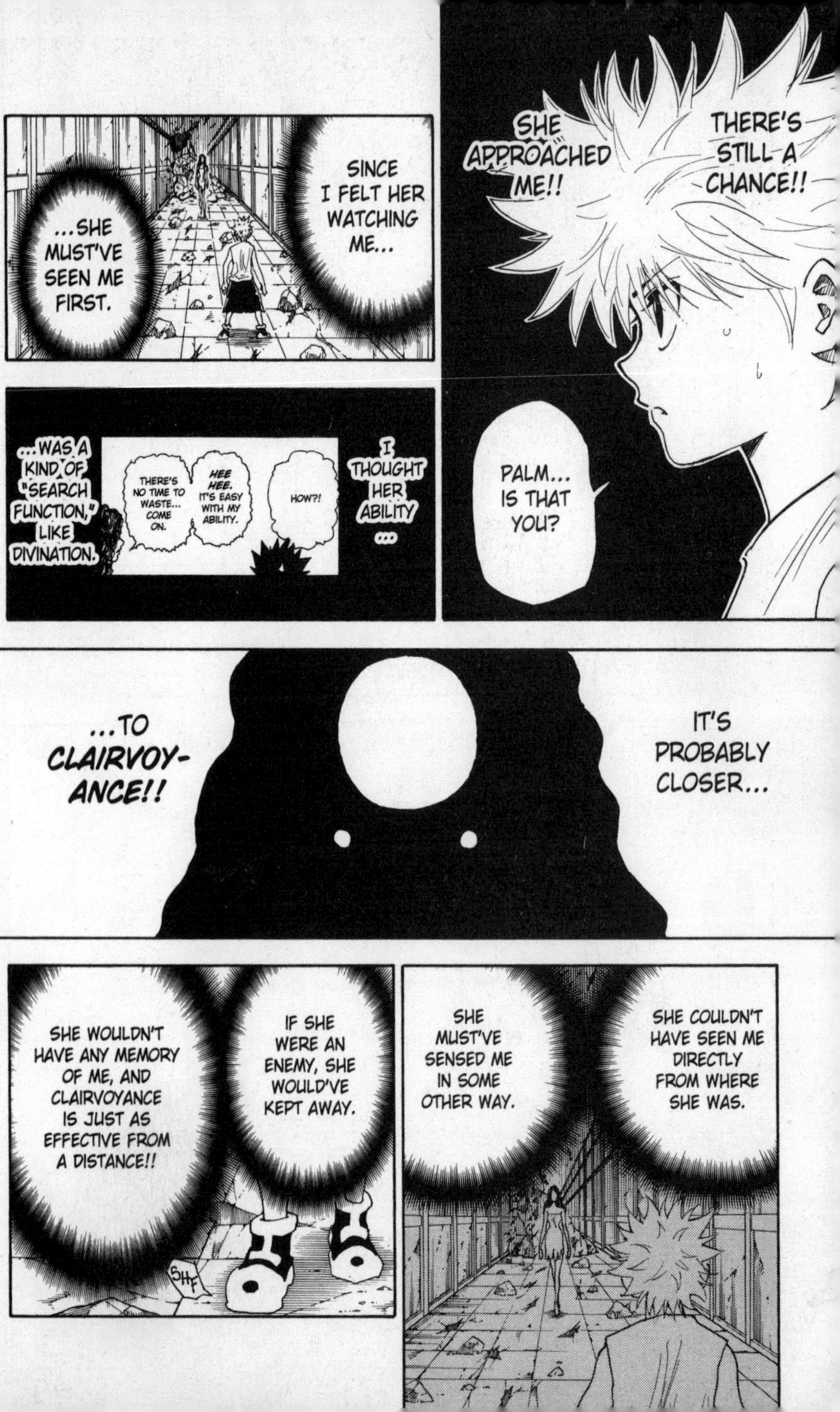
THERE'S STILL A CHANCE!!
SHE APPROACHED ME!!
PALM... IS THAT YOU?
SINCE I FELT HER WATCHING ME...
...SHE MUST'VE SEEN ME FIRST.
I THOUGHT HER ABILITY...
HOW?!
HEE HEE. IT'S EASY WITH MY ABILITY.
THERE'S NO TIME TO WASTE... COME ON.
...WAS A KIND OF "SEARCH FUNCTION," LIKE DIVINATION.
IT'S PROBABLY CLOSER...
...TO CLAIRVOYANCE!!
SHE COULDN'T HAVE SEEN ME DIRECTLY FROM WHERE SHE WAS.
SHE MUST'VE SENSED ME IN SOME OTHER WAY.
IF SHE WERE AN ENEMY, SHE WOULD'VE KEPT AWAY.
SHE WOULDN'T HAVE ANY MEMORY OF ME, AND CLAIRVOYANCE IS JUST AS EFFECTIVE FROM A DISTANCE!!
SHF

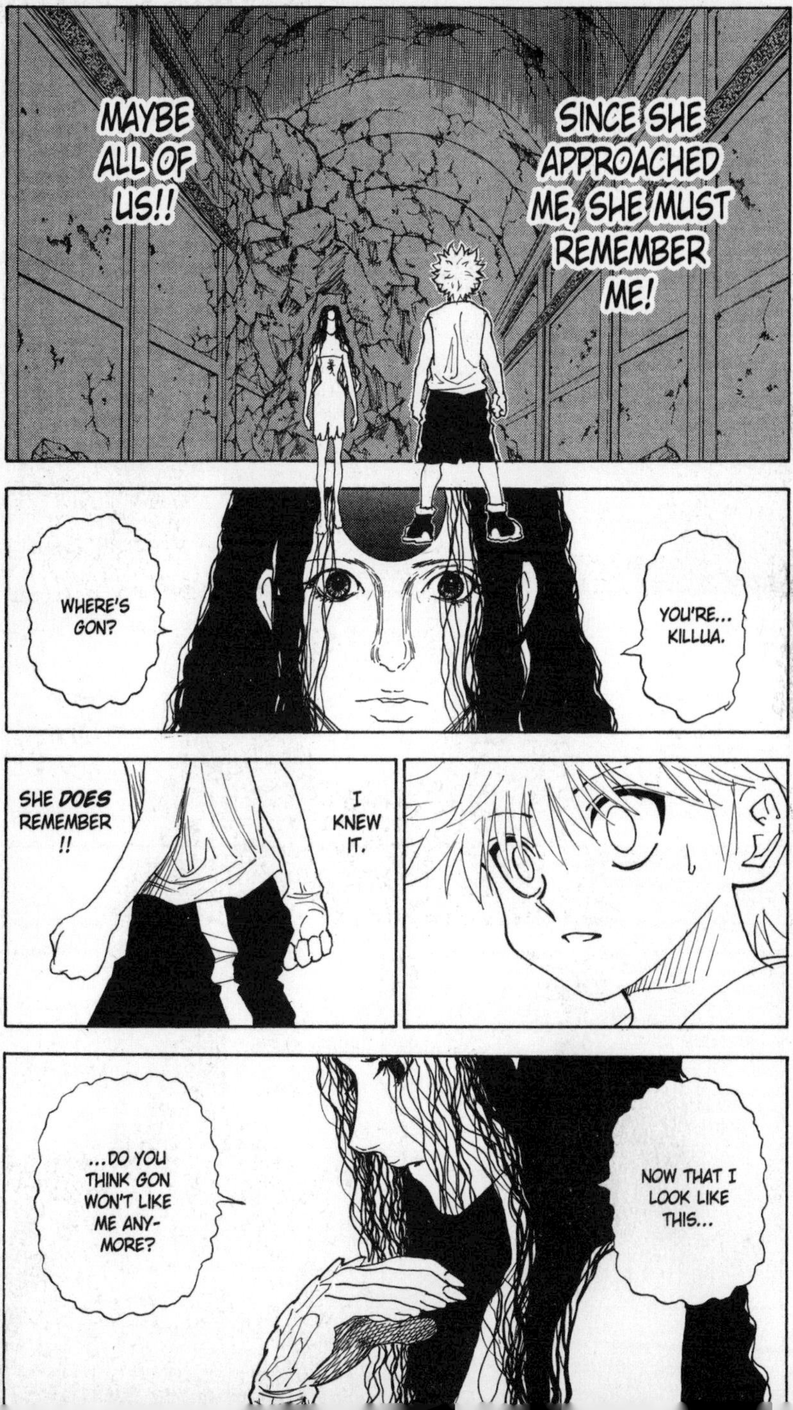
SINCE SHE APPROACHED ME, SHE MUST REMEMBER ME!
MAYBE ALL OF US!!
YOU'RE... KILLUA.
WHERE'S GON?
I KNEW IT.
SHE *DOES* REMEMBER !!
NOW THAT I LOOK LIKE THIS...
...DO YOU THINK GON WON'T LIKE ME ANY-MORE?

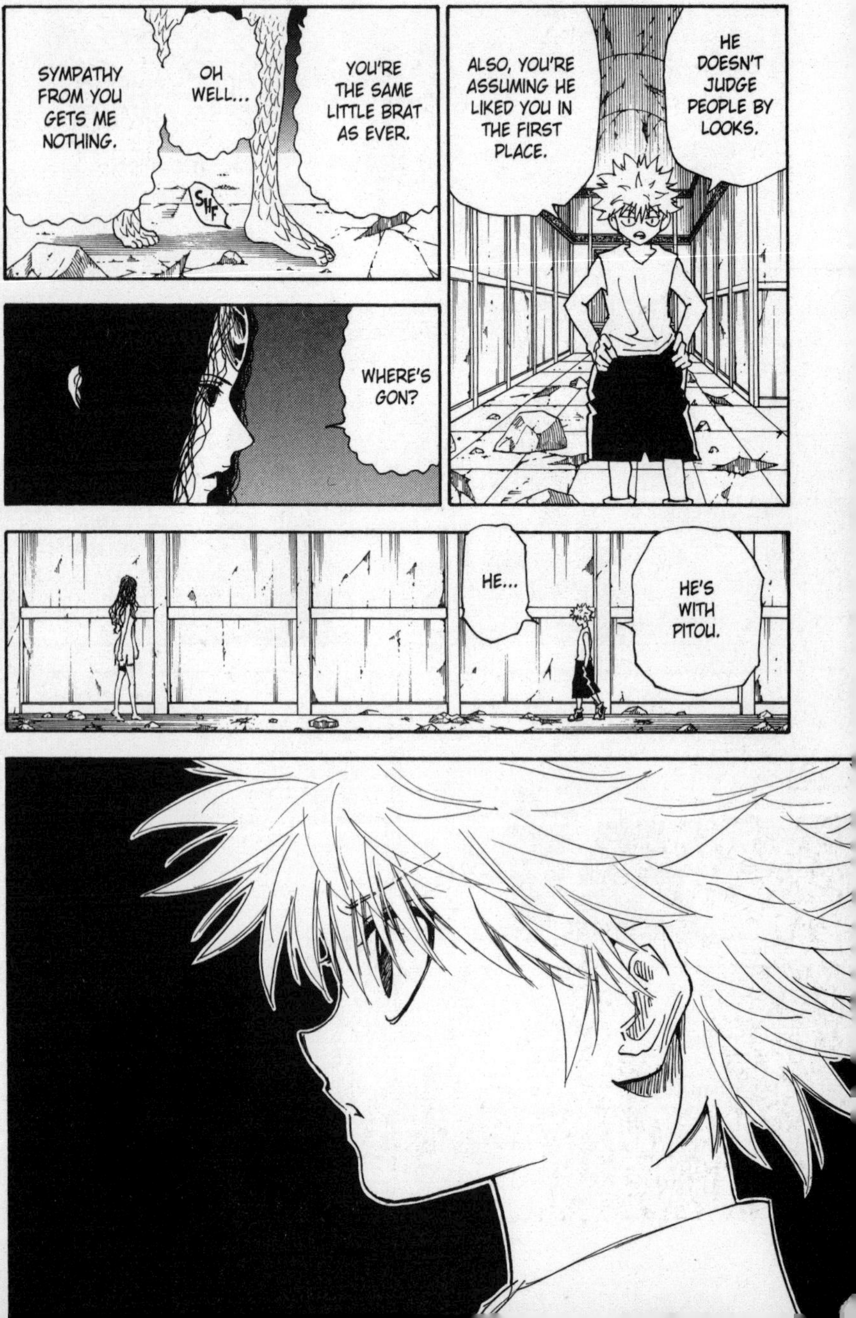
HE DOESN'T JUDGE PEOPLE BY LOOKS.
ALSO, YOU'RE ASSUMING HE LIKED YOU IN THE FIRST PLACE.
YOU'RE THE SAME LITTLE BRAT AS EVER.
OH WELL...
SYMPATHY FROM YOU GETS ME NOTHING.
SHF
WHERE'S GON?
HE...
HE'S WITH PITOU.

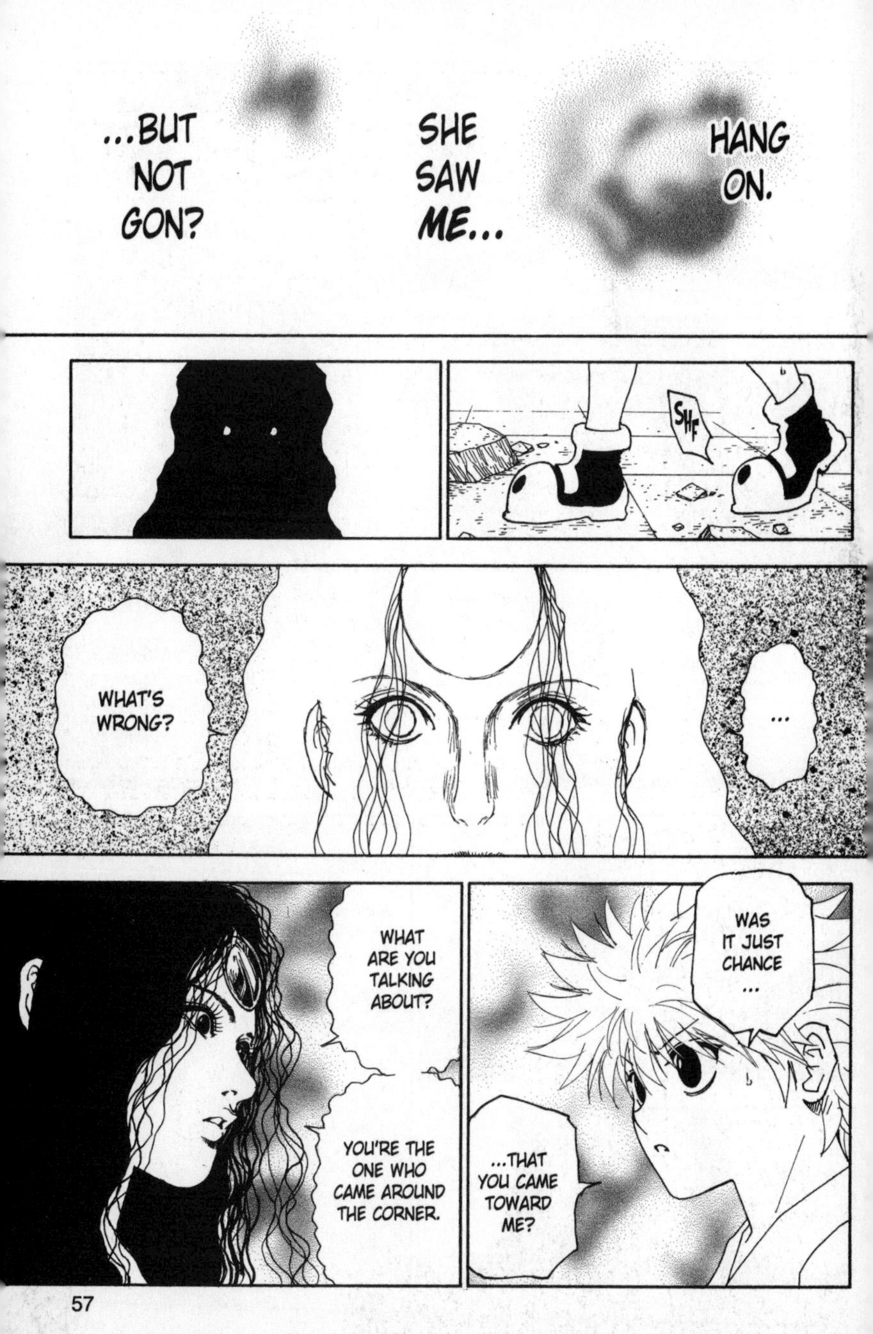
HANG ON.
SHE SAW ME...
...BUT NOT GON?
SHF
...
WHAT'S WRONG?
WAS IT JUST CHANCE ...
...THAT YOU CAME TOWARD ME?
WHAT ARE YOU TALKING ABOUT?
YOU'RE THE ONE WHO CAME AROUND THE CORNER.

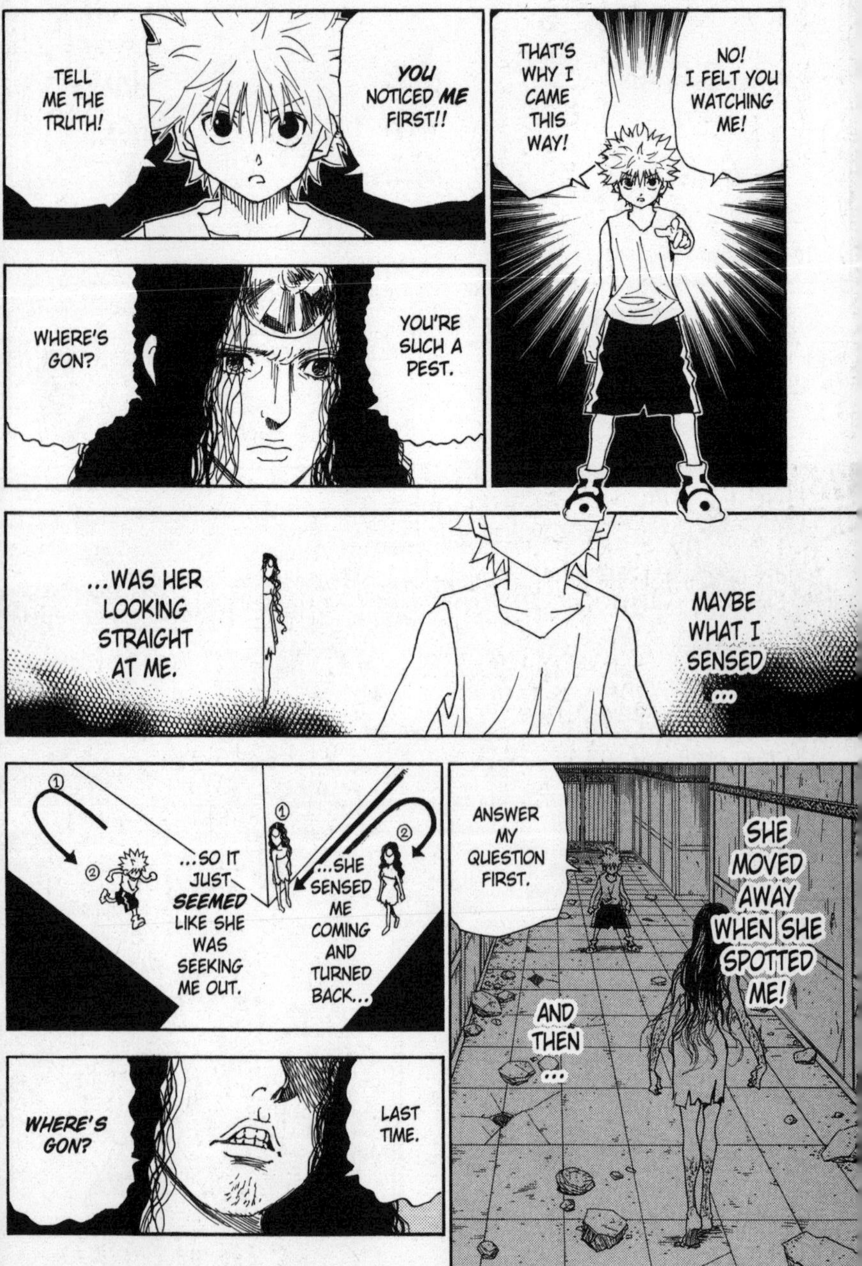
NO! I FELT YOU WATCHING ME!
THAT'S WHY I CAME THIS WAY!
YOU NOTICED *ME* FIRST!!
TELL ME THE TRUTH!
YOU'RE SUCH A PEST.
WHERE'S GON?
MAYBE WHAT I SENSED...
...WAS HER LOOKING STRAIGHT AT ME.
SHE MOVED AWAY WHEN SHE SPOTTED ME!
ANSWER MY QUESTION FIRST.
AND THEN...
...SHE SENSED ME COMING AND TURNED BACK...
...SO IT JUST *SEEMED* LIKE SHE WAS SEEKING ME OUT.
LAST TIME.
WHERE'S GON?

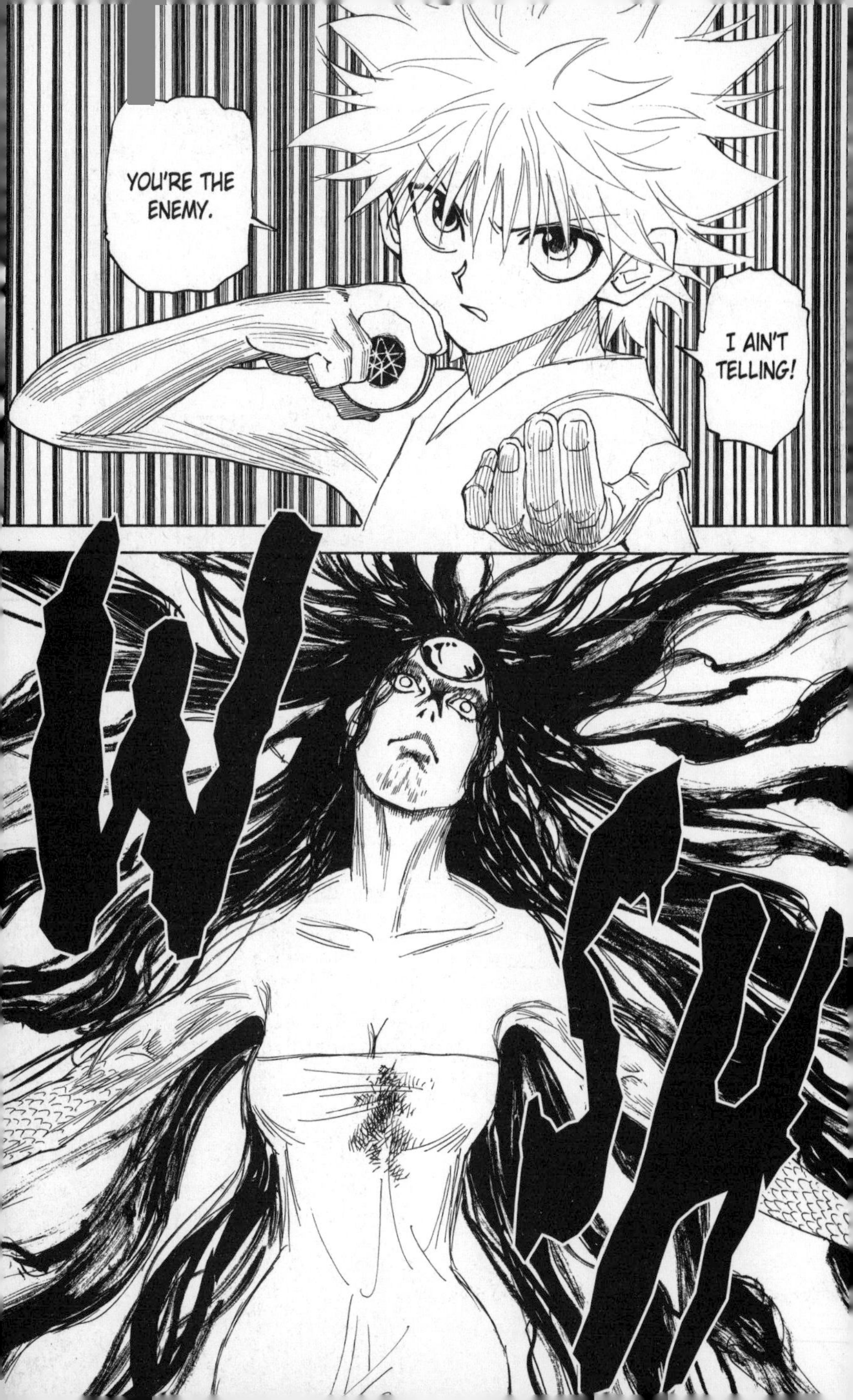
I AIN'T TELLING!
YOU'RE THE ENEMY.

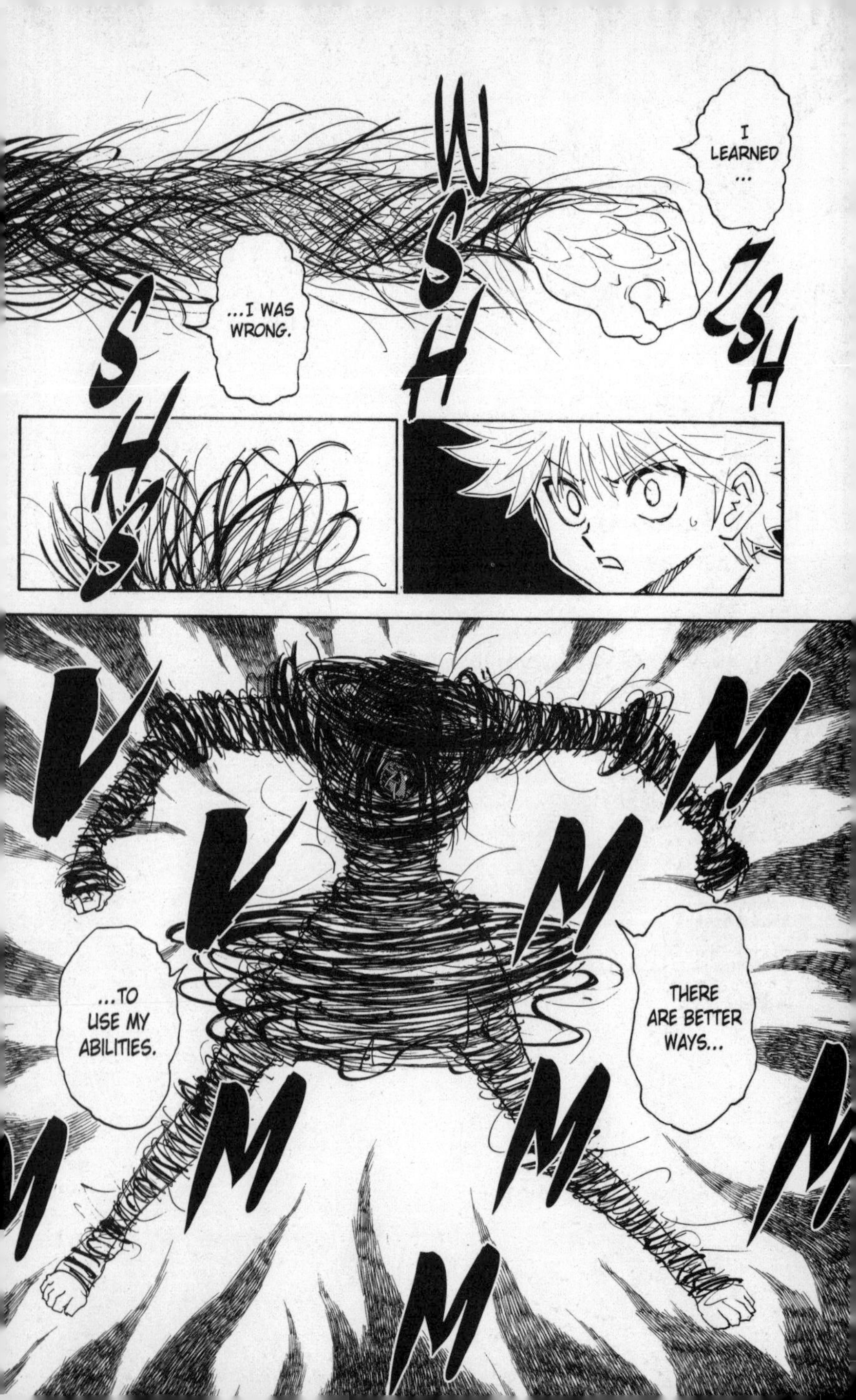
I LEARNED ...
ZSH
WSH
...I WAS WRONG.
THERE ARE BETTER WAYS...
...TO USE MY ABILITIES.

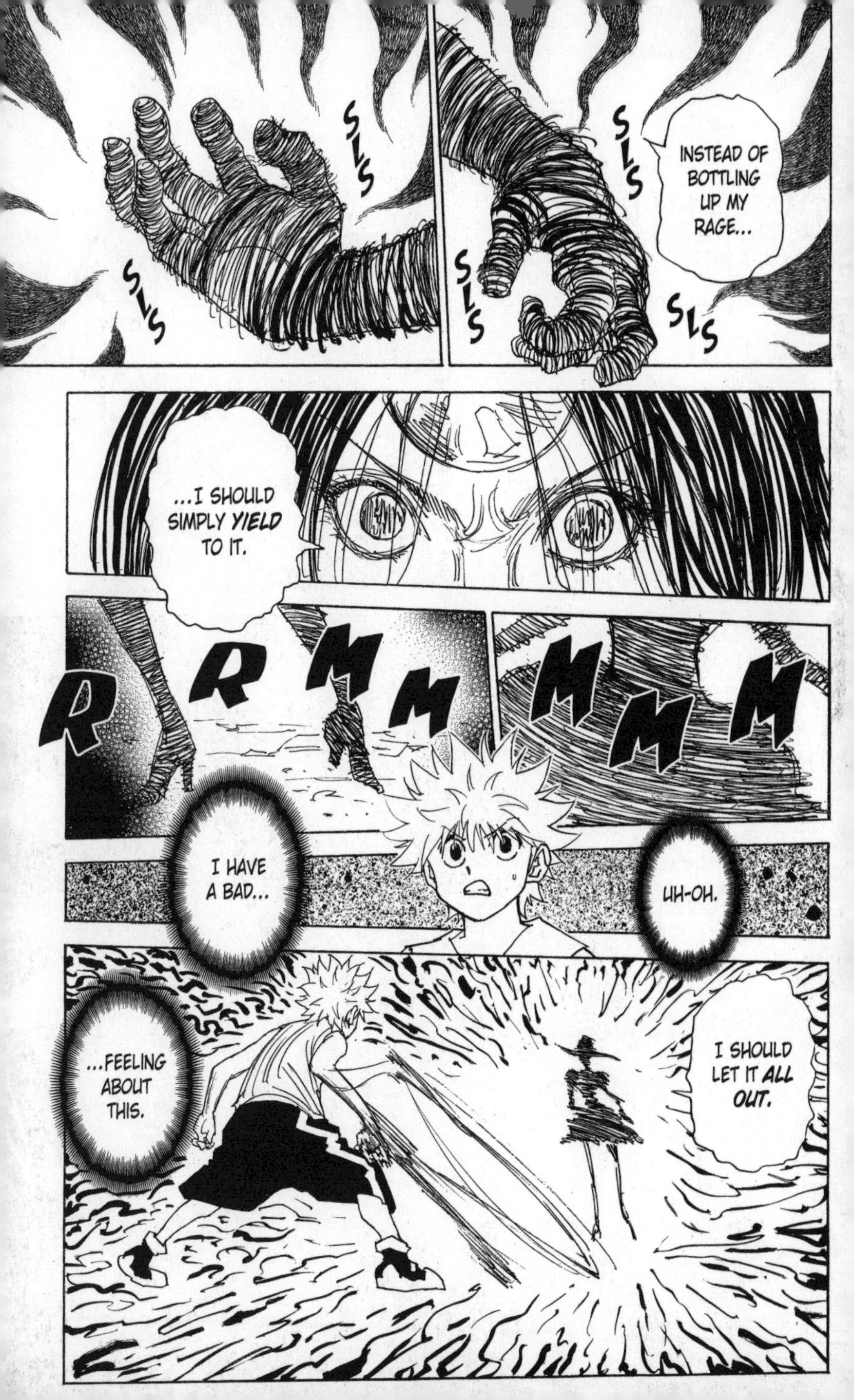
SLS
INSTEAD OF BOTTLING UP MY RAGE...
SLS
SLS
SLS
SLS
...I SHOULD SIMPLY *YIELD* TO IT.
RRMMMMMM
UH-OH.
I HAVE A BAD...
I SHOULD LET IT *ALL OUT.*
...FEELING ABOUT THIS.

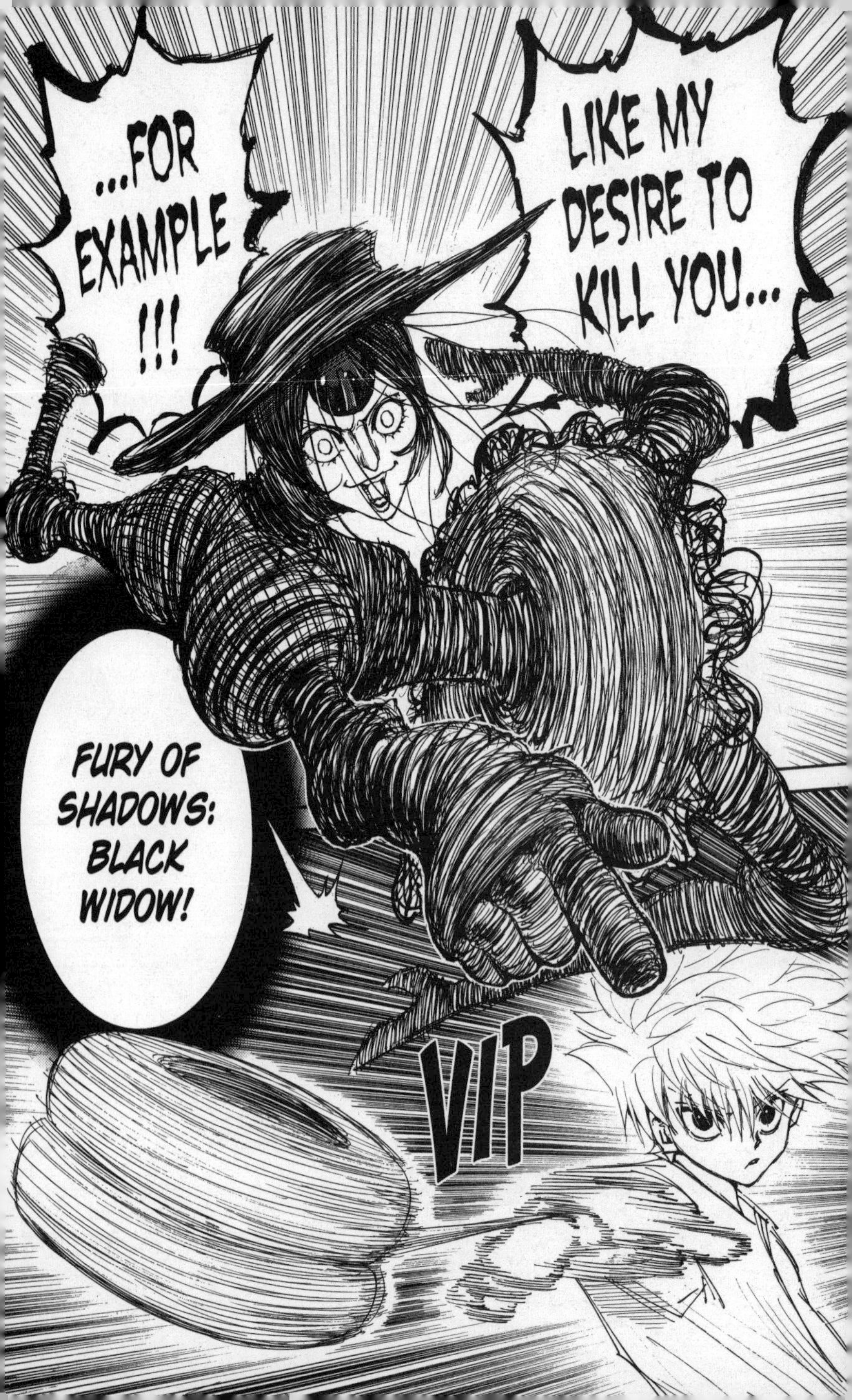
LIKE MY DESIRE TO KILL YOU...
...FOR EXAMPLE !!!
FURY OF SHADOWS: BLACK WIDOW!
VIP

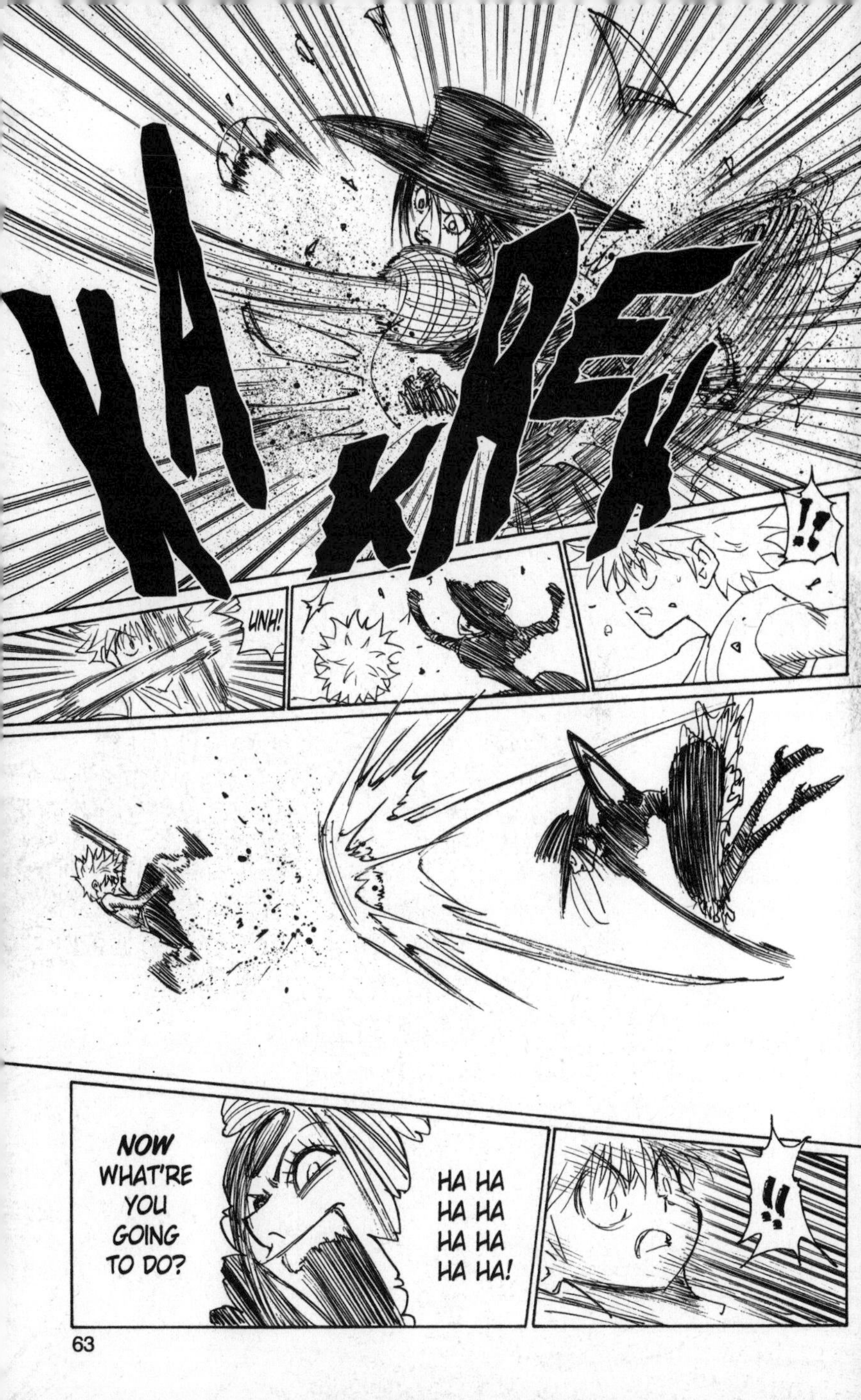
KA KRACK
!!
UNH!
!!
HA HA
HA HA
HA HA
HA HA!
NOW
WHAT'RE
YOU
GOING
TO DO?

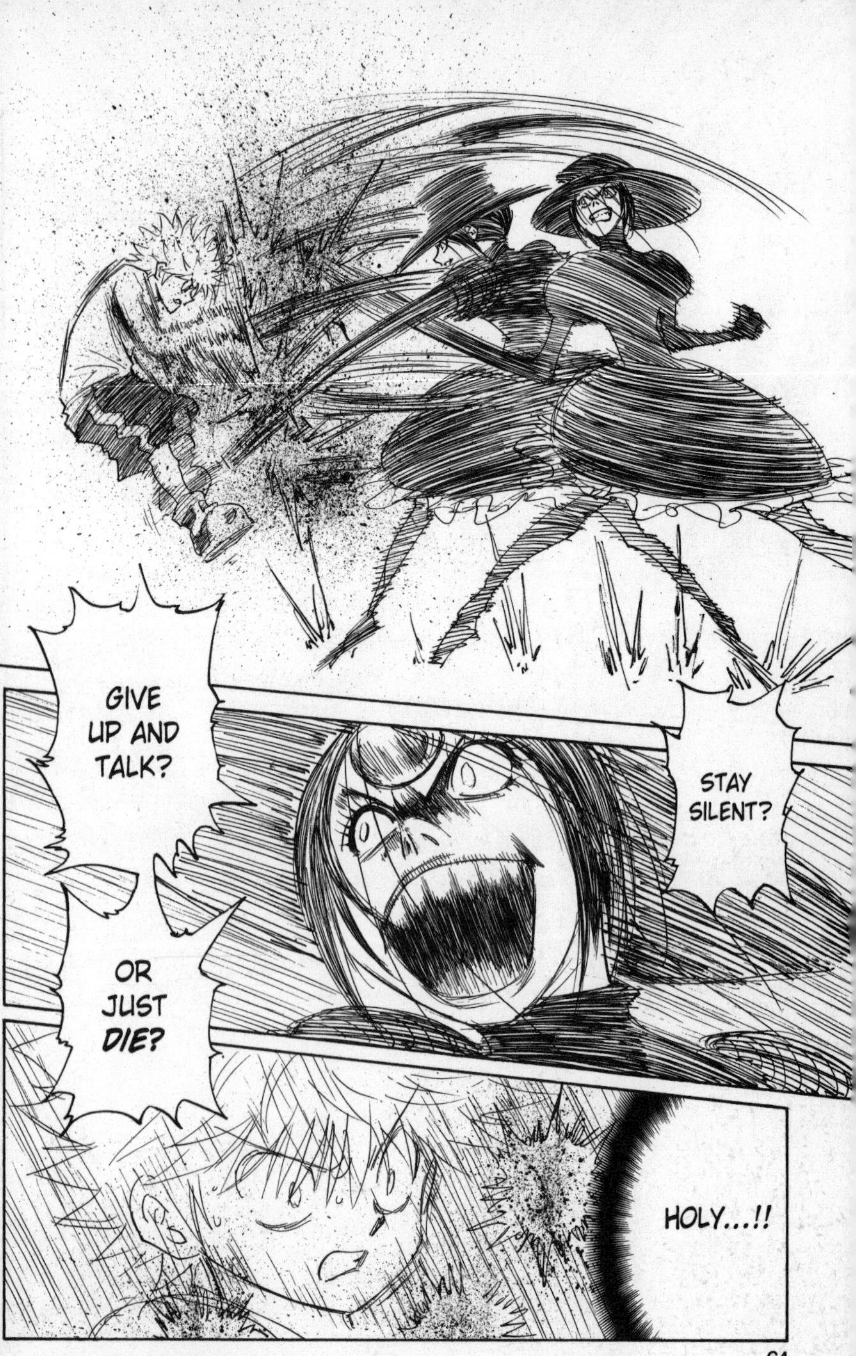
STAY SILENT?
GIVE UP AND TALK?
OR JUST DIE?
HOLY...!!

READ THIS WAY

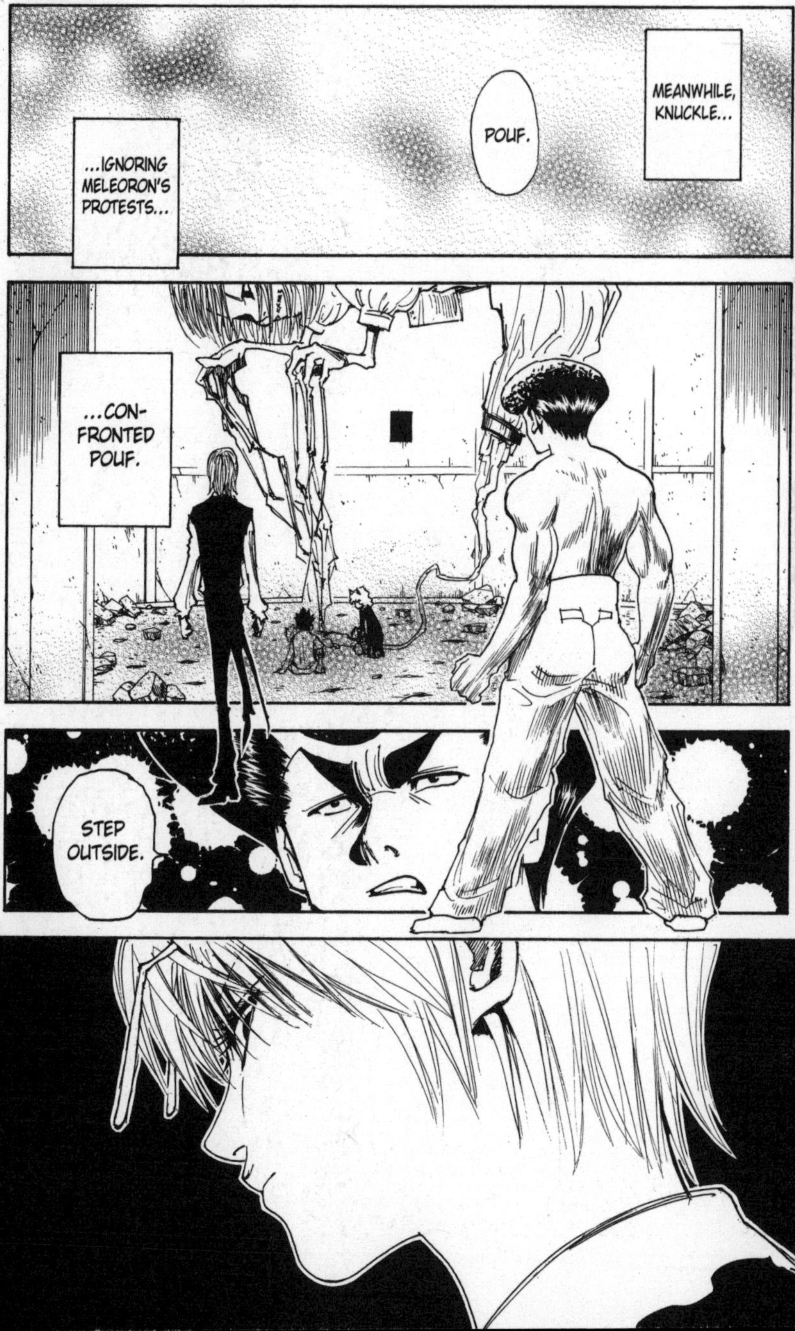
MEANWHILE, KNUCKLE...
POUF.
...IGNORING MELEORON'S PROTESTS...
...CON-FRONTED POUF.
STEP OUTSIDE.

Chapter 294: Breakdown

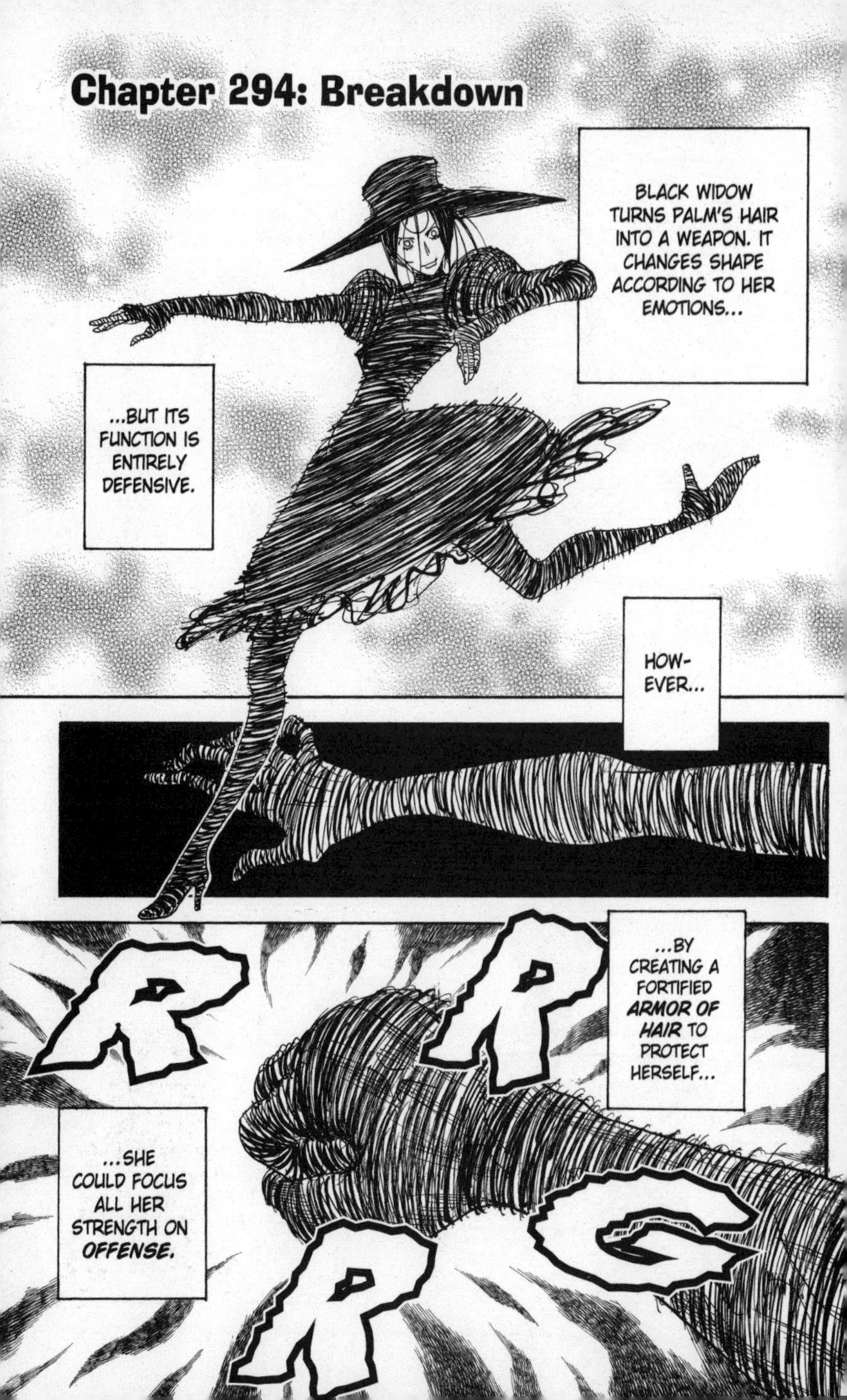
BLACK WIDOW TURNS PALM'S HAIR INTO A WEAPON. IT CHANGES SHAPE ACCORDING TO HER EMOTIONS...
...BUT ITS FUNCTION IS ENTIRELY DEFENSIVE.
HOW-EVER...
...BY CREATING A FORTIFIED **ARMOR OF HAIR** TO PROTECT HERSELF...
...SHE COULD FOCUS ALL HER STRENGTH ON **OFFENSE.**

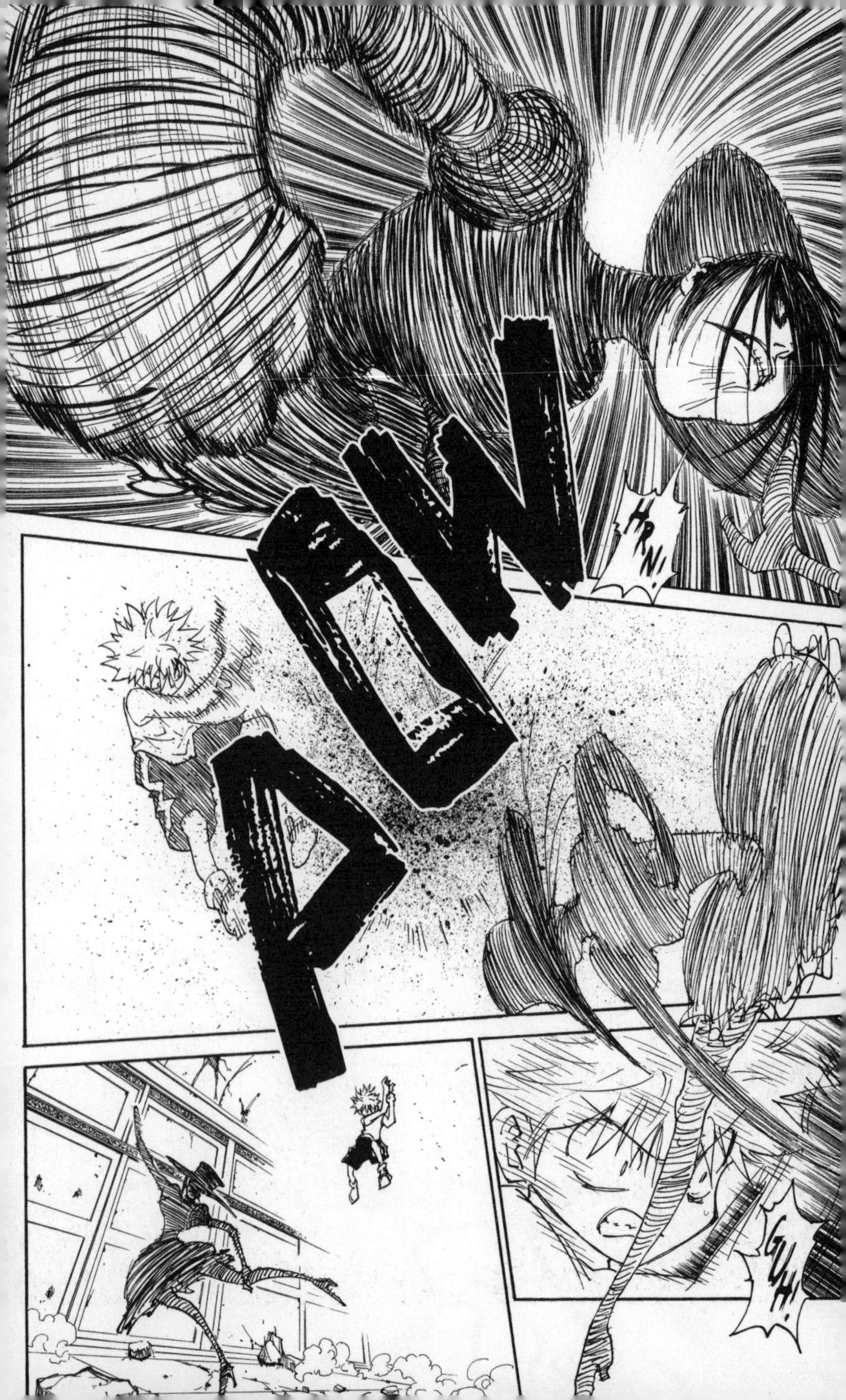
HRN!
POW
GUH!

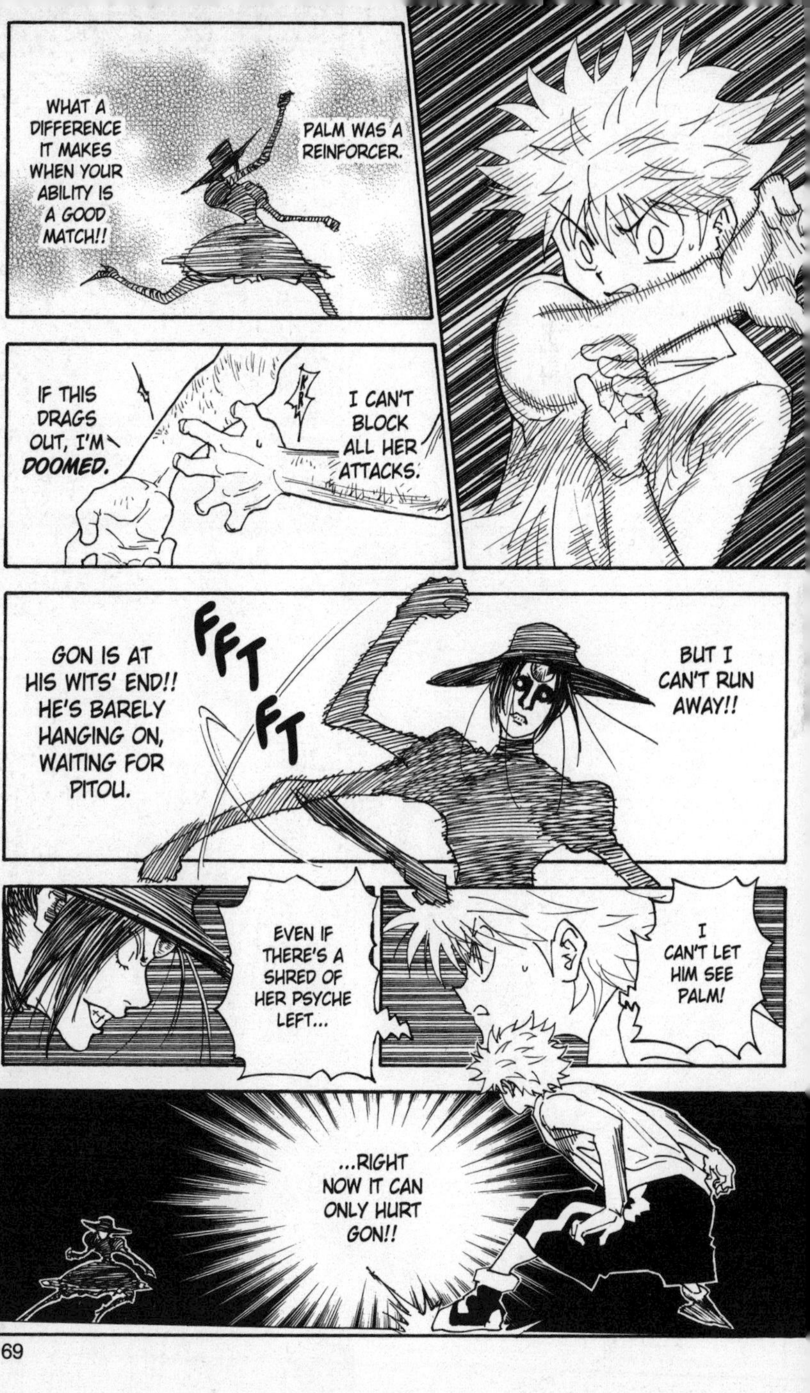
PALM WAS A REINFORCER.
WHAT A DIFFERENCE IT MAKES WHEN YOUR ABILITY IS A GOOD MATCH!!
I CAN'T BLOCK ALL HER ATTACKS.
IF THIS DRAGS OUT, I'M **DOOMED.**
BUT I CAN'T RUN AWAY!!
FFT FT
GON IS AT HIS WITS' END!! HE'S BARELY HANGING ON, WAITING FOR PITOU.
I CAN'T LET HIM SEE PALM!
EVEN IF THERE'S A SHRED OF HER PSYCHE LEFT...
...RIGHT NOW IT CAN ONLY HURT GON!!

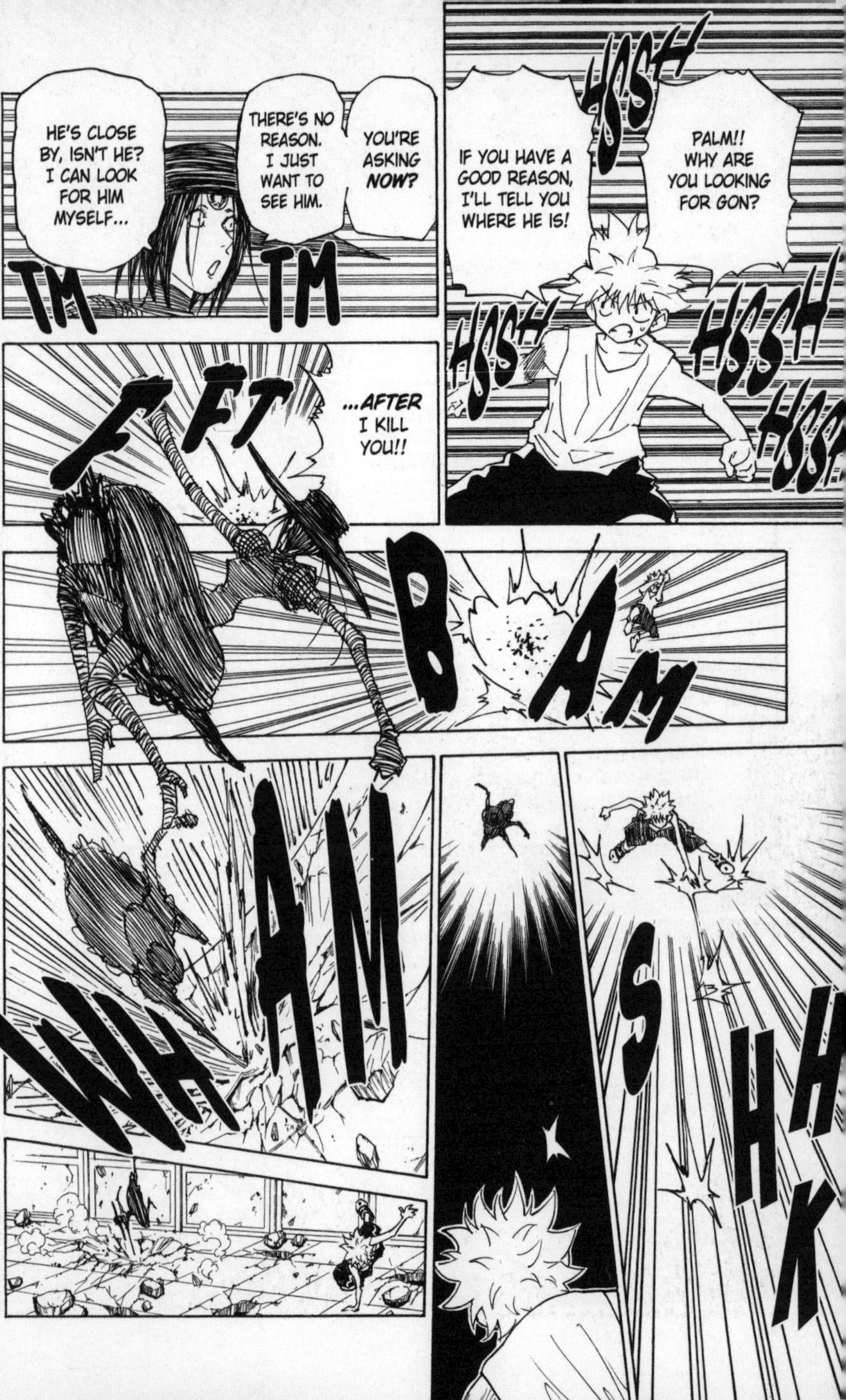

HSSH
PALM!! WHY ARE YOU LOOKING FOR GON?
IF YOU HAVE A GOOD REASON, I'LL TELL YOU WHERE HE IS!
HSSH
HSSH
HSSH
YOU'RE ASKING NOW?
THERE'S NO REASON. I JUST WANT TO SEE HIM.
HE'S CLOSE BY, ISN'T HE? I CAN LOOK FOR HIM MYSELF...
TM
TM
FFT
...AFTER I KILL YOU!!
BAM
SHHK
WHAM

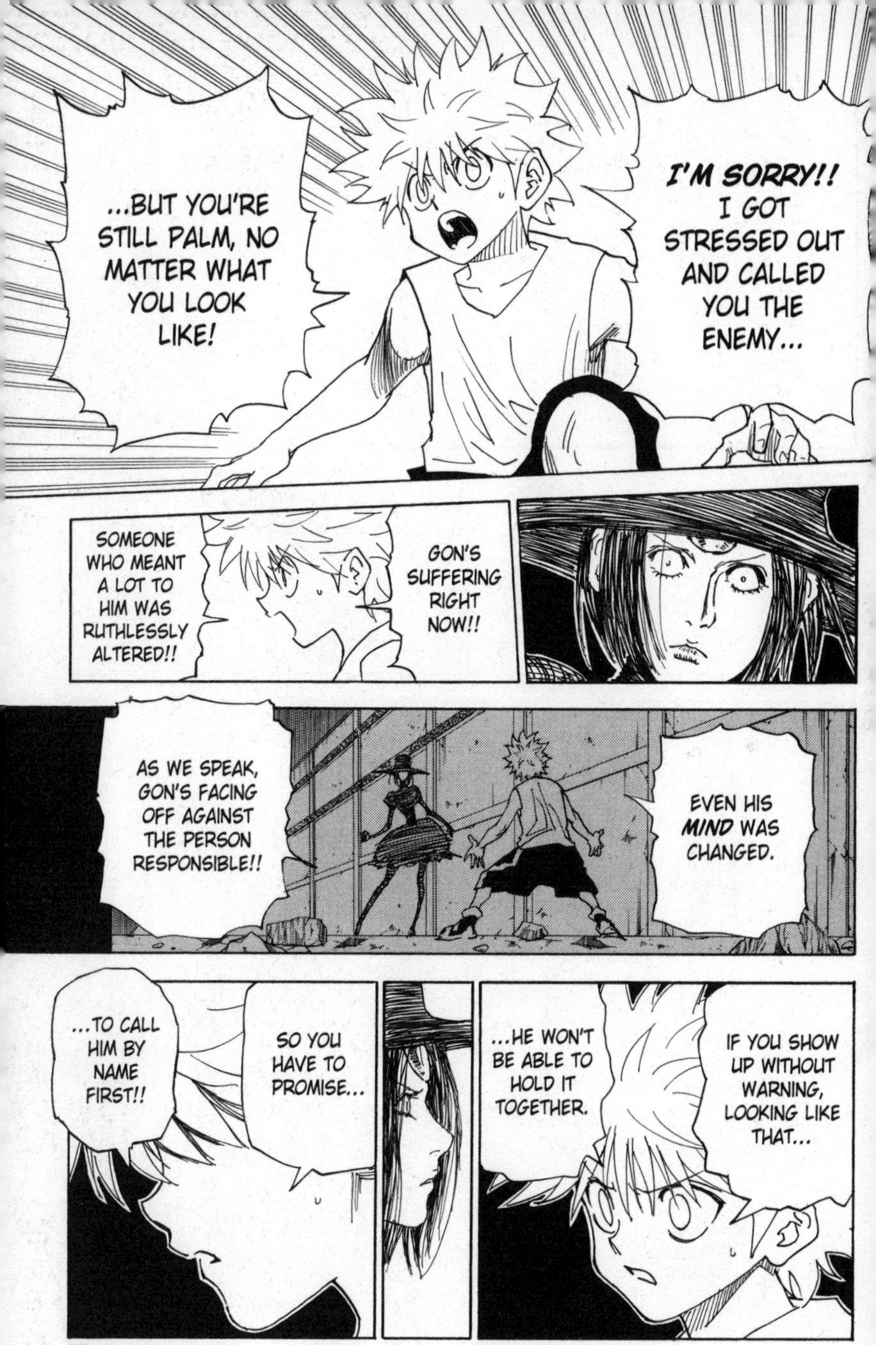
I'M SORRY!! I GOT STRESSED OUT AND CALLED YOU THE ENEMY...
...BUT YOU'RE STILL PALM, NO MATTER WHAT YOU LOOK LIKE!
GON'S SUFFERING RIGHT NOW!!
SOMEONE WHO MEANT A LOT TO HIM WAS RUTHLESSLY ALTERED!!
EVEN HIS *MIND* WAS CHANGED.
AS WE SPEAK, GON'S FACING OFF AGAINST THE PERSON RESPONSIBLE!!
IF YOU SHOW UP WITHOUT WARNING, LOOKING LIKE THAT...
...HE WON'T BE ABLE TO HOLD IT TOGETHER.
SO YOU HAVE TO PROMISE...
...TO CALL HIM BY NAME FIRST!!

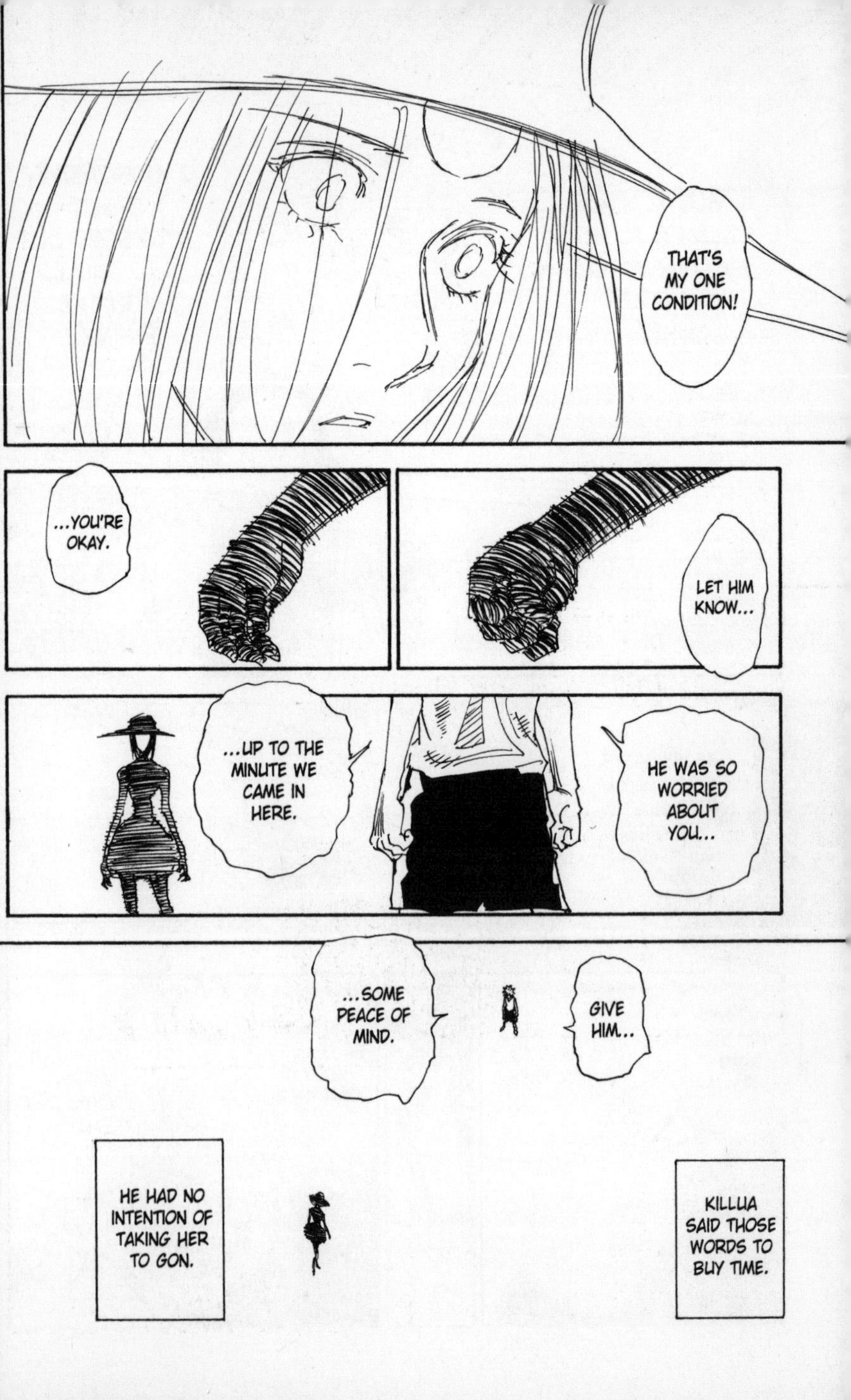
THAT'S MY ONE CONDITION!
LET HIM KNOW...
...YOU'RE OKAY.
HE WAS SO WORRIED ABOUT YOU...
...UP TO THE MINUTE WE CAME IN HERE.
GIVE HIM...
...SOME PEACE OF MIND.
KILLUA SAID THOSE WORDS TO BUY TIME.
HE HAD NO INTENTION OF TAKING HER TO GON.

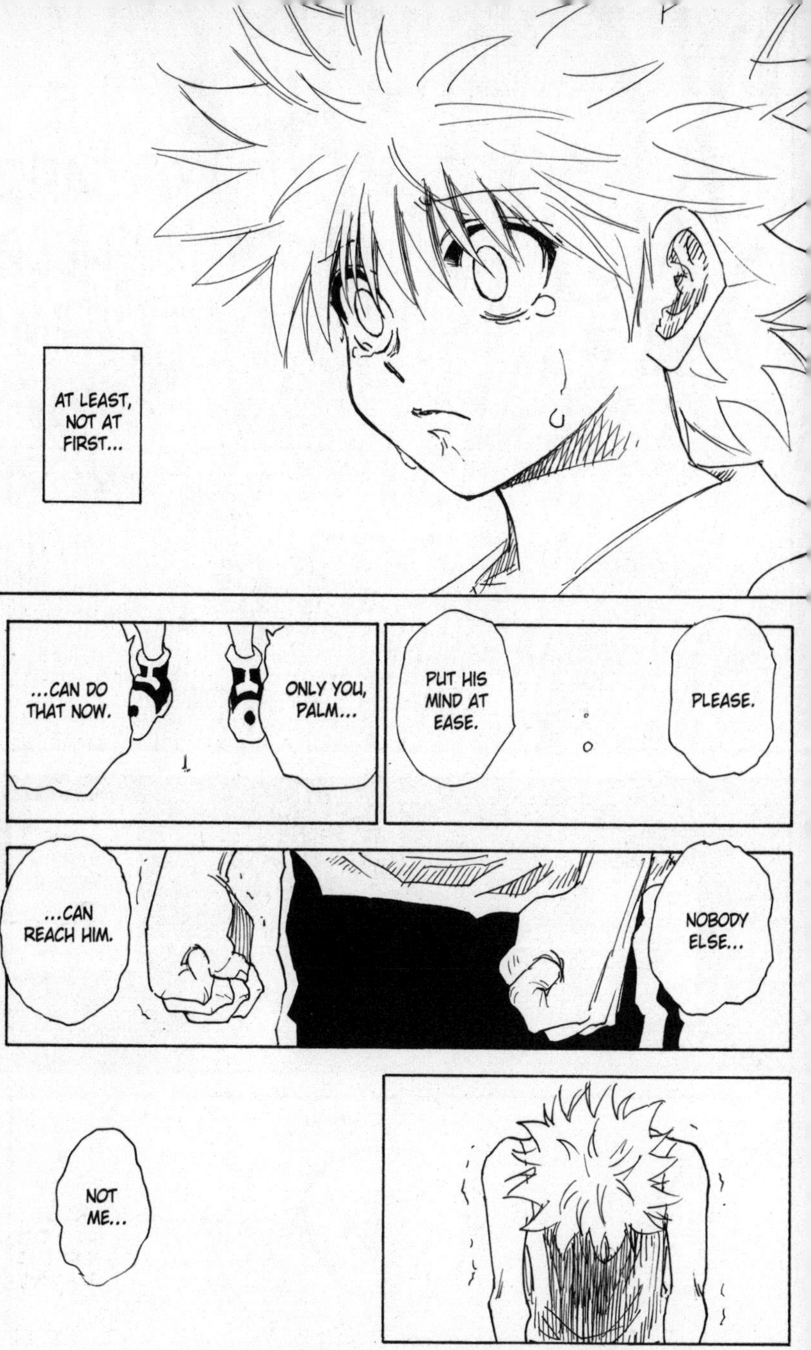
AT LEAST, NOT AT FIRST...
PLEASE.
PUT HIS MIND AT EASE.
ONLY YOU, PALM...
...CAN DO THAT NOW.
NOBODY ELSE...
...CAN REACH HIM.
NOT ME...

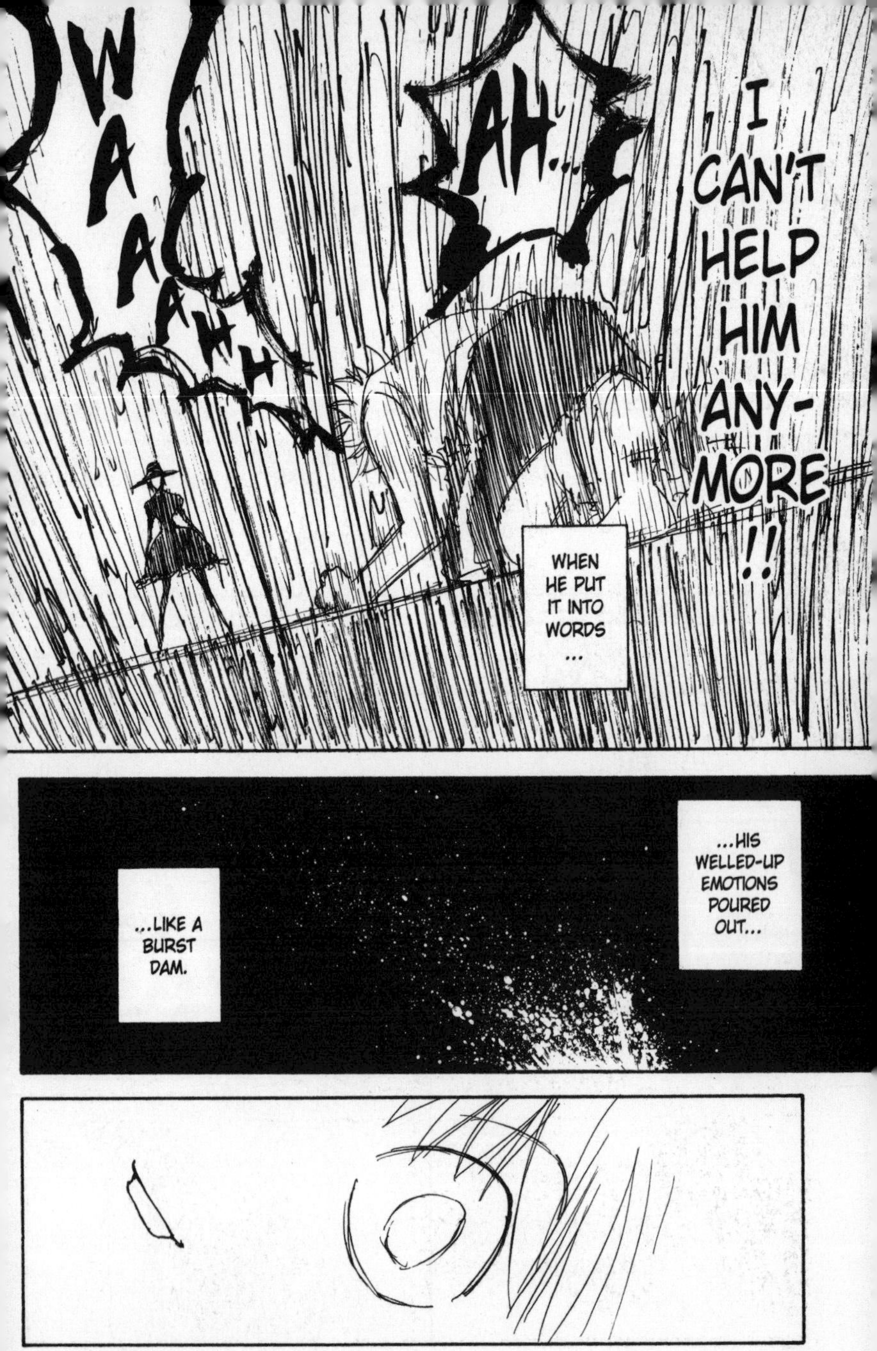

I CAN'T HELP HIM ANY-MORE!!
AH...!
WAAAHH
WHEN HE PUT IT INTO WORDS...
...HIS WELLED-UP EMOTIONS POURED OUT...
...LIKE A BURST DAM.

CHANGE OF PLANS.

HE'S WIDE OPEN.

...NUMBER ONE.

KILL HIM...

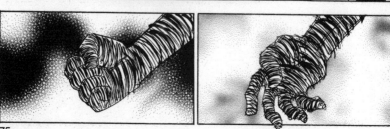

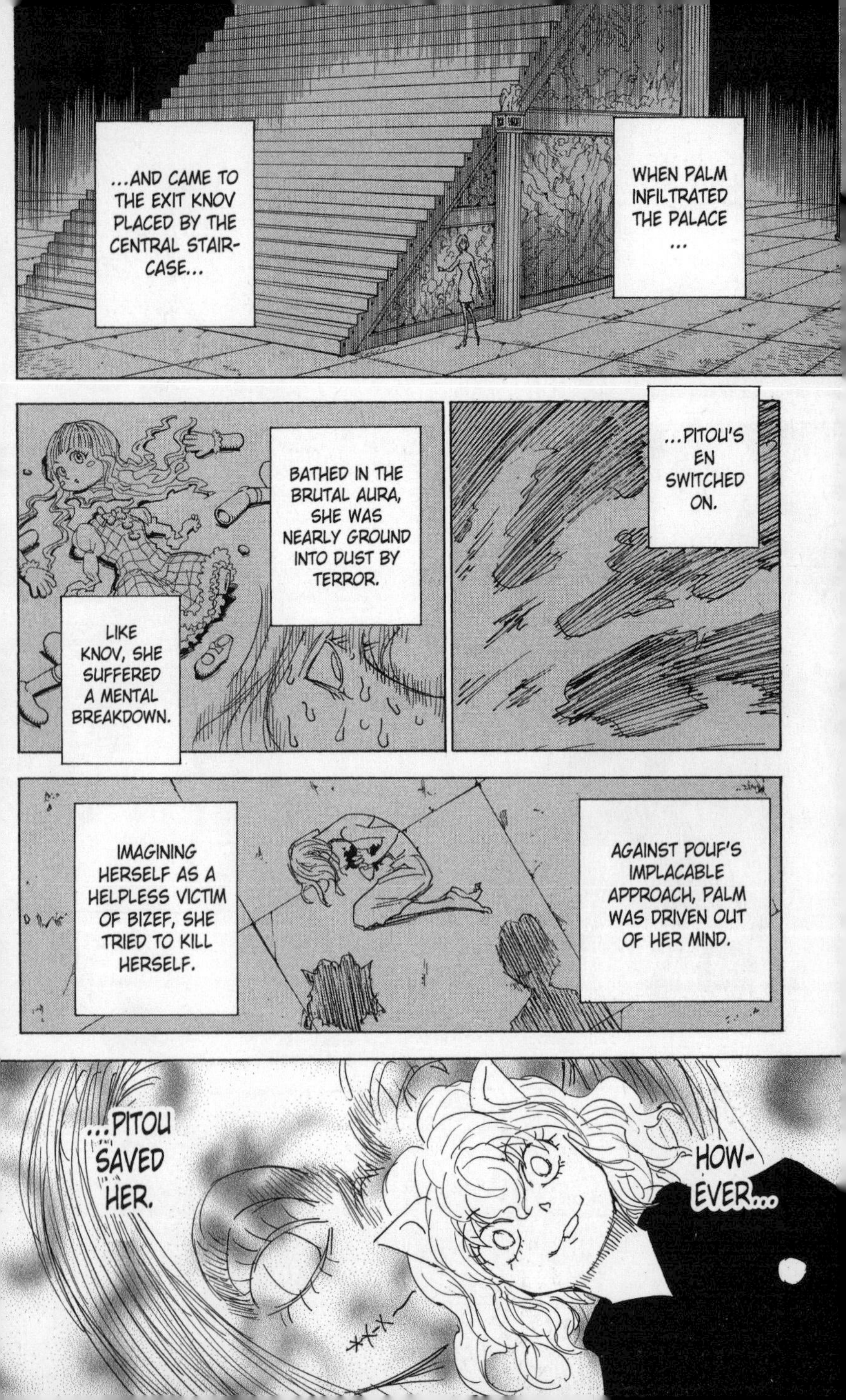
WHEN PALM INFILTRATED THE PALACE ...
...AND CAME TO THE EXIT KNOV PLACED BY THE CENTRAL STAIR-CASE...
...PITOU'S EN SWITCHED ON.
BATHED IN THE BRUTAL AURA, SHE WAS NEARLY GROUND INTO DUST BY TERROR.
LIKE KNOV, SHE SUFFERED A MENTAL BREAKDOWN.
AGAINST POUF'S IMPLACABLE APPROACH, PALM WAS DRIVEN OUT OF HER MIND.
IMAGINING HERSELF AS A HELPLESS VICTIM OF BIZEF, SHE TRIED TO KILL HERSELF.
HOW-EVER...
...PITOU SAVED HER.

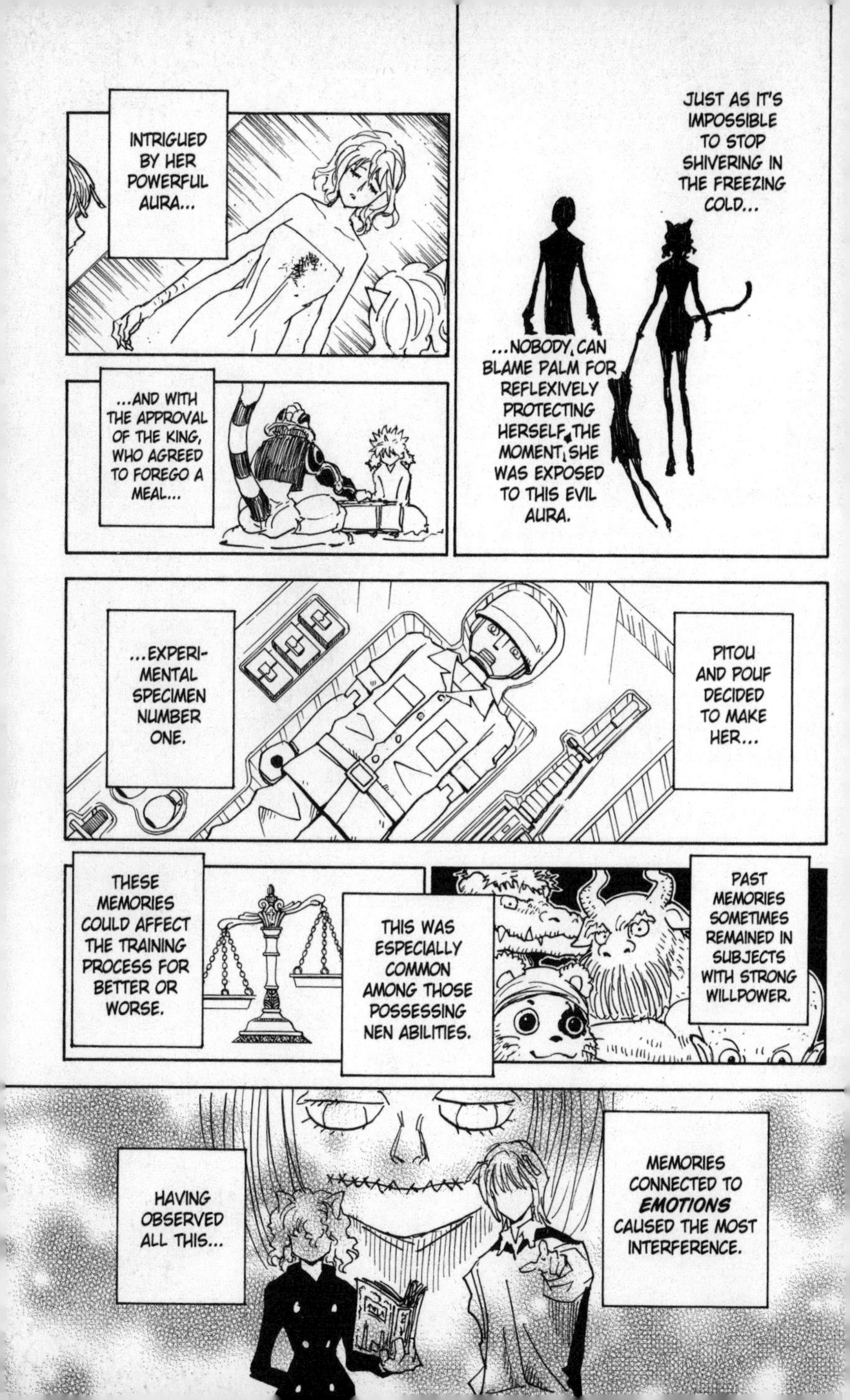
JUST AS IT'S IMPOSSIBLE TO STOP SHIVERING IN THE FREEZING COLD...
...NOBODY CAN BLAME PALM FOR REFLEXIVELY PROTECTING HERSELF THE MOMENT SHE WAS EXPOSED TO THIS EVIL AURA.
INTRIGUED BY HER POWERFUL AURA...
...AND WITH THE APPROVAL OF THE KING, WHO AGREED TO FOREGO A MEAL...
PITOU AND POUF DECIDED TO MAKE HER...
...EXPERI-MENTAL SPECIMEN NUMBER ONE.
PAST MEMORIES SOMETIMES REMAINED IN SUBJECTS WITH STRONG WILLPOWER.
THIS WAS ESPECIALLY COMMON AMONG THOSE POSSESSING NEN ABILITIES.
THESE MEMORIES COULD AFFECT THE TRAINING PROCESS FOR BETTER OR WORSE.
MEMORIES CONNECTED TO ***EMOTIONS*** CAUSED THE MOST INTERFERENCE.
HAVING OBSERVED ALL THIS...

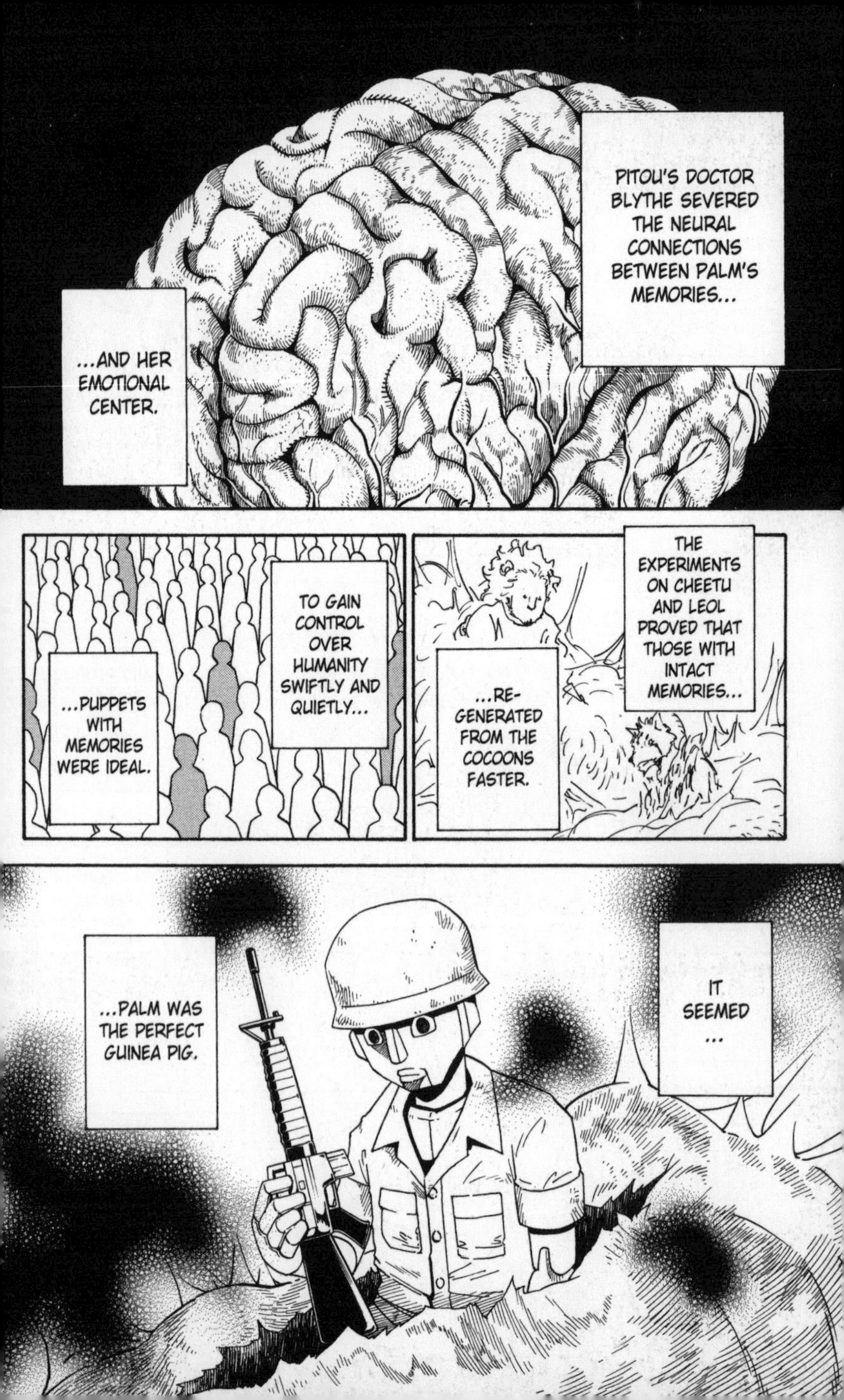
PITOU'S DOCTOR BLYTHE SEVERED THE NEURAL CONNECTIONS BETWEEN PALM'S MEMORIES...
...AND HER EMOTIONAL CENTER.
THE EXPERIMENTS ON CHEETU AND LEOL PROVED THAT THOSE WITH INTACT MEMORIES...
...RE-GENERATED FROM THE COCOONS FASTER.
TO GAIN CONTROL OVER HUMANITY SWIFTLY AND QUIETLY...
...PUPPETS WITH MEMORIES WERE IDEAL.
IT SEEMED ...
...PALM WAS THE PERFECT GUINEA PIG.

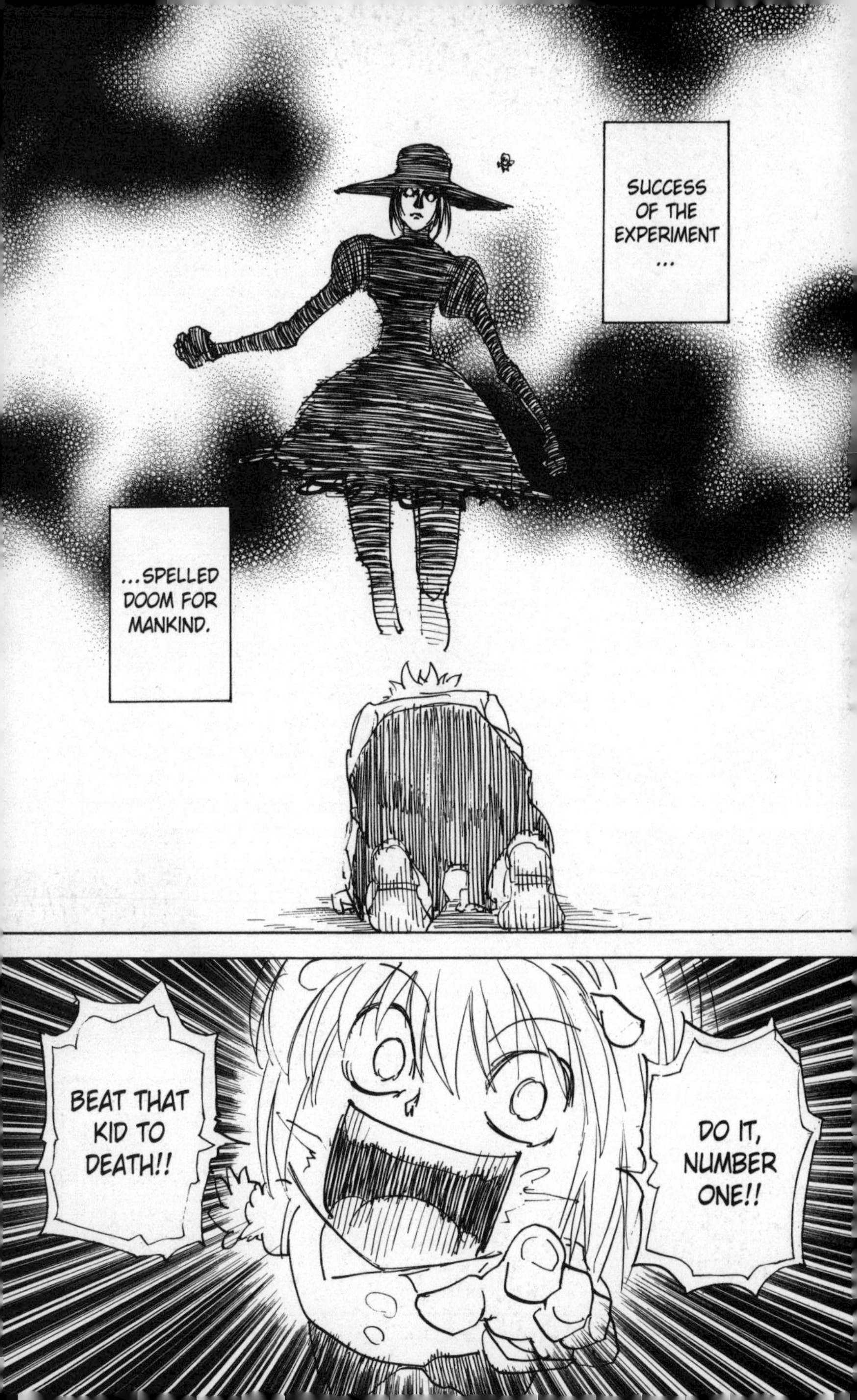
SUCCESS OF THE EXPERIMENT ...
...SPELLED DOOM FOR MANKIND.
DO IT, NUMBER ONE!!
BEAT THAT KID TO DEATH!!

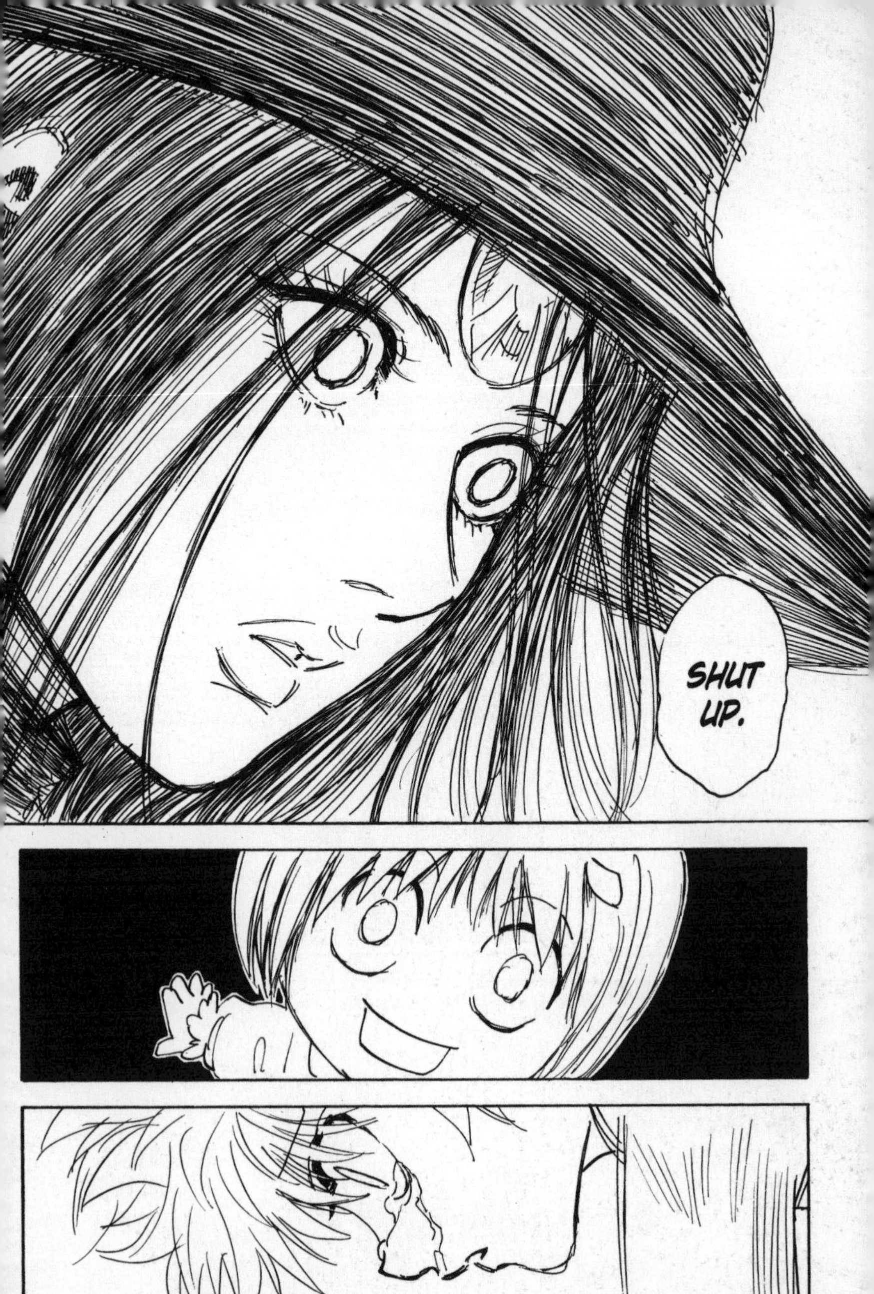
SHUT UP.

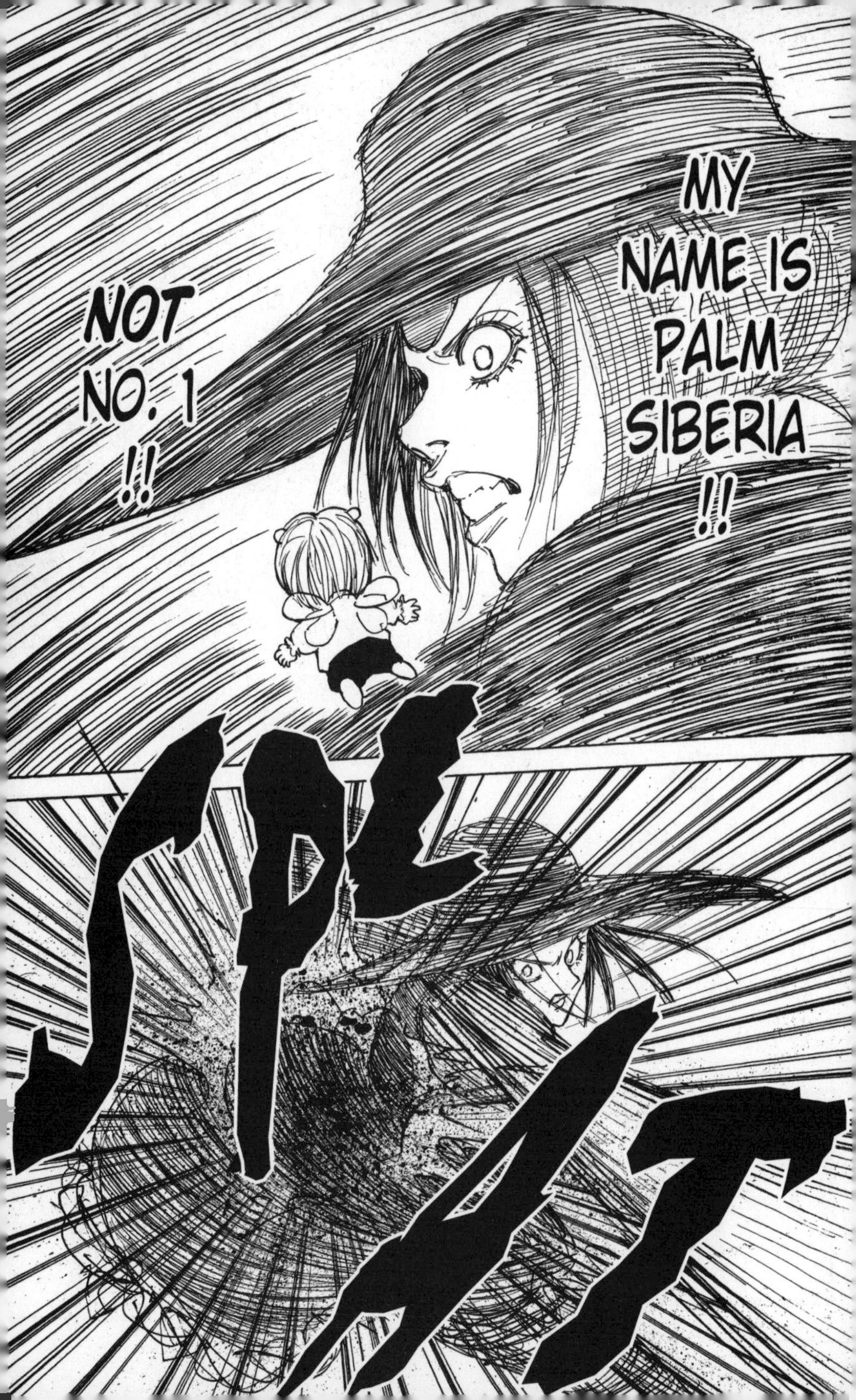
MY NAME IS PALM SIBERIA !!
NOT NO. 1 !!

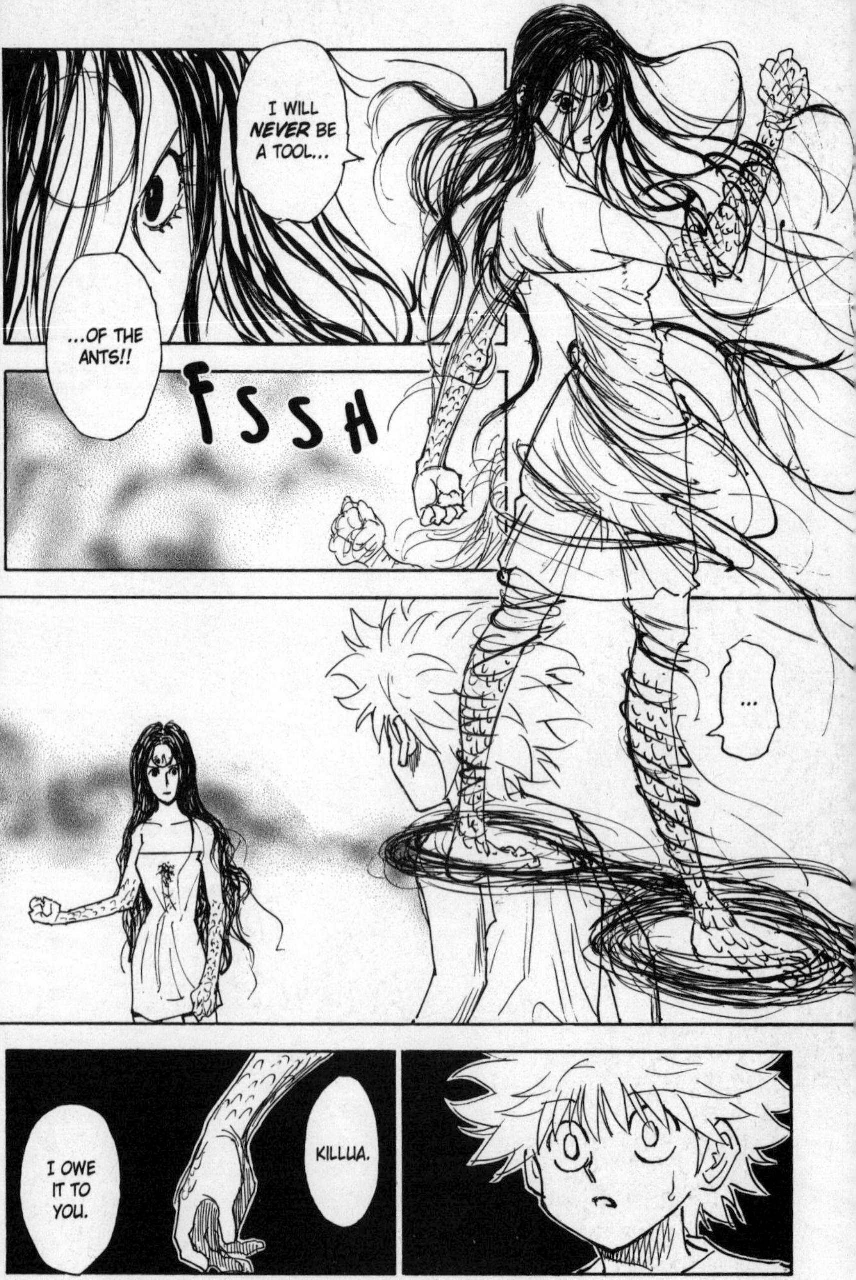
I WILL *NEVER* BE A TOOL...
...OF THE ANTS!!
FSSH
...
KILLUA.
I OWE IT TO YOU.

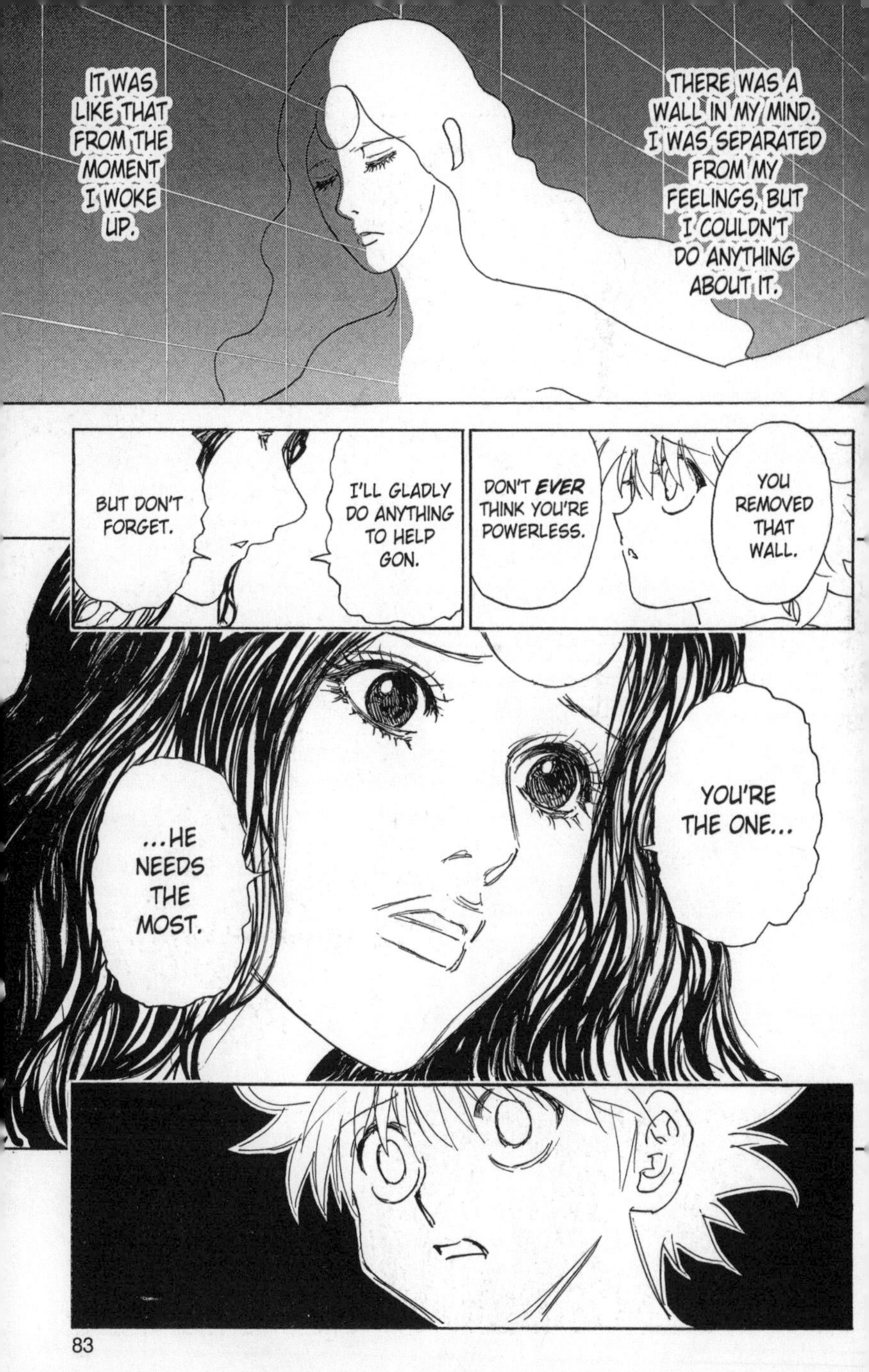
THERE WAS A WALL IN MY MIND. I WAS SEPARATED FROM MY FEELINGS, BUT I COULDN'T DO ANYTHING ABOUT IT.
IT WAS LIKE THAT FROM THE MOMENT I WOKE UP.
YOU REMOVED THAT WALL.
DON'T **EVER** THINK YOU'RE POWERLESS.
I'LL GLADLY DO ANYTHING TO HELP GON.
BUT DON'T FORGET.
YOU'RE THE ONE...
...HE NEEDS THE MOST.

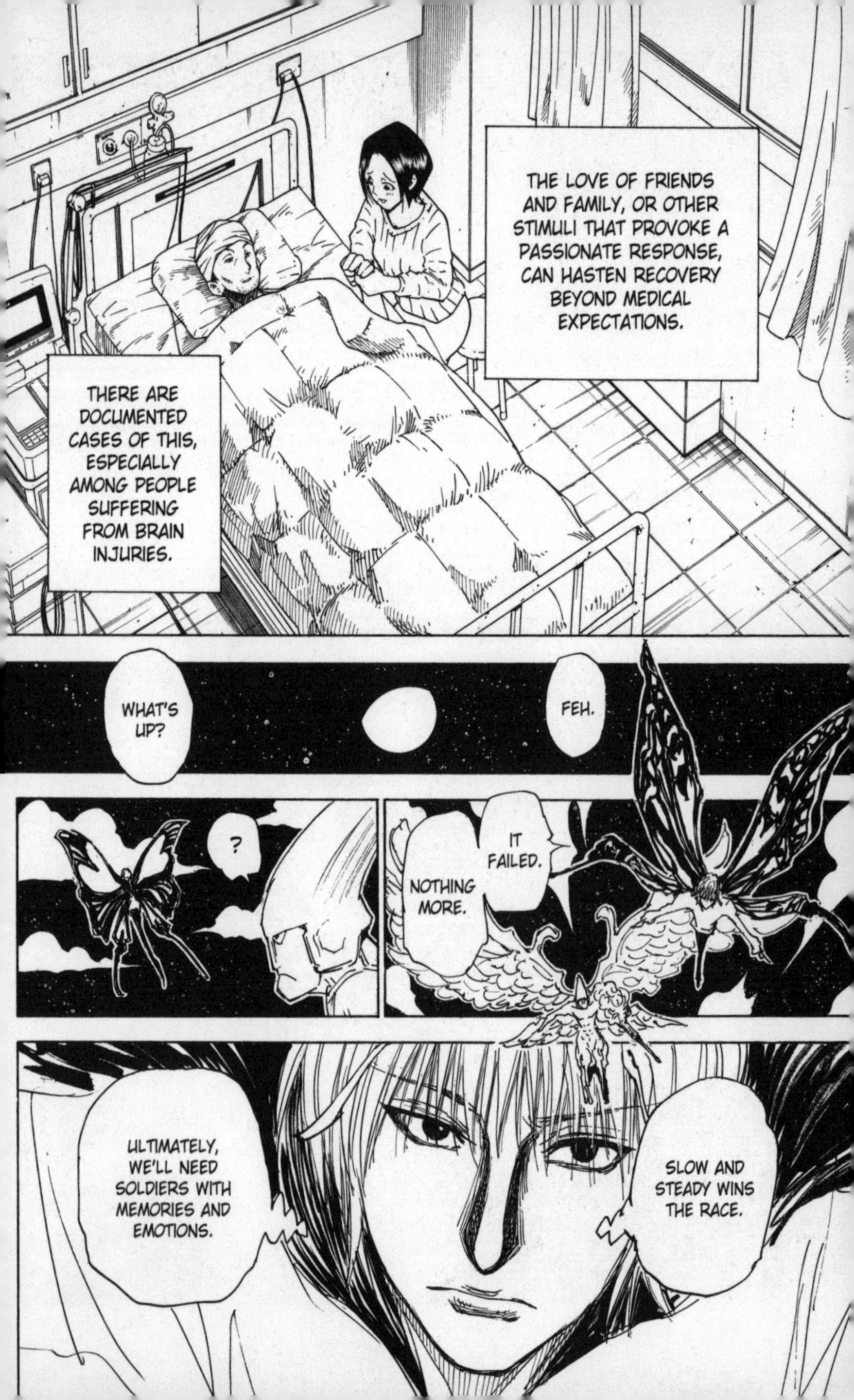
THE LOVE OF FRIENDS AND FAMILY, OR OTHER STIMULI THAT PROVOKE A PASSIONATE RESPONSE, CAN HASTEN RECOVERY BEYOND MEDICAL EXPECTATIONS.
THERE ARE DOCUMENTED CASES OF THIS, ESPECIALLY AMONG PEOPLE SUFFERING FROM BRAIN INJURIES.
FEH.
WHAT'S UP?
IT FAILED.
NOTHING MORE.
?
SLOW AND STEADY WINS THE RACE.
ULTIMATELY, WE'LL NEED SOLDIERS WITH MEMORIES AND EMOTIONS.

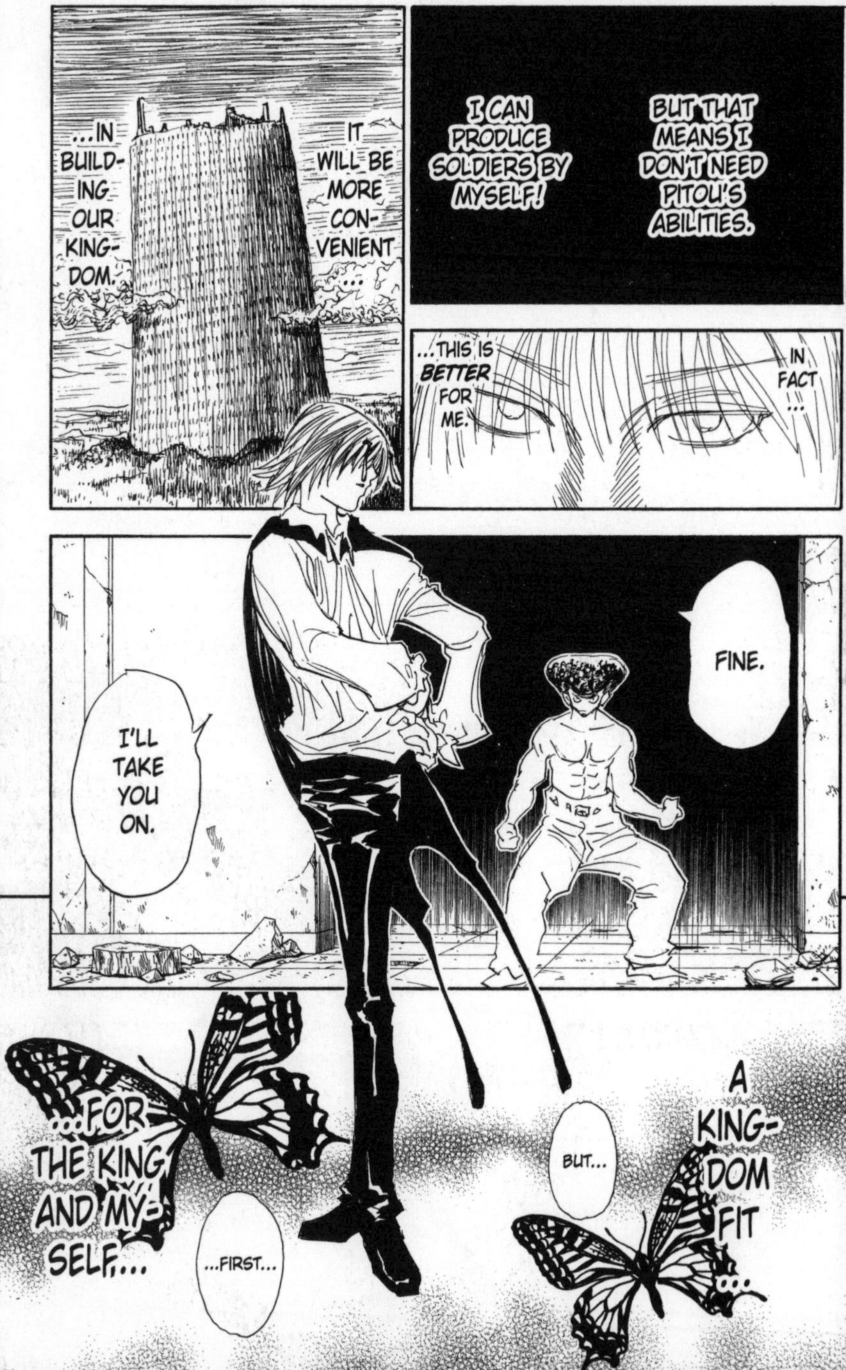
BUT THAT MEANS I DON'T NEED PITOU'S ABILITIES.
I CAN PRODUCE SOLDIERS BY MYSELF!
IN FACT...
...THIS IS BETTER FOR ME.
IT WILL BE MORE CONVENIENT...
...IN BUILDING OUR KINGDOM.
FINE.
I'LL TAKE YOU ON.
A KINGDOM FIT...
BUT...
...FIRST...
...FOR THE KING AND MYSELF...

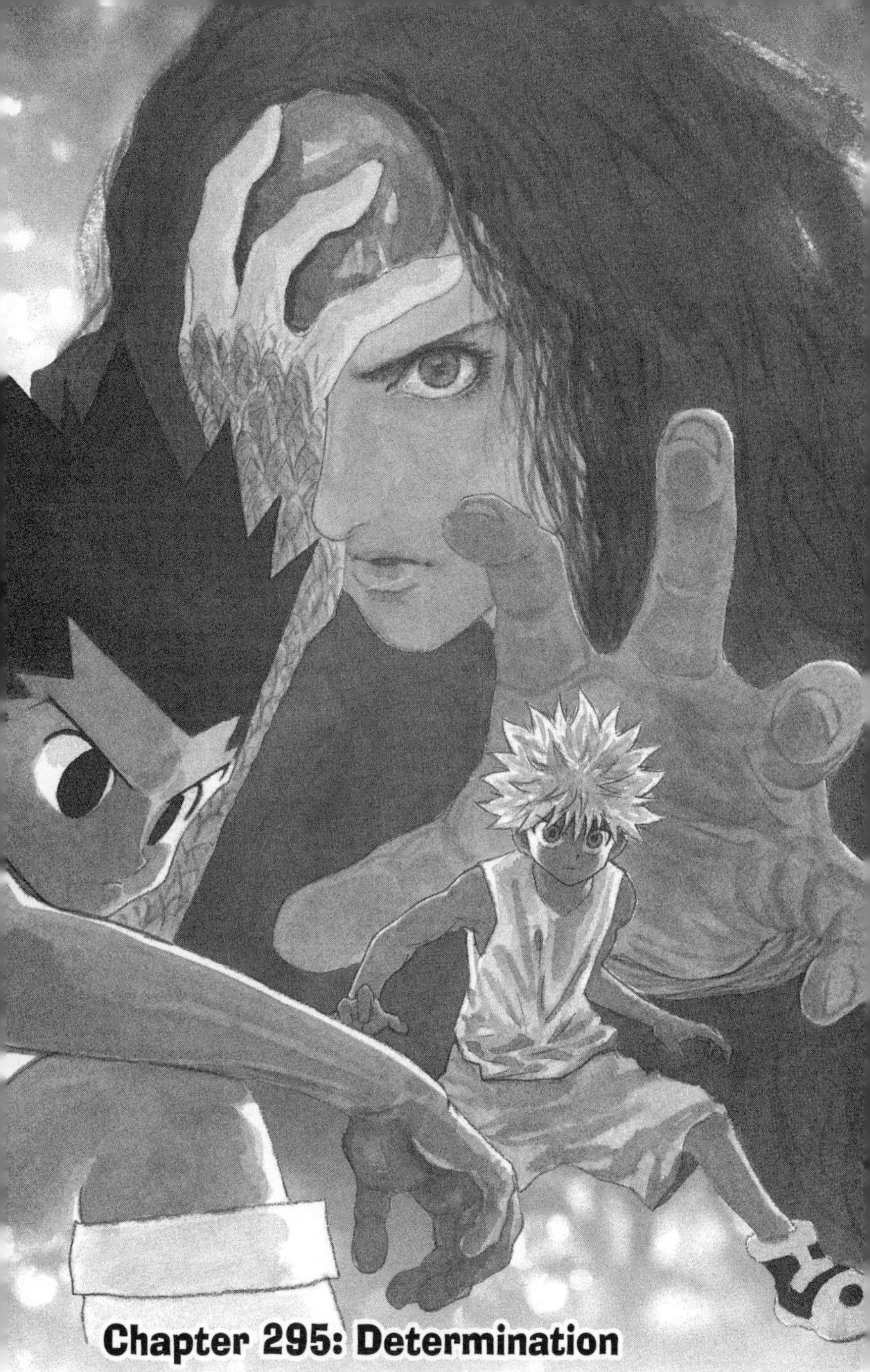

Chapter 295: Determination

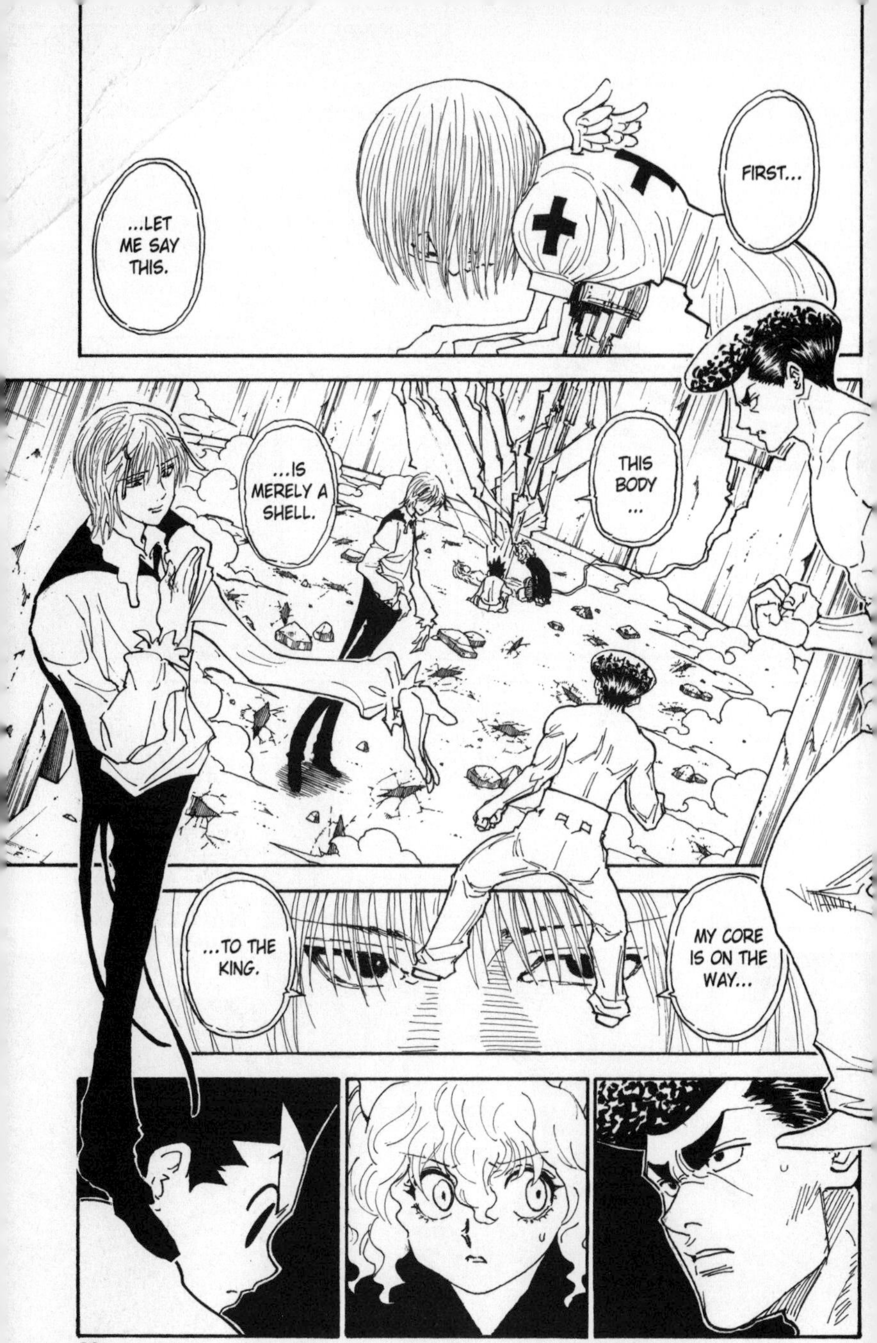
FIRST...
...LET ME SAY THIS.
THIS BODY...
...IS MERELY A SHELL.
MY CORE IS ON THE WAY...
...TO THE KING.

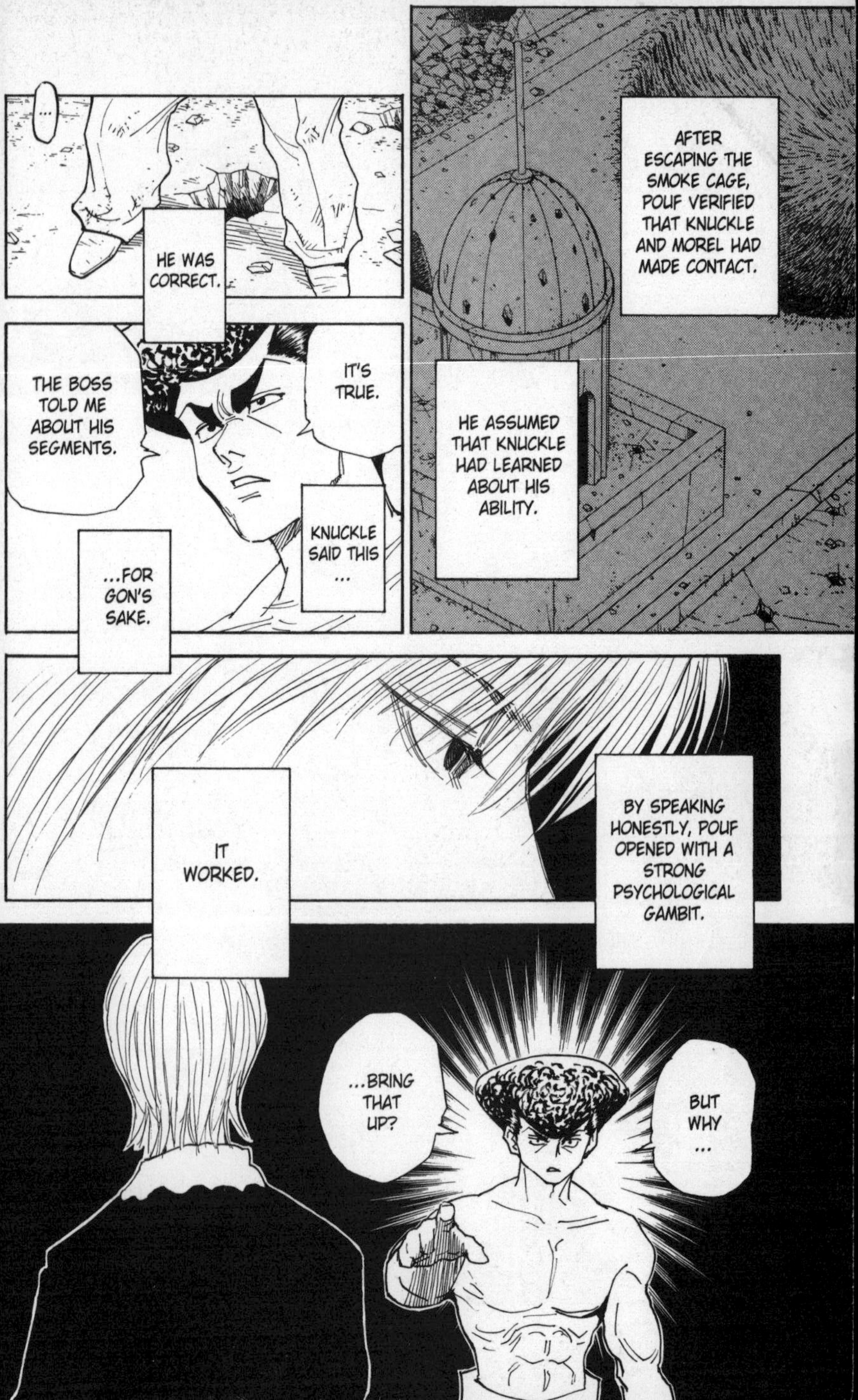
AFTER ESCAPING THE SMOKE CAGE, POUF VERIFIED THAT KNUCKLE AND MOREL HAD MADE CONTACT.
HE ASSUMED THAT KNUCKLE HAD LEARNED ABOUT HIS ABILITY.
...
HE WAS CORRECT.
IT'S TRUE.
THE BOSS TOLD ME ABOUT HIS SEGMENTS.
KNUCKLE SAID THIS ...
...FOR GON'S SAKE.
BY SPEAKING HONESTLY, POUF OPENED WITH A STRONG PSYCHOLOGICAL GAMBIT.
IT WORKED.
BUT WHY ...
...BRING THAT UP?

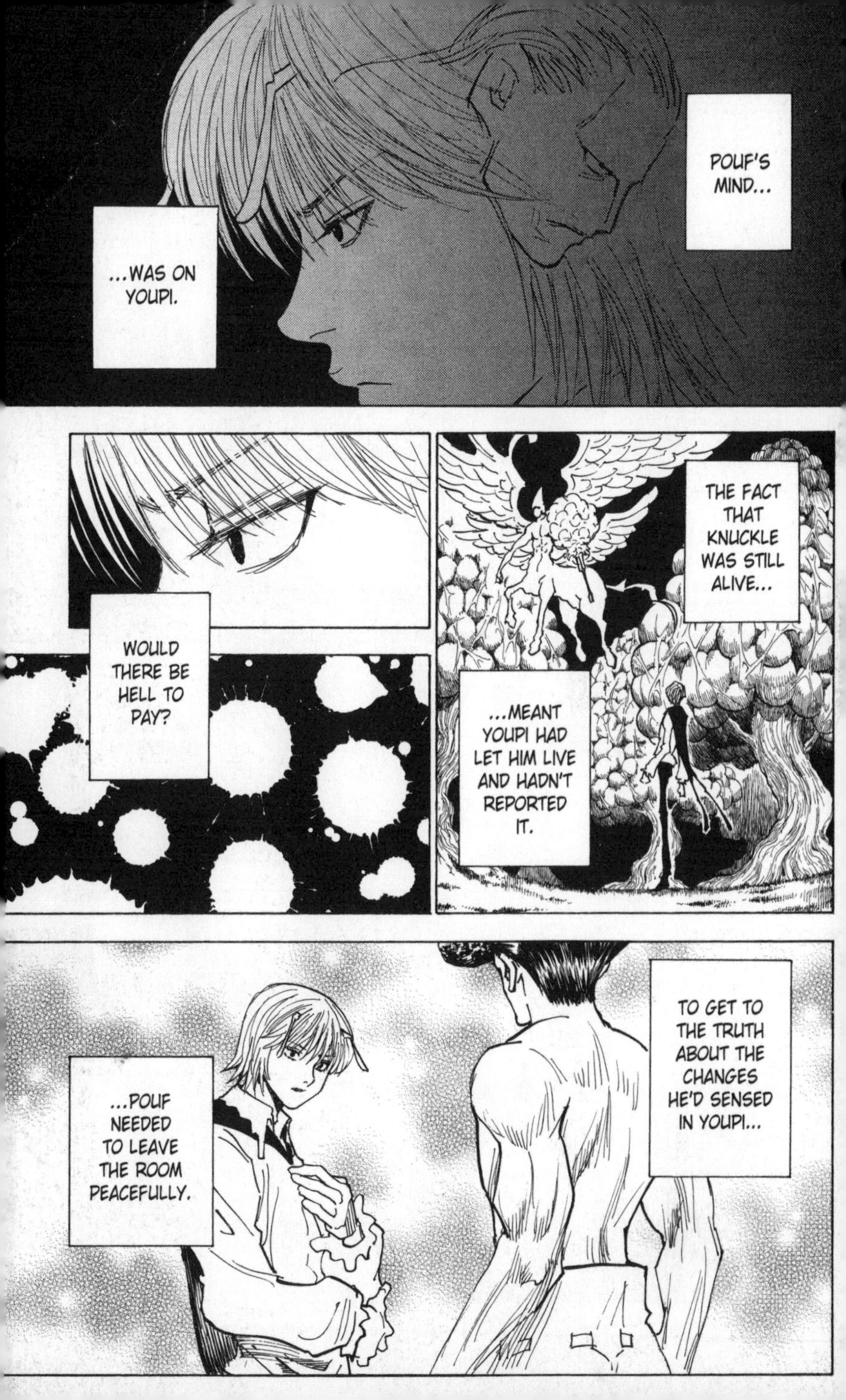
POUF'S MIND...
...WAS ON YOUPI.
THE FACT THAT KNUCKLE WAS STILL ALIVE...
...MEANT YOUPI HAD LET HIM LIVE AND HADN'T REPORTED IT.
WOULD THERE BE HELL TO PAY?
TO GET TO THE TRUTH ABOUT THE CHANGES HE'D SENSED IN YOUPI...
...POUF NEEDED TO LEAVE THE ROOM PEACEFULLY.

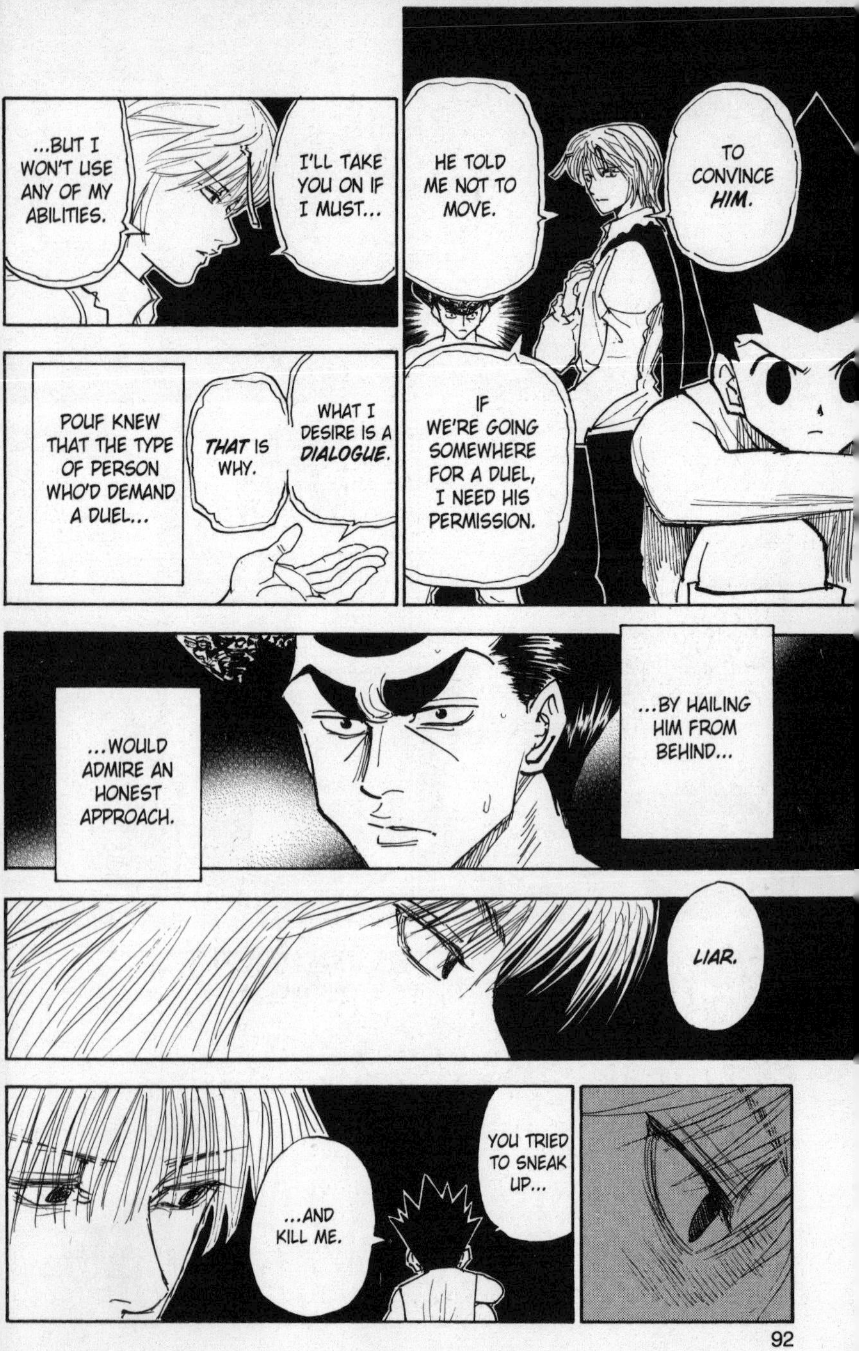
TO CONVINCE HIM.
HE TOLD ME NOT TO MOVE.
IF WE'RE GOING SOMEWHERE FOR A DUEL, I NEED HIS PERMISSION.
I'LL TAKE YOU ON IF I MUST...
...BUT I WON'T USE ANY OF MY ABILITIES.
WHAT I DESIRE IS A DIALOGUE.
THAT IS WHY.
POUF KNEW THAT THE TYPE OF PERSON WHO'D DEMAND A DUEL...
...BY HAILING HIM FROM BEHIND...
...WOULD ADMIRE AN HONEST APPROACH.
LIAR.
YOU TRIED TO SNEAK UP...
...AND KILL ME.

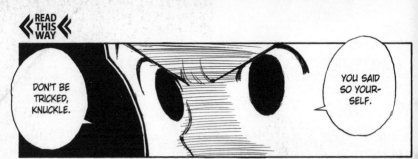

READ THIS WAY

YOU SAID SO YOURSELF.
DON'T BE TRICKED, KNUCKLE.
YOU'RE A SHELL AND NOT THE REAL POUF?
HOW DO WE EVEN KNOW THAT'S TRUE?
OH YEAH ...
...
THIS KID...
...IS TROUBLE.

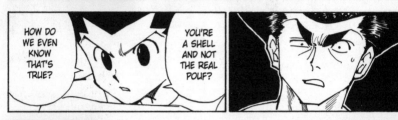

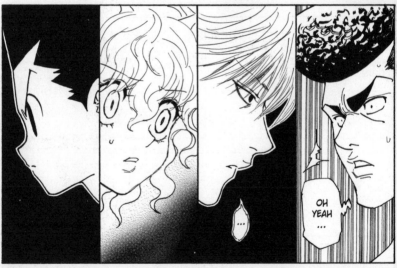

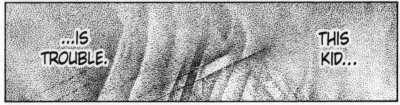

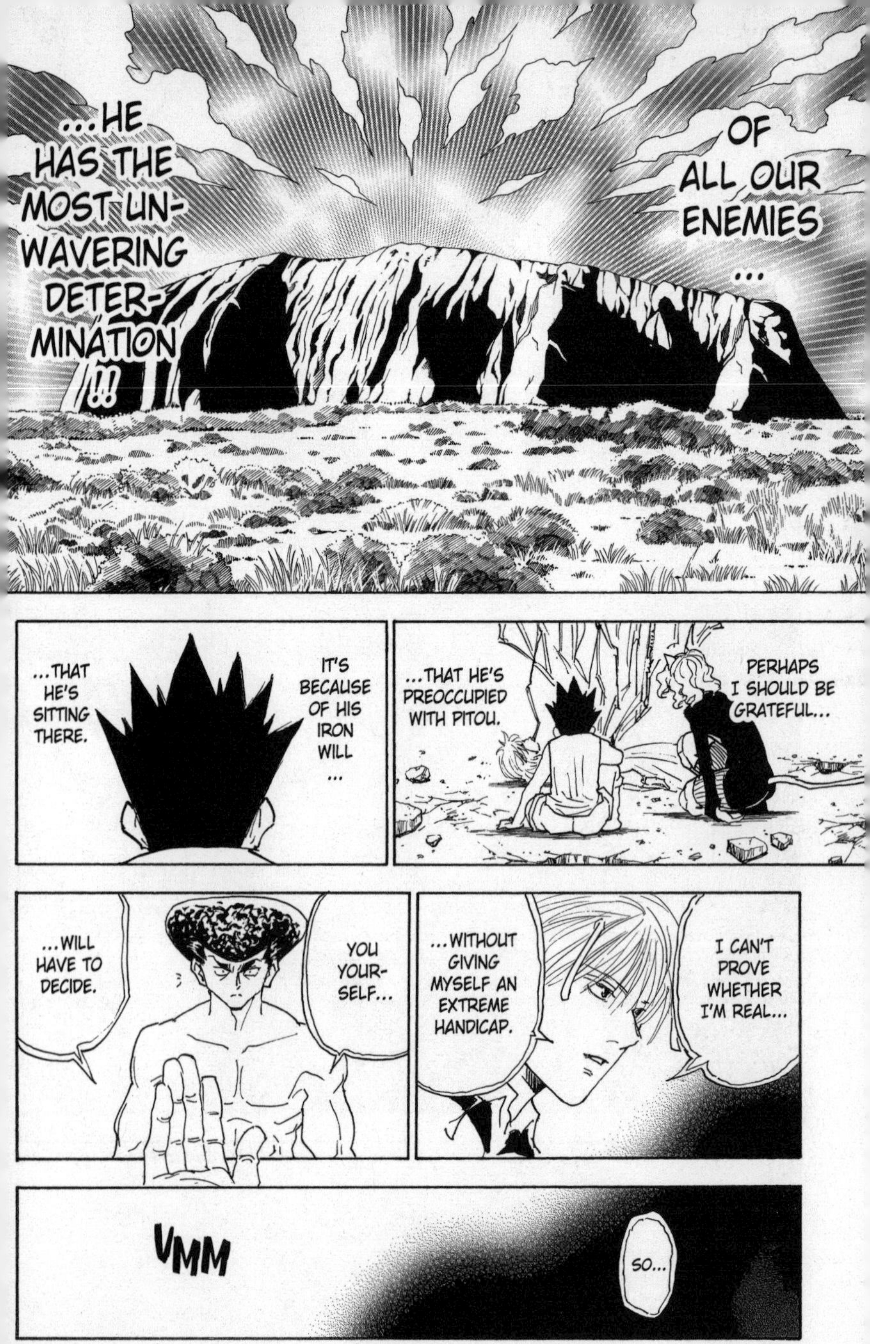
OF ALL OUR ENEMIES ...
...HE HAS THE MOST UN-WAVERING DETER-MINATION!!
PERHAPS I SHOULD BE GRATEFUL...
...THAT HE'S PREOCCUPIED WITH PITOU.
IT'S BECAUSE OF HIS IRON WILL ...
...THAT HE'S SITTING THERE.
I CAN'T PROVE WHETHER I'M REAL...
...WITHOUT GIVING MYSELF AN EXTREME HANDICAP.
YOU YOUR-SELF...
...WILL HAVE TO DECIDE.
SO...
VMM

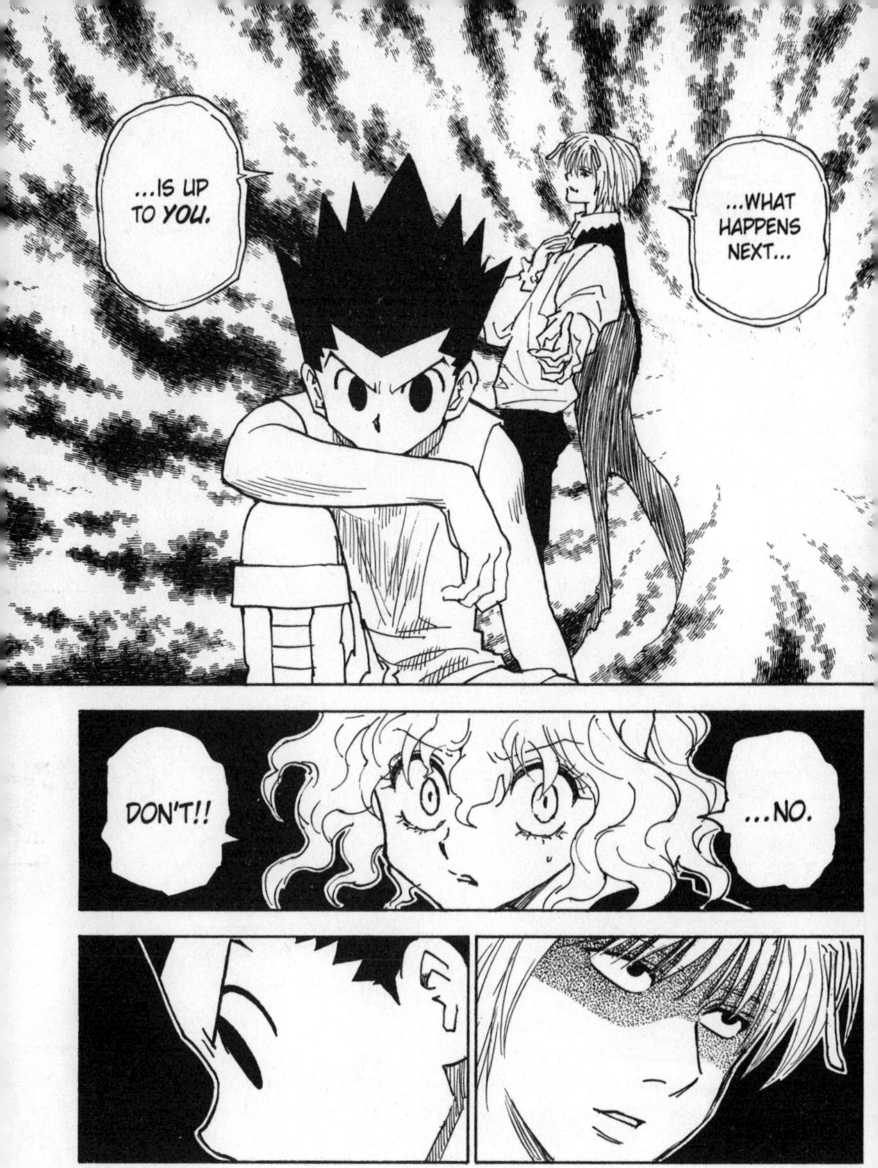
...WHAT HAPPENS NEXT...
...IS UP TO YOU.
...NO.
DON'T!!

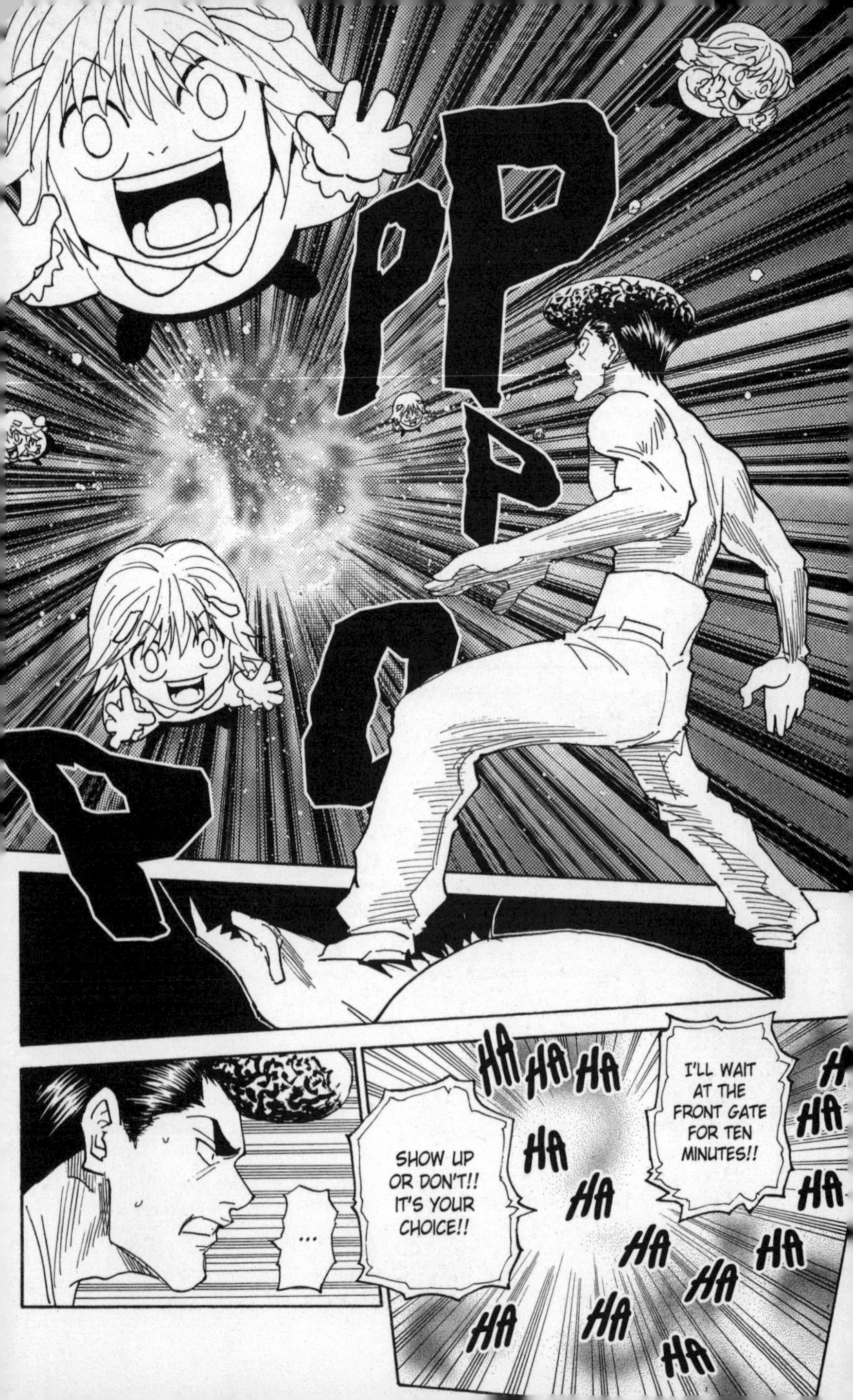
PPPP
I'LL WAIT AT THE FRONT GATE FOR TEN MINUTES!!
SHOW UP OR DON'T!! IT'S YOUR CHOICE!!
HA HA HA HA HA HA HA HA HA HA HA HA HA HA HA HA
...

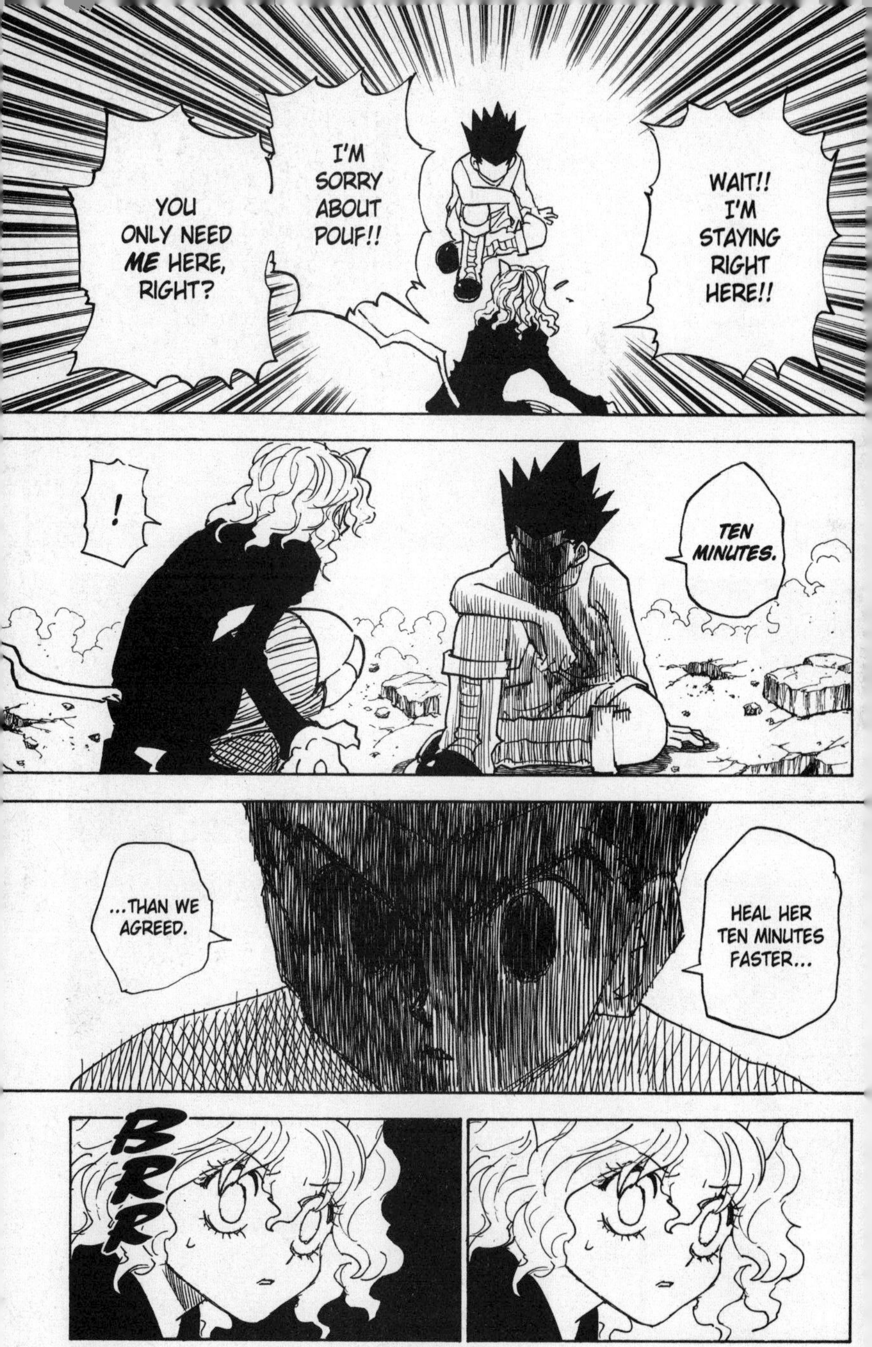
WAIT!! I'M STAYING RIGHT HERE!!
I'M SORRY ABOUT POUF!!
YOU ONLY NEED *ME* HERE, RIGHT?
TEN MINUTES.
!
HEAL HER TEN MINUTES FASTER...
...THAN WE AGREED.
BRR

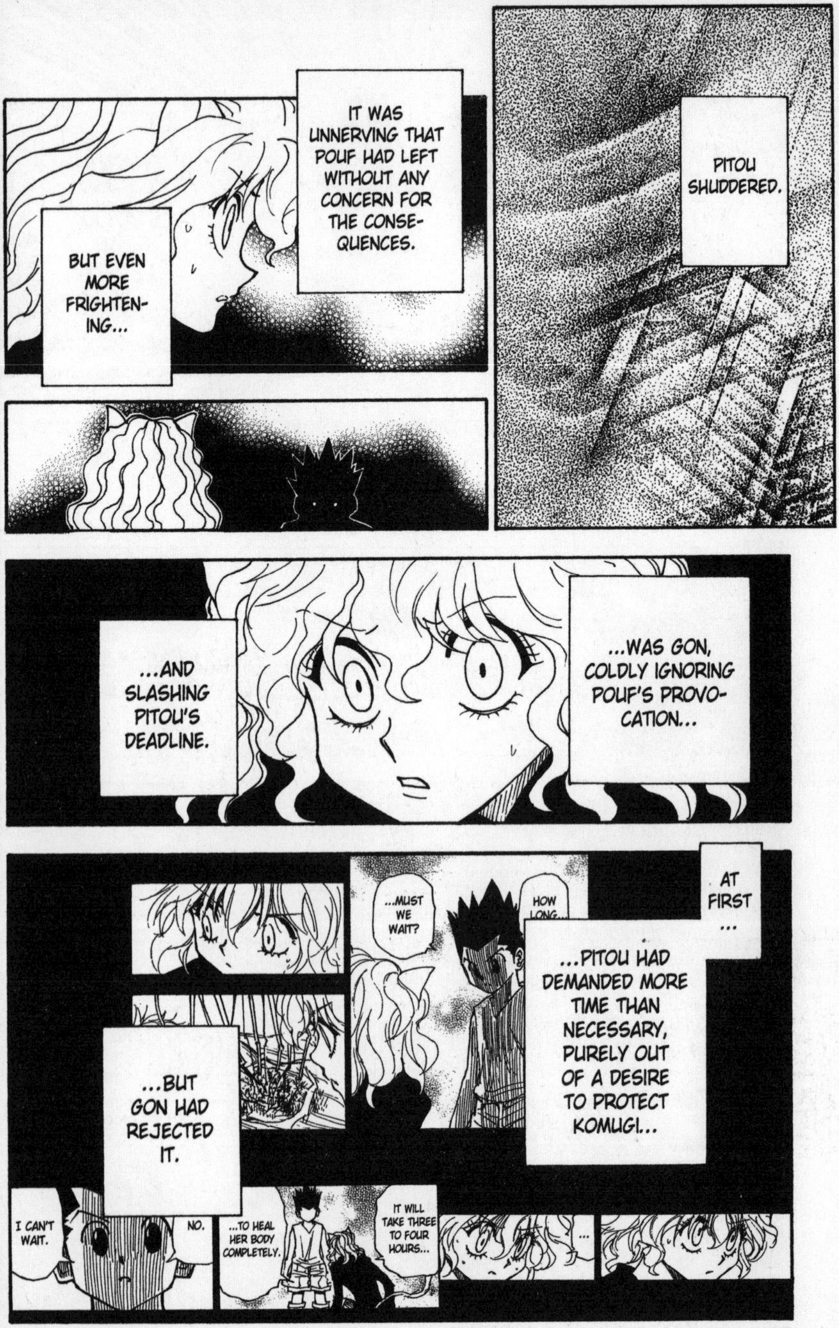
PITOU SHUDDERED.
IT WAS UNNERVING THAT POUF HAD LEFT WITHOUT ANY CONCERN FOR THE CONSE-QUENCES.
BUT EVEN MORE FRIGHTEN-ING...
...WAS GON, COLDLY IGNORING POUF'S PROVO-CATION...
...AND SLASHING PITOU'S DEADLINE.
AT FIRST ...
...PITOU HAD DEMANDED MORE TIME THAN NECESSARY, PURELY OUT OF A DESIRE TO PROTECT KOMUGI...
HOW LONG...
...MUST WE WAIT?
...BUT GON HAD REJECTED IT.
...
IT WILL TAKE THREE TO FOUR HOURS...
...TO HEAL HER BODY COMPLETELY.
NO.
I CAN'T WAIT.

READ THIS WAY

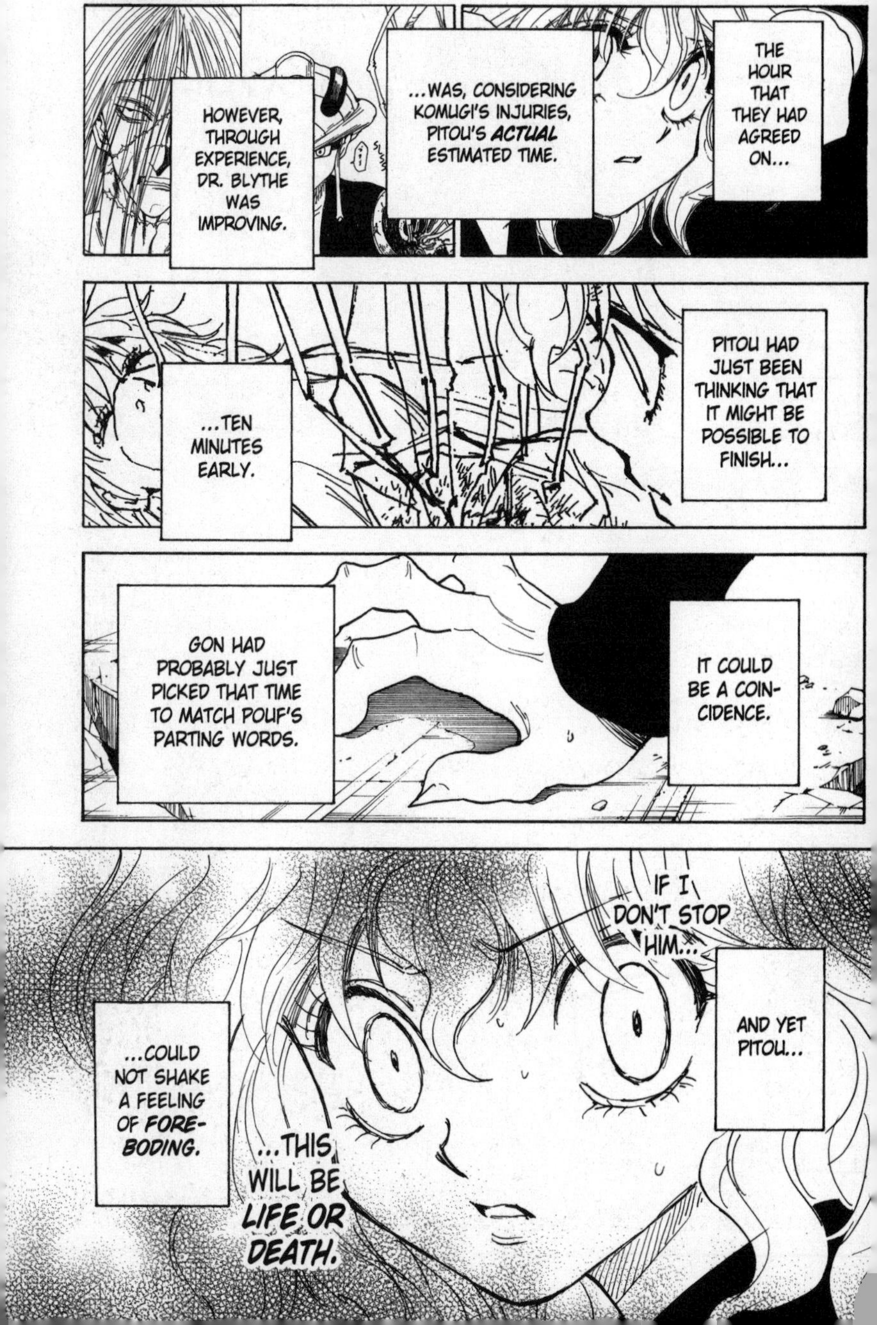
THE HOUR THAT THEY HAD AGREED ON...
...WAS, CONSIDERING KOMUGI'S INJURIES, PITOU'S *ACTUAL* ESTIMATED TIME.
HOWEVER, THROUGH EXPERIENCE, DR. BLYTHE WAS IMPROVING.
PITOU HAD JUST BEEN THINKING THAT IT MIGHT BE POSSIBLE TO FINISH...
...TEN MINUTES EARLY.
IT COULD BE A COINCIDENCE.
GON HAD PROBABLY JUST PICKED THAT TIME TO MATCH POUF'S PARTING WORDS.
IF I DON'T STOP HIM...
AND YET PITOU...
...COULD NOT SHAKE A FEELING OF *FOREBODING.*
...THIS WILL BE *LIFE OR DEATH.*

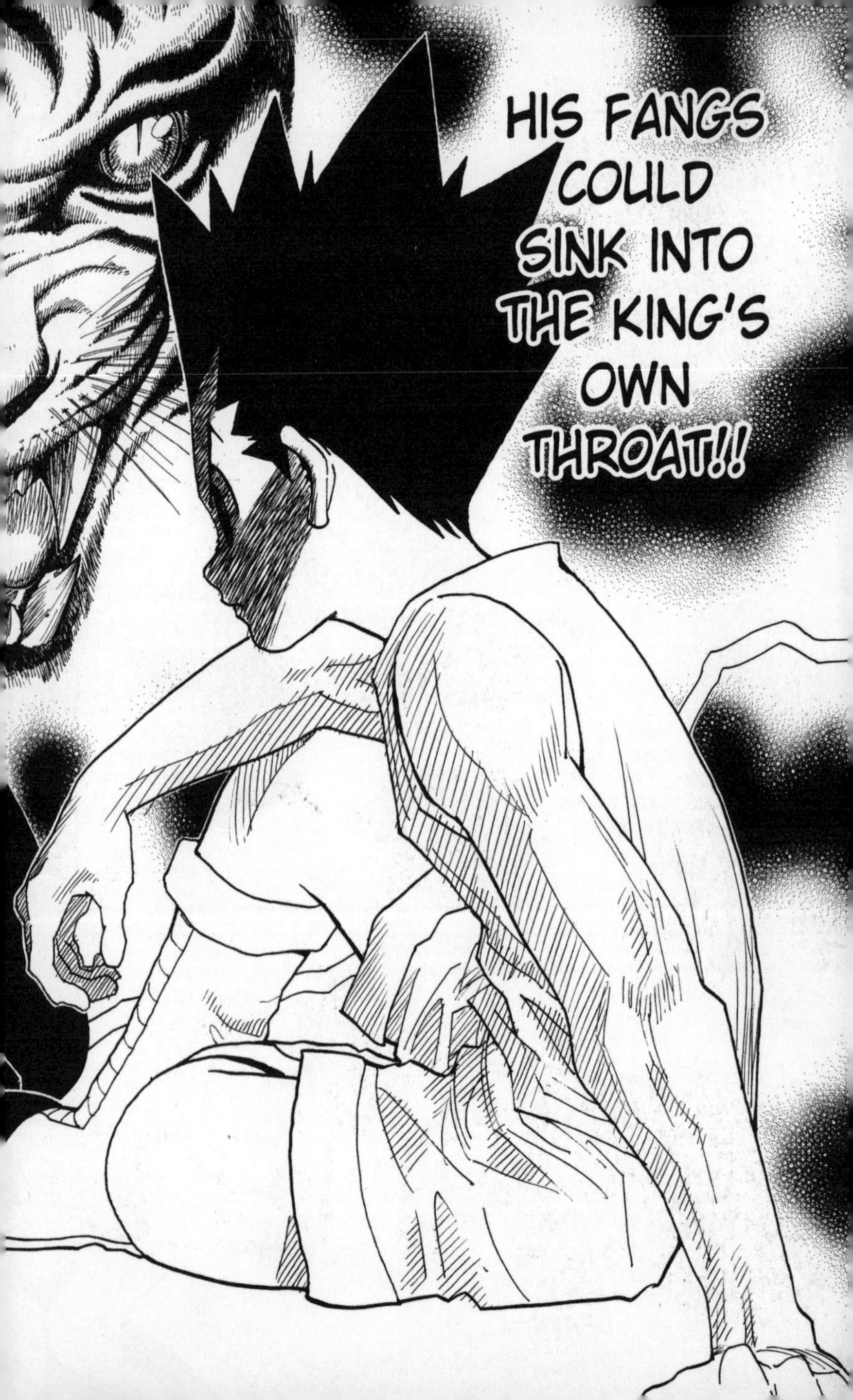
HIS FANGS COULD SINK INTO THE KING'S OWN THROAT!!

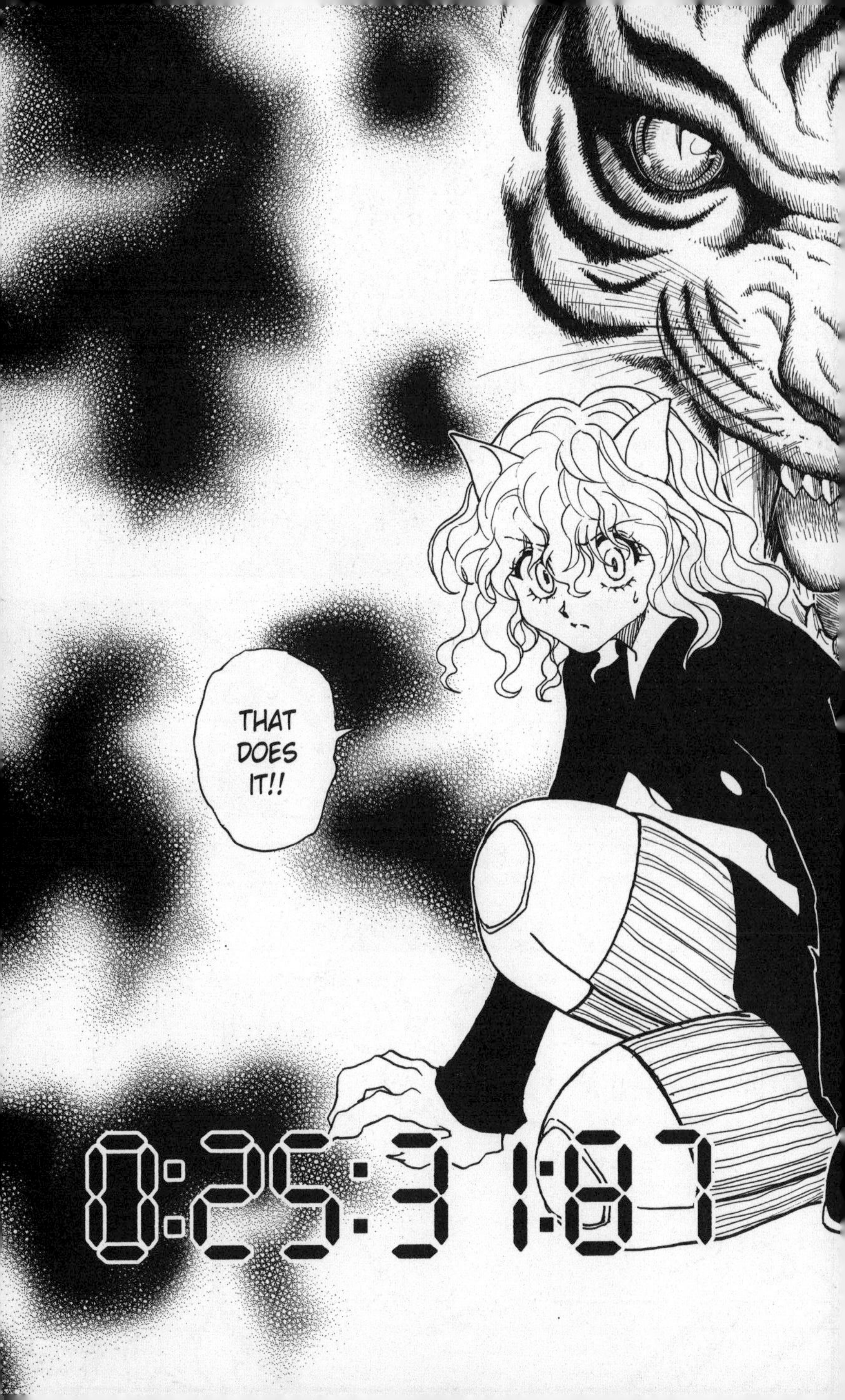
THAT DOES IT!!
0:25:31:87

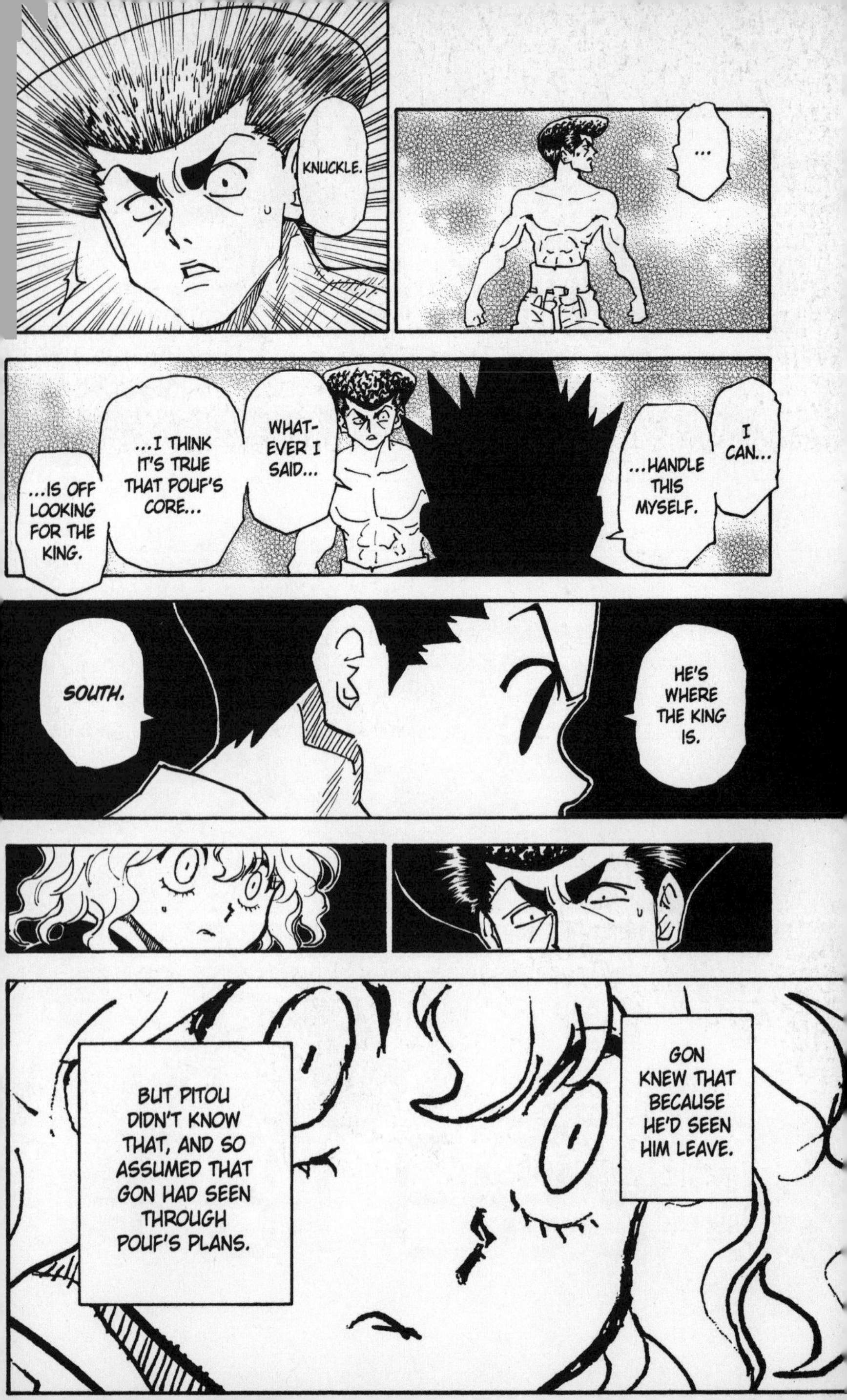
...
KNUCKLE.
I CAN...
...HANDLE THIS MYSELF.
WHATEVER I SAID...
...I THINK IT'S TRUE THAT POUF'S CORE...
...IS OFF LOOKING FOR THE KING.
HE'S WHERE THE KING IS.
SOUTH.
GON KNEW THAT BECAUSE HE'D SEEN HIM LEAVE.
BUT PITOU DIDN'T KNOW THAT, AND SO ASSUMED THAT GON HAD SEEN THROUGH POUF'S PLANS.

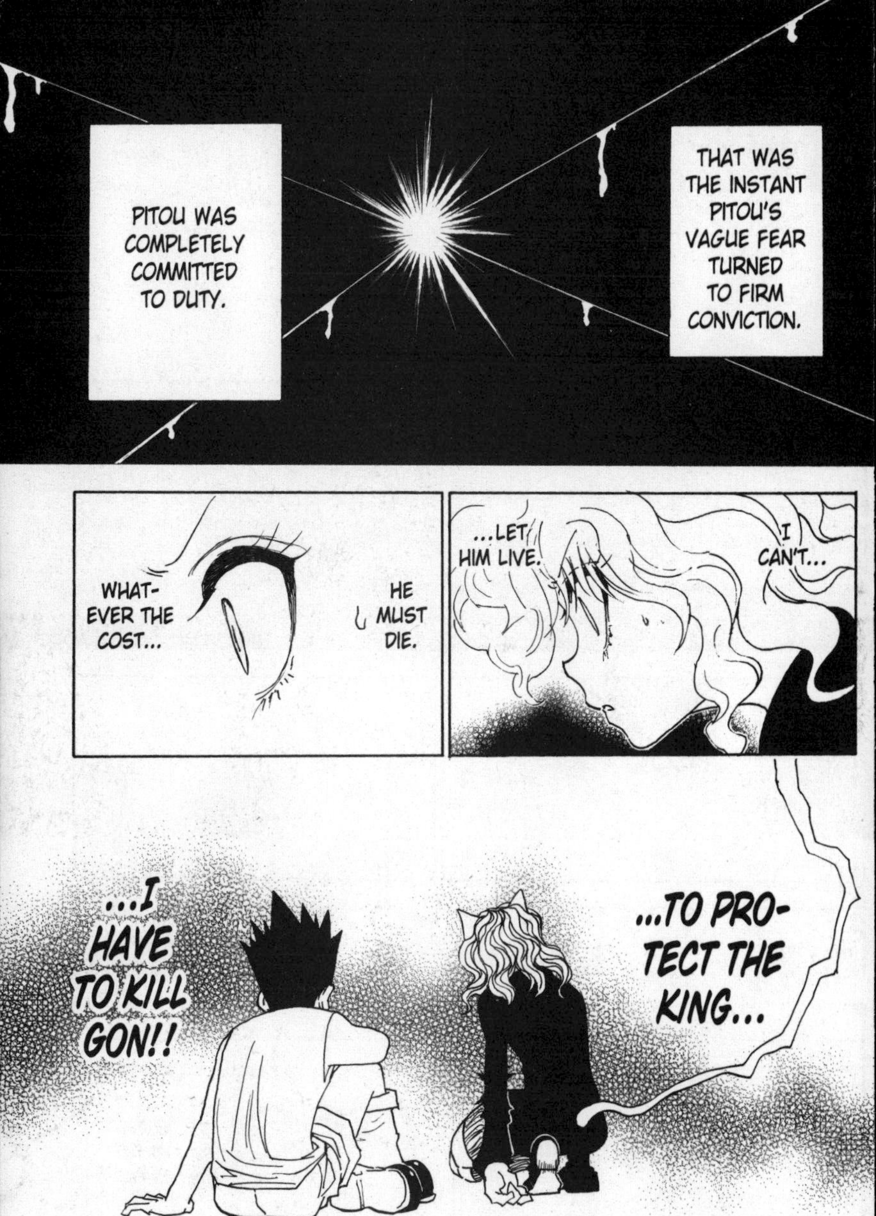
THAT WAS THE INSTANT PITOU'S VAGUE FEAR TURNED TO FIRM CONVICTION.
PITOU WAS COMPLETELY COMMITTED TO DUTY.
I CAN'T...
...LET HIM LIVE.
HE MUST DIE.
WHATEVER THE COST...
...TO PROTECT THE KING...
...I HAVE TO KILL GON!!

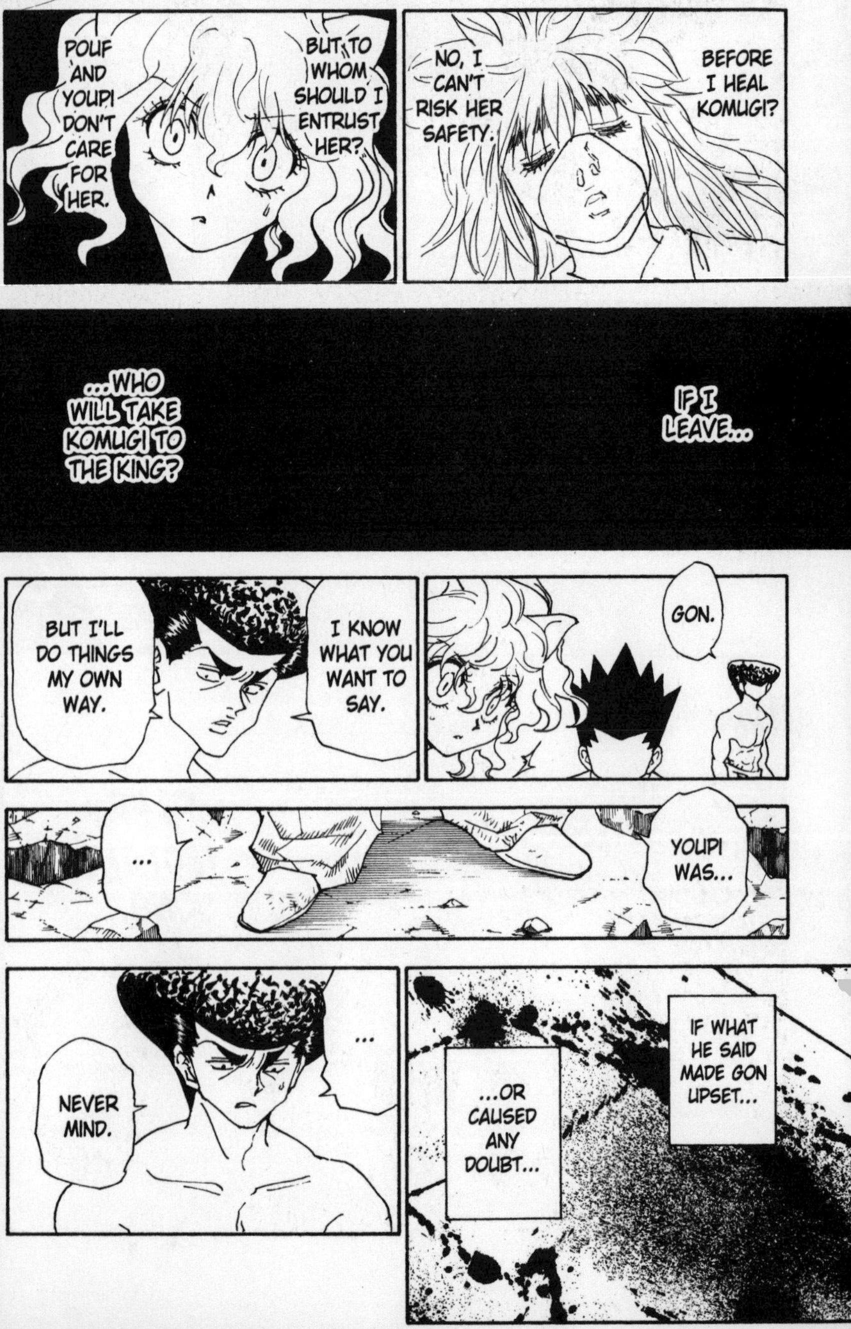
BEFORE I HEAL KOMUGI?
NO, I CAN'T RISK HER SAFETY.
BUT TO WHOM SHOULD I ENTRUST HER?
POUF AND YOUPI DON'T CARE FOR HER.
IF I LEAVE...
...WHO WILL TAKE KOMUGI TO THE KING?
GON.
I KNOW WHAT YOU WANT TO SAY.
BUT I'LL DO THINGS MY OWN WAY.
YOUPI WAS...
...
IF WHAT HE SAID MADE GON UPSET...
...OR CAUSED ANY DOUBT...
...
NEVER MIND.

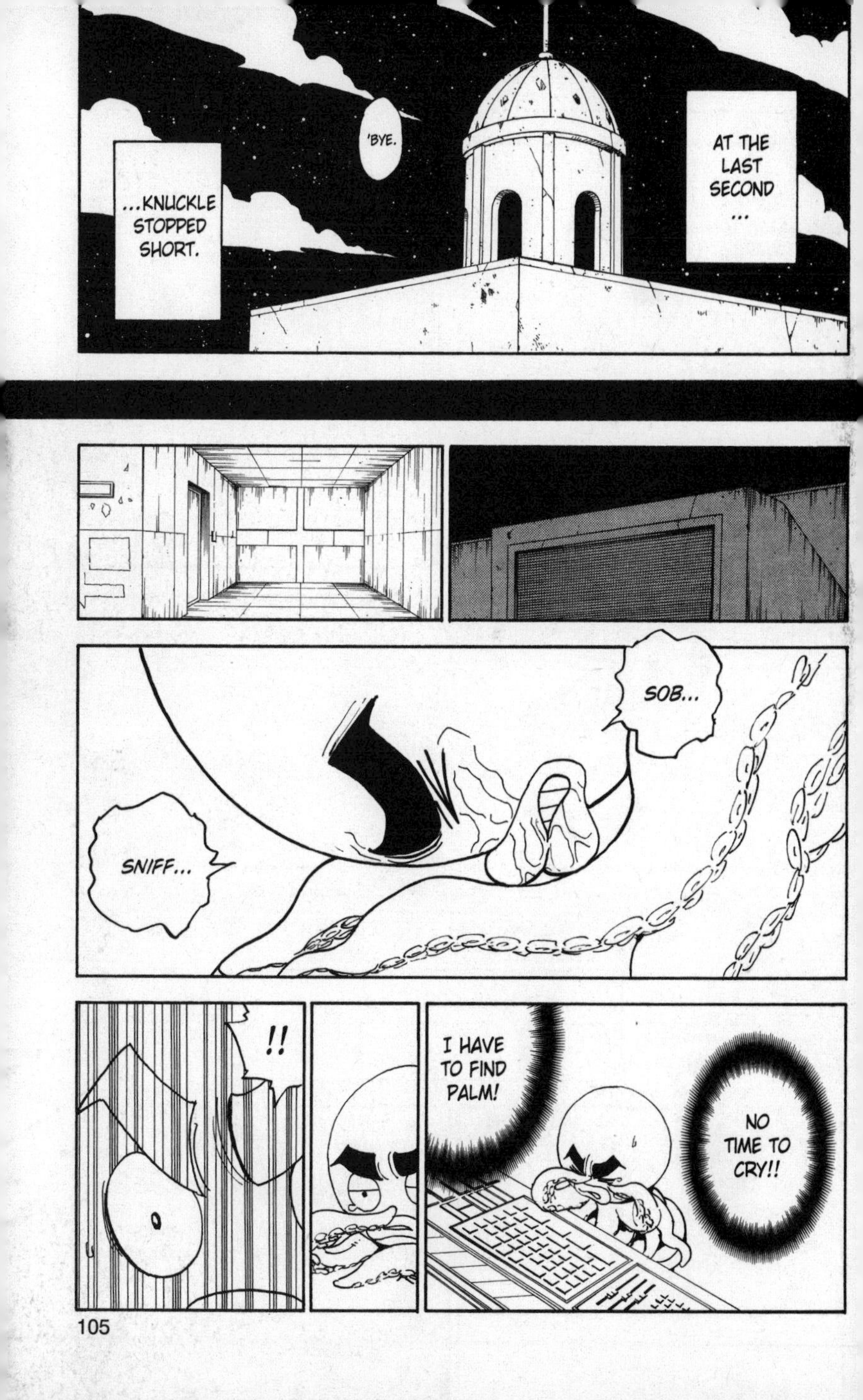
AT THE LAST SECOND ...
'BYE.
...KNUCKLE STOPPED SHORT.
SOB...
SNIFF...
NO TIME TO CRY!!
I HAVE TO FIND PALM!
!!

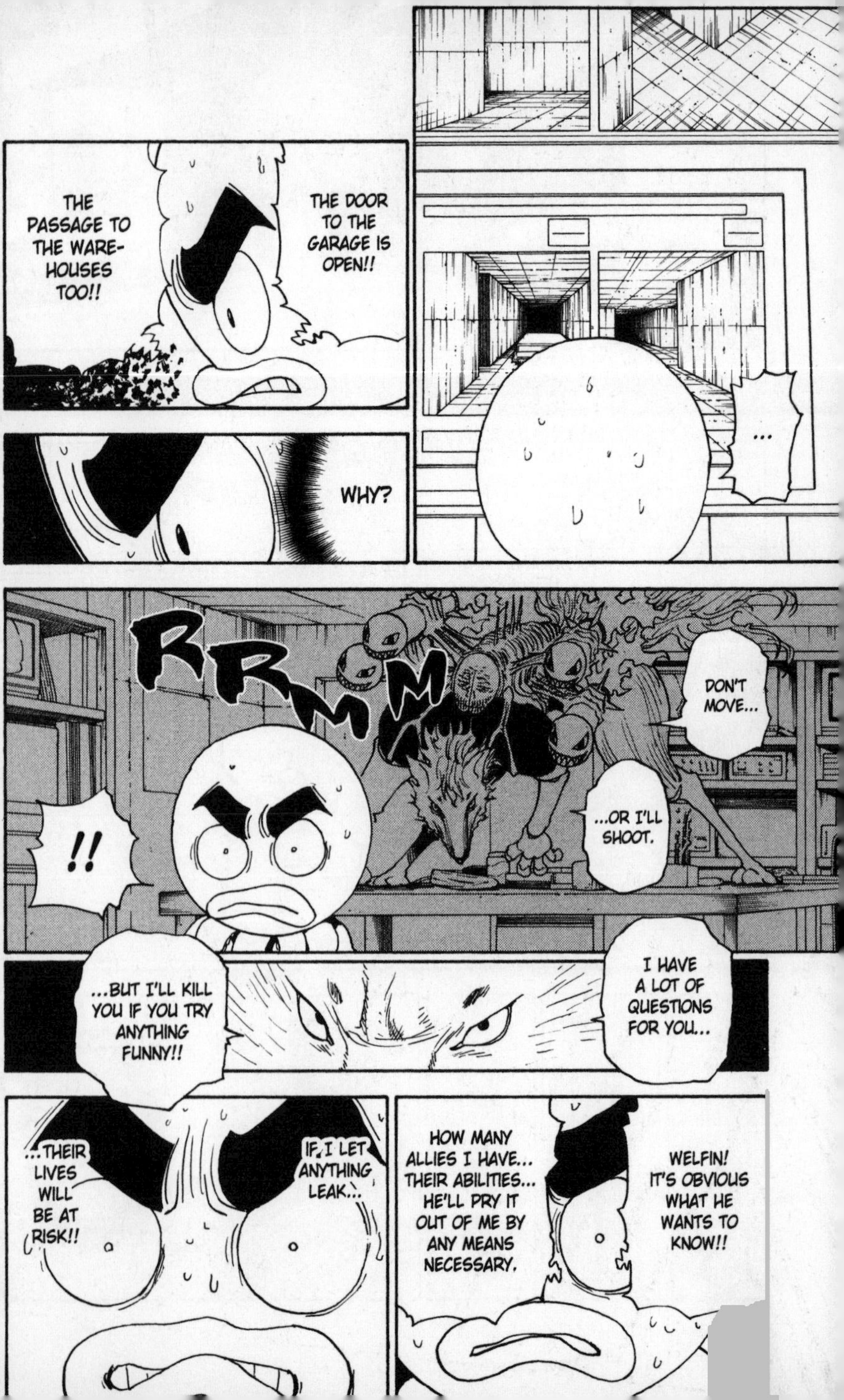
...
THE DOOR TO THE GARAGE IS OPEN!!
THE PASSAGE TO THE WARE-HOUSES TOO!!
WHY?
DON'T MOVE...
...OR I'LL SHOOT.
RRMM
!!
I HAVE A LOT OF QUESTIONS FOR YOU...
...BUT I'LL KILL YOU IF YOU TRY ANYTHING FUNNY!!
WELFIN! IT'S OBVIOUS WHAT HE WANTS TO KNOW!!
HOW MANY ALLIES I HAVE... THEIR ABILITIES... HE'LL PRY IT OUT OF ME BY ANY MEANS NECESSARY.
IF I LET ANYTHING LEAK...
...THEIR LIVES WILL BE AT RISK!!

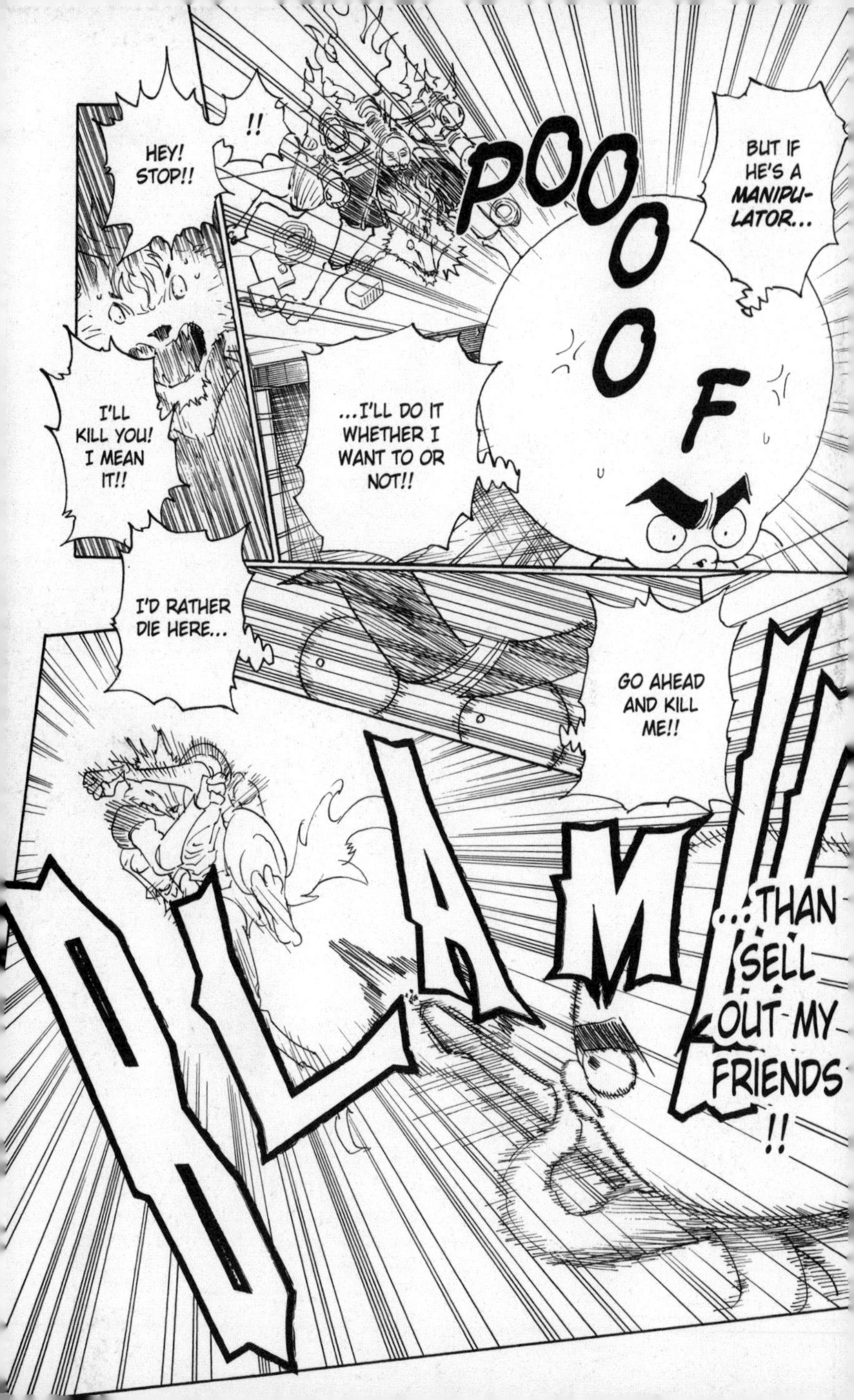
BUT IF HE'S A MANIPULATOR...
POOOOF
...I'LL DO IT WHETHER I WANT TO OR NOT!!
!!
HEY! STOP!!
I'LL KILL YOU! I MEAN IT!!
GO AHEAD AND KILL ME!!
I'D RATHER DIE HERE...
...THAN SELL OUT MY FRIENDS!!
BLAM

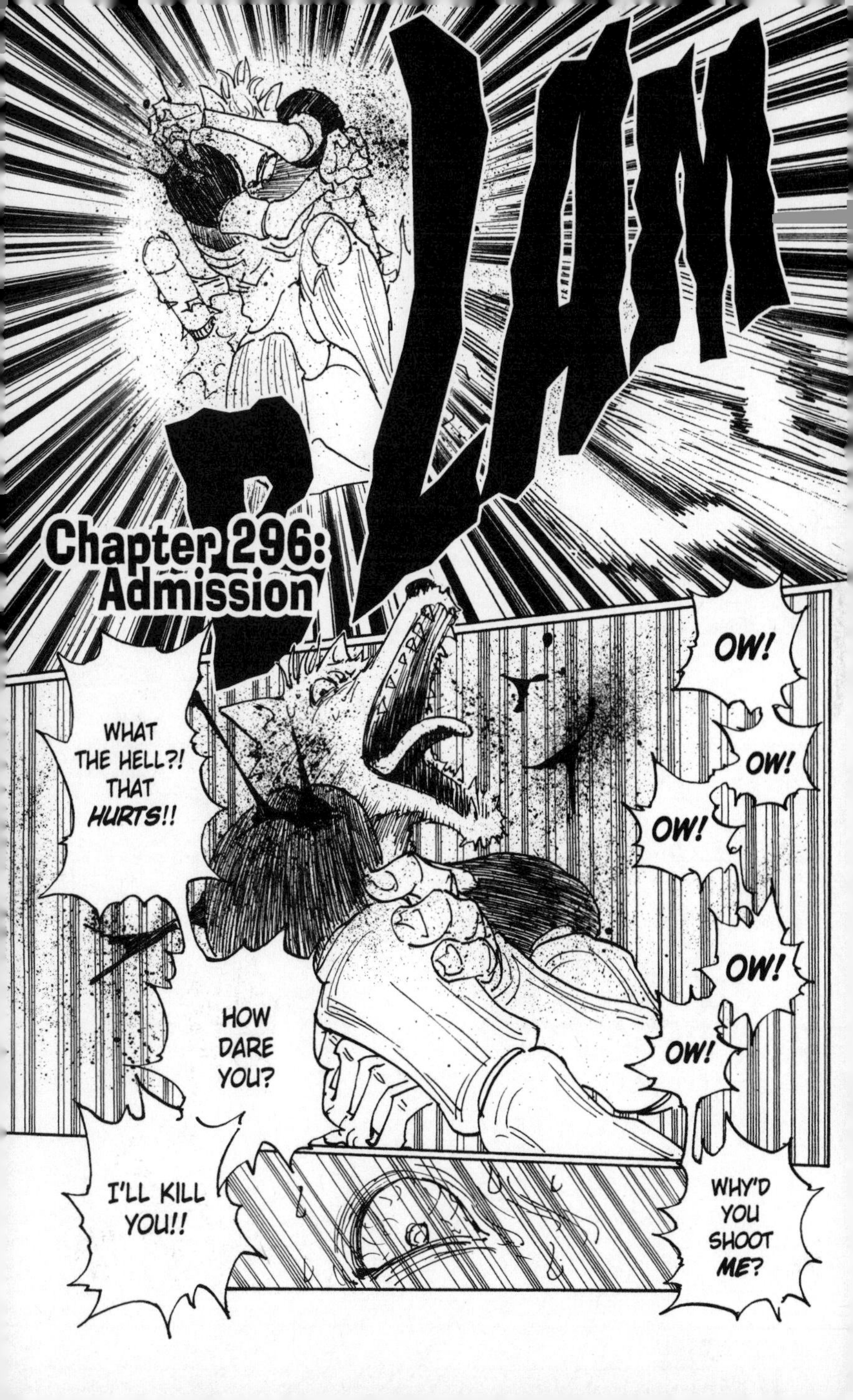
BLAM
Chapter 296: Admission
OW!
OW!
OW!
OW!
OW!
WHAT THE HELL?! THAT HURTS!!
HOW DARE YOU?
WHY'D YOU SHOOT ME?
I'LL KILL YOU!!

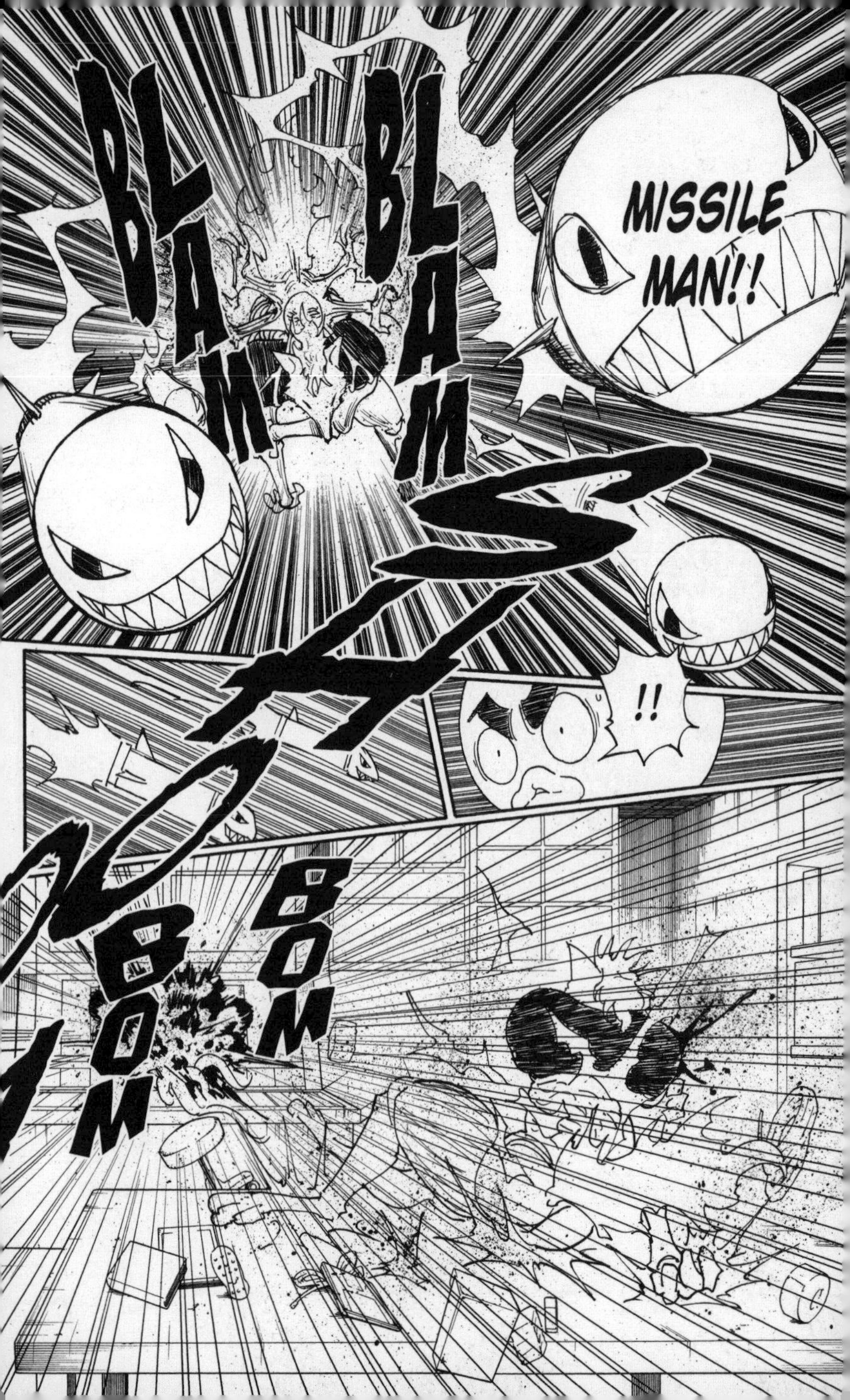
MISSILE MAN!!
BLAM
BLAM
!!
BOOM
BOOM

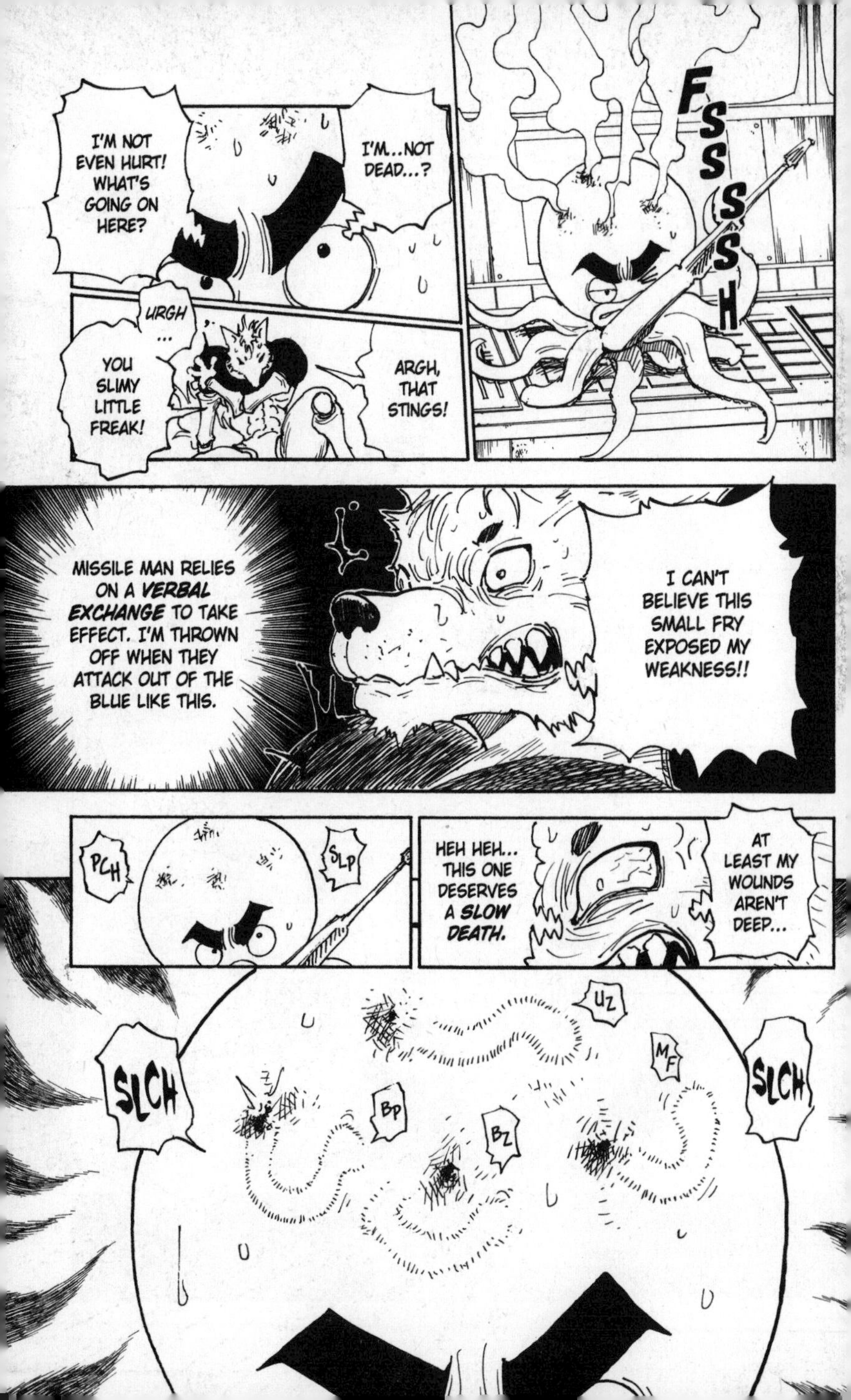
FSSSSH
I'M...NOT DEAD...?
I'M NOT EVEN HURT! WHAT'S GOING ON HERE?
ARGH, THAT STINGS!
URGH...
YOU SLIMY LITTLE FREAK!
I CAN'T BELIEVE THIS SMALL FRY EXPOSED MY WEAKNESS!!
MISSILE MAN RELIES ON A *VERBAL EXCHANGE* TO TAKE EFFECT. I'M THROWN OFF WHEN THEY ATTACK OUT OF THE BLUE LIKE THIS.
AT LEAST MY WOUNDS AREN'T DEEP...
HEH HEH... THIS ONE DESERVES A *SLOW DEATH.*
SLP
PCH
SLCH
UZ
MF
BZ
BP
SLCH

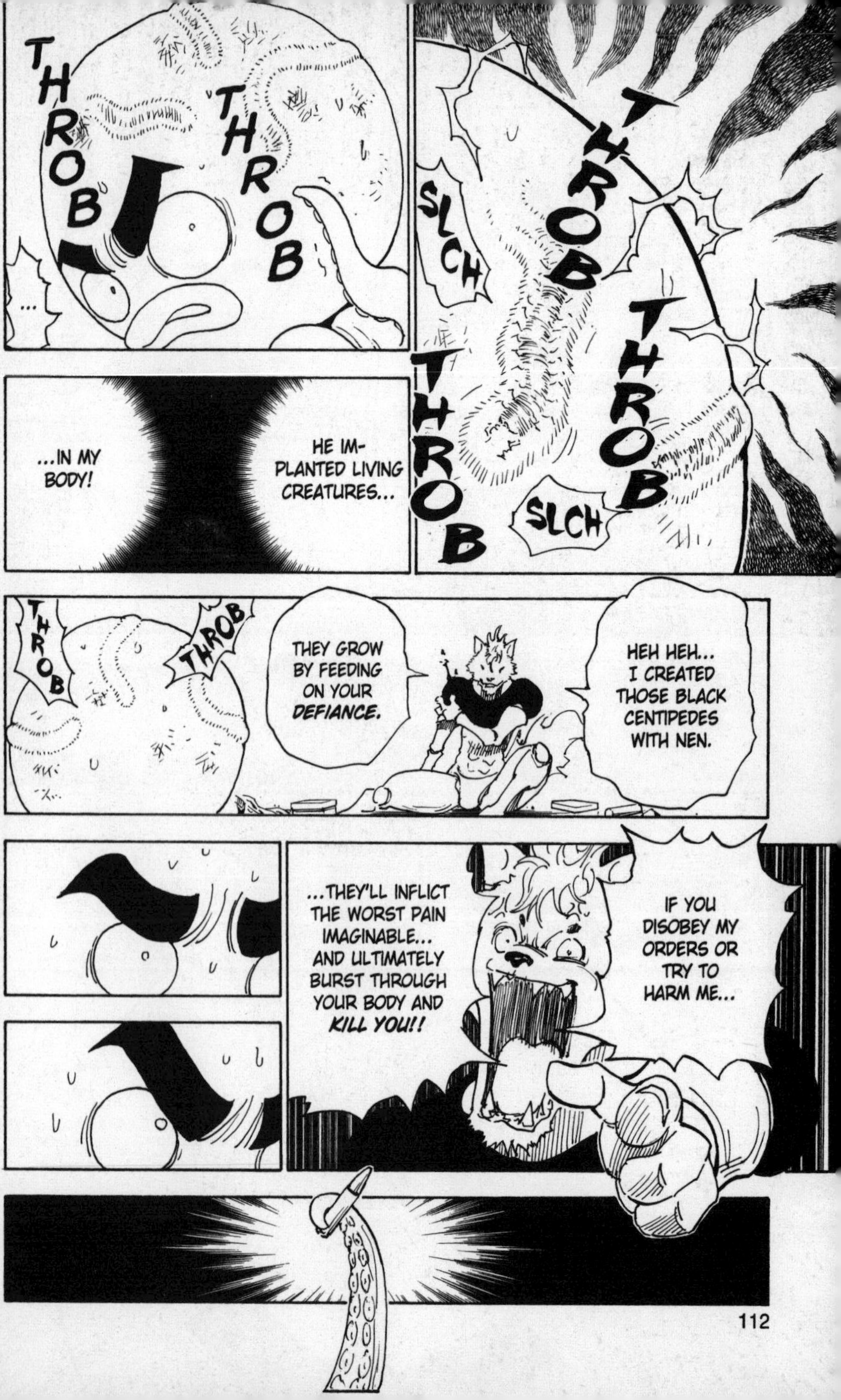
THROB
THROB
SLCH
THROB
SLCH
THROB
THROB
...
HE IM-
PLANTED LIVING
CREATURES...
...IN MY
BODY!
HEH HEH...
I CREATED
THOSE BLACK
CENTIPEDES
WITH NEN.
THEY GROW
BY FEEDING
ON YOUR
DEFIANCE.
THROB
THROB
IF YOU
DISOBEY MY
ORDERS OR
TRY TO
HARM ME...
...THEY'LL INFLICT
THE WORST PAIN
IMAGINABLE...
AND ULTIMATELY
BURST THROUGH
YOUR BODY AND
KILL YOU!!

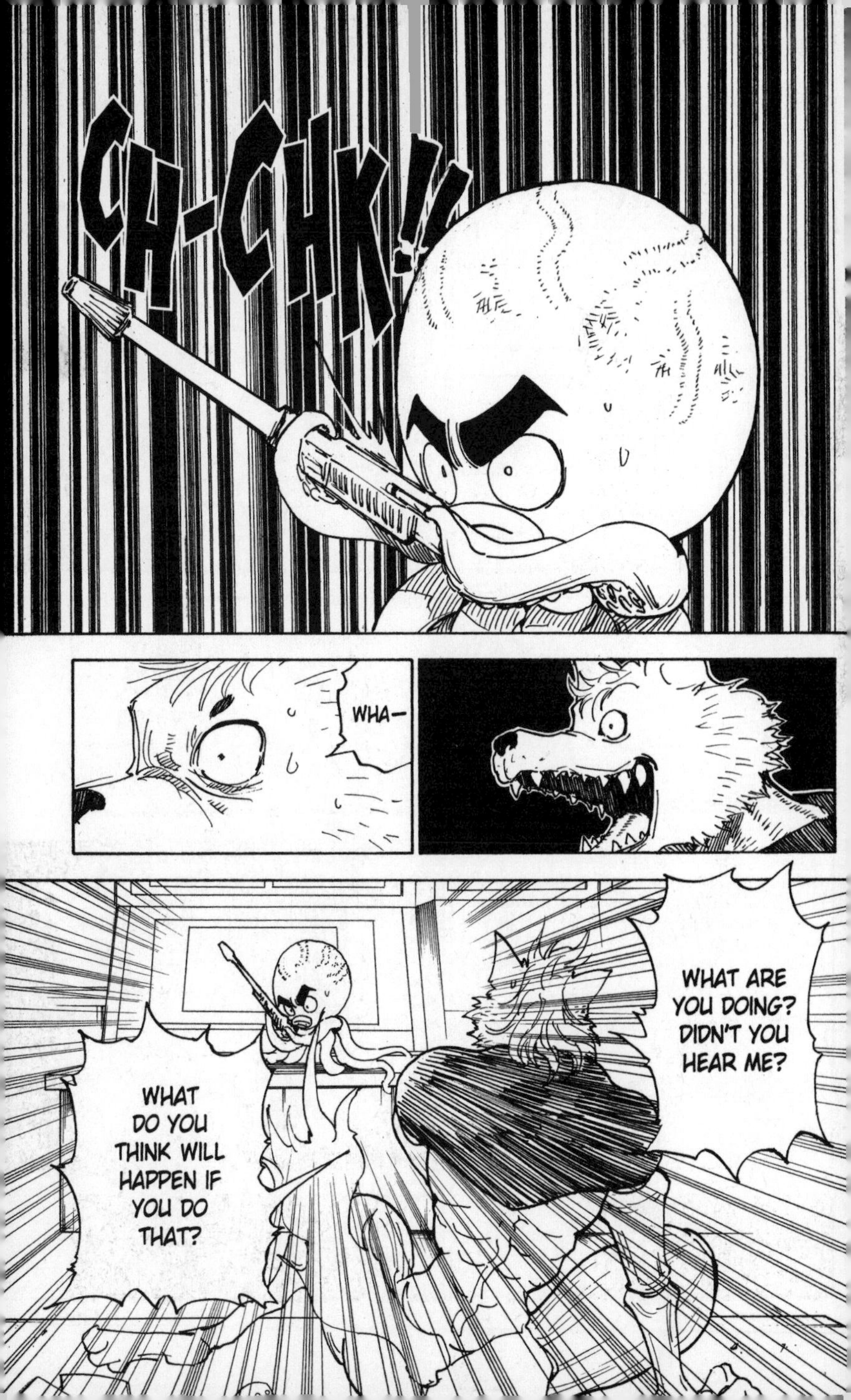
CH-CHK!!
WHA—
WHAT ARE YOU DOING? DIDN'T YOU HEAR ME?
WHAT DO YOU THINK WILL HAPPEN IF YOU DO THAT?

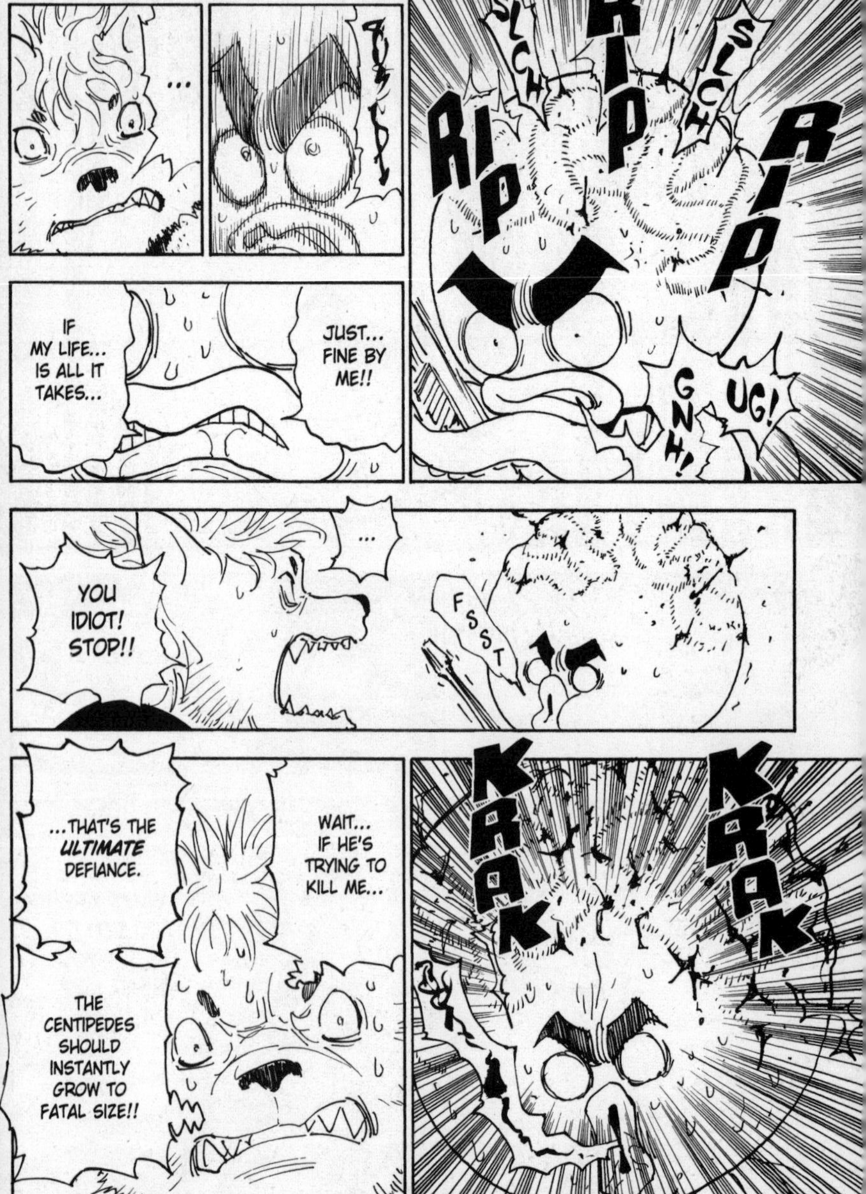
RIP
SLCH
RIP
SLCH
RIP
UG!
GNH!
...
IF MY LIFE... IS ALL IT TAKES...
JUST... FINE BY ME!!
...
FSST
YOU IDIOT! STOP!!
KRAK
KRAK
WAIT... IF HE'S TRYING TO KILL ME...
...THAT'S THE *ULTIMATE* DEFIANCE.
THE CENTIPEDES SHOULD INSTANTLY GROW TO FATAL SIZE!!

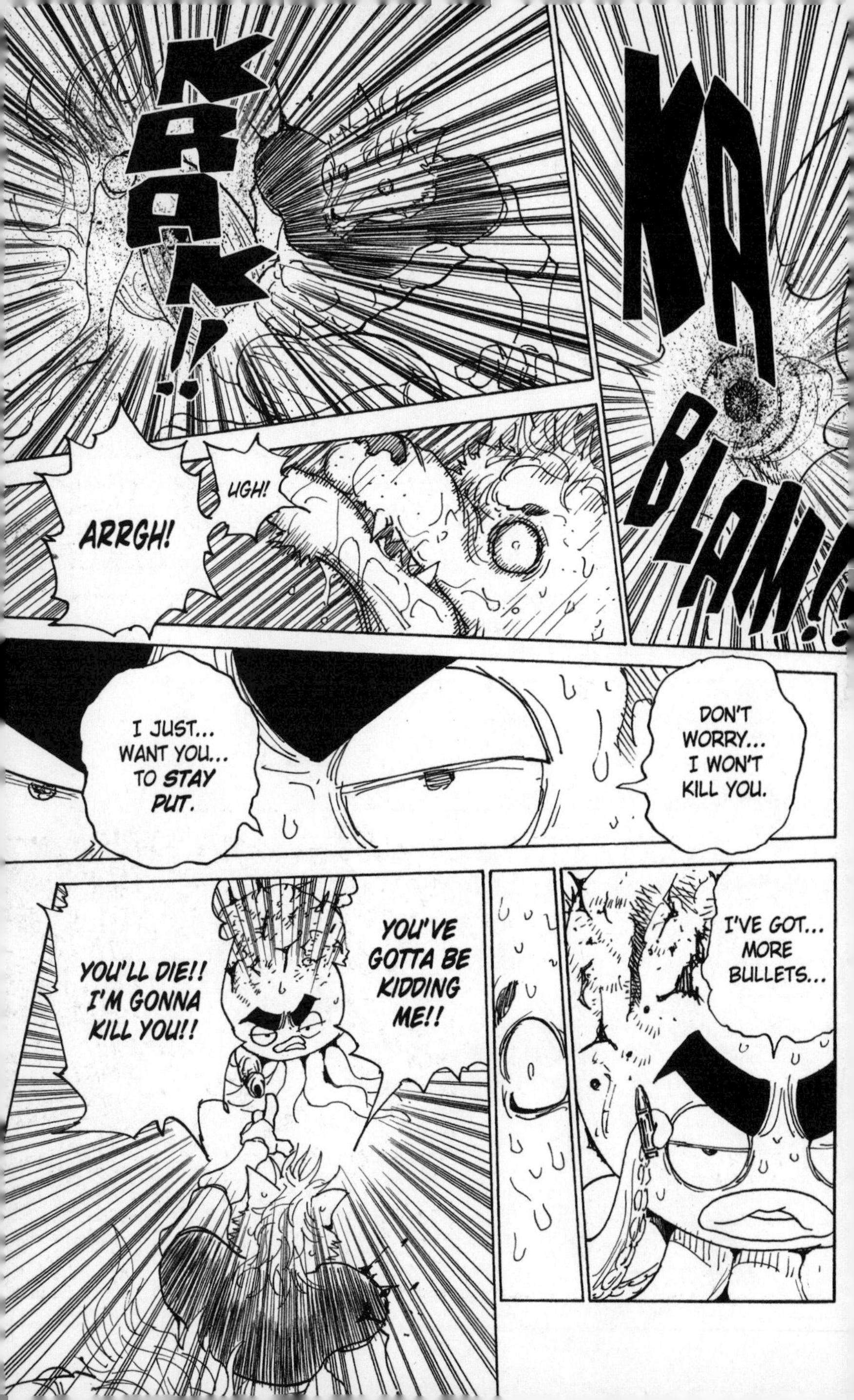
KA BLAM!!
KRAK!!
UGH!
ARRGH!
DON'T WORRY... I WON'T KILL YOU.
I JUST... WANT YOU... TO STAY PUT.
I'VE GOT... MORE BULLETS...
YOU'VE GOTTA BE KIDDING ME!!
YOU'LL DIE!! I'M GONNA KILL YOU!!

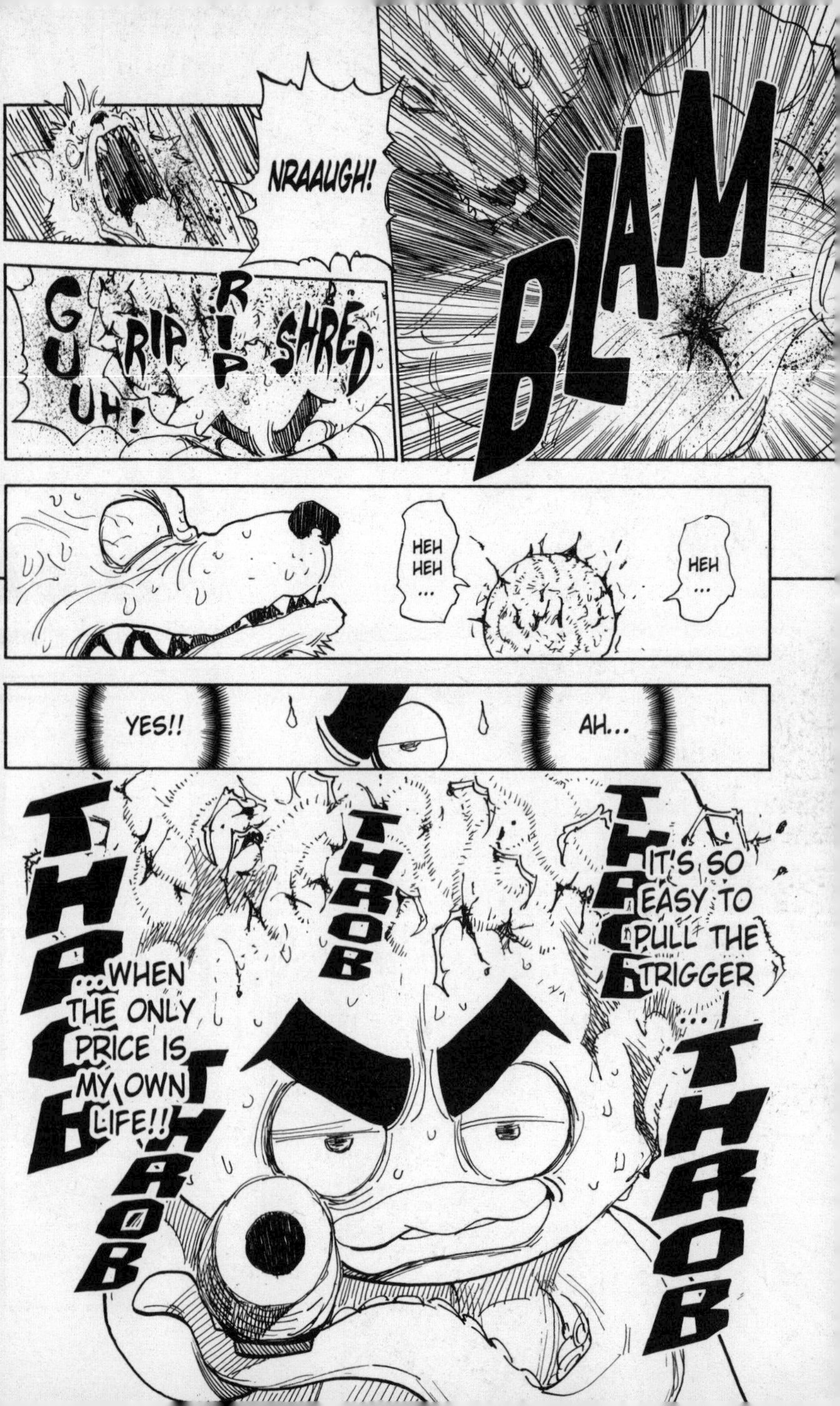
BLAM
NRAAUGH!
SHRED
RIP
RIP
GUUH!
HEH ...
HEH HEH ...
AH...
YES!!
THROB
IT'S SO EASY TO PULL THE TRIGGER...
THROB
THROB
...WHEN THE ONLY PRICE IS MY OWN LIFE!!
THROB
THROB

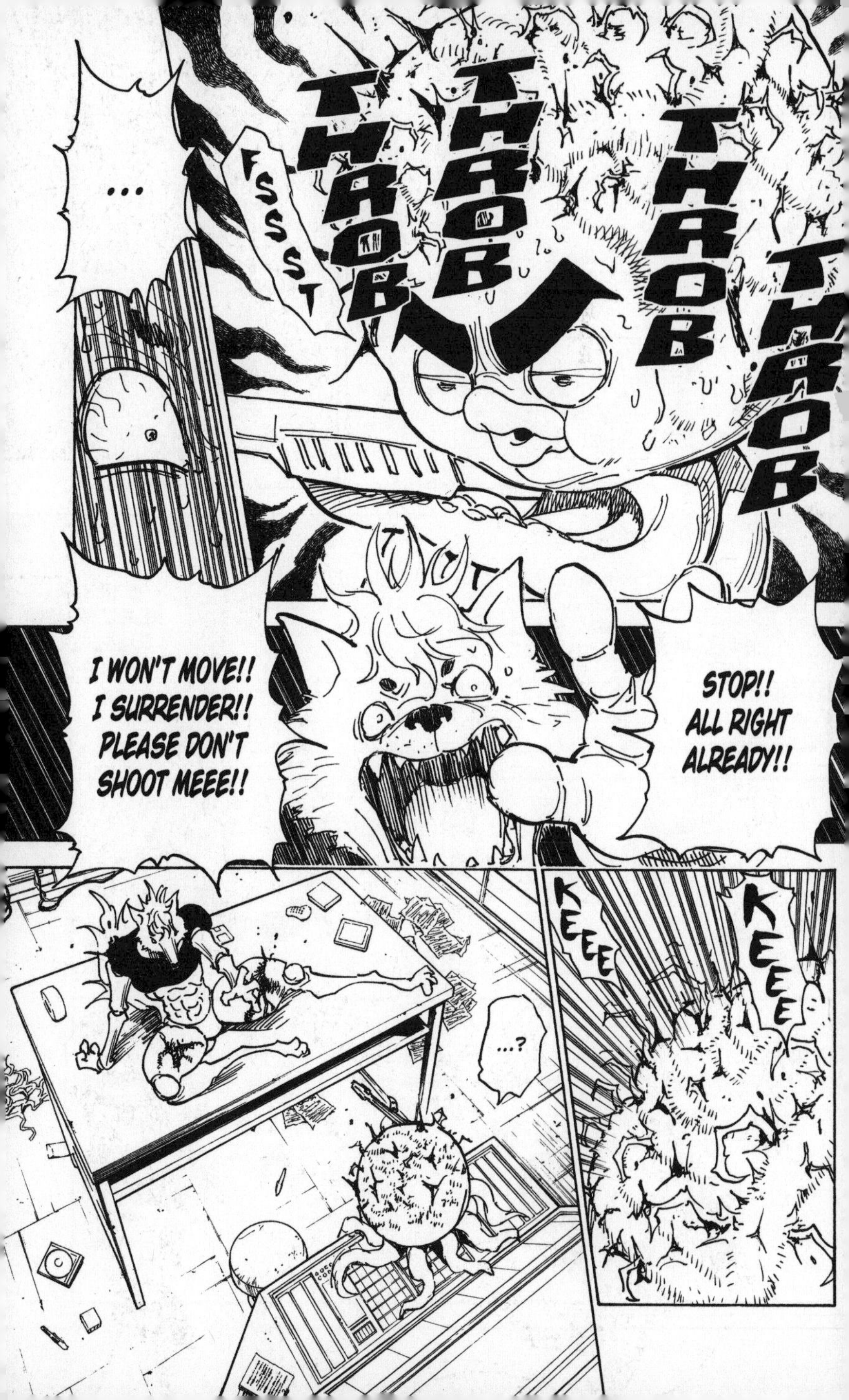

THROB
THROB
THROB
THROB
THROB
FSSST
...
STOP!! ALL RIGHT ALREADY!!
I WON'T MOVE!! I SURRENDER!! PLEASE DON'T SHOOT MEEE!!
KEEE
KEEE
...?

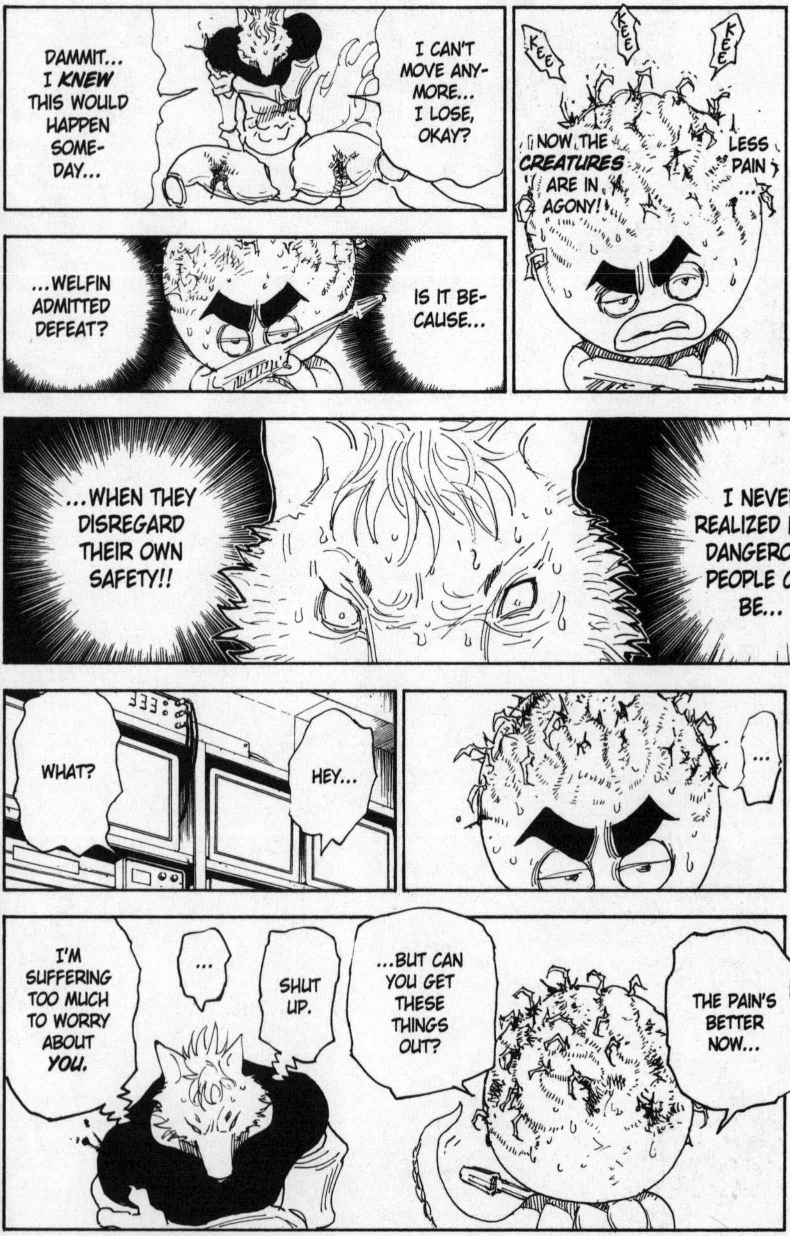
KEE
KEE
KEE
LESS PAIN...
NOW THE *CREATURES* ARE IN AGONY!
I CAN'T MOVE ANYMORE... I LOSE, OKAY?
DAMMIT... I *KNEW* THIS WOULD HAPPEN SOMEDAY...
IS IT BECAUSE...
...WELFIN ADMITTED DEFEAT?
I NEVER REALIZED HOW DANGEROUS PEOPLE CAN BE...
...WHEN THEY DISREGARD THEIR OWN SAFETY!!
...
HEY...
WHAT?
THE PAIN'S BETTER NOW...
...BUT CAN YOU GET THESE THINGS OUT?
SHUT UP.
...
I'M SUFFERING TOO MUCH TO WORRY ABOUT *YOU*.

READ THIS WAY

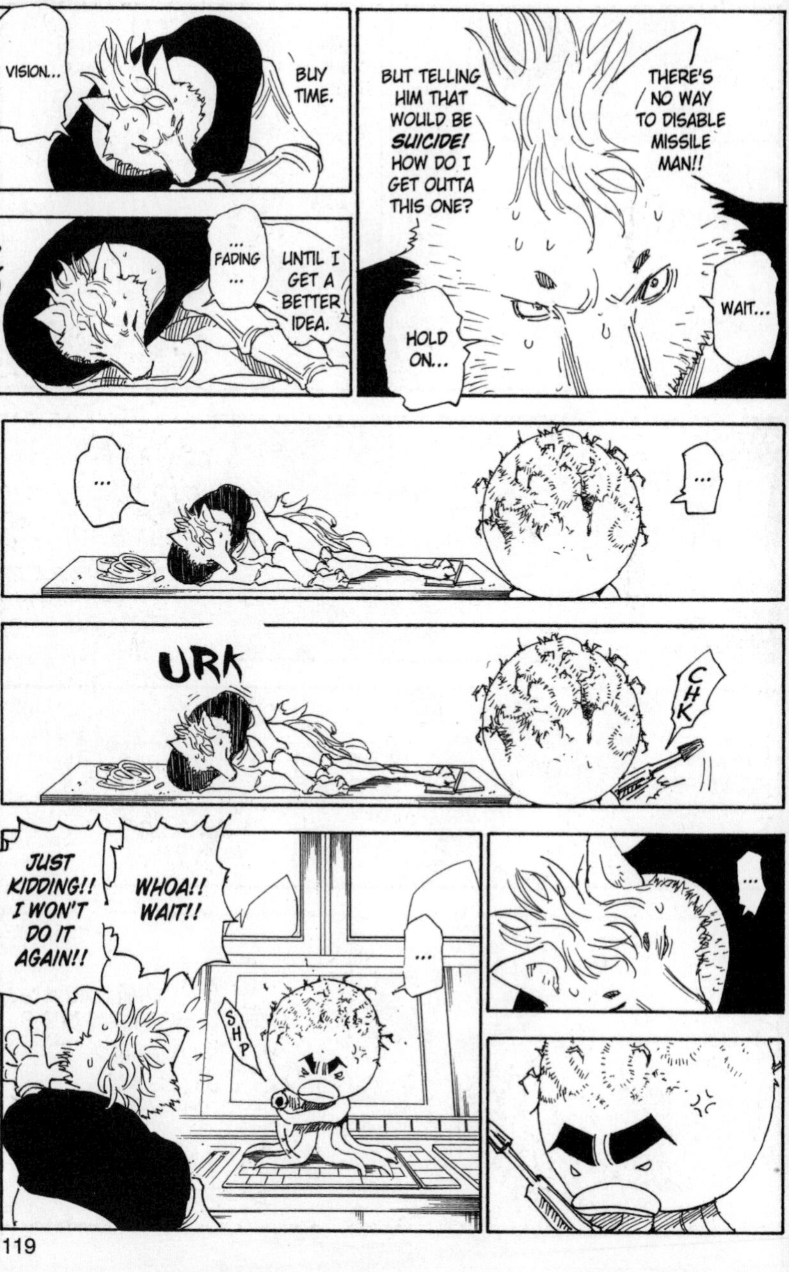
THERE'S NO WAY TO DISABLE MISSILE MAN!!
BUT TELLING HIM THAT WOULD BE SUICIDE! HOW DO I GET OUTTA THIS ONE?
WAIT...
HOLD ON...
BUY TIME.
VISION...
UNTIL I GET A BETTER IDEA.
... FADING ...
SLUMP
...
...
CHK
URK
...
...
SHP
WHOA!! WAIT!!
JUST KIDDING!! I WON'T DO IT AGAIN!!

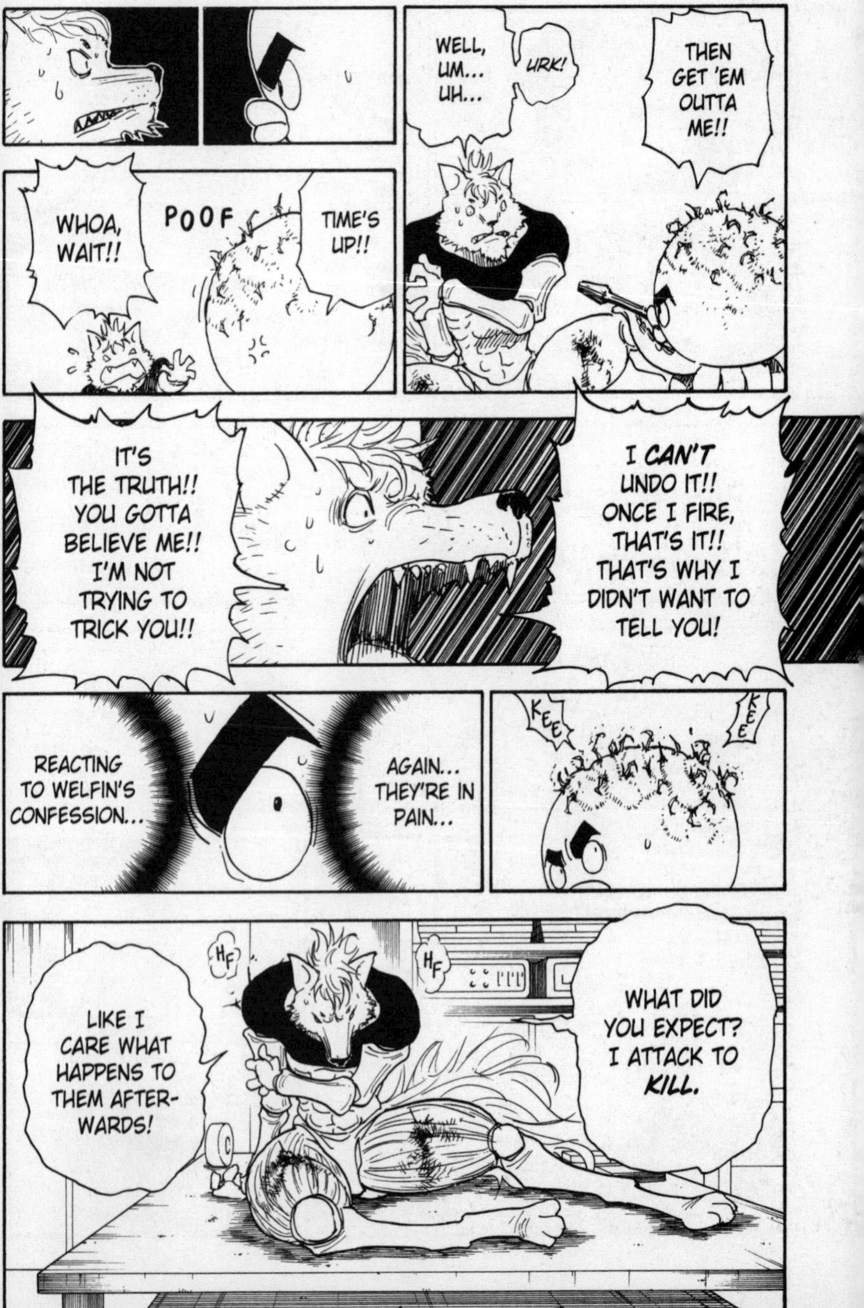
THEN GET 'EM OUTTA ME!!
URK!
WELL, UM... UH...
TIME'S UP!!
POOF
WHOA, WAIT!!
I CAN'T UNDO IT!! ONCE I FIRE, THAT'S IT!! THAT'S WHY I DIDN'T WANT TO TELL YOU!
IT'S THE TRUTH!! YOU GOTTA BELIEVE ME!! I'M NOT TRYING TO TRICK YOU!!
KEE
KEE
AGAIN... THEY'RE IN PAIN...
REACTING TO WELFIN'S CONFESSION...
WHAT DID YOU EXPECT? I ATTACK TO KILL.
HF
HF
LIKE I CARE WHAT HAPPENS TO THEM AFTER-WARDS!

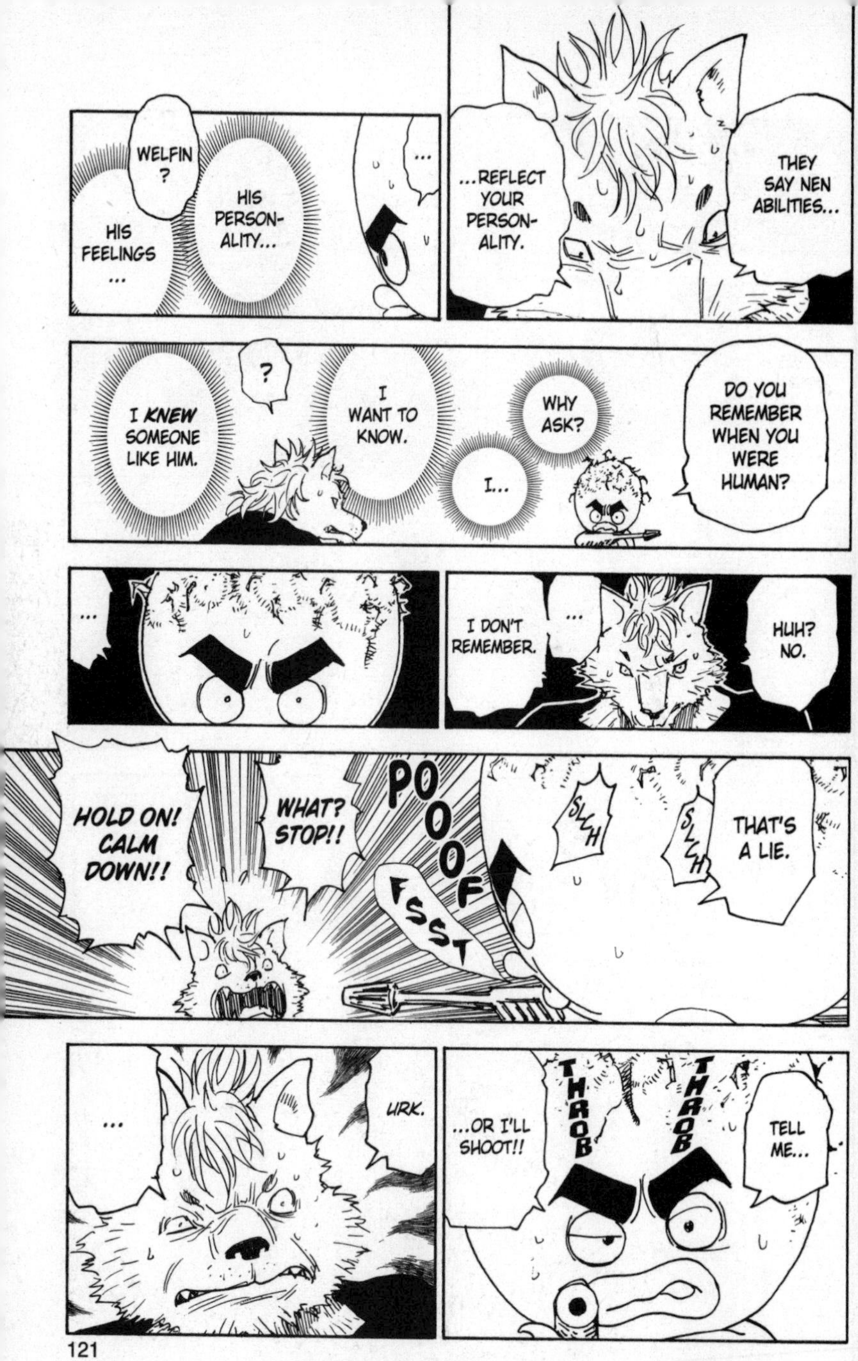
THEY SAY NEN ABILITIES...
...REFLECT YOUR PERSONALITY.
...
WELFIN?
HIS PERSONALITY...
HIS FEELINGS...
DO YOU REMEMBER WHEN YOU WERE HUMAN?
WHY ASK?
I...
I WANT TO KNOW.
?
I KNEW SOMEONE LIKE HIM.
HUH? NO.
...
I DON'T REMEMBER.
...
THAT'S A LIE.
SLSH
SLSH
POOOOF
FSSST
WHAT? STOP!!
HOLD ON! CALM DOWN!!
TELL ME...
THROB
THROB
...OR I'LL SHOOT!!
URK.
...

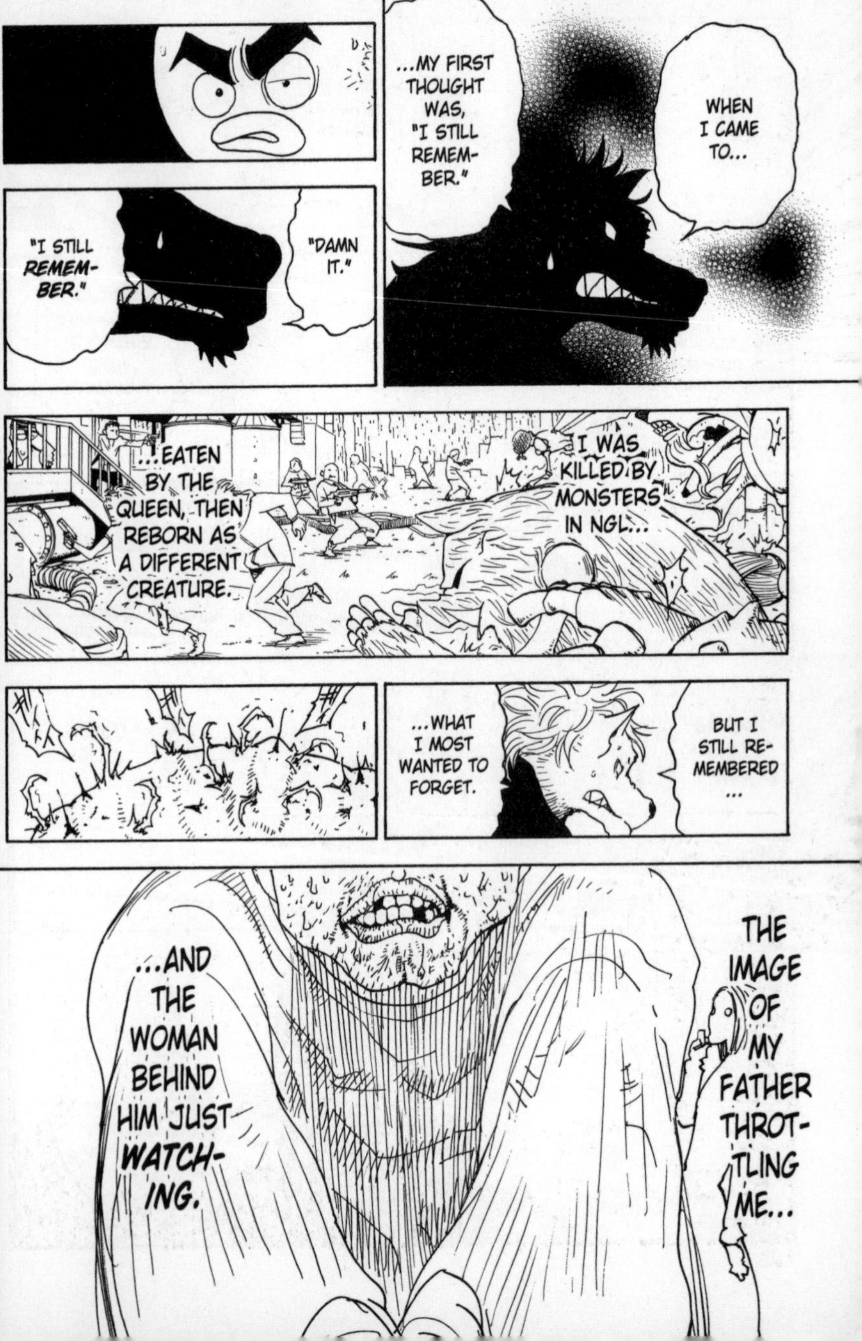
WHEN I CAME TO...
...MY FIRST THOUGHT WAS, "I STILL REMEMBER."
"DAMN IT."
"I STILL *REMEMBER.*"
I WAS KILLED BY MONSTERS IN NGL...
...EATEN BY THE QUEEN, THEN REBORN AS A DIFFERENT CREATURE.
BUT I STILL REMEMBERED ...
...WHAT I MOST WANTED TO FORGET.
THE IMAGE OF MY FATHER THROTTLING ME...
...AND THE WOMAN BEHIND HIM JUST *WATCHING.*

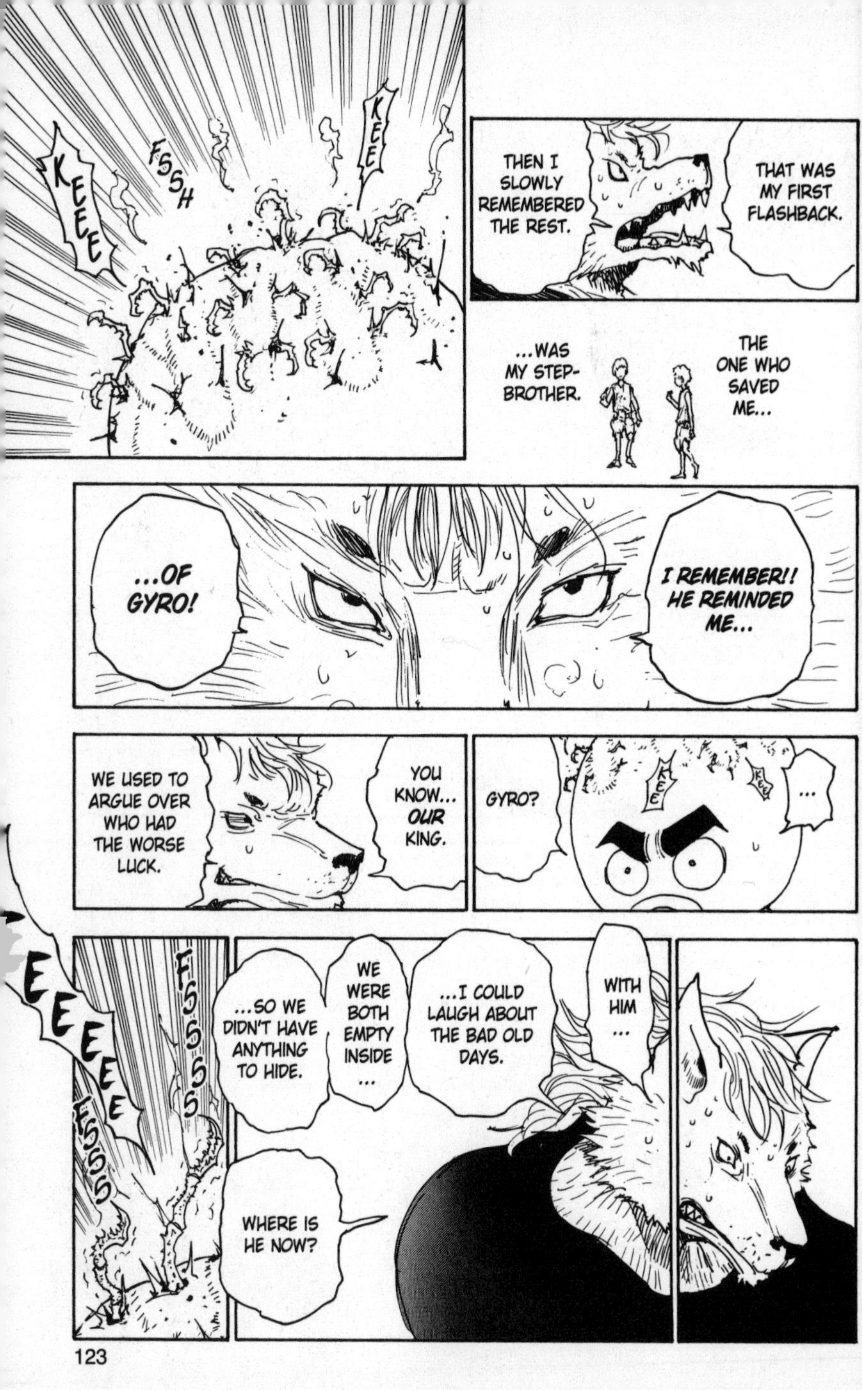
THAT WAS MY FIRST FLASHBACK.
THEN I SLOWLY REMEMBERED THE REST.
THE ONE WHO SAVED ME...
...WAS MY STEP-BROTHER.
KEE
FSSH
KEEE
I REMEMBER!! HE REMINDED ME...
...OF GYRO!
...
KEE
KEE
GYRO?
YOU KNOW... OUR KING.
WE USED TO ARGUE OVER WHO HAD THE WORSE LUCK.
WITH HIM...
...I COULD LAUGH ABOUT THE BAD OLD DAYS.
WE WERE BOTH EMPTY INSIDE...
...SO WE DIDN'T HAVE ANYTHING TO HIDE.
WHERE IS HE NOW?
FSSSS
EEEEEE
FSSS

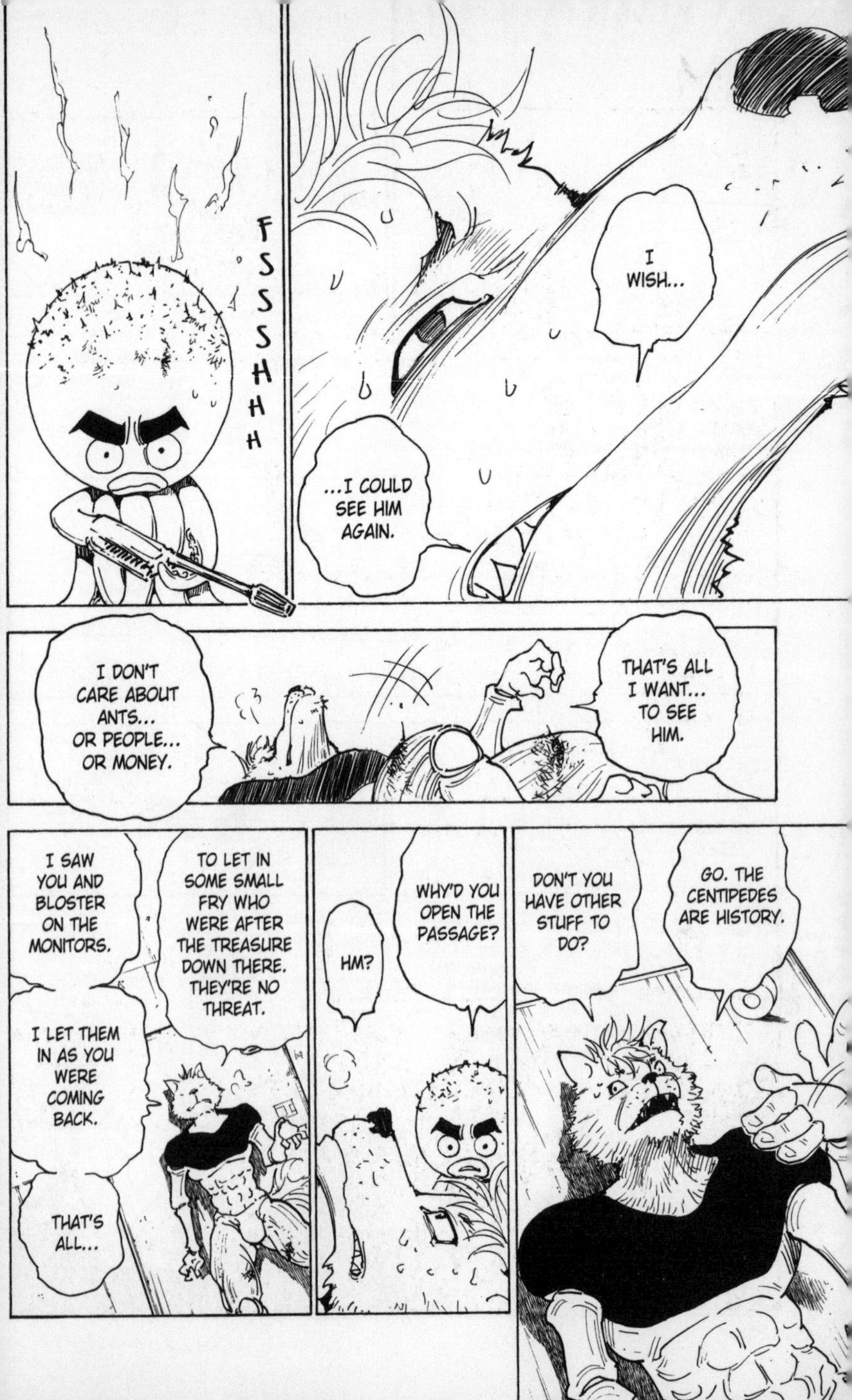
I WISH...
...I COULD SEE HIM AGAIN.
FSSSHHH
THAT'S ALL I WANT... TO SEE HIM.
I DON'T CARE ABOUT ANTS... OR PEOPLE... OR MONEY.
GO. THE CENTIPEDES ARE HISTORY.
DON'T YOU HAVE OTHER STUFF TO DO?
WHY'D YOU OPEN THE PASSAGE?
HM?
TO LET IN SOME SMALL FRY WHO WERE AFTER THE TREASURE DOWN THERE. THEY'RE NO THREAT.
I SAW YOU AND BLOSTER ON THE MONITORS.
I LET THEM IN AS YOU WERE COMING BACK.
THAT'S ALL...

READ THIS WAY

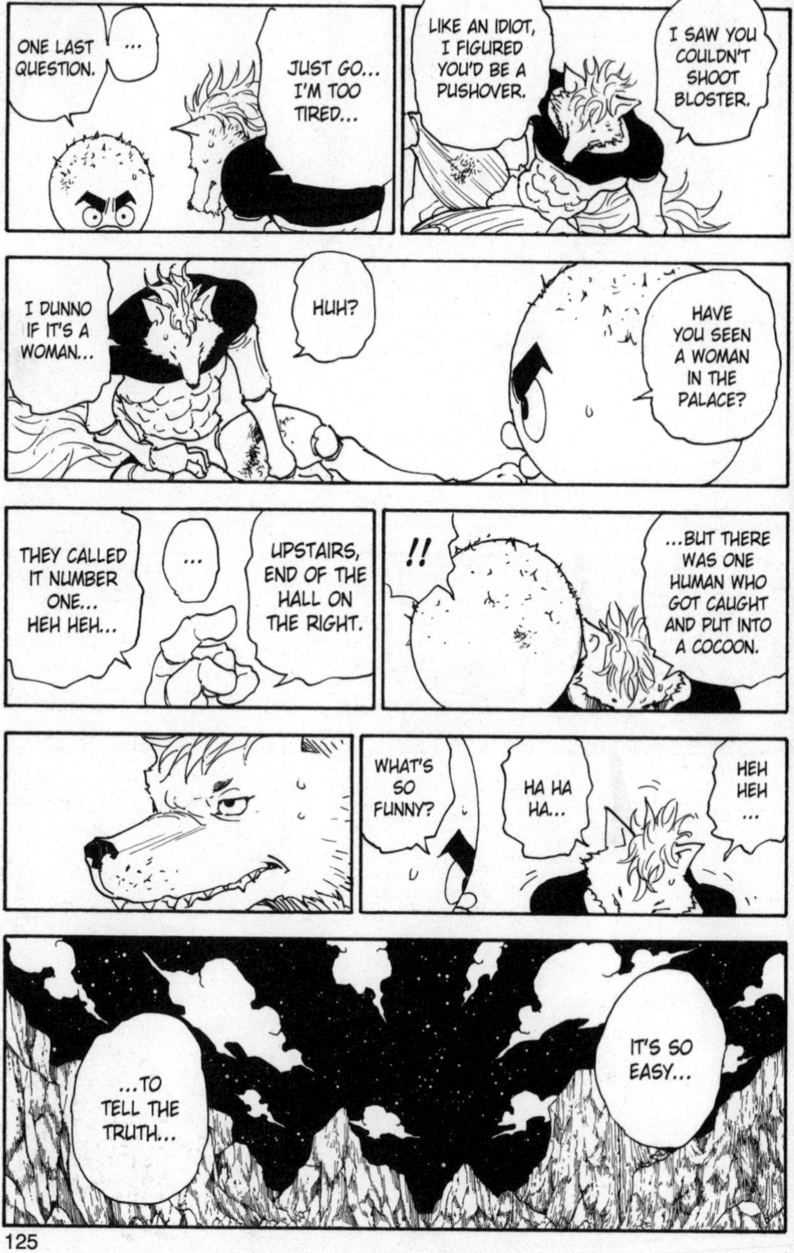
I SAW YOU COULDN'T SHOOT BLOSTER.
LIKE AN IDIOT, I FIGURED YOU'D BE A PUSHOVER.
JUST GO... I'M TOO TIRED...
...
ONE LAST QUESTION.
HAVE YOU SEEN A WOMAN IN THE PALACE?
HUH?
I DUNNO IF IT'S A WOMAN...
...BUT THERE WAS ONE HUMAN WHO GOT CAUGHT AND PUT INTO A COCOON.
!!
UPSTAIRS, END OF THE HALL ON THE RIGHT.
...
THEY CALLED IT NUMBER ONE... HEH HEH...
HEH HEH ...
HA HA HA...
WHAT'S SO FUNNY?
IT'S SO EASY...
...TO TELL THE TRUTH...

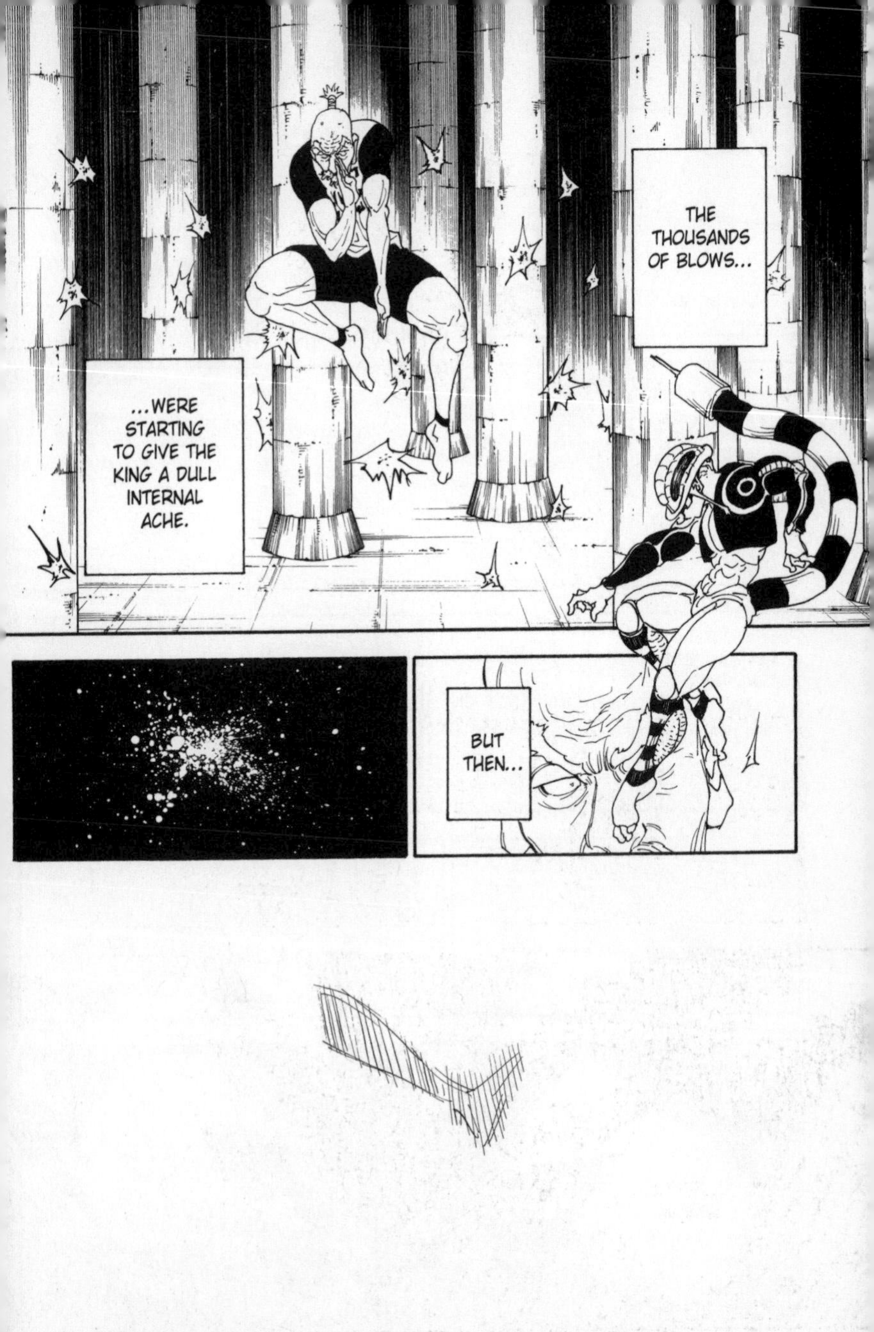
THE THOUSANDS OF BLOWS...
...WERE STARTING TO GIVE THE KING A DULL INTERNAL ACHE.
BUT THEN...

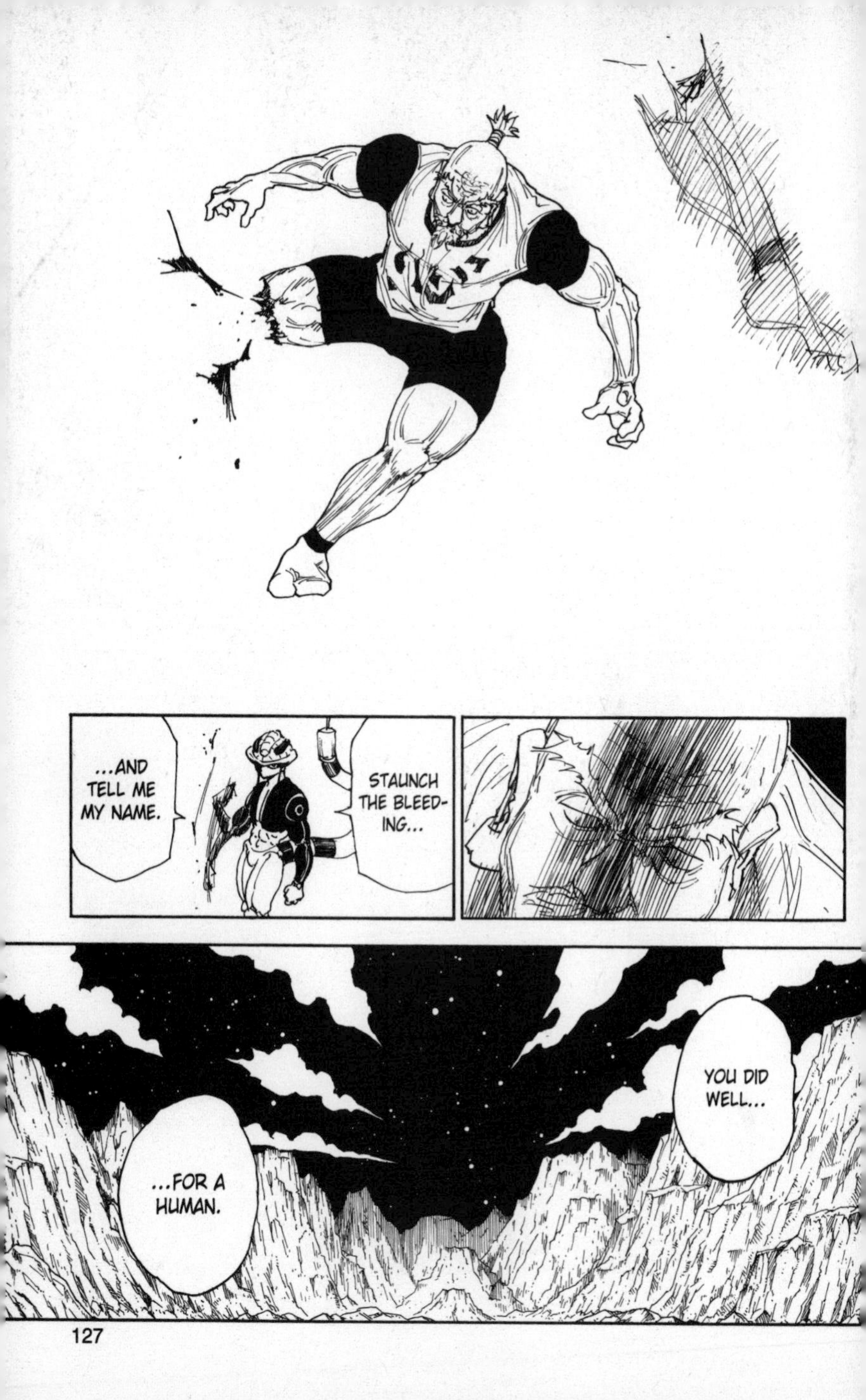
STAUNCH THE BLEED-ING...
...AND TELL ME MY NAME.
YOU DID WELL...
...FOR A HUMAN.

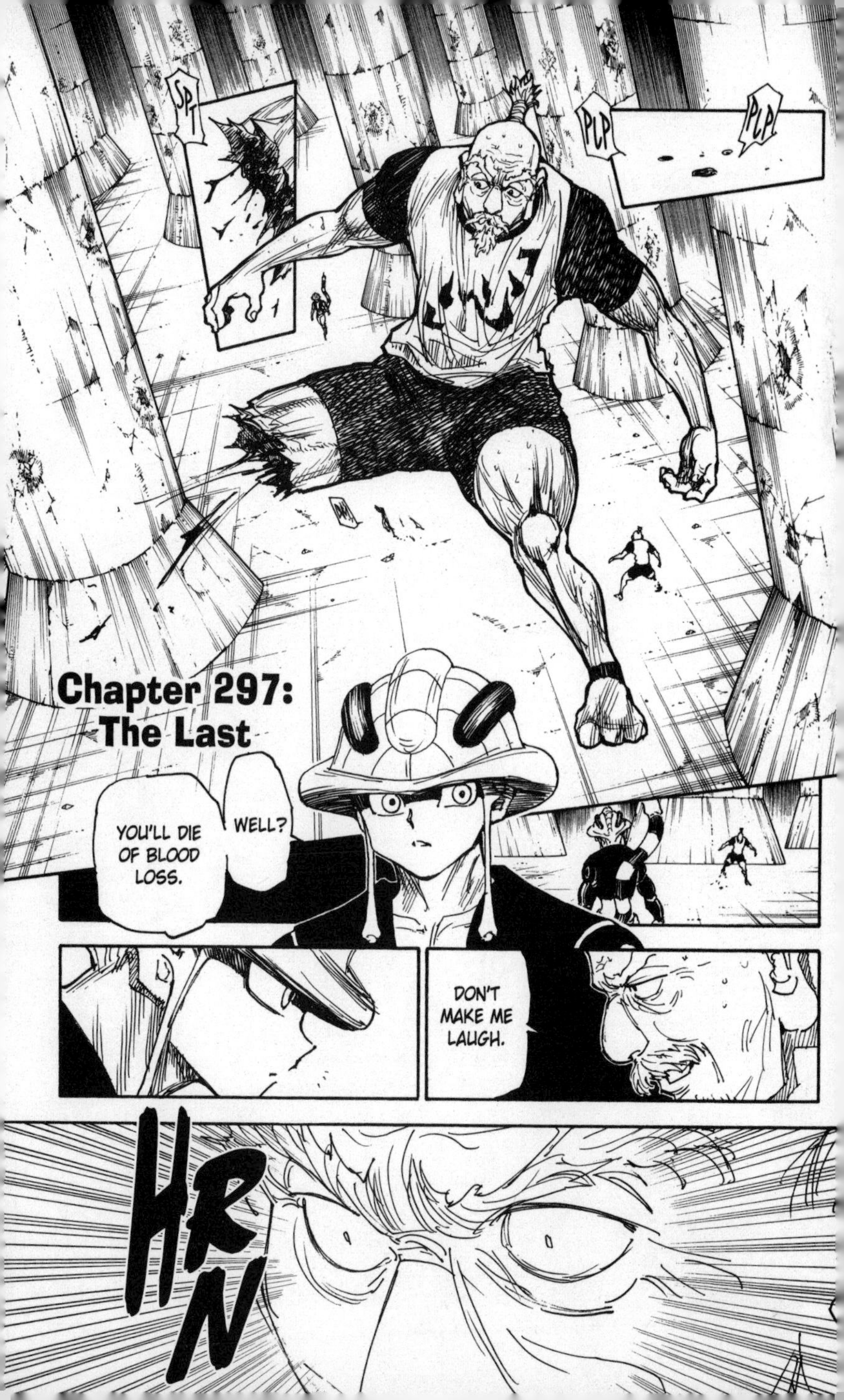
PLP
PLP
SPT
Chapter 297: The Last
WELL?
YOU'LL DIE OF BLOOD LOSS.
DON'T MAKE ME LAUGH.
HRN

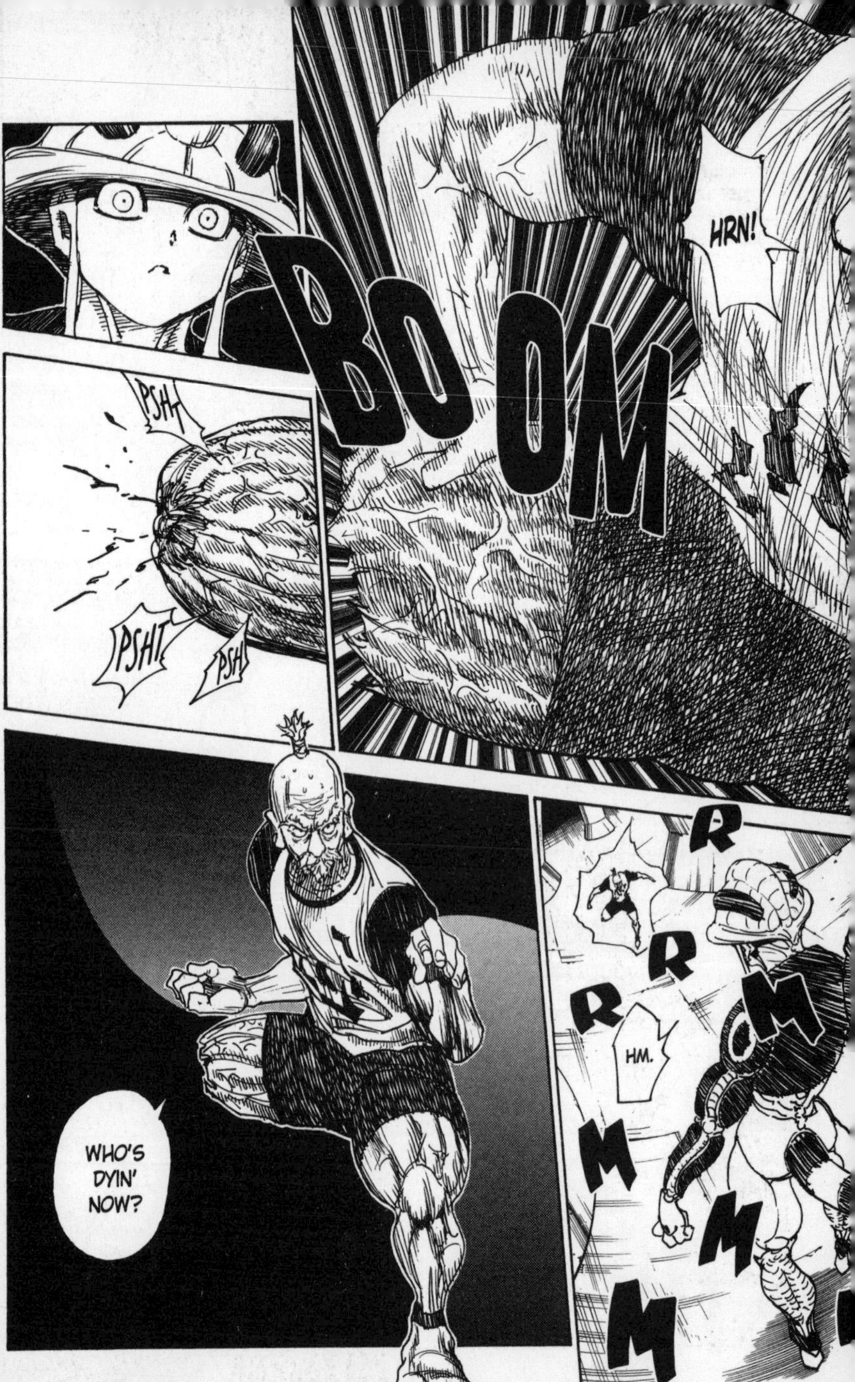
HRN!
BOOM
PSHT
PSHT
PSH
RRRMMMM
HM.
WHO'S DYIN' NOW?

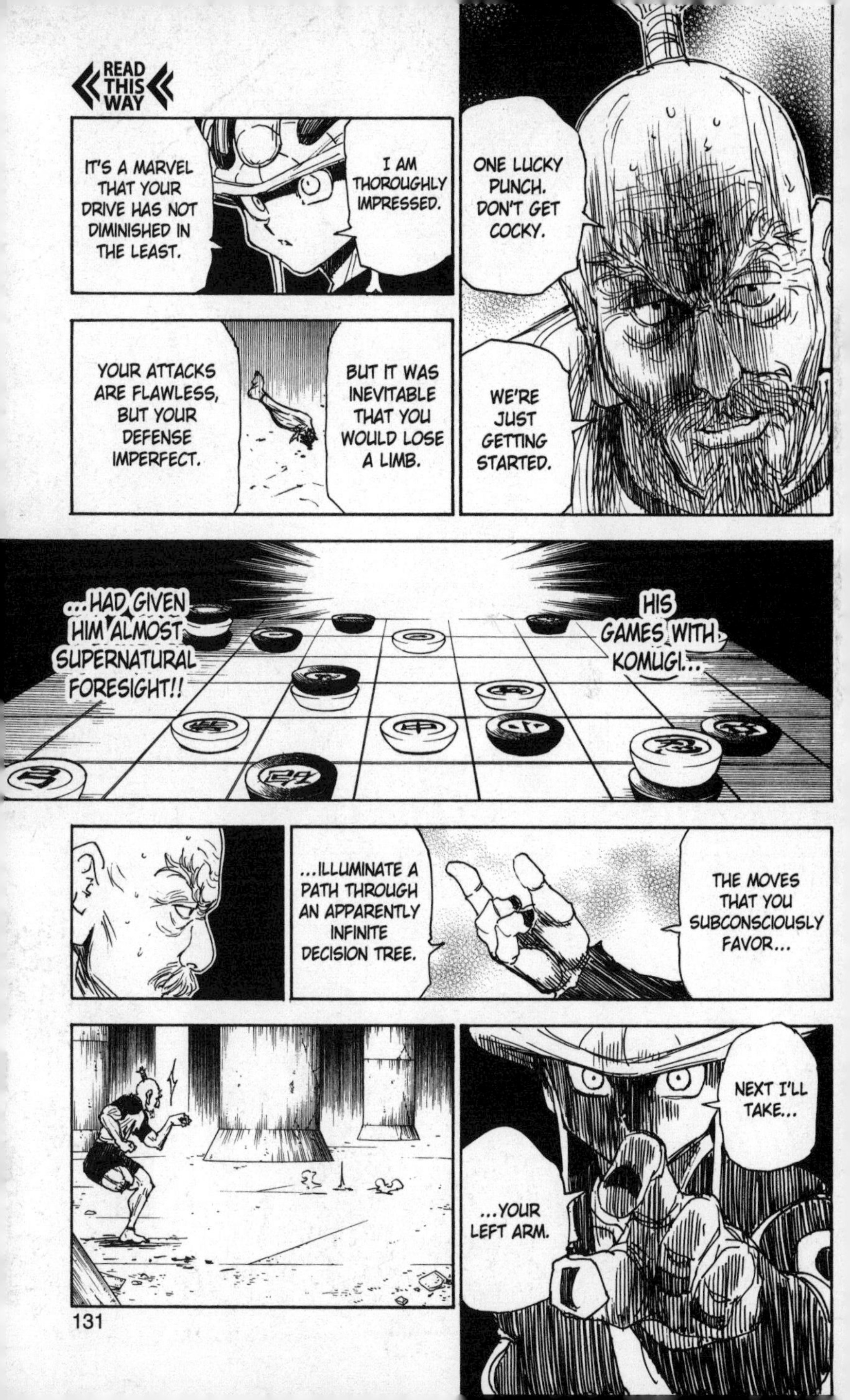
READ THIS WAY
ONE LUCKY PUNCH. DON'T GET COCKY.
WE'RE JUST GETTING STARTED.
I AM THOROUGHLY IMPRESSED.
IT'S A MARVEL THAT YOUR DRIVE HAS NOT DIMINISHED IN THE LEAST.
BUT IT WAS INEVITABLE THAT YOU WOULD LOSE A LIMB.
YOUR ATTACKS ARE FLAWLESS, BUT YOUR DEFENSE IMPERFECT.
HIS GAMES WITH KOMUGI...
...HAD GIVEN HIM ALMOST SUPERNATURAL FORESIGHT!!
THE MOVES THAT YOU SUBCONSCIOUSLY FAVOR...
...ILLUMINATE A PATH THROUGH AN APPARENTLY INFINITE DECISION TREE.
NEXT I'LL TAKE...
...YOUR LEFT ARM.

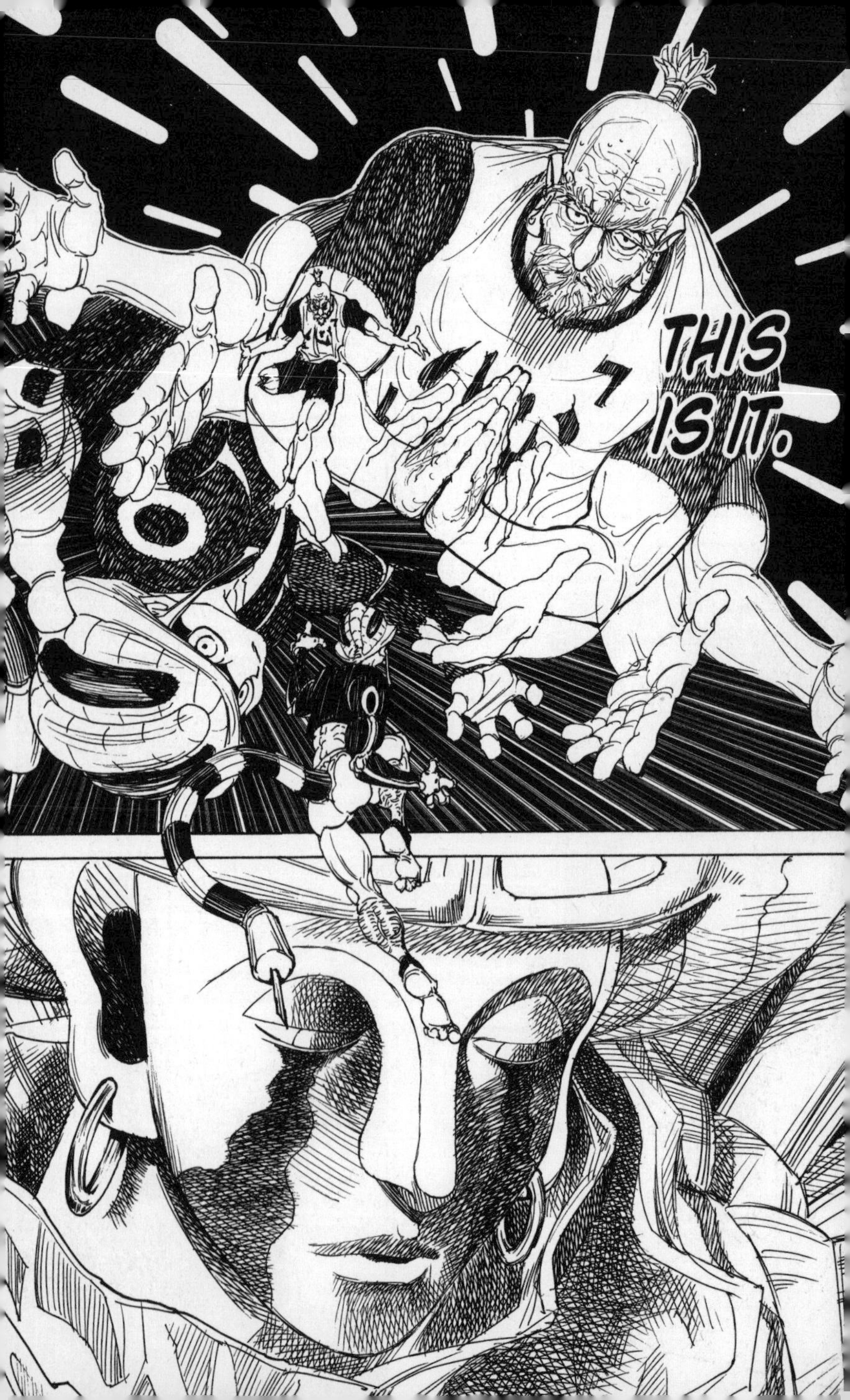
THIS IS IT.

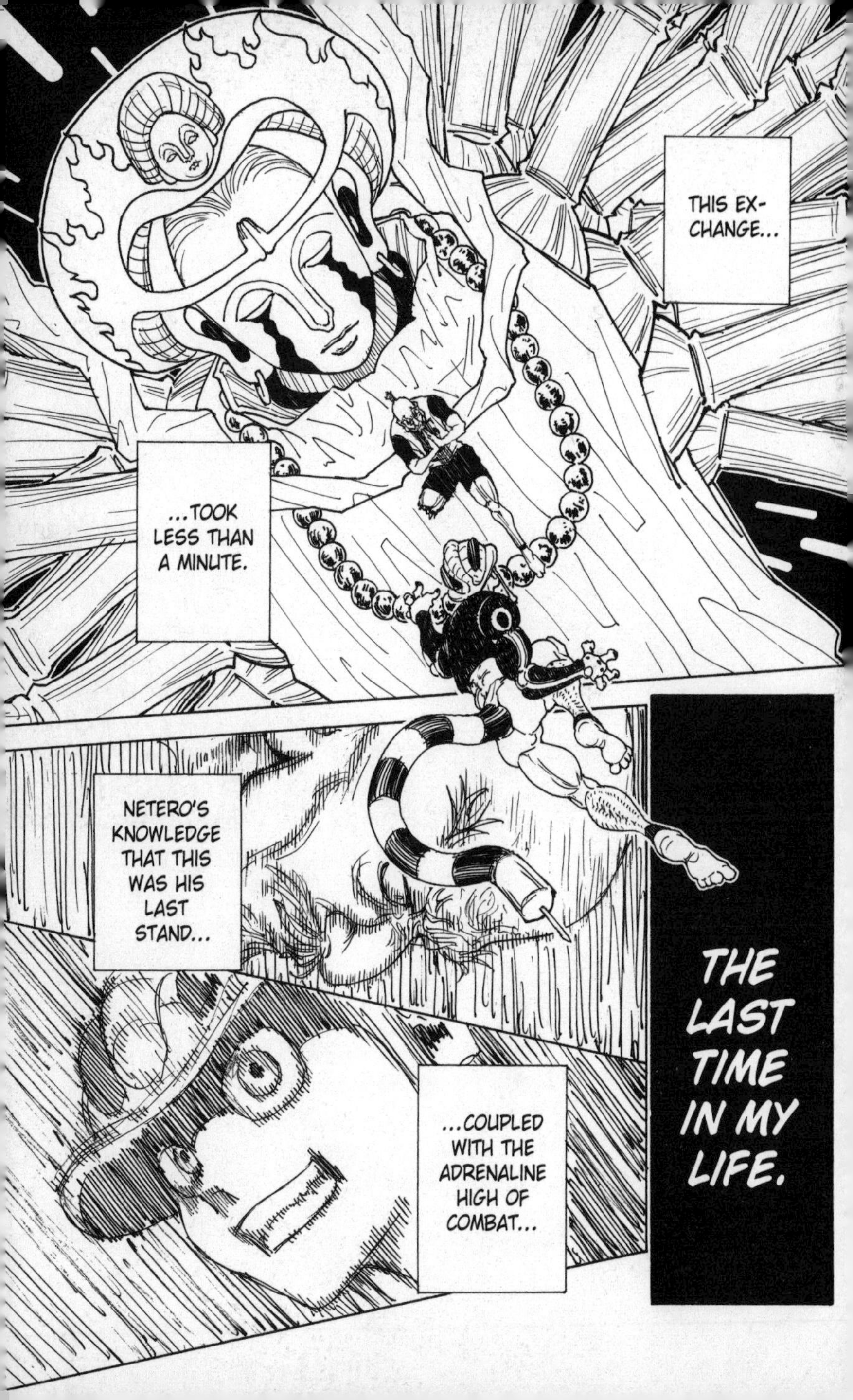
THIS EX-
CHANGE...
...TOOK LESS THAN A MINUTE.
THE LAST TIME IN MY LIFE.
NETERO'S KNOWLEDGE THAT THIS WAS HIS LAST STAND...
...COUPLED WITH THE ADRENALINE HIGH OF COMBAT...

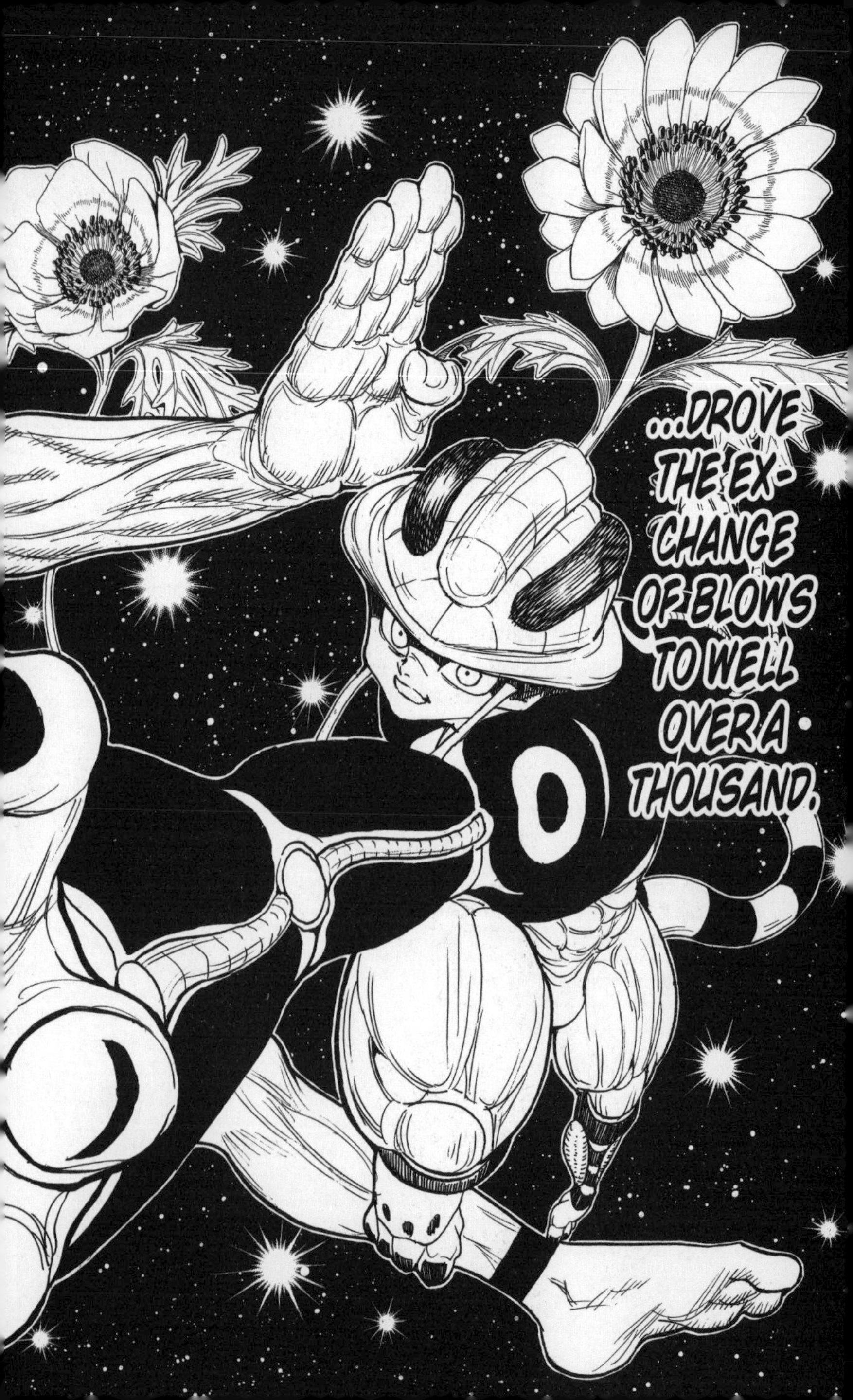
...DROVE THE EX-CHANGE OF BLOWS TO WELL OVER A THOUSAND.

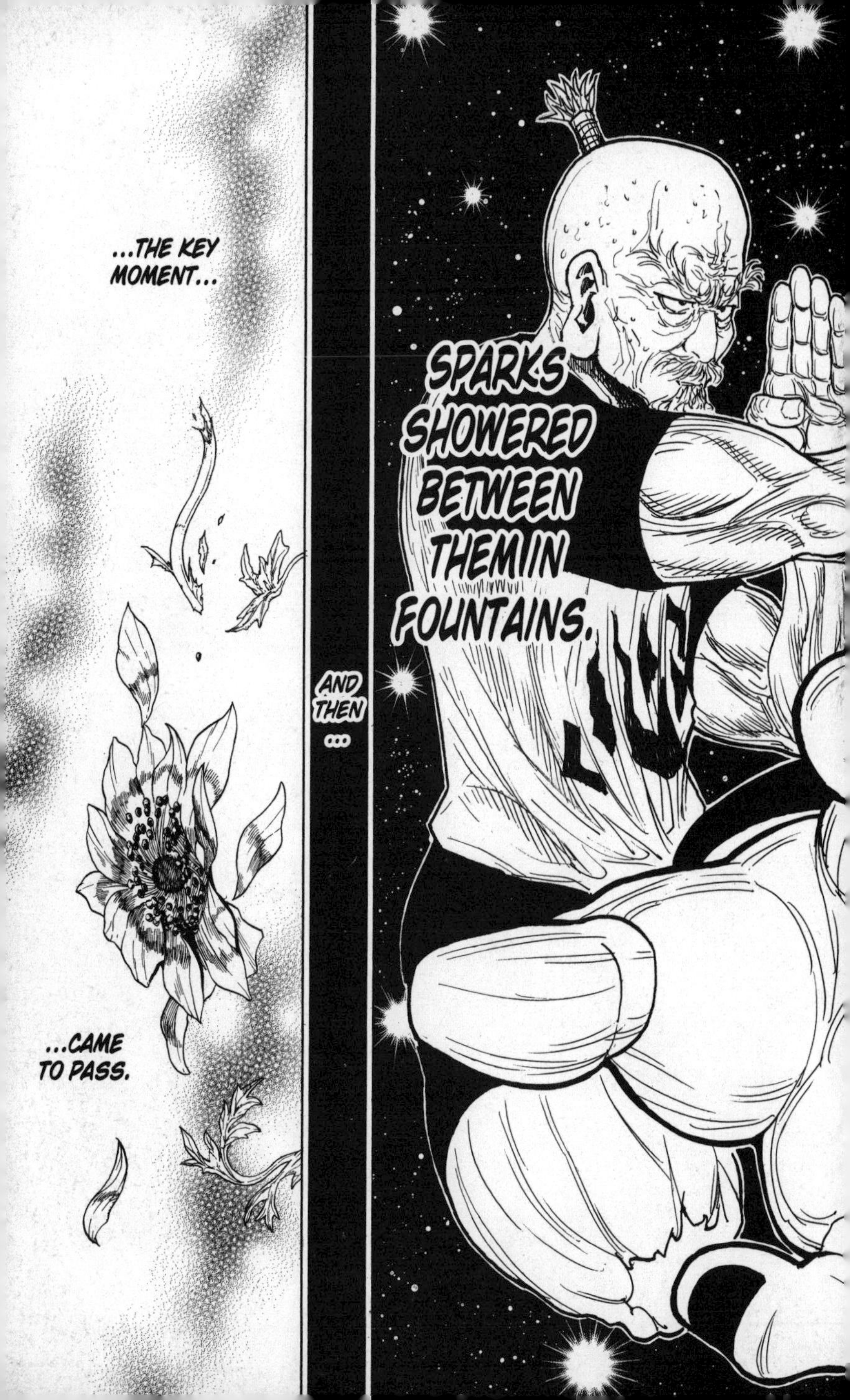
SPARKS SHOWERED BETWEEN THEM IN FOUNTAINS.
AND THEN...
...THE KEY MOMENT...
...CAME TO PASS.

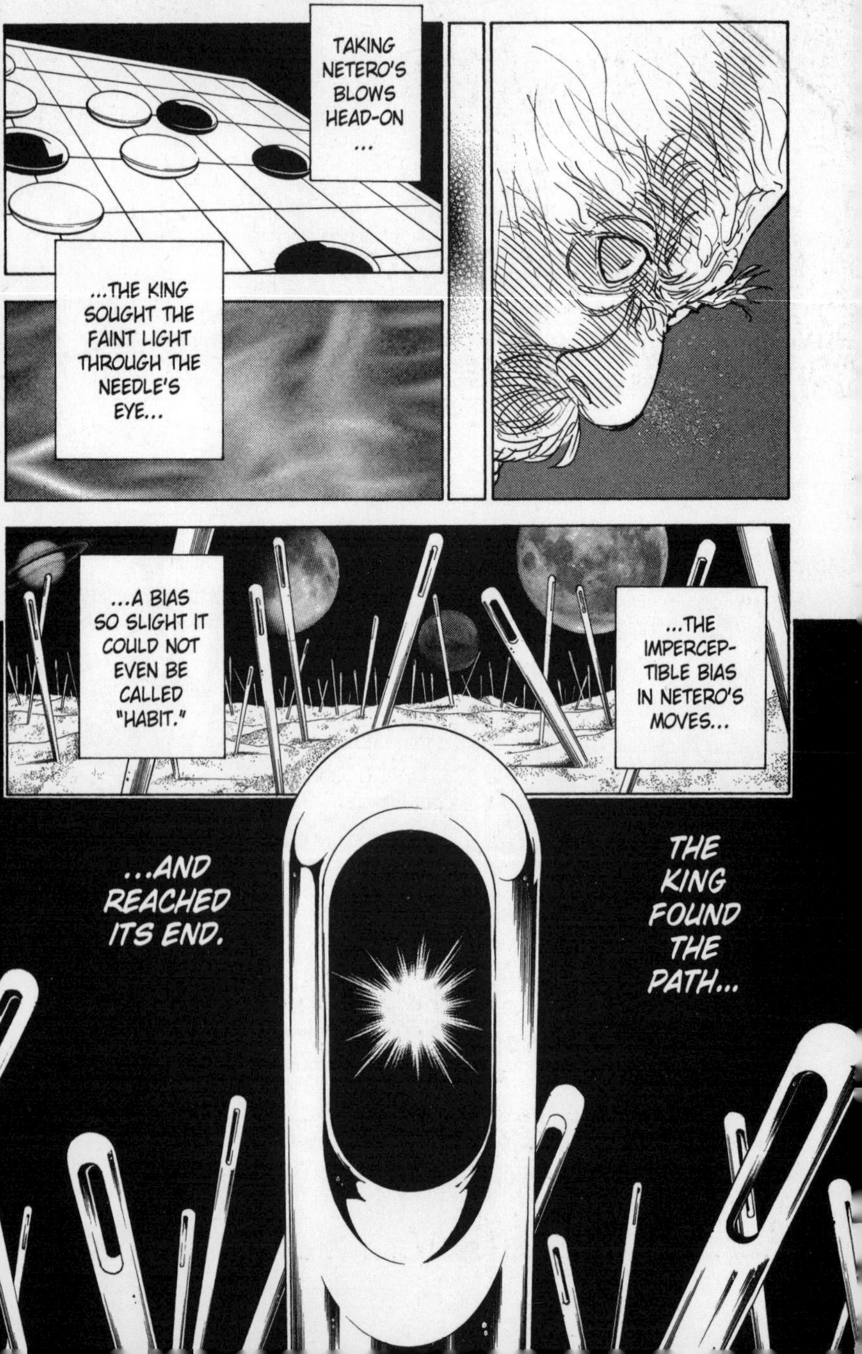
TAKING NETERO'S BLOWS HEAD-ON ...
...THE KING SOUGHT THE FAINT LIGHT THROUGH THE NEEDLE'S EYE...
...THE IMPERCEP-TIBLE BIAS IN NETERO'S MOVES...
...A BIAS SO SLIGHT IT COULD NOT EVEN BE CALLED "HABIT."
THE KING FOUND THE PATH...
...AND REACHED ITS END.

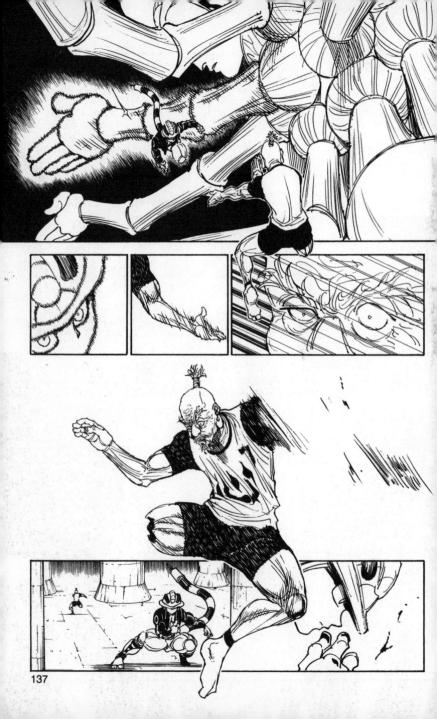

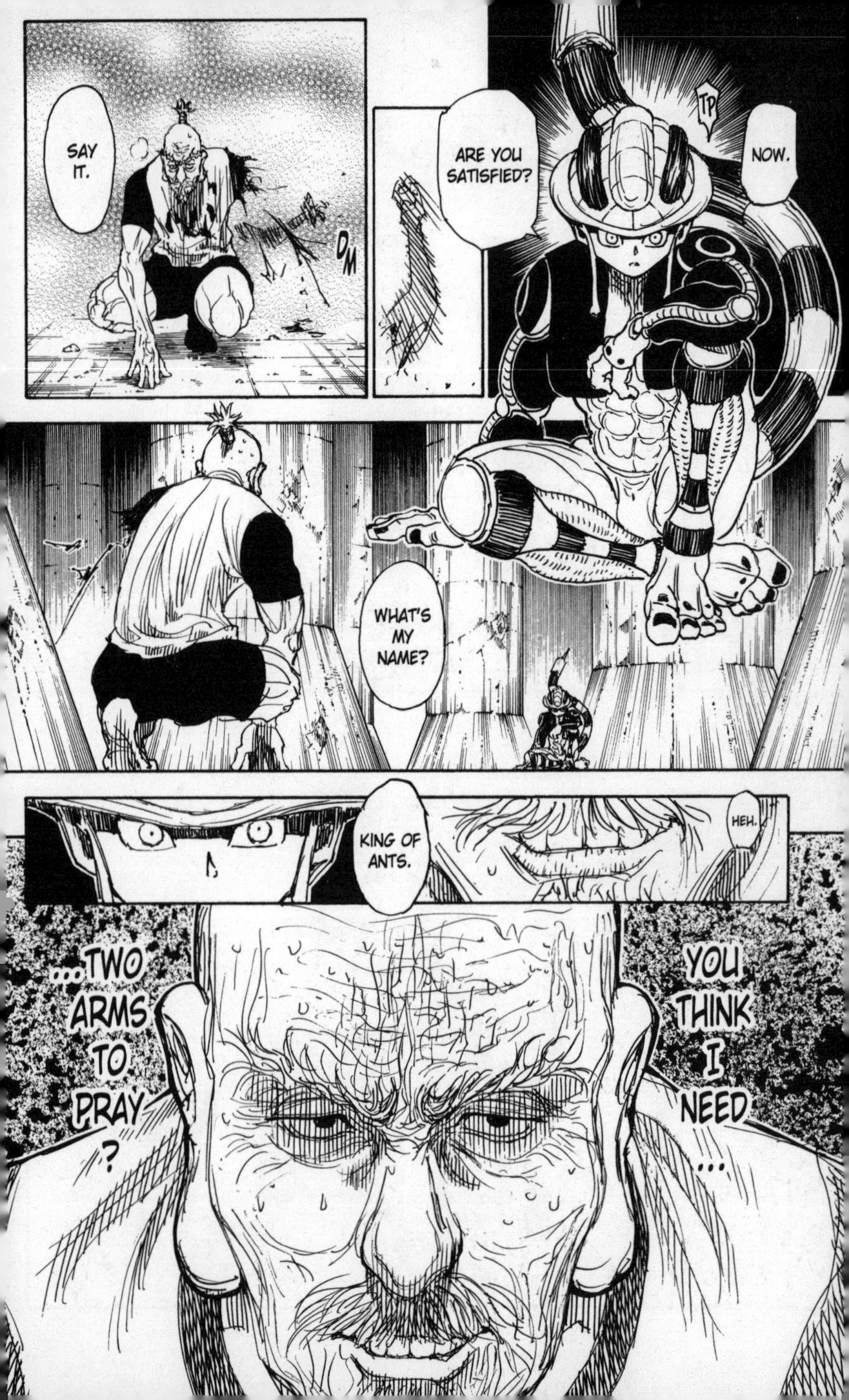
TP
NOW.
ARE YOU SATISFIED?
SAY IT.
DM
WHAT'S MY NAME?
HEH.
KING OF ANTS.
YOU THINK I NEED...
...TWO ARMS TO PRAY?

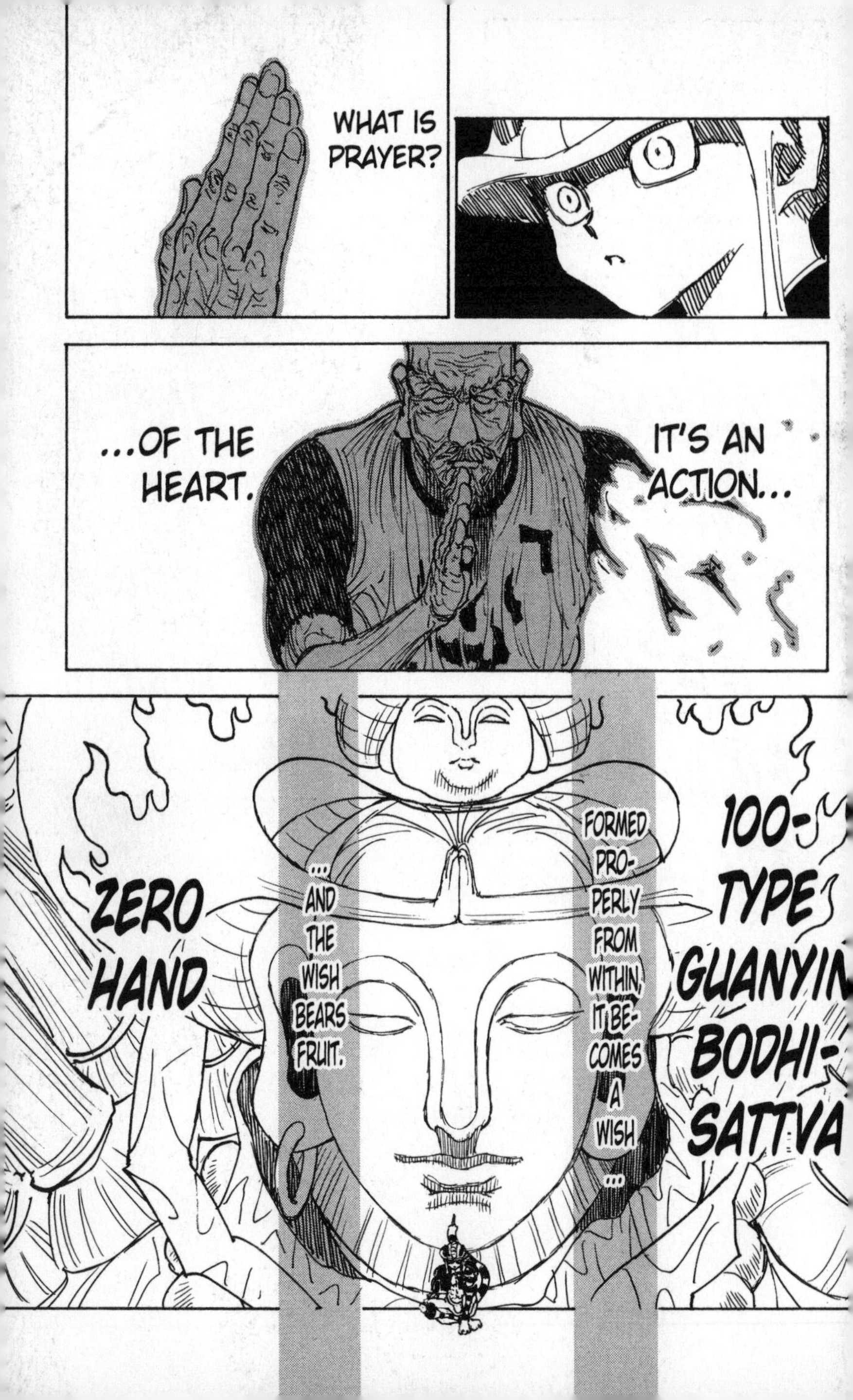
WHAT IS PRAYER?
IT'S AN ACTION...
...OF THE HEART.
100-TYPE GUANYIN BODHISATTVA
FORMED PROPERLY FROM WITHIN, IT BECOMES A WISH...
...AND THE WISH BEARS FRUIT.
ZERO HAND

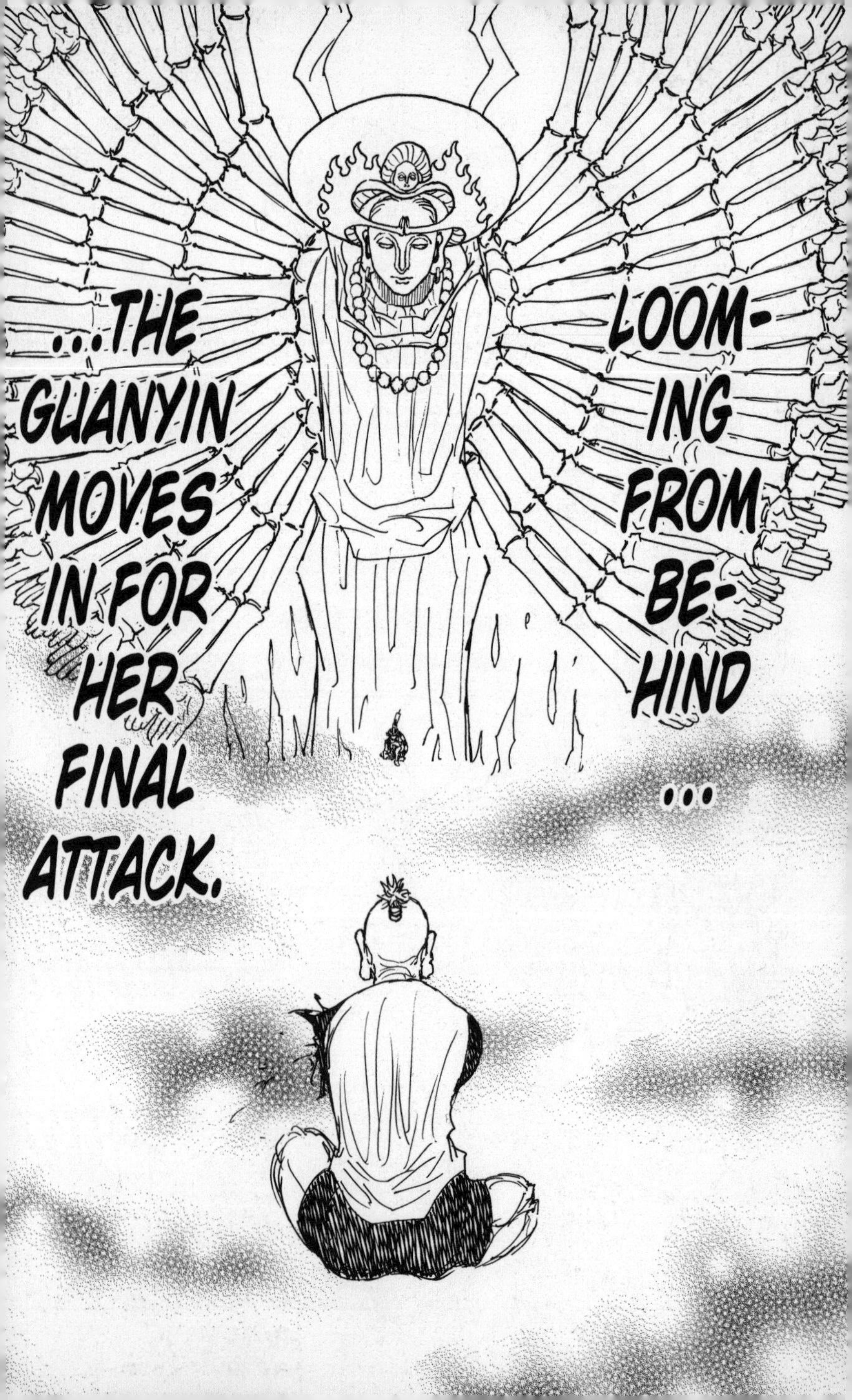
LOOMING FROM BEHIND...
...THE GUANYIN MOVES IN FOR HER FINAL ATTACK.

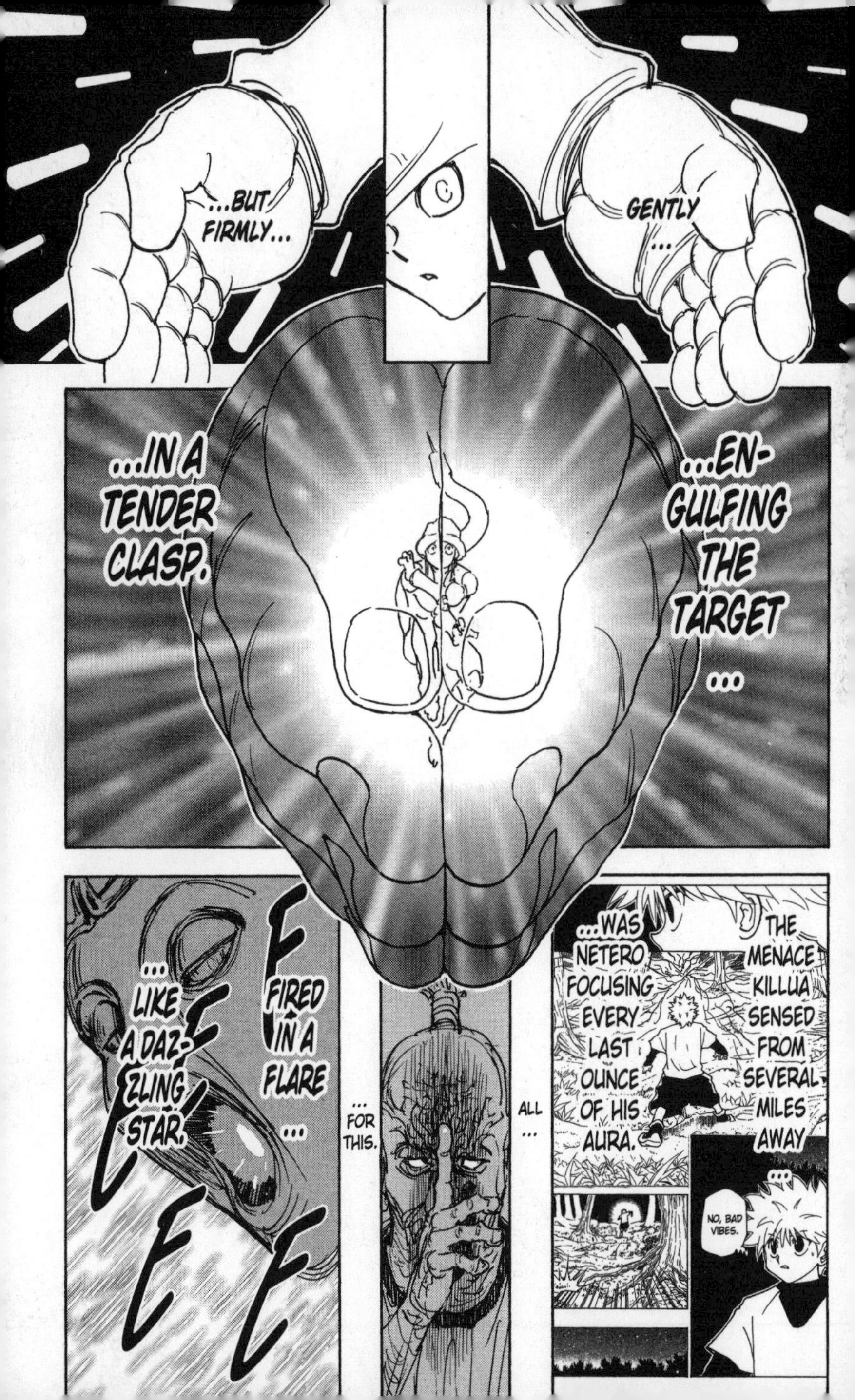
GENTLY...
...BUT FIRMLY...
...EN-GULFING THE TARGET...
...IN A TENDER CLASP.
THE MENACE KILLUA SENSED FROM SEVERAL MILES AWAY...
...WAS NETERO FOCUSING EVERY LAST OUNCE OF HIS AURA.
NO, BAD VIBES.
ALL...
...FOR THIS.
FIRED IN A FLARE...
...LIKE A DAZ-ZLING STAR.

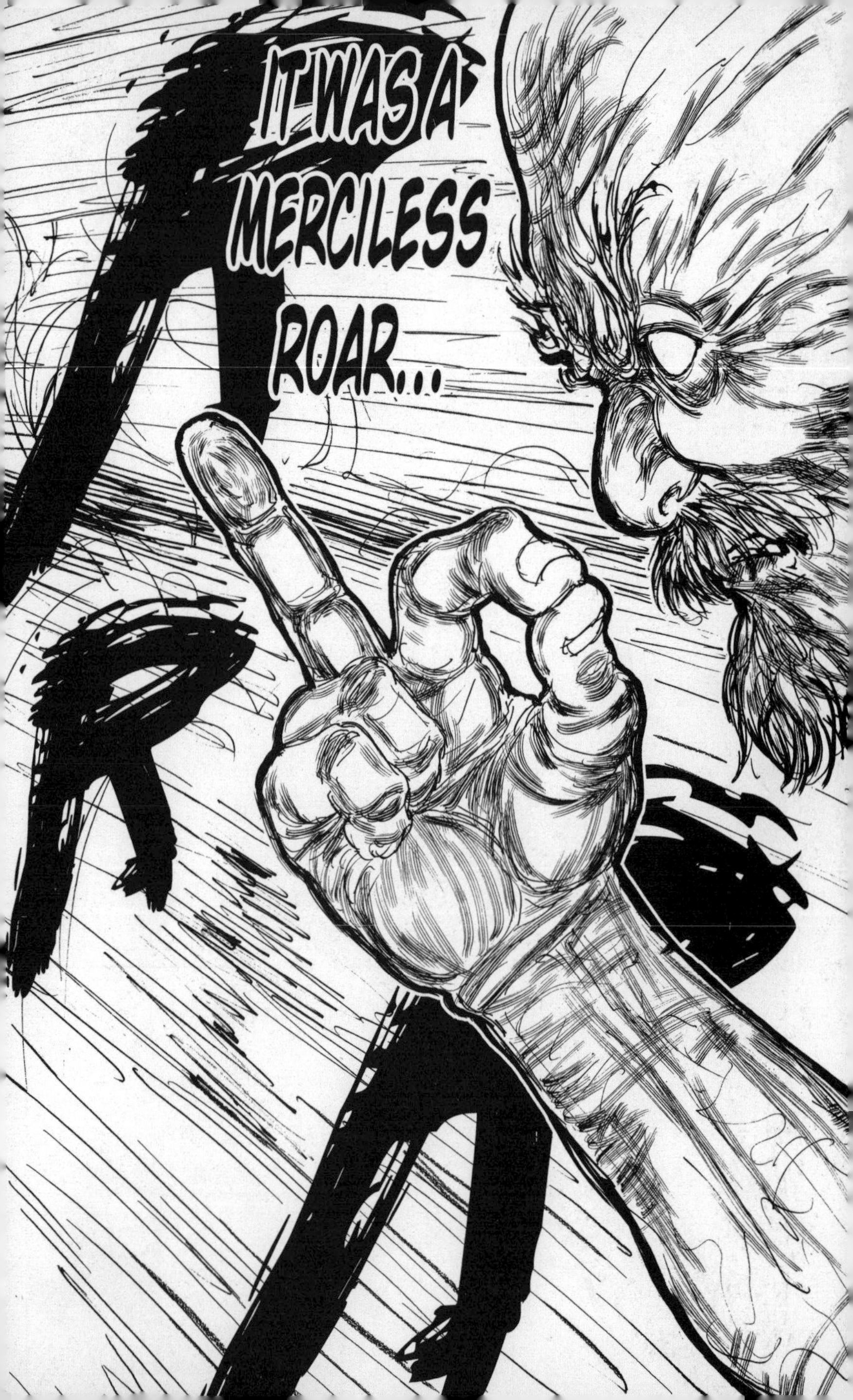
IT WAS A MERCILESS ROAR...

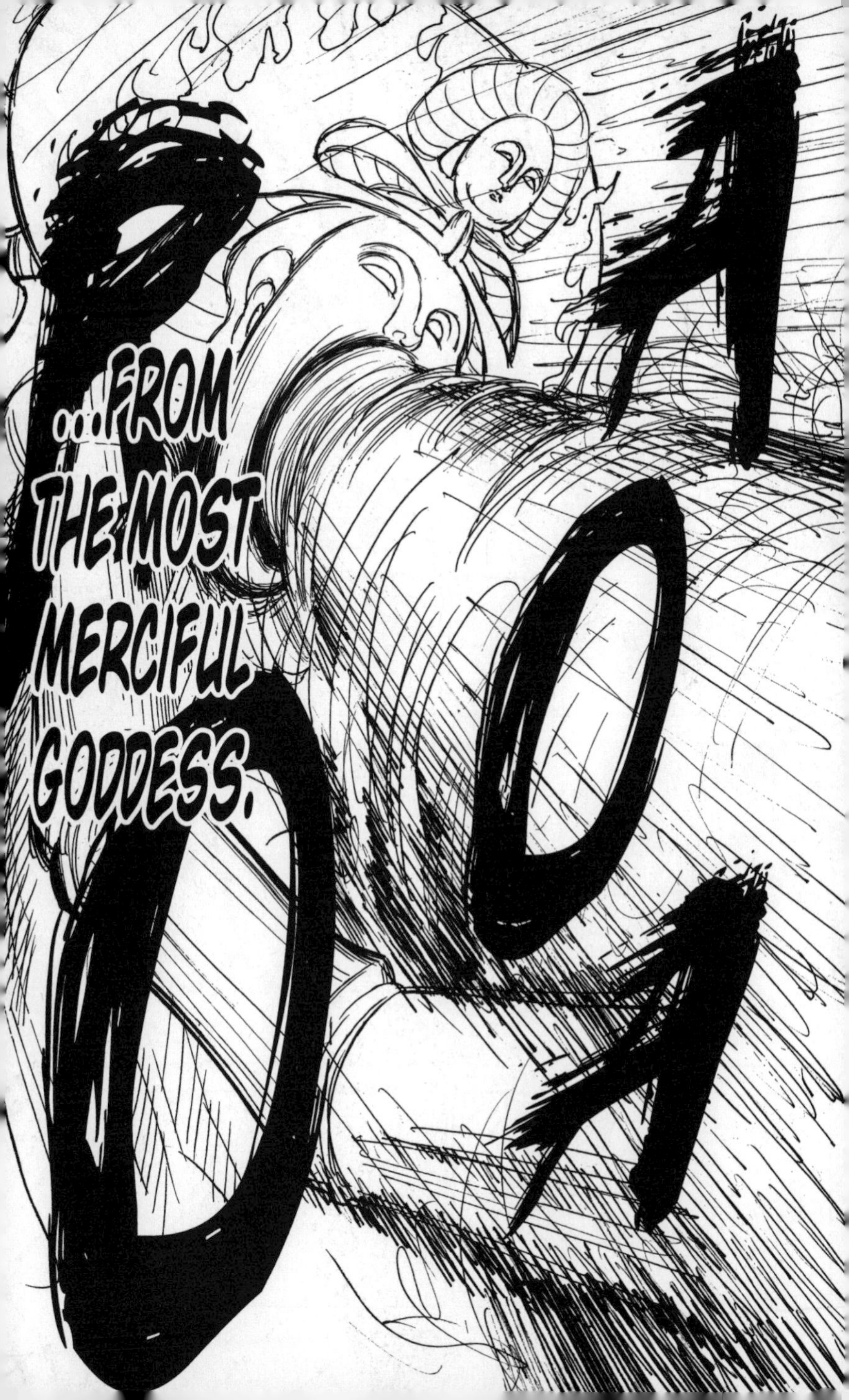
...FROM THE MOST MERCIFUL GODDESS.

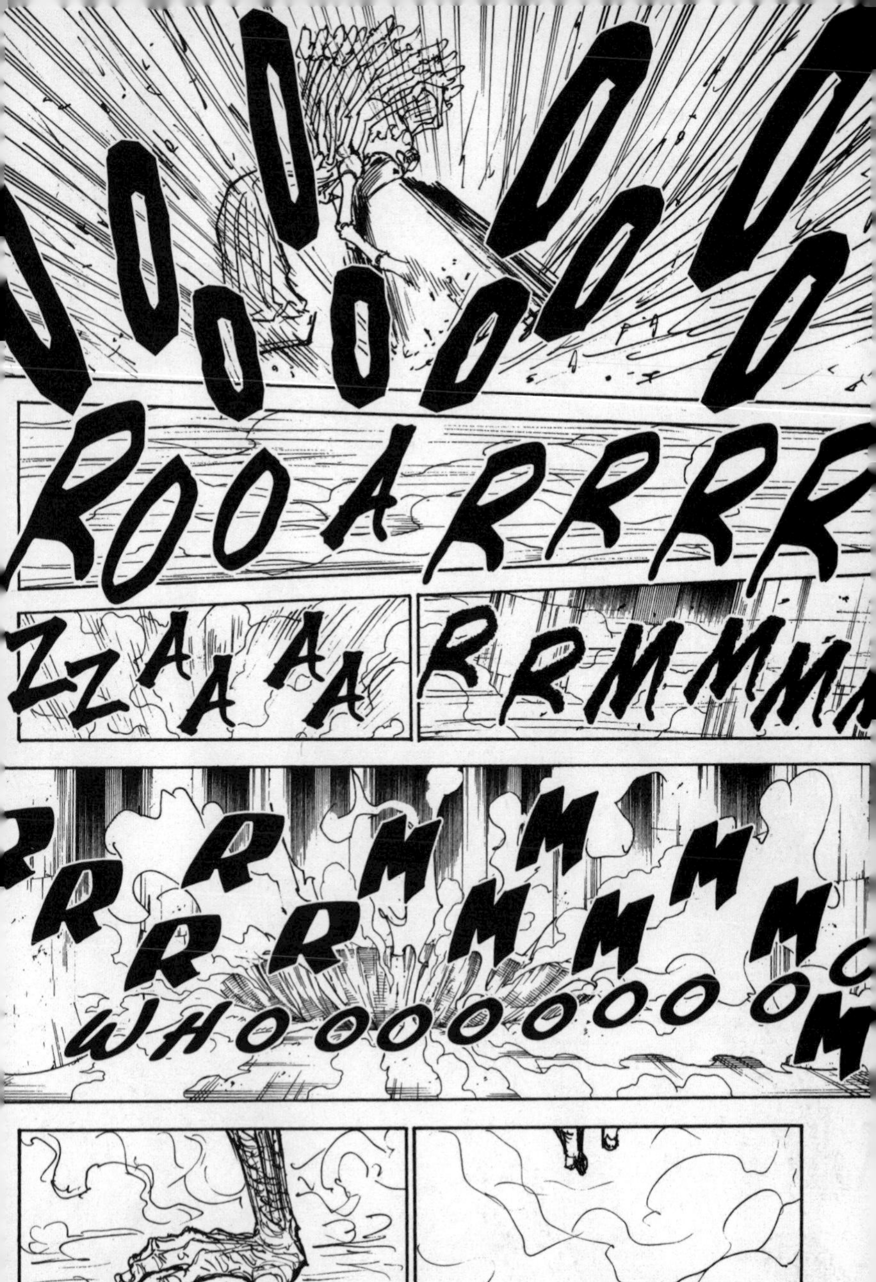
ROOARRRRR
RRMMMM
ZZAAAA
RRRRRMMMMMM
WHOOOOOOOOM

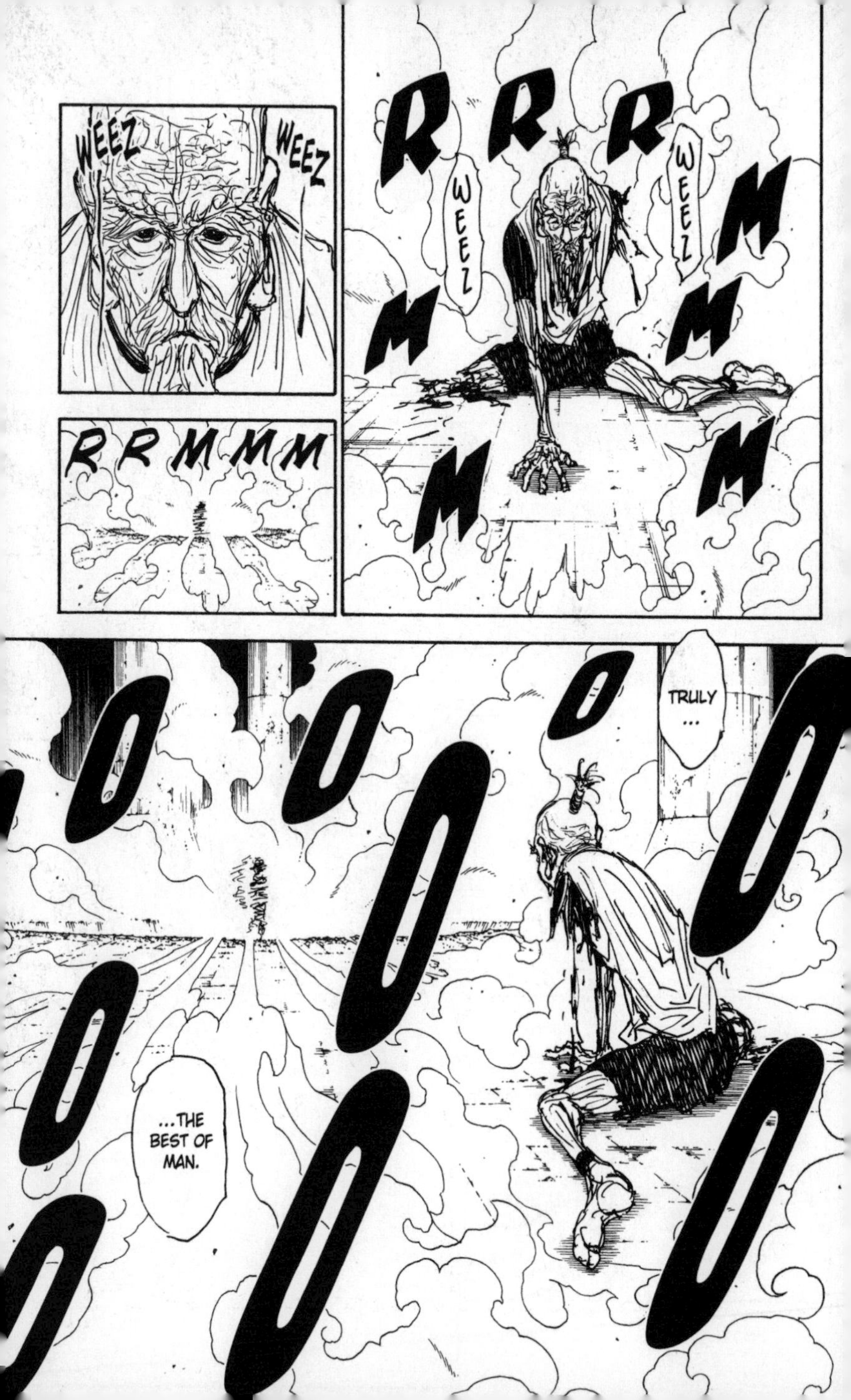
RRRMMMMMM
WEEZ
WEEZ
WEEZ
WEEZ
RRMMM
OOOOOOOOOO
TRULY ...
...THE BEST OF MAN.

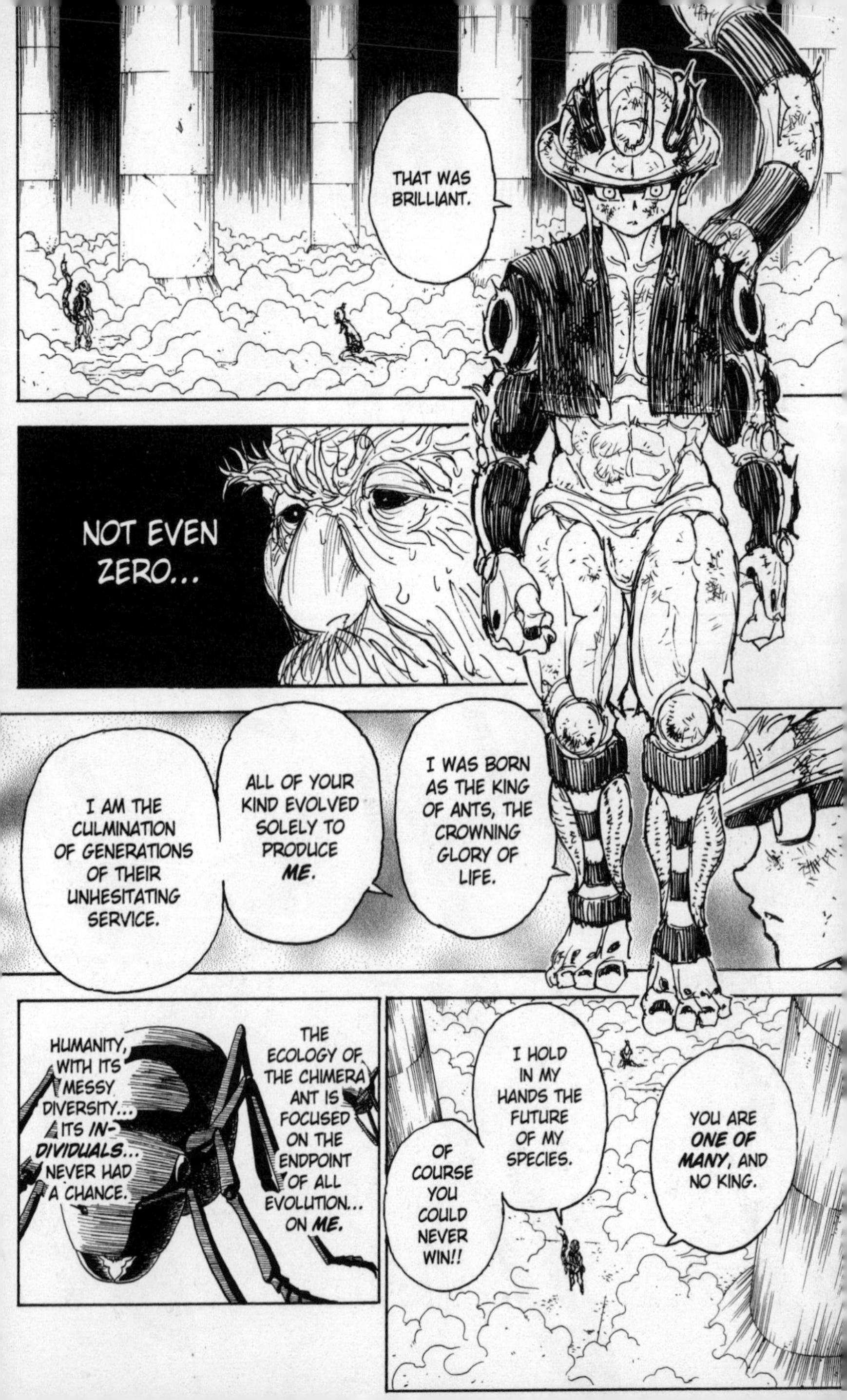
THAT WAS BRILLIANT.
NOT EVEN ZERO...
I WAS BORN AS THE KING OF ANTS, THE CROWNING GLORY OF LIFE.
ALL OF YOUR KIND EVOLVED SOLELY TO PRODUCE *ME*.
I AM THE CULMINATION OF GENERATIONS OF THEIR UNHESITATING SERVICE.
YOU ARE *ONE OF MANY*, AND NO KING.
I HOLD IN MY HANDS THE FUTURE OF MY SPECIES.
OF COURSE YOU COULD NEVER WIN!!
THE ECOLOGY OF THE CHIMERA ANT IS FOCUSED ON THE ENDPOINT OF ALL EVOLUTION... ON *ME*.
HUMANITY, WITH ITS MESSY DIVERSITY... ITS *IN-DIVIDUALS*... NEVER HAD A CHANCE.

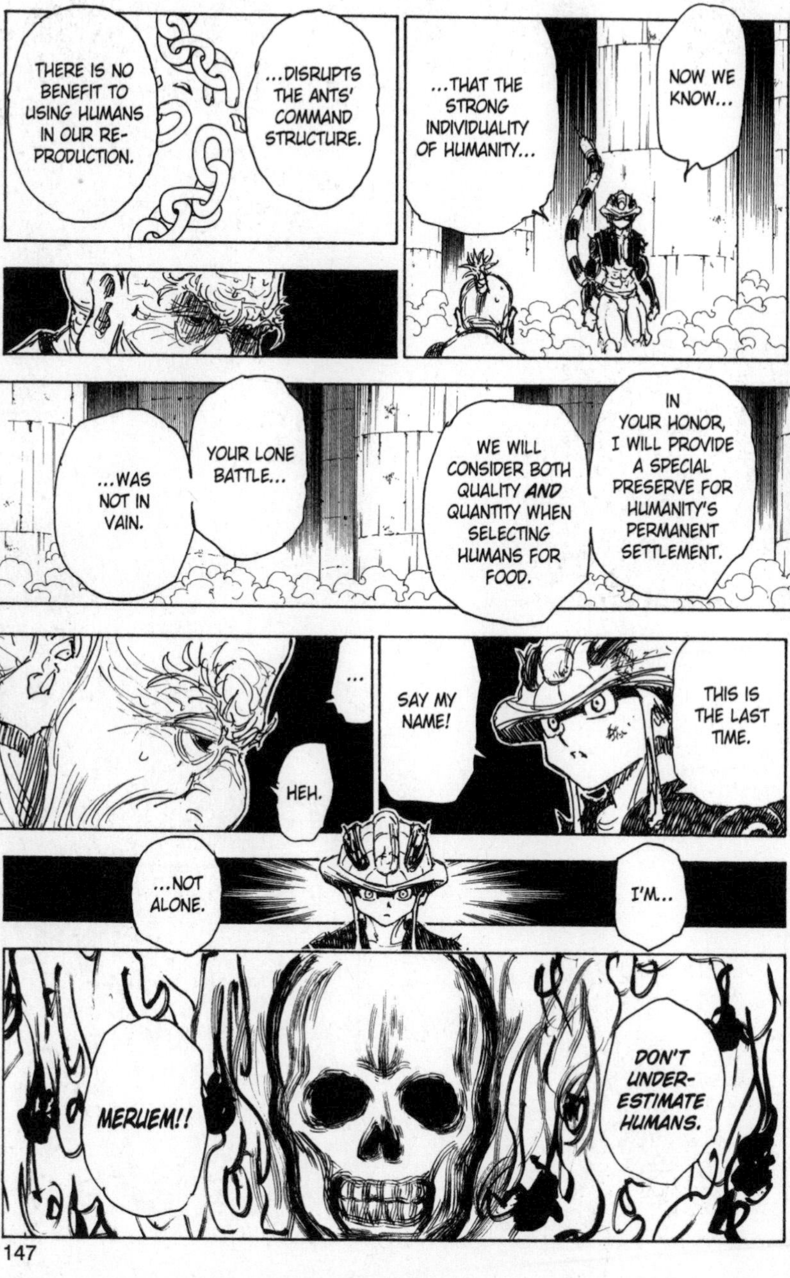
NOW WE KNOW...
...THAT THE STRONG INDIVIDUALITY OF HUMANITY...
...DISRUPTS THE ANTS' COMMAND STRUCTURE.
THERE IS NO BENEFIT TO USING HUMANS IN OUR RE-PRODUCTION.
IN YOUR HONOR, I WILL PROVIDE A SPECIAL PRESERVE FOR HUMANITY'S PERMANENT SETTLEMENT.
WE WILL CONSIDER BOTH QUALITY *AND* QUANTITY WHEN SELECTING HUMANS FOR FOOD.
YOUR LONE BATTLE...
...WAS NOT IN VAIN.
THIS IS THE LAST TIME.
SAY MY NAME!
...
HEH.
I'M...
...NOT ALONE.
DON'T UNDER-ESTIMATE HUMANS.
MERUEM!!

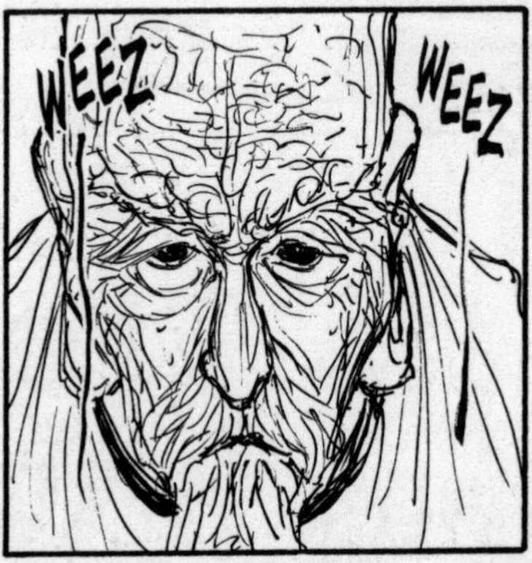
WEEZ
WEEZ

Chapter 298: Rose

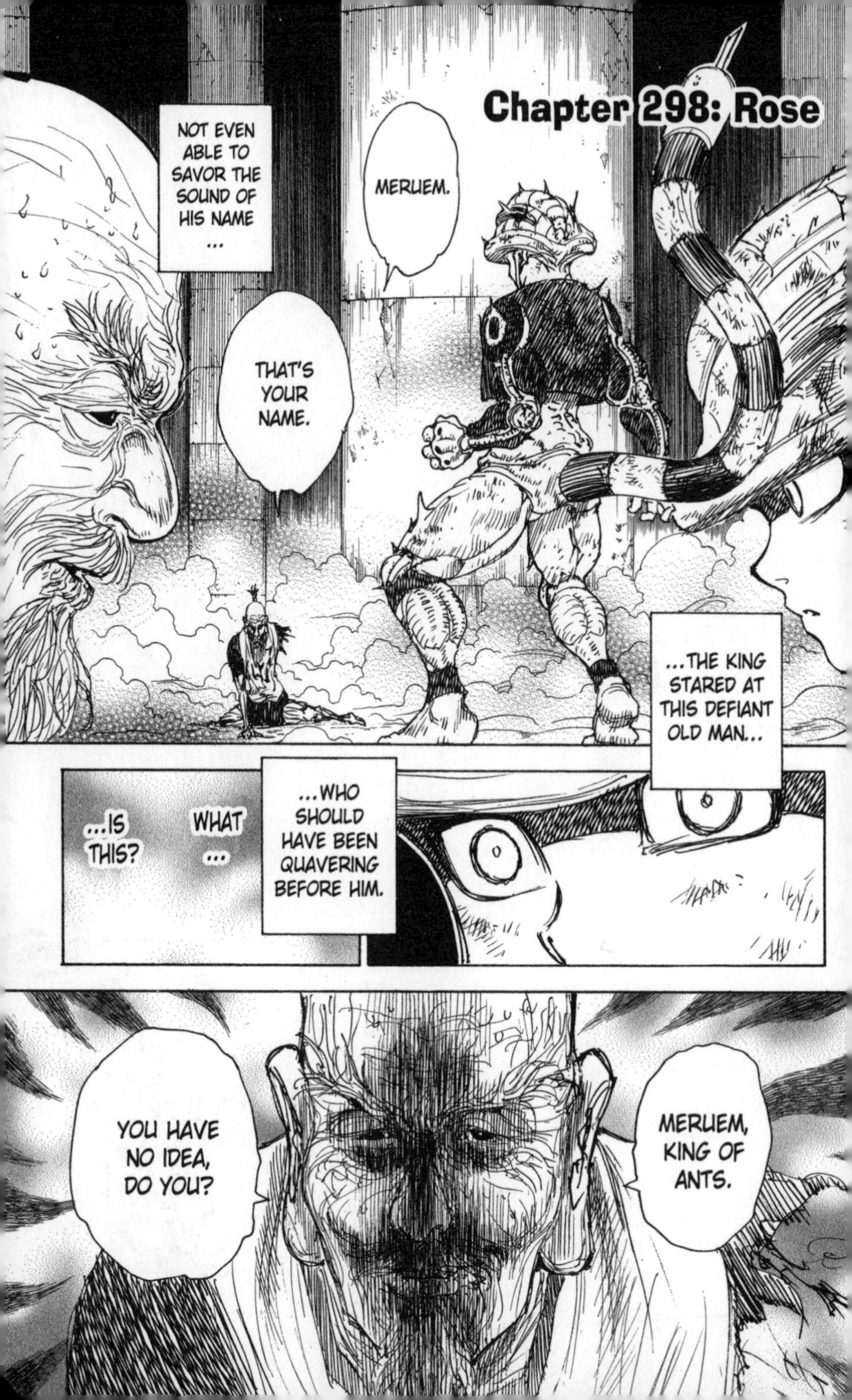
MERUEM.
NOT EVEN ABLE TO SAVOR THE SOUND OF HIS NAME ...
THAT'S YOUR NAME.
...THE KING STARED AT THIS DEFIANT OLD MAN...
...WHO SHOULD HAVE BEEN QUAVERING BEFORE HIM.
WHAT ...
...IS THIS?
MERUEM, KING OF ANTS.
YOU HAVE NO IDEA, DO YOU?

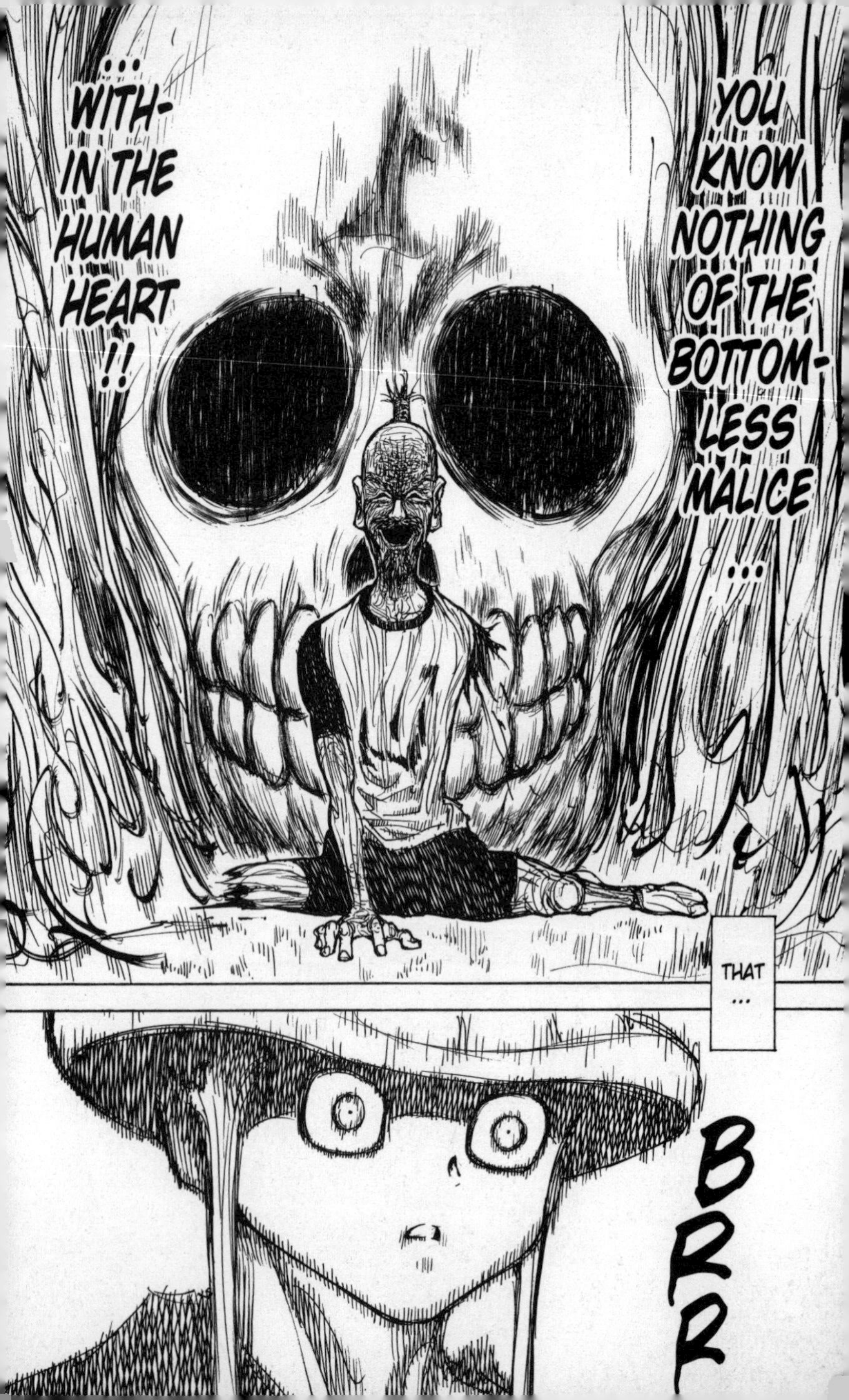
YOU KNOW NOTHING OF THE BOTTOM-LESS MALICE ...
... WITH-IN THE HUMAN HEART !!
THAT ...
BRRR

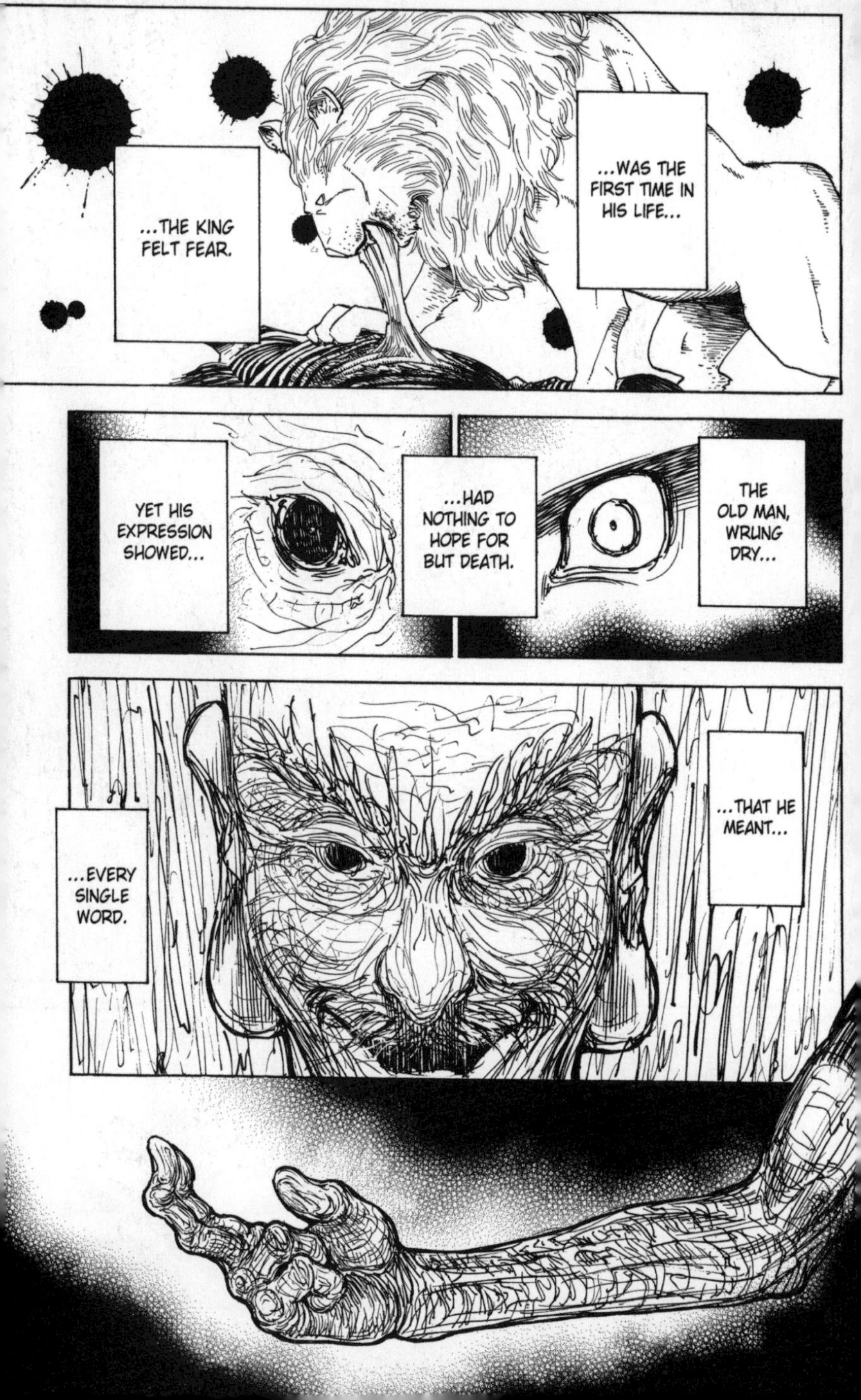
...WAS THE FIRST TIME IN HIS LIFE...
...THE KING FELT FEAR.
THE OLD MAN, WRUNG DRY...
...HAD NOTHING TO HOPE FOR BUT DEATH.
YET HIS EXPRESSION SHOWED...
...THAT HE MEANT...
...EVERY SINGLE WORD.

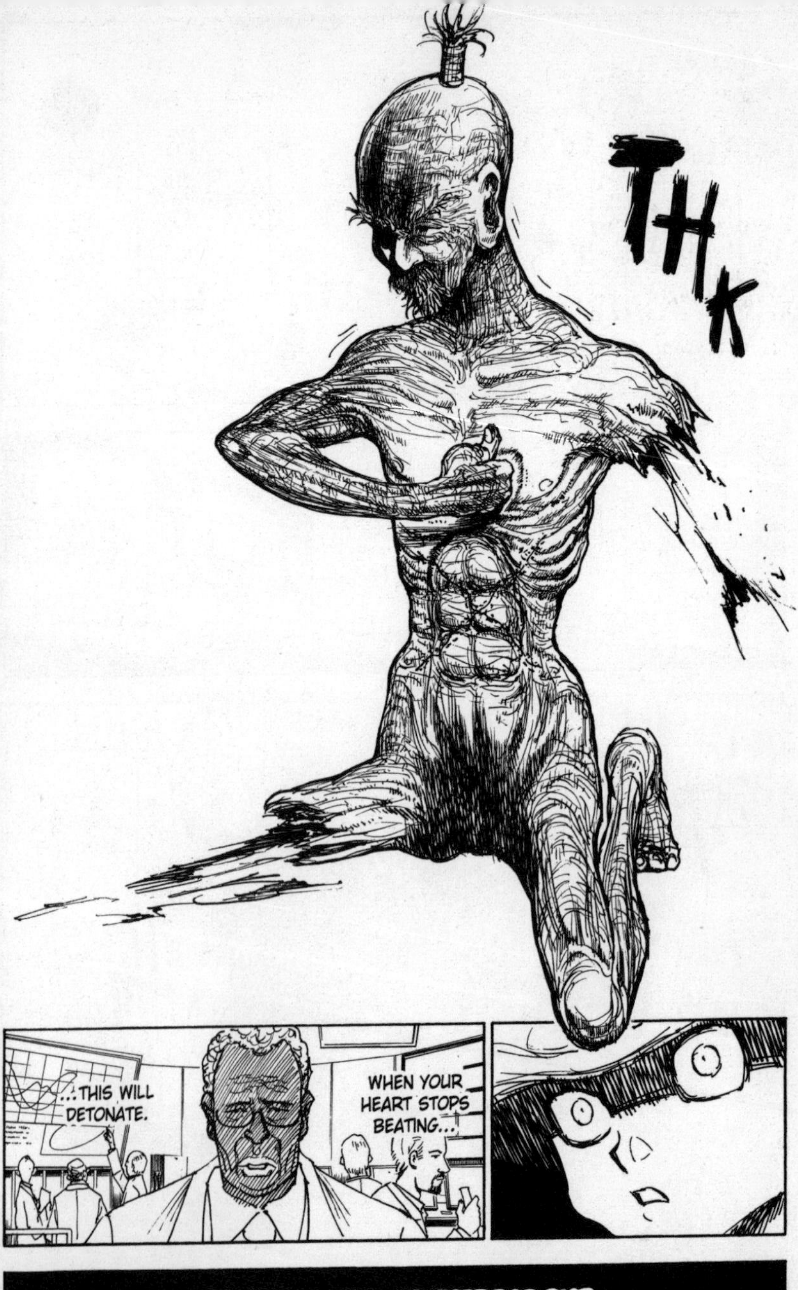
THK
WHEN YOUR HEART STOPS BEATING...
...THIS WILL DETONATE.
SEE YOU IN HELL, IF THERE IS ONE.

OLD MAN...

WHAT HAVE YOU DONE?

THE GAME WAS OVER
...

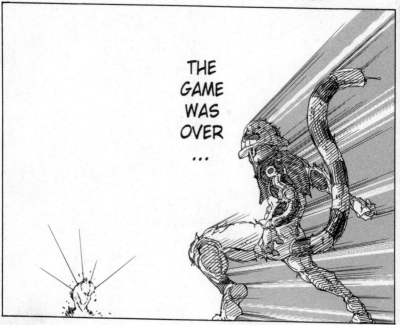

...BEFORE WE EVEN STARTED.

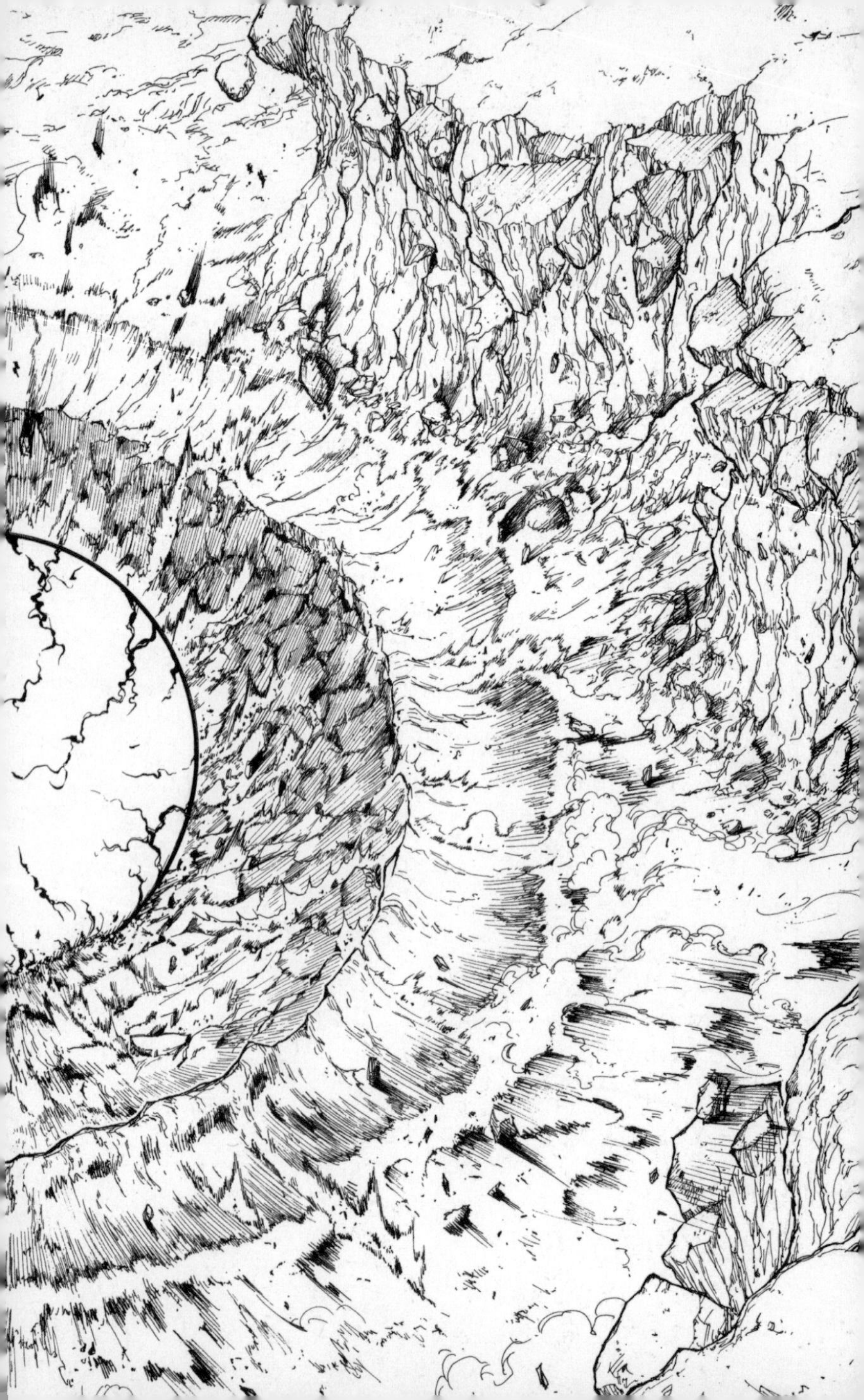

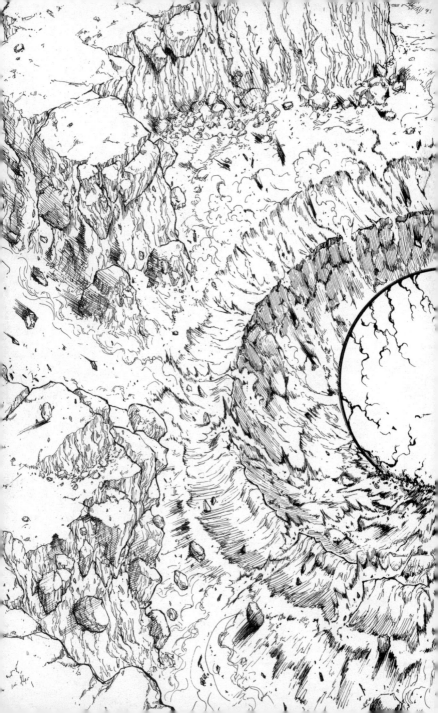

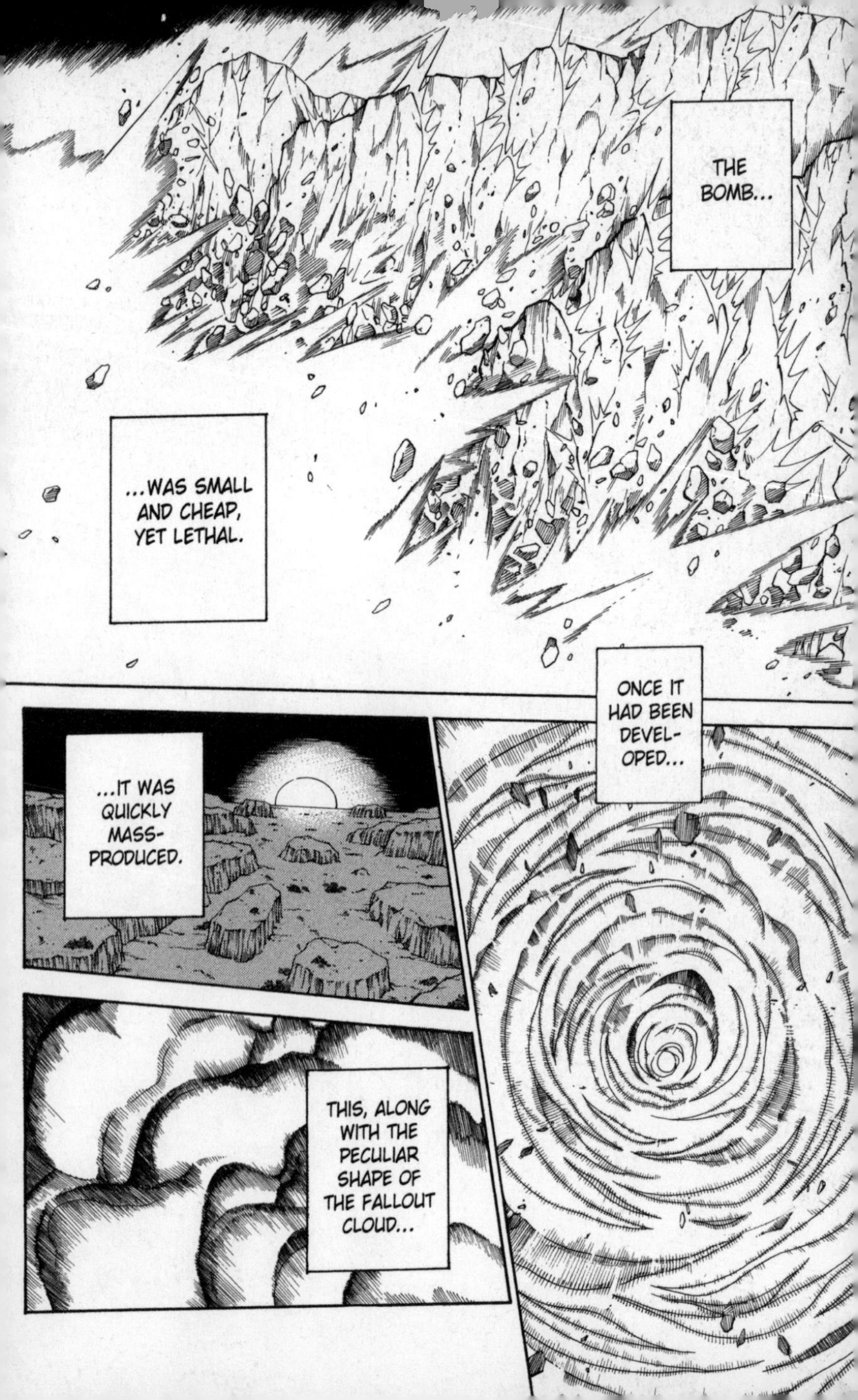
THE BOMB...
...WAS SMALL AND CHEAP, YET LETHAL.
ONCE IT HAD BEEN DEVEL-OPED...
...IT WAS QUICKLY MASS-PRODUCED.
THIS, ALONG WITH THE PECULIAR SHAPE OF THE FALLOUT CLOUD...

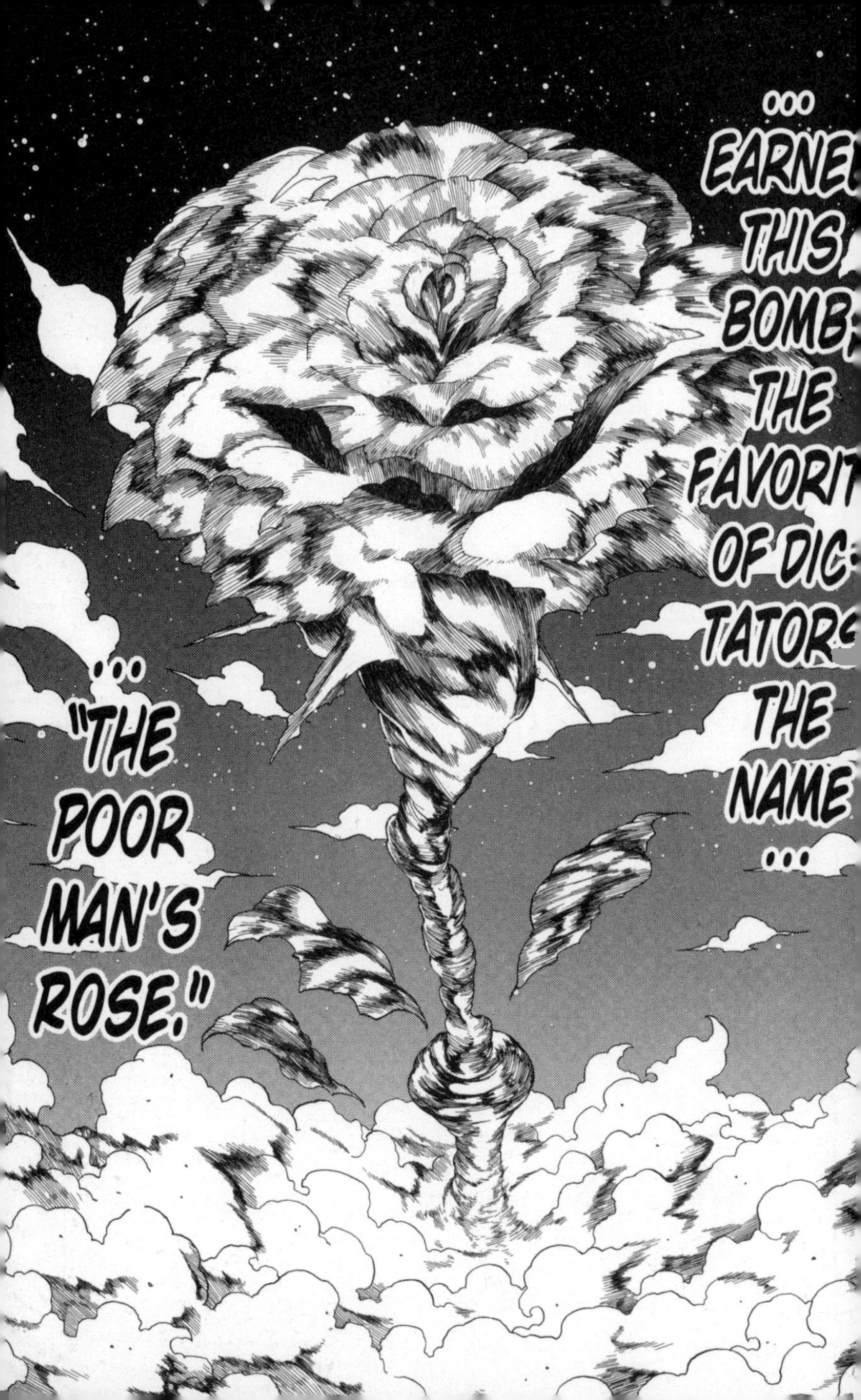
... EARNE THIS BOMB, THE FAVORIT OF DIC- TATOR THE NAME ...
... "THE POOR MAN'S ROSE."

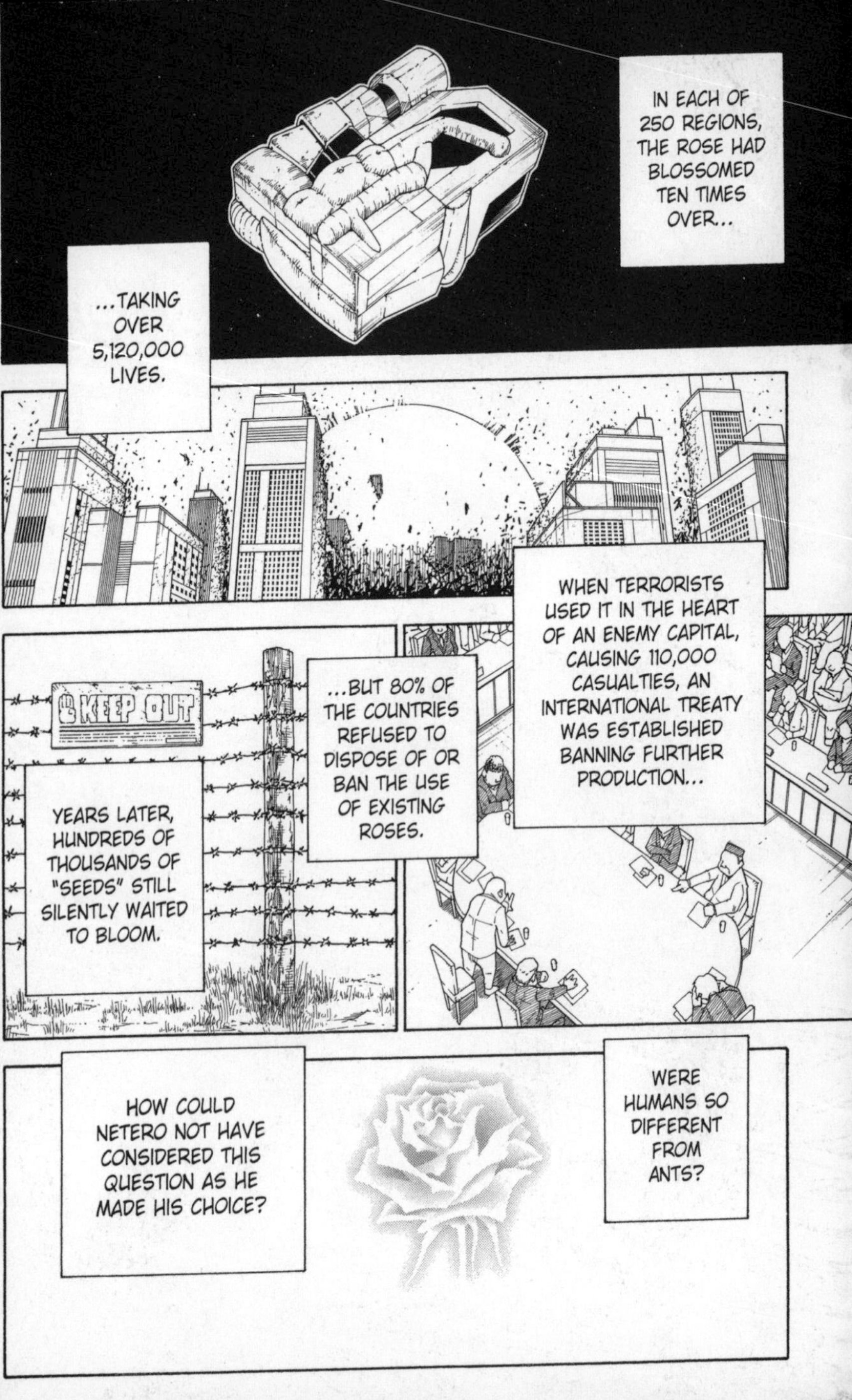
IN EACH OF 250 REGIONS, THE ROSE HAD BLOSSOMED TEN TIMES OVER...
...TAKING OVER 5,120,000 LIVES.
WHEN TERRORISTS USED IT IN THE HEART OF AN ENEMY CAPITAL, CAUSING 110,000 CASUALTIES, AN INTERNATIONAL TREATY WAS ESTABLISHED BANNING FURTHER PRODUCTION...
...BUT 80% OF THE COUNTRIES REFUSED TO DISPOSE OF OR BAN THE USE OF EXISTING ROSES.
KEEP OUT
YEARS LATER, HUNDREDS OF THOUSANDS OF "SEEDS" STILL SILENTLY WAITED TO BLOOM.
WERE HUMANS SO DIFFERENT FROM ANTS?
HOW COULD NETERO NOT HAVE CONSIDERED THIS QUESTION AS HE MADE HIS CHOICE?

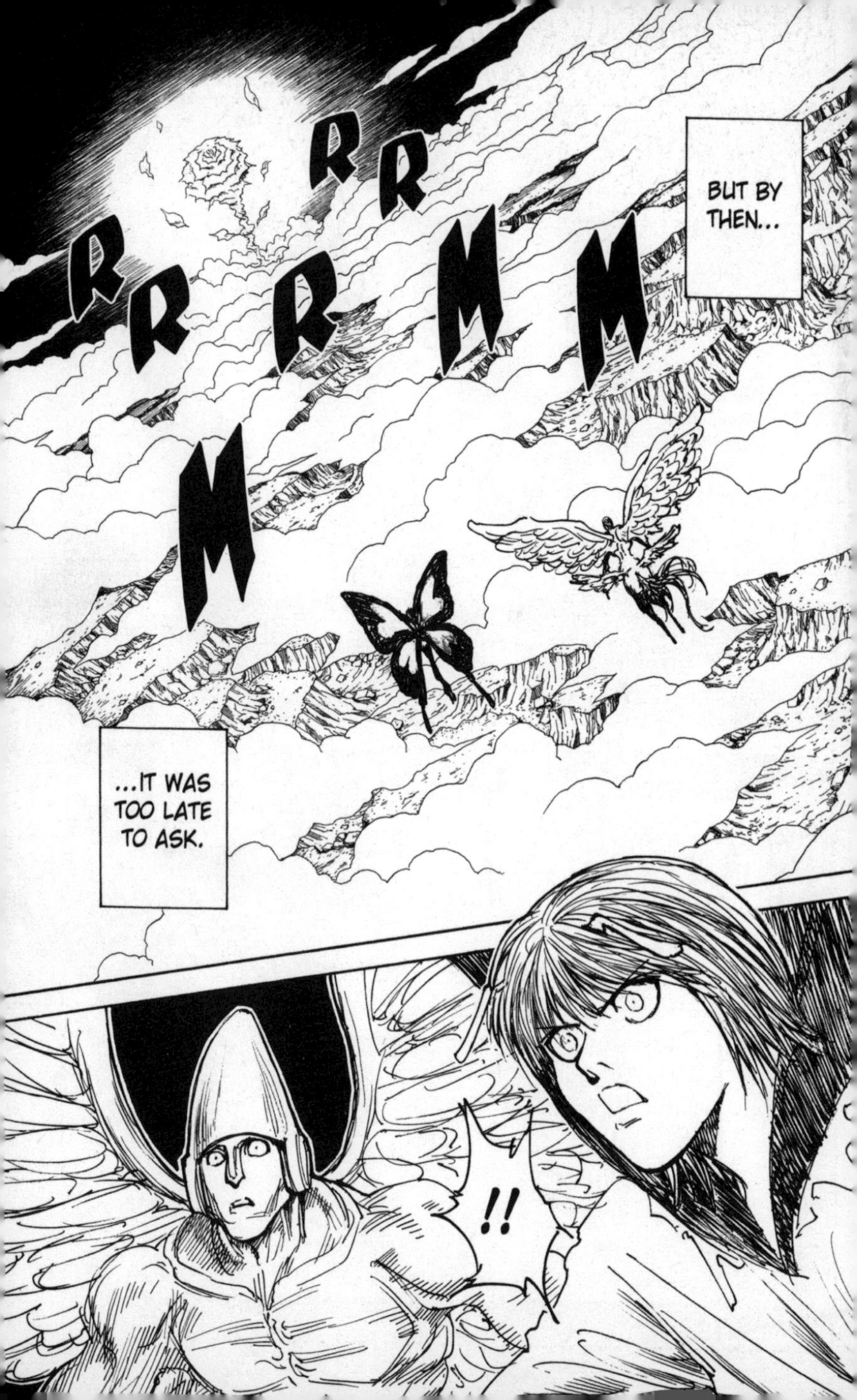
BUT BY THEN...
RRRRRRMMMM
...IT WAS TOO LATE TO ASK.
!!

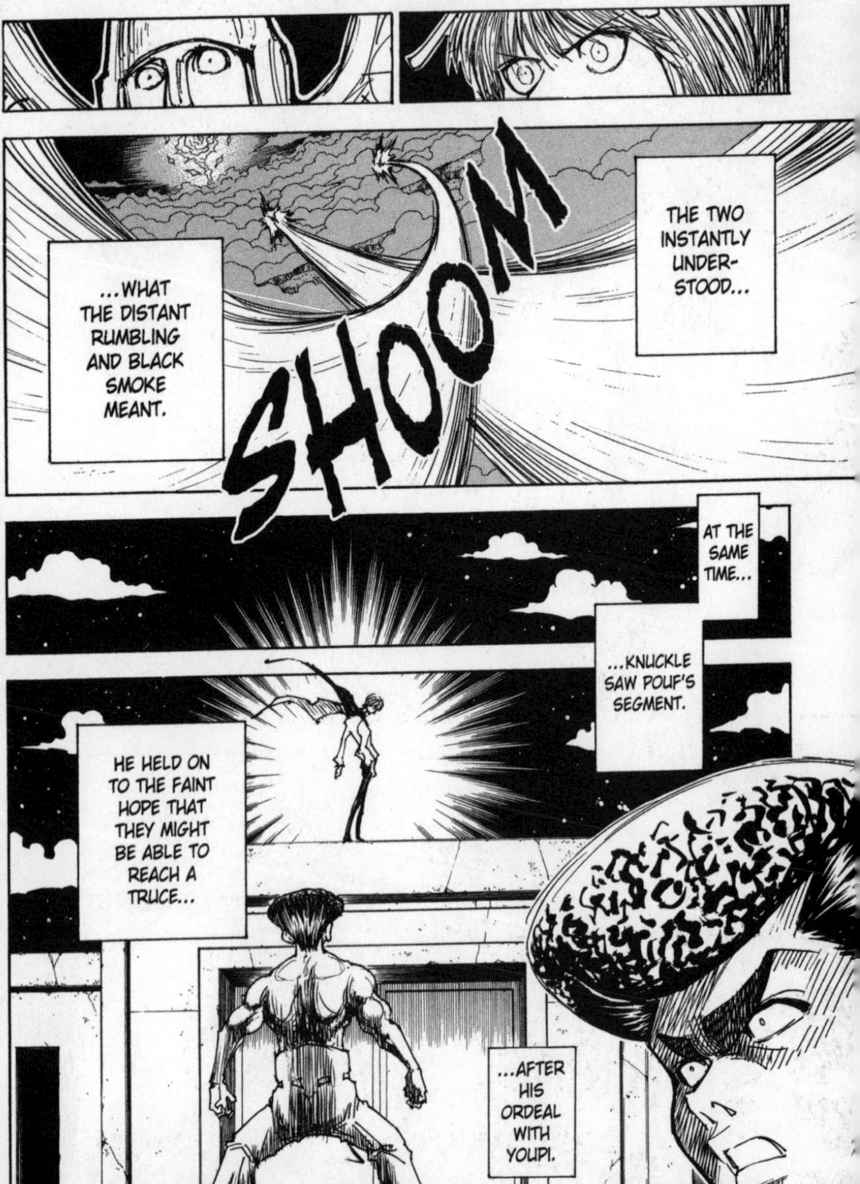
THE TWO INSTANTLY UNDER-STOOD...
SHOOM
...WHAT THE DISTANT RUMBLING AND BLACK SMOKE MEANT.
AT THE SAME TIME...
...KNUCKLE SAW POUF'S SEGMENT.
HE HELD ON TO THE FAINT HOPE THAT THEY MIGHT BE ABLE TO REACH A TRUCE...
...AFTER HIS ORDEAL WITH YOUPI.

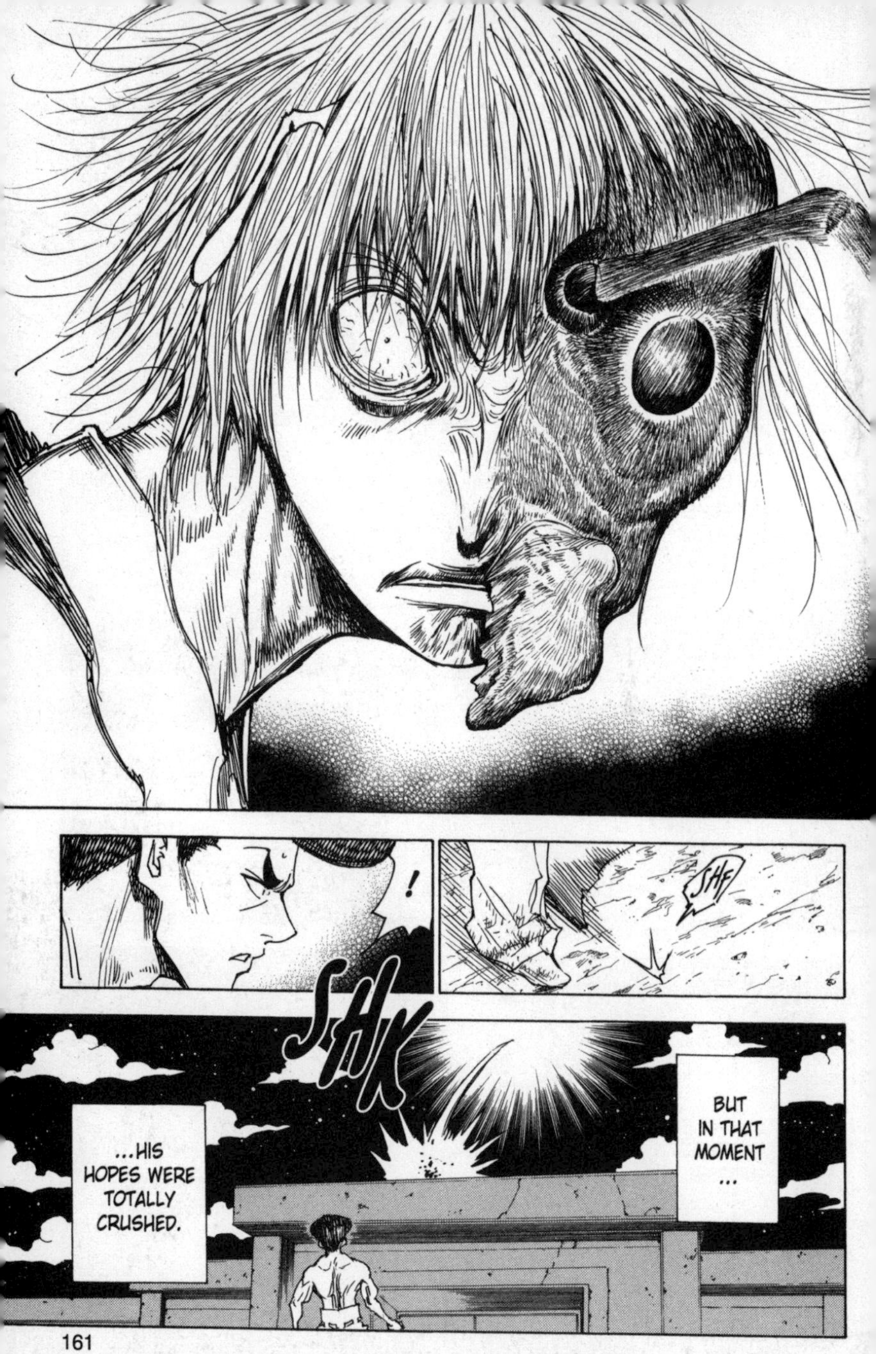
SHF
!
SHK
BUT IN THAT MOMENT ...
...HIS HOPES WERE TOTALLY CRUSHED.

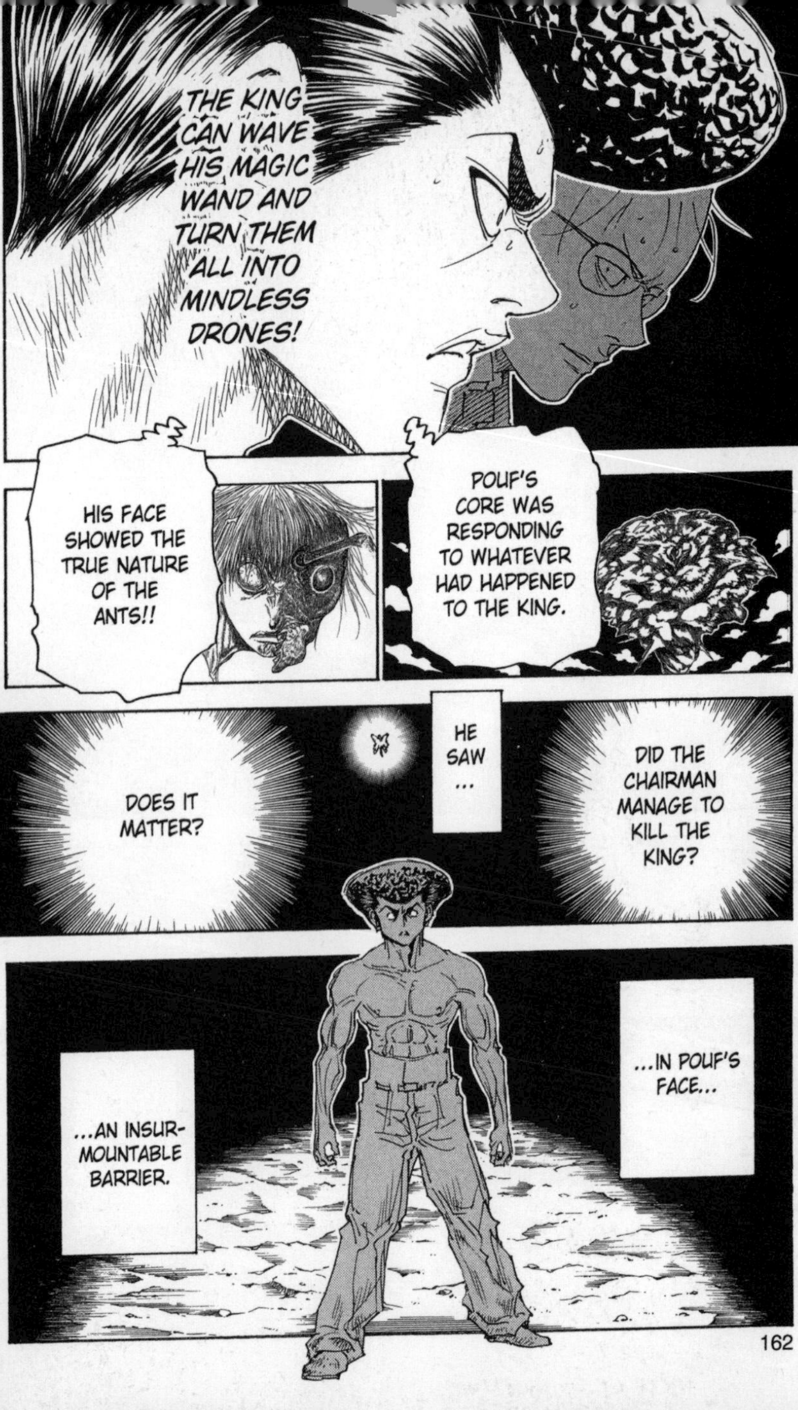
THE KING CAN WAVE HIS MAGIC WAND AND TURN THEM ALL INTO MINDLESS DRONES!
POUF'S CORE WAS RESPONDING TO WHATEVER HAD HAPPENED TO THE KING.
HIS FACE SHOWED THE TRUE NATURE OF THE ANTS!!
DID THE CHAIRMAN MANAGE TO KILL THE KING?
DOES IT MATTER?
HE SAW ...
...IN POUF'S FACE...
...AN INSUR-MOUNTABLE BARRIER.

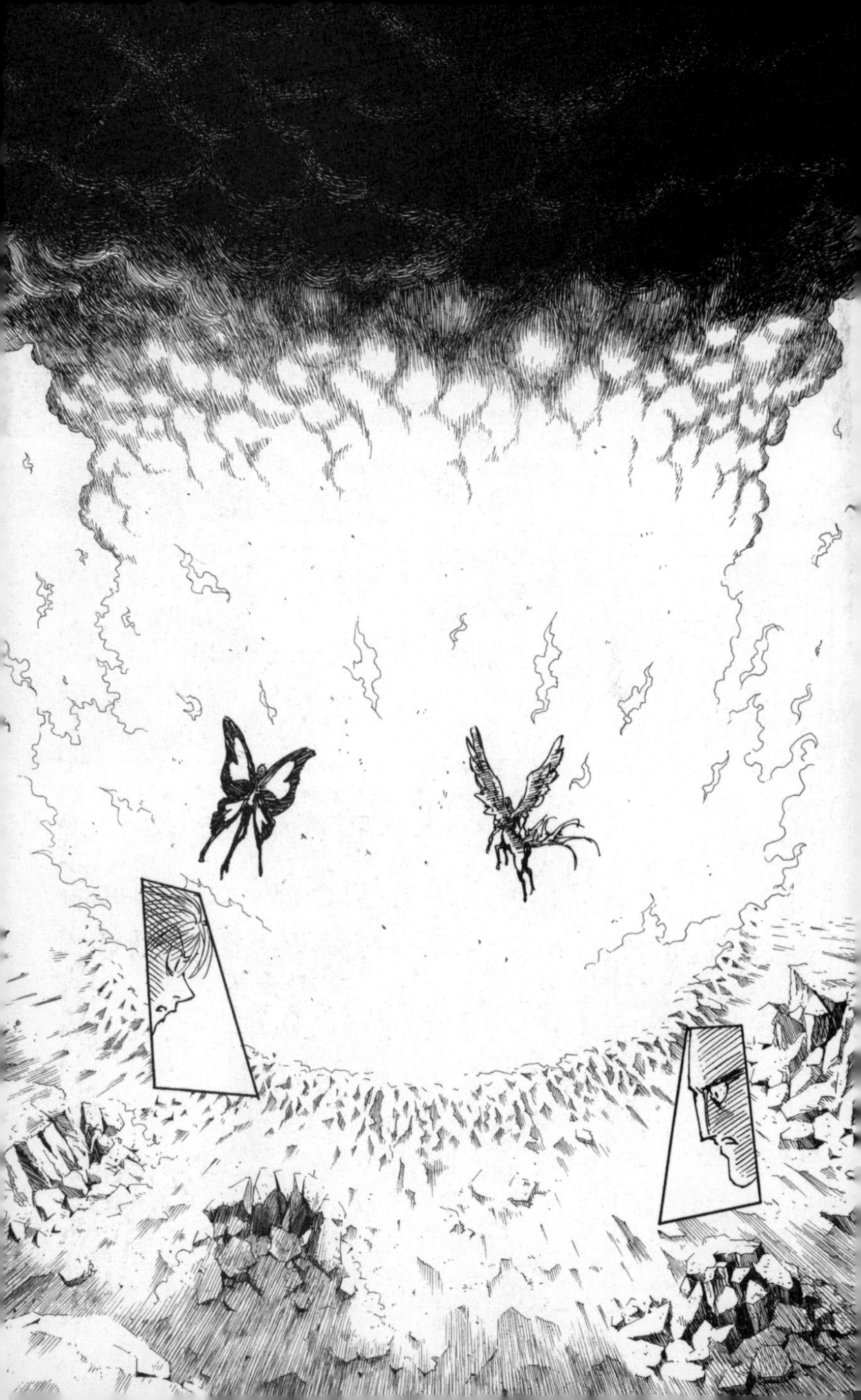

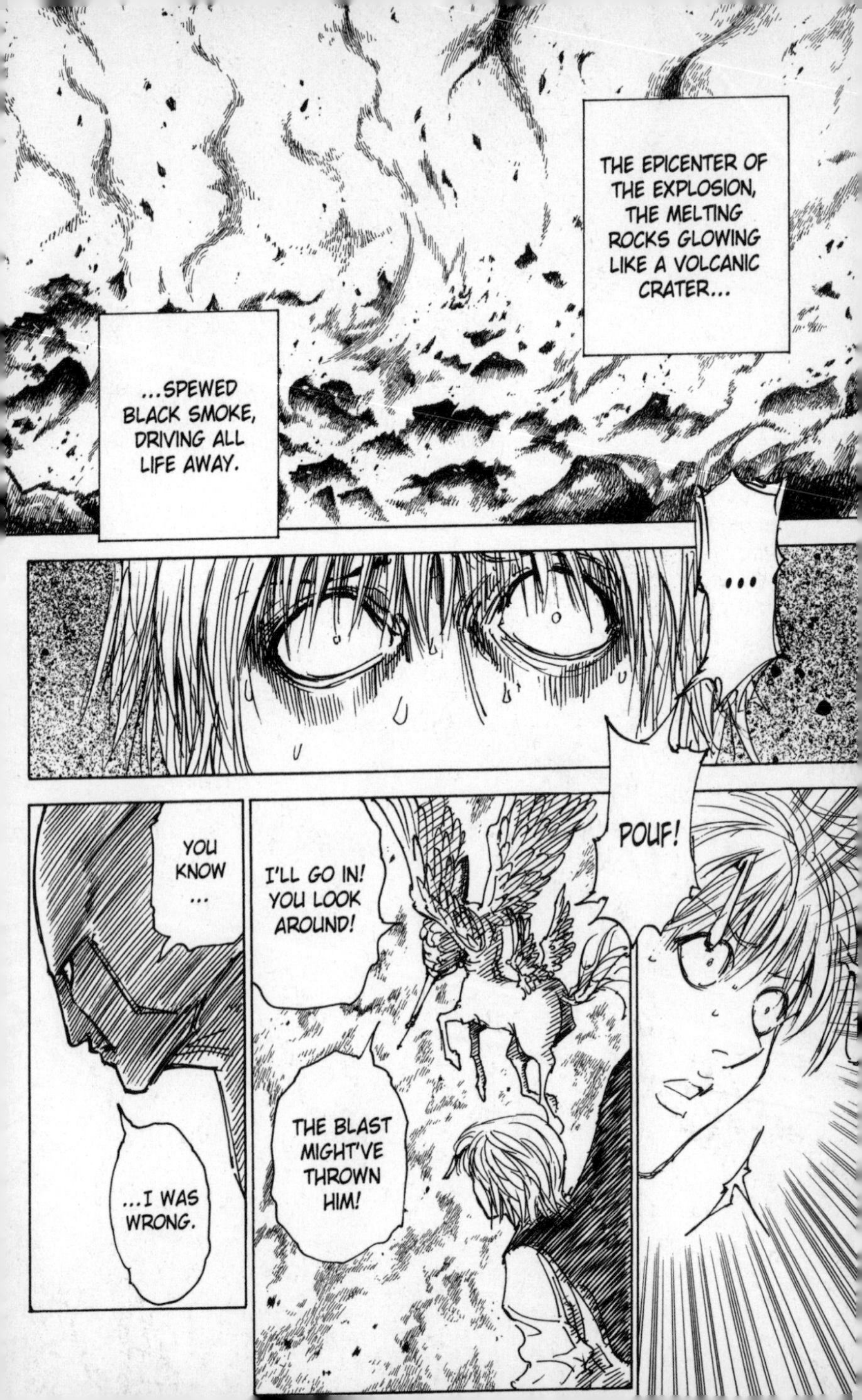
THE EPICENTER OF THE EXPLOSION, THE MELTING ROCKS GLOWING LIKE A VOLCANIC CRATER...
...SPEWED BLACK SMOKE, DRIVING ALL LIFE AWAY.
...
POUF!
I'LL GO IN! YOU LOOK AROUND!
THE BLAST MIGHT'VE THROWN HIM!
YOU KNOW ...
...I WAS WRONG.

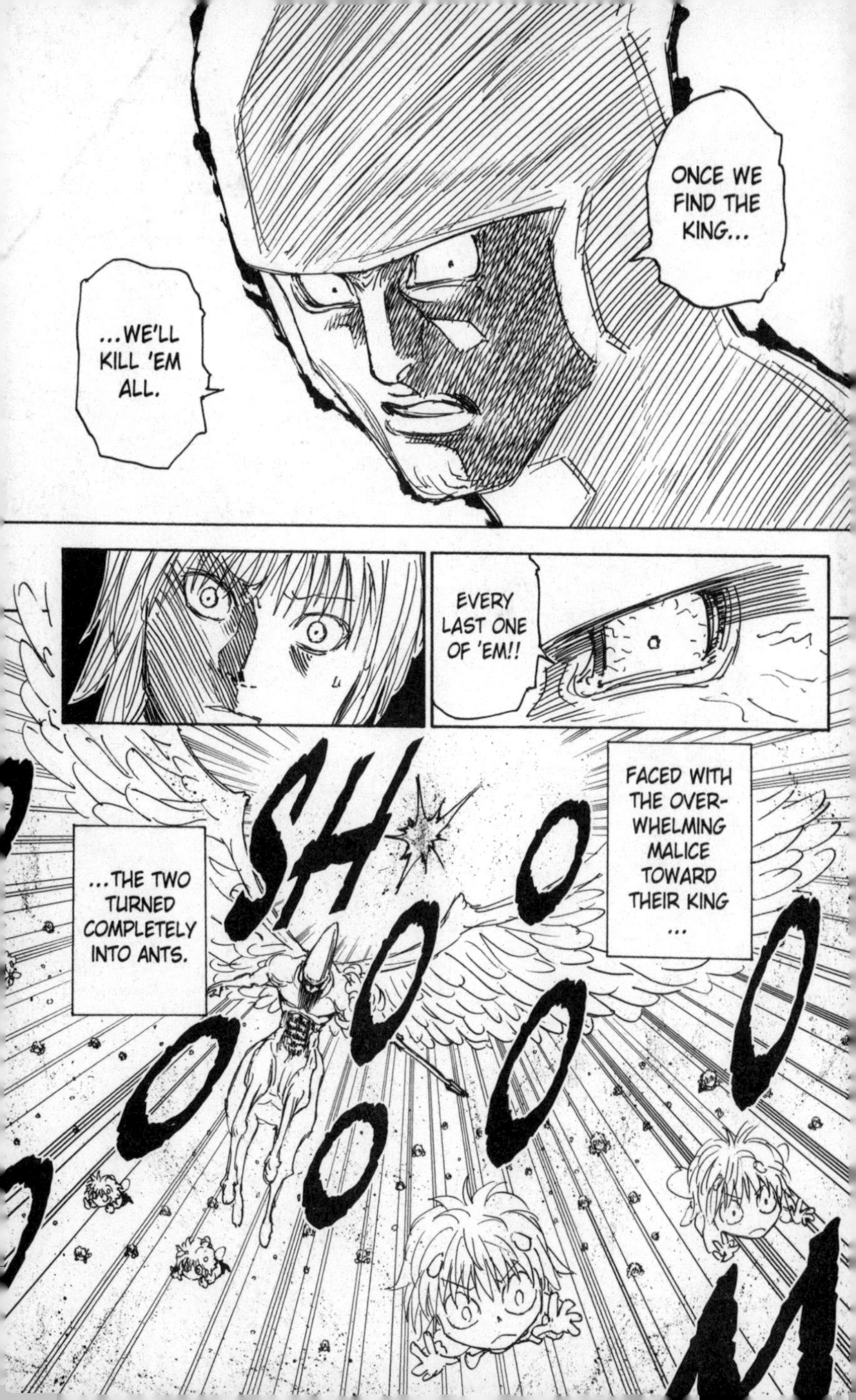
ONCE WE FIND THE KING...
...WE'LL KILL 'EM ALL.
EVERY LAST ONE OF 'EM!!
FACED WITH THE OVER-WHELMING MALICE TOWARD THEIR KING ...
...THE TWO TURNED COMPLETELY INTO ANTS.
SHOOOOOOOOM

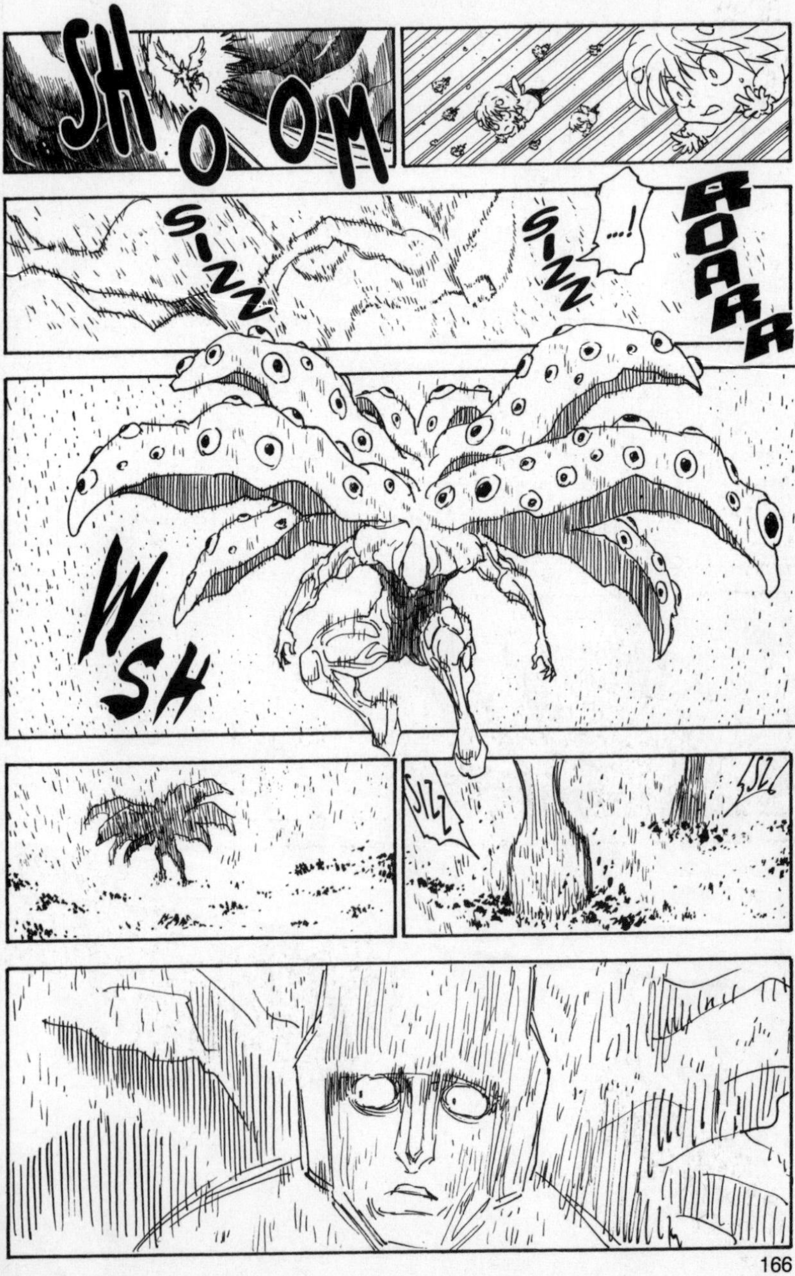
SHOOM
ROARRR
...!
SIZZ
SIZZ
WSH
SIZZ
SIZZ

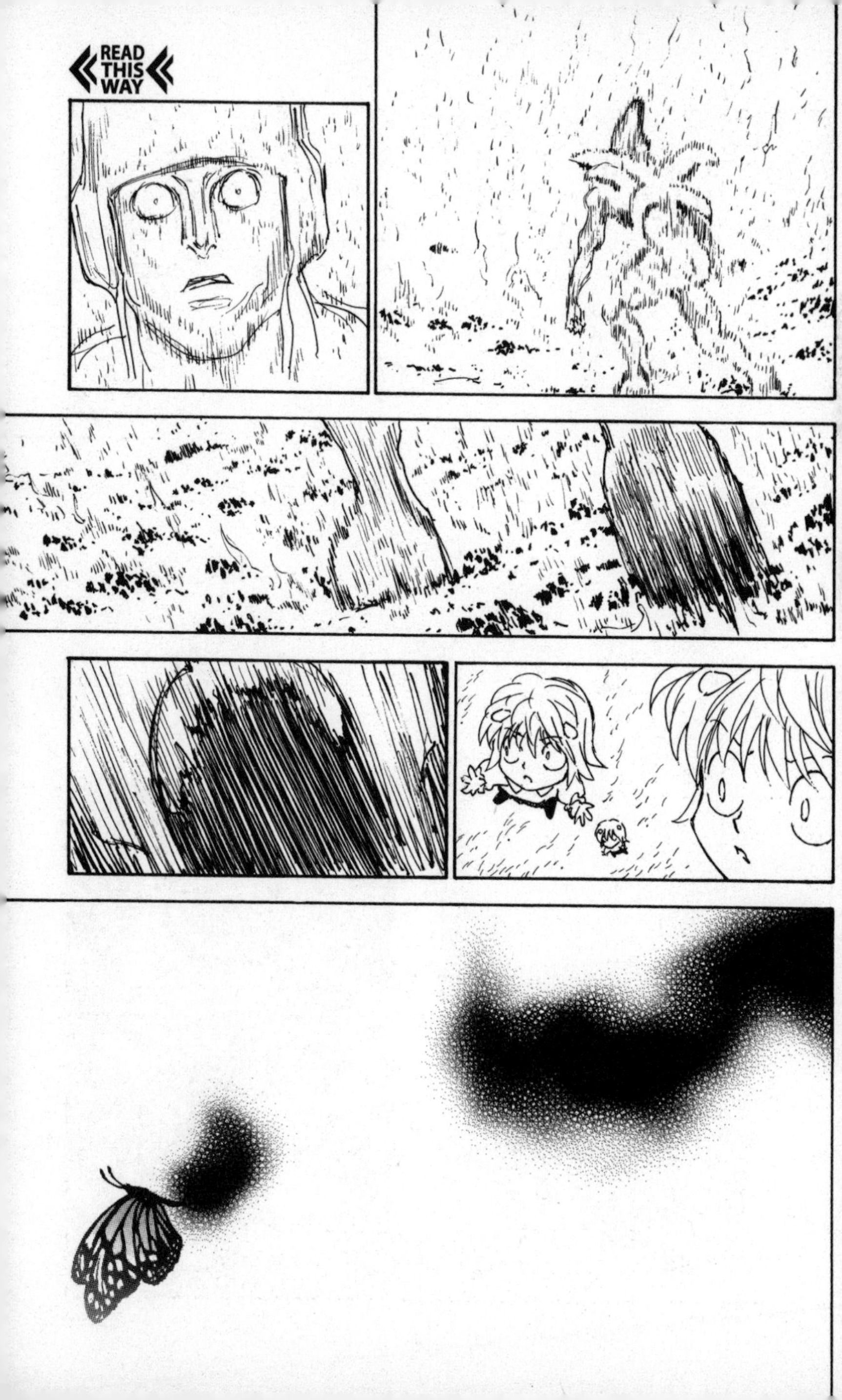
READ THIS WAY

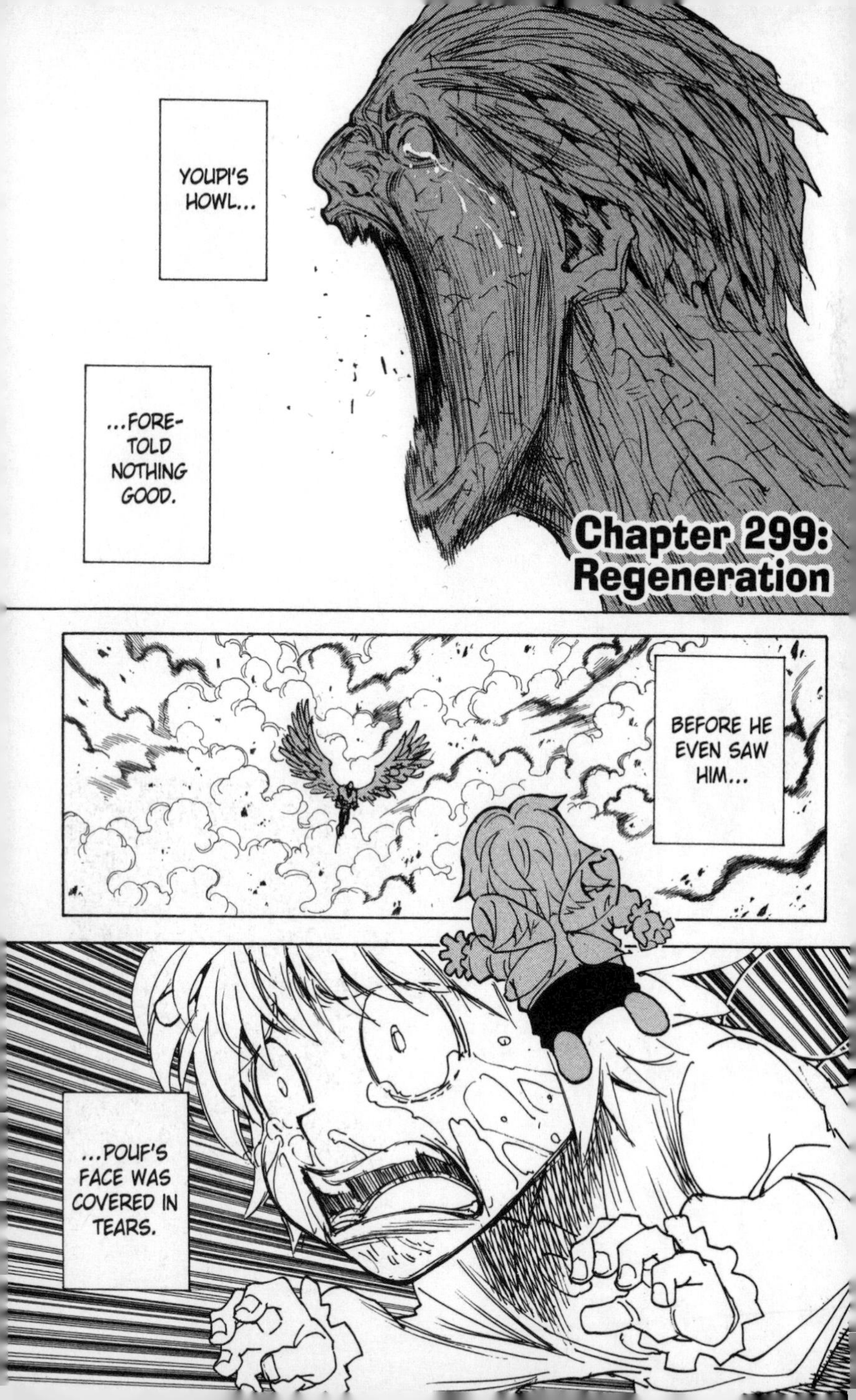
YOUPI'S HOWL...
...FORE-TOLD NOTHING GOOD.
Chapter 299: Regeneration
BEFORE HE EVEN SAW HIM...
...POUF'S FACE WAS COVERED IN TEARS.

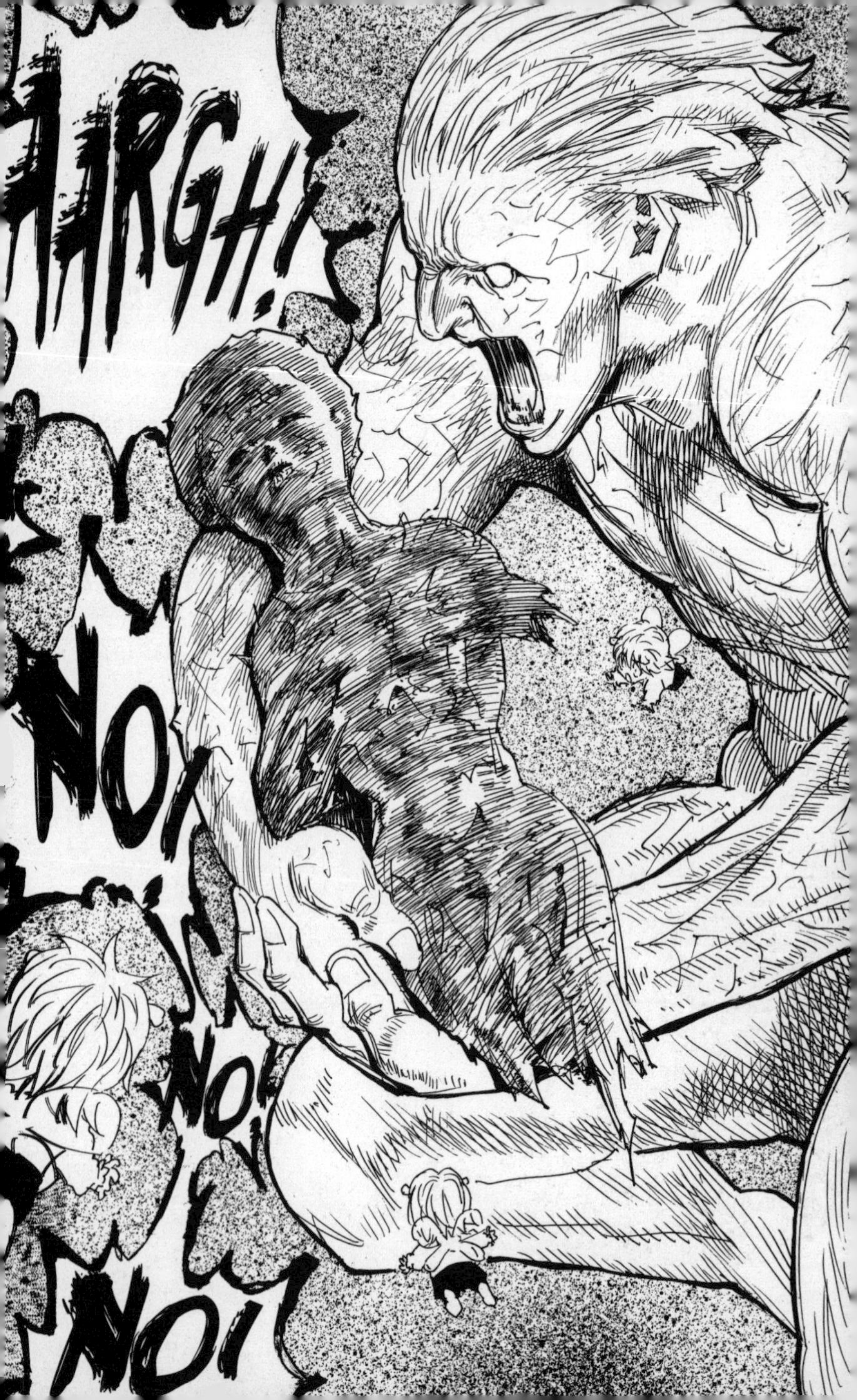
ARGH!
NO!
NO!
NO!

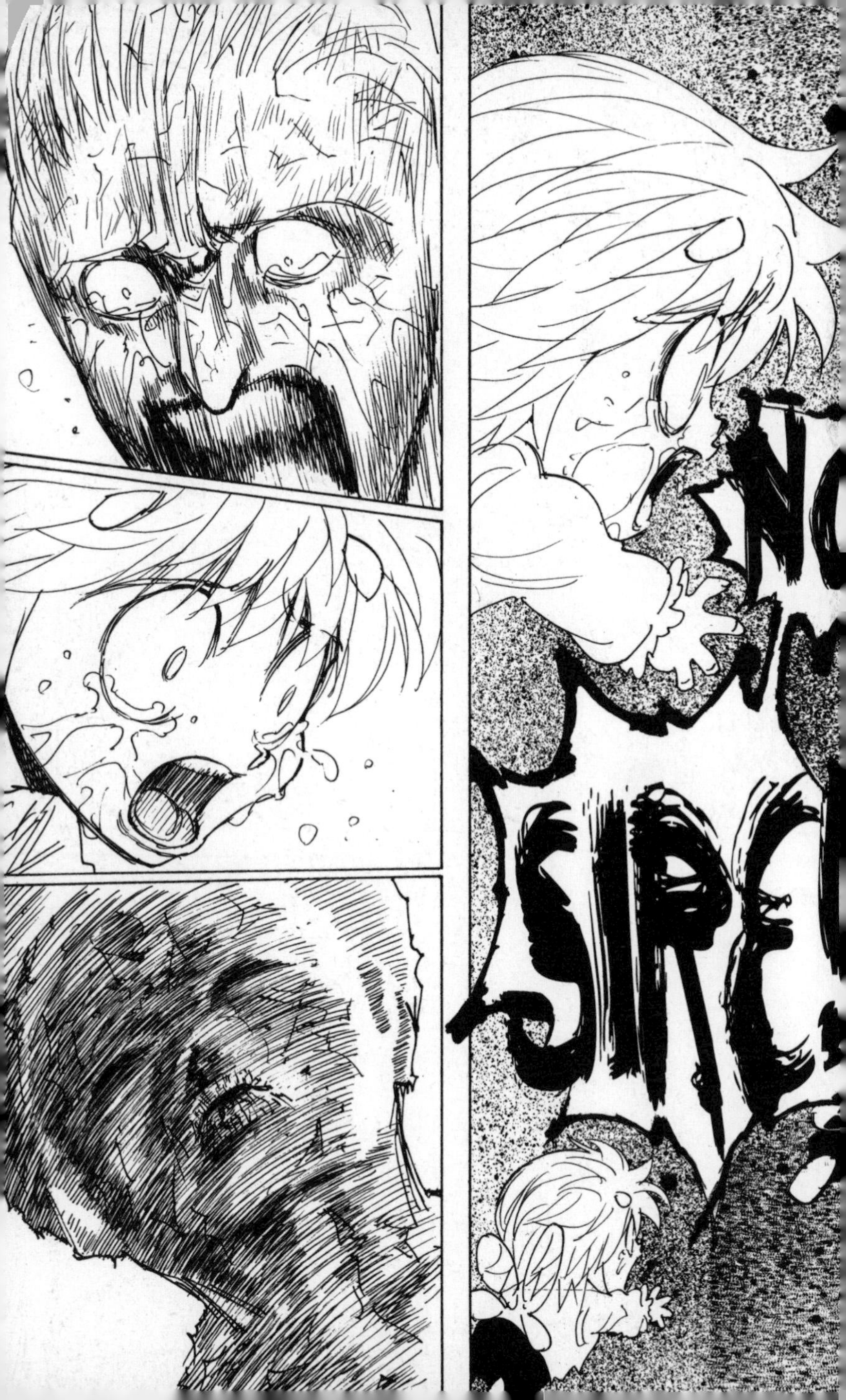
NO
SIR

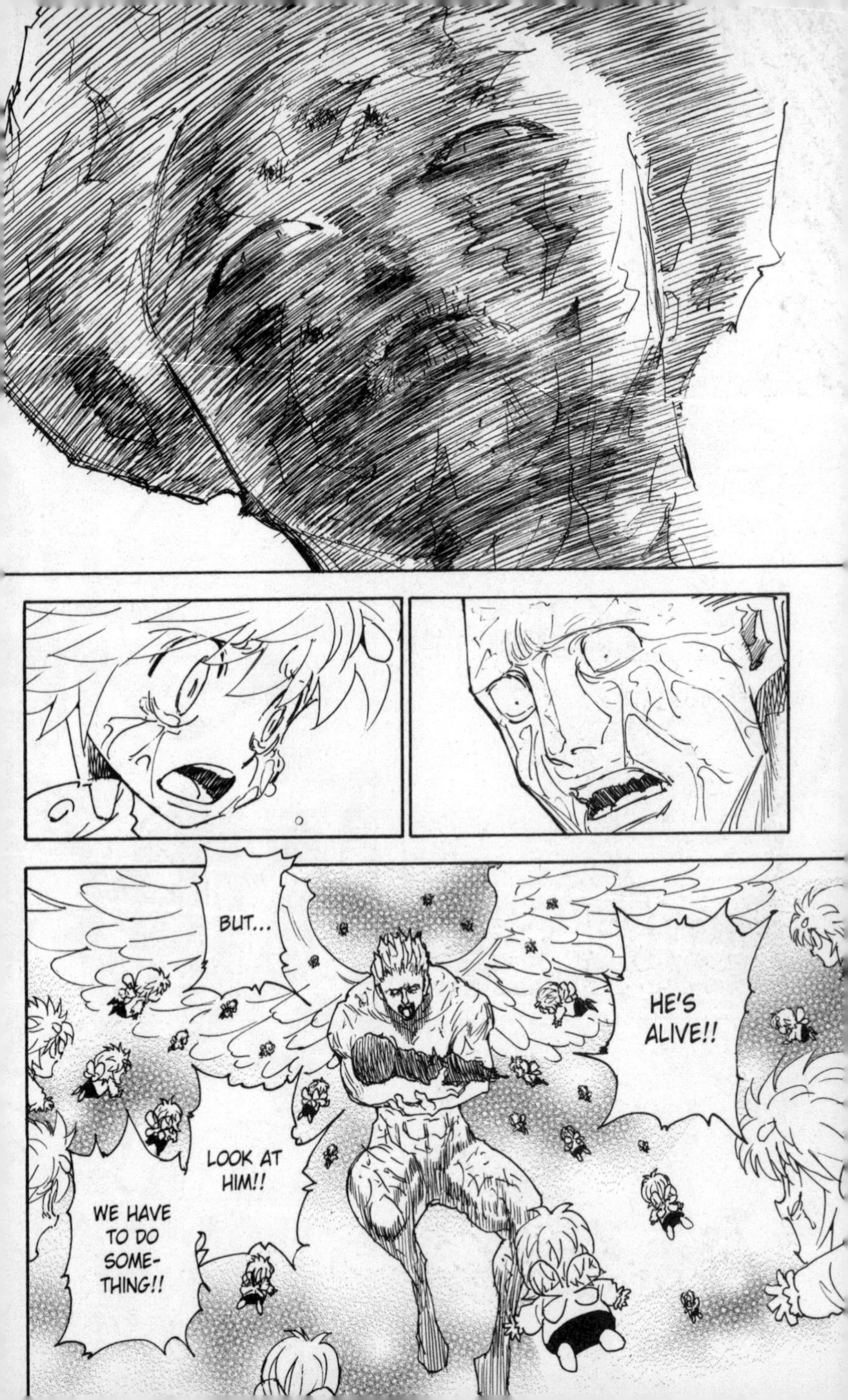
HE'S ALIVE!!
BUT...
LOOK AT HIM!!
WE HAVE TO DO SOMETHING!!

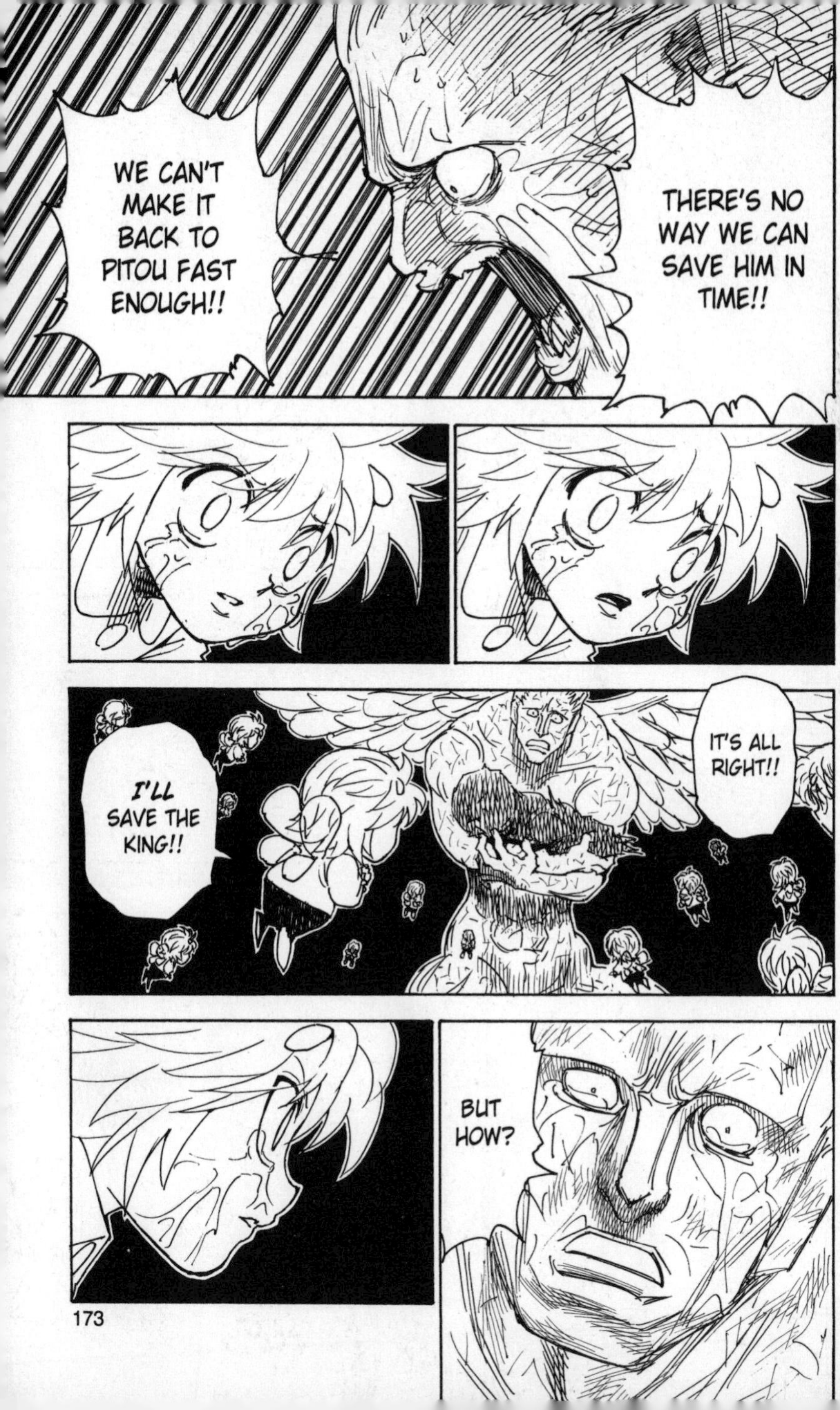
THERE'S NO WAY WE CAN SAVE HIM IN TIME!!
WE CAN'T MAKE IT BACK TO PITOU FAST ENOUGH!!
IT'S ALL RIGHT!!
I'LL SAVE THE KING!!
BUT HOW?

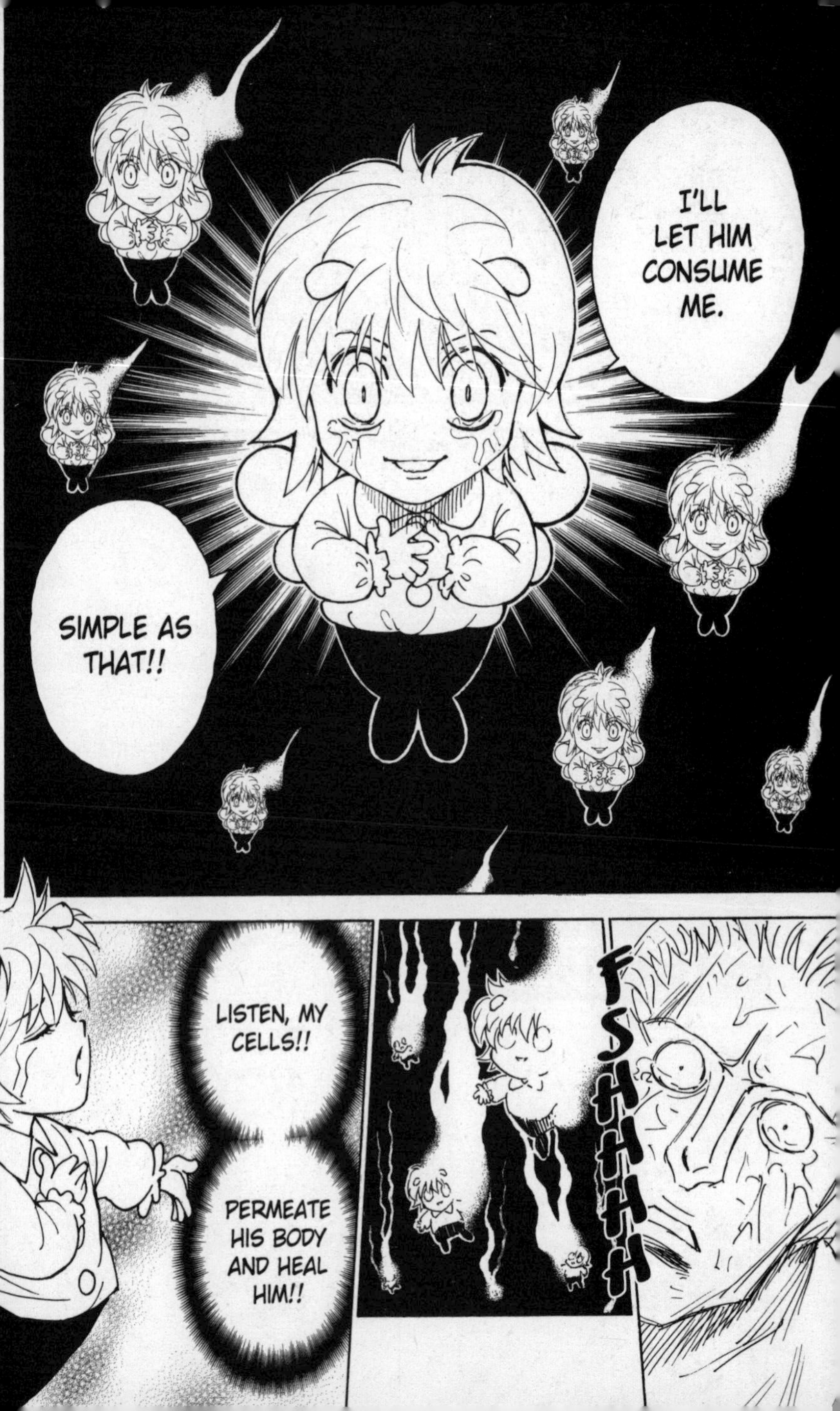
I'LL LET HIM CONSUME ME.
SIMPLE AS THAT!!
FSHHHHH
LISTEN, MY CELLS!!
PERMEATE HIS BODY AND HEAL HIM!!

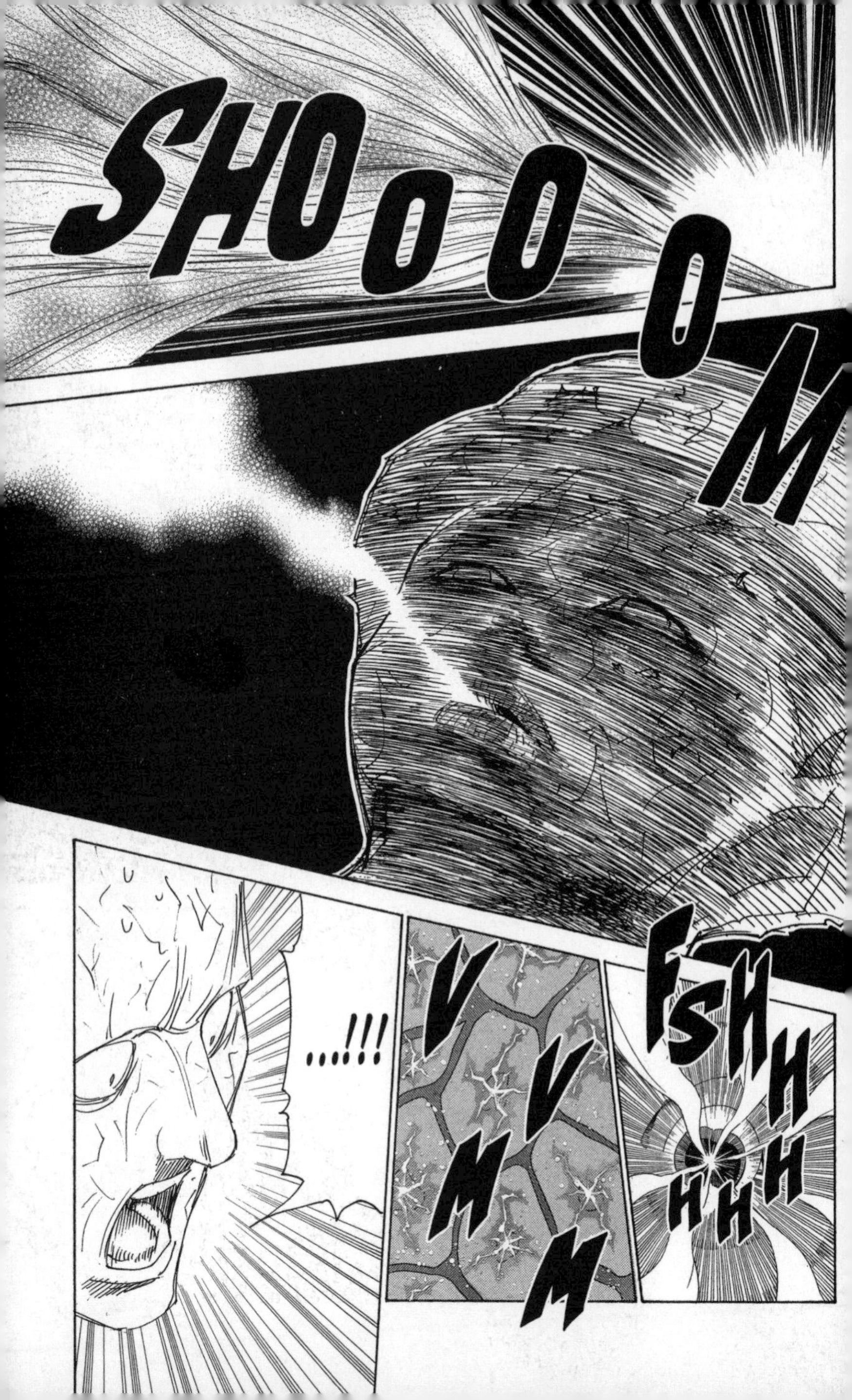
SHOOOOM
FSHHHHHH
VVMMM
...!!!

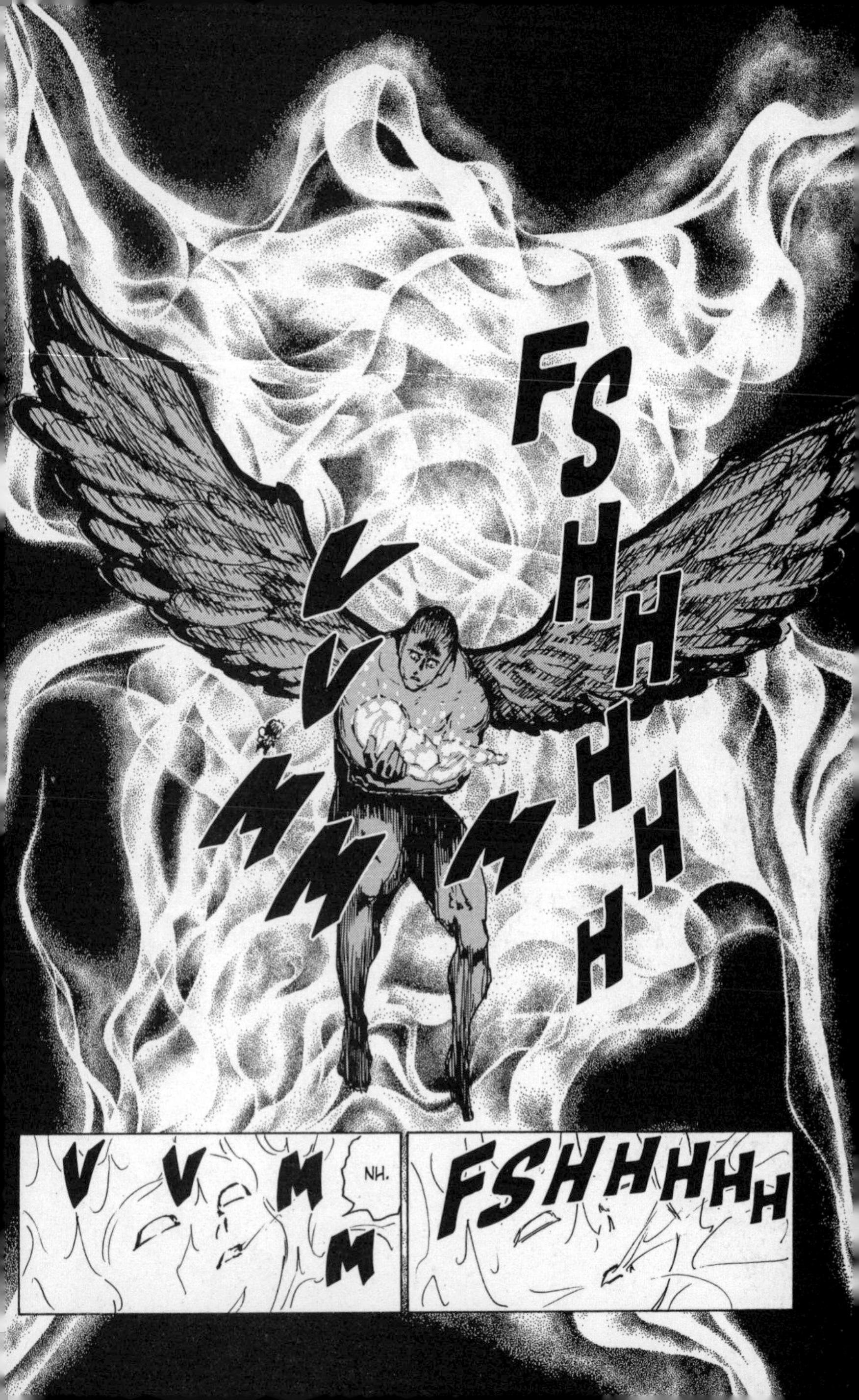
FSHHHHHH
VVMMMM
FSHHHHHH
VVMM
NH.

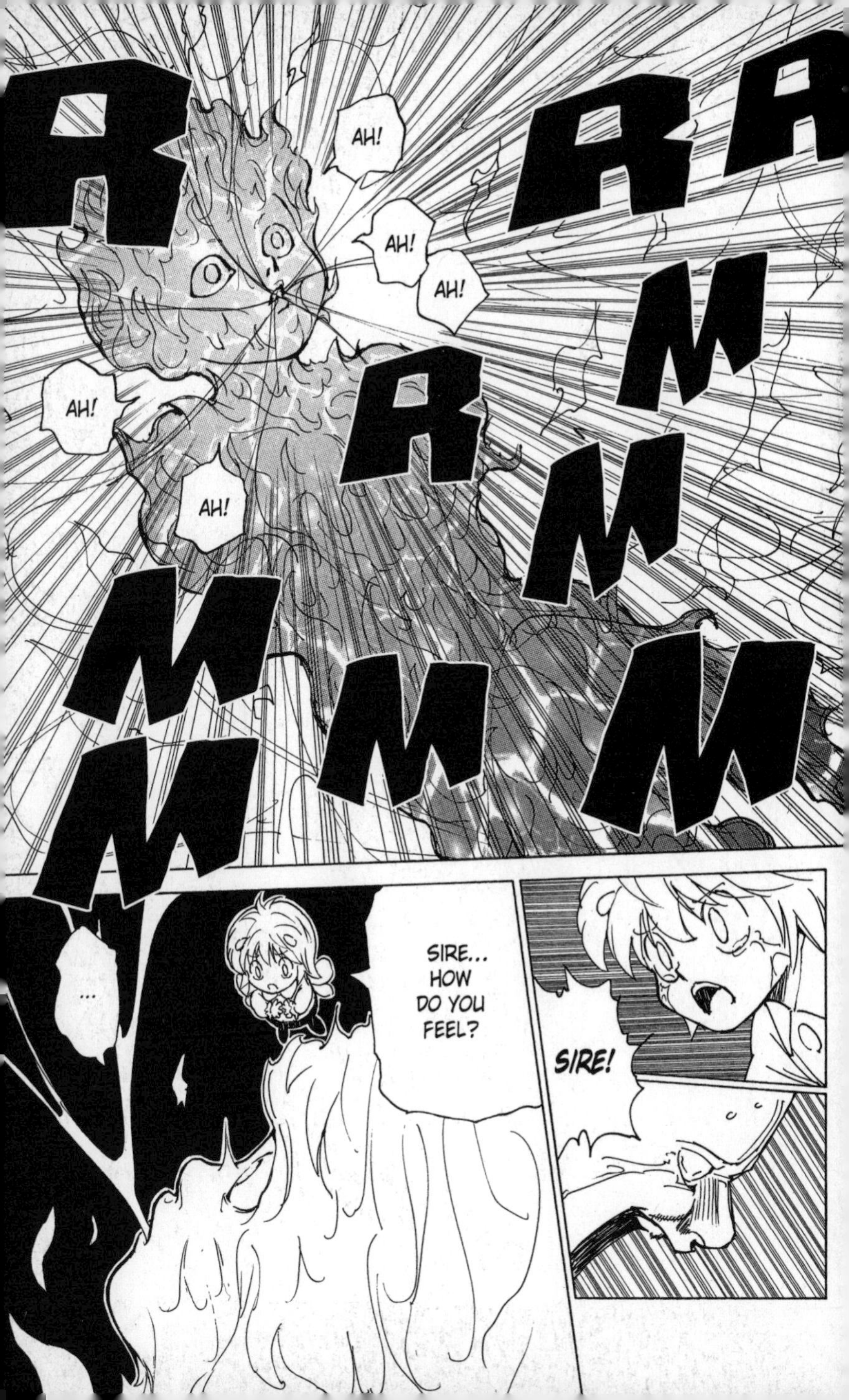
RRRRMMMMMMM
AH!
AH!
AH!
AH!
AH!
SIRE!
SIRE... HOW DO YOU FEEL?
...

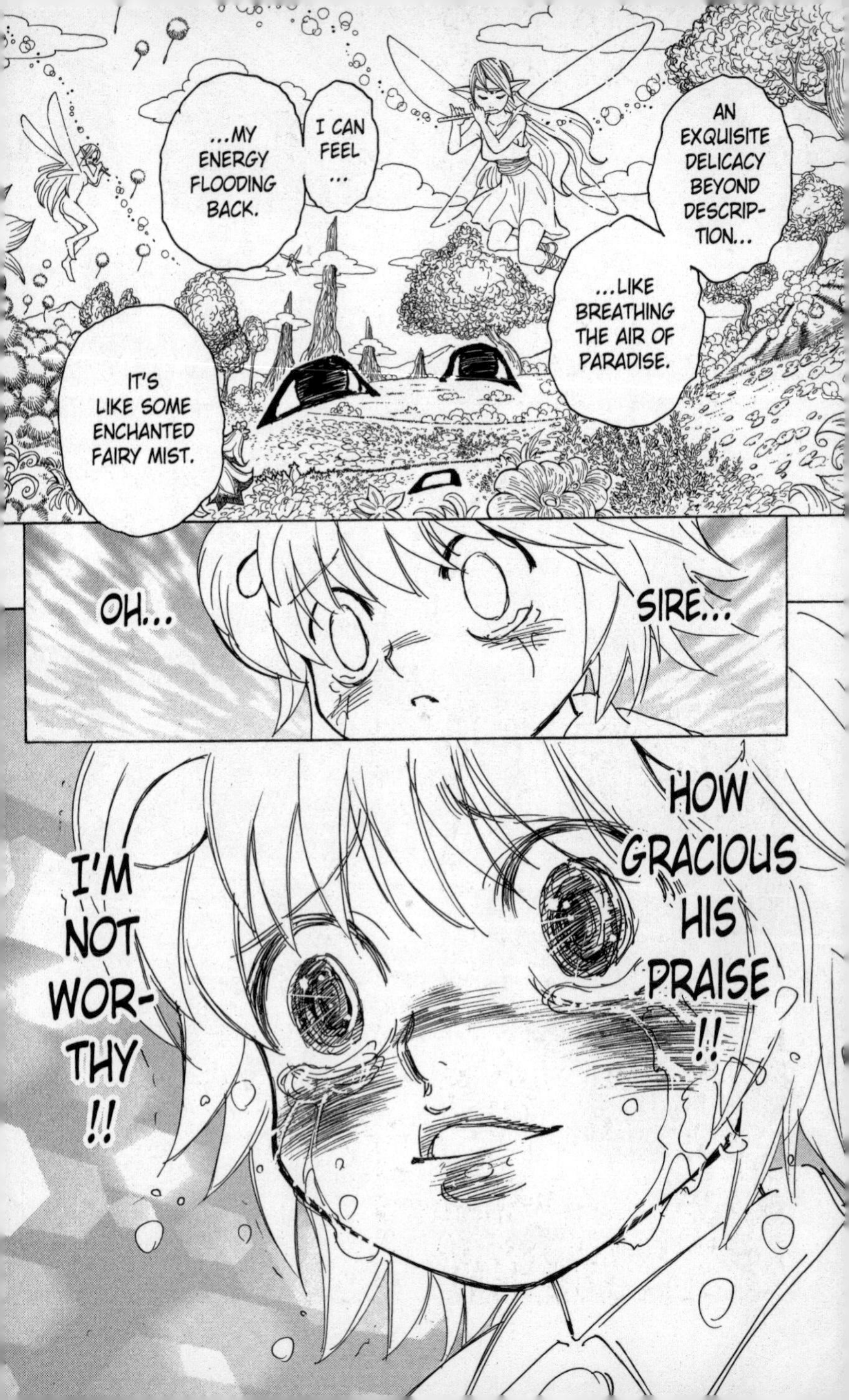
AN EXQUISITE DELICACY BEYOND DESCRIPTION...
...LIKE BREATHING THE AIR OF PARADISE.
I CAN FEEL ...
...MY ENERGY FLOODING BACK.
IT'S LIKE SOME ENCHANTED FAIRY MIST.
SIRE...
OH...
HOW GRACIOUS HIS PRAISE!!
I'M NOT WORTHY!!

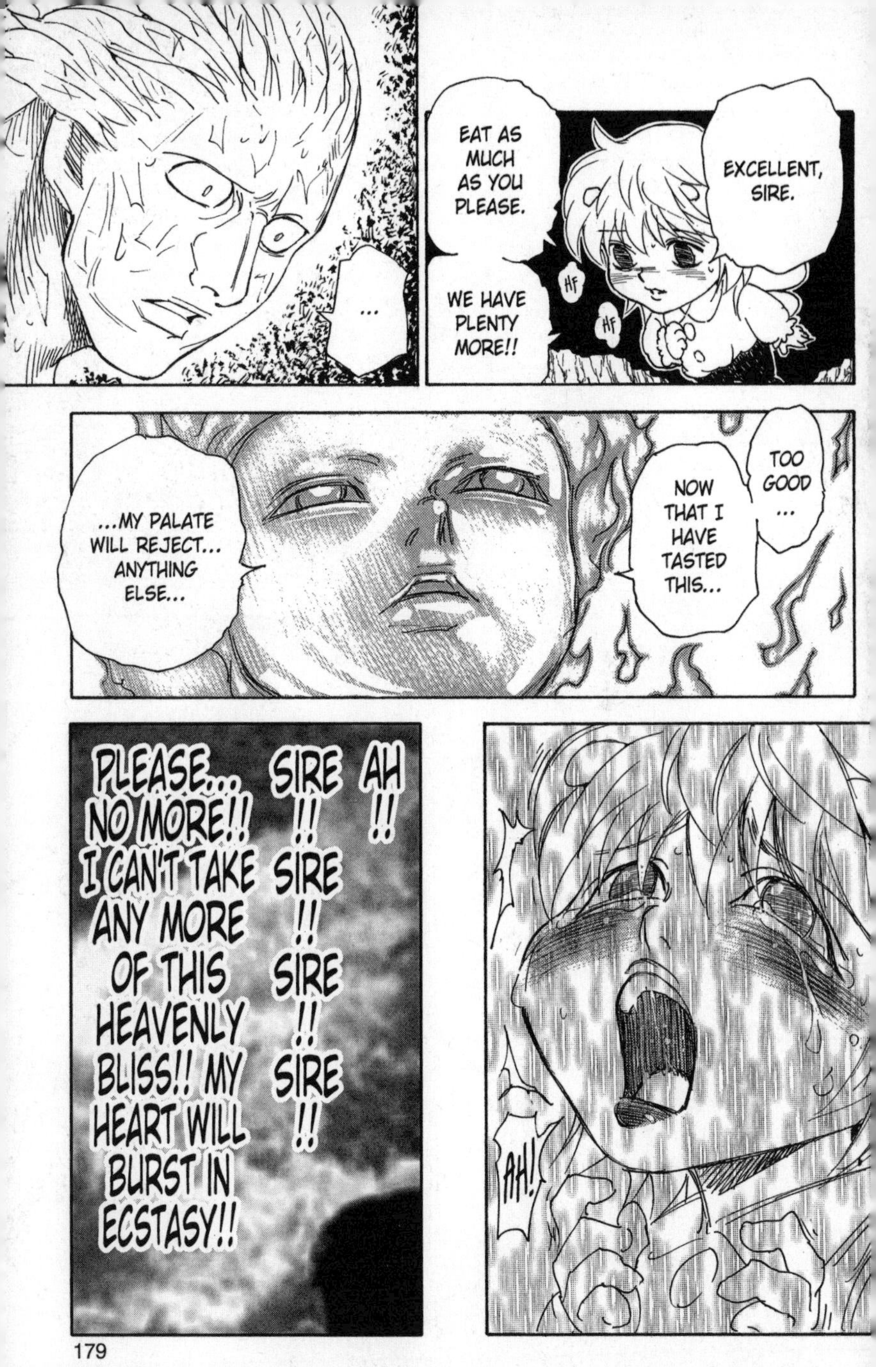
EXCELLENT, SIRE.
EAT AS MUCH AS YOU PLEASE.
HF
HF
WE HAVE PLENTY MORE!!
...
TOO GOOD...
NOW THAT I HAVE TASTED THIS...
...MY PALATE WILL REJECT... ANYTHING ELSE...
AH!
AH!!
SIRE!! SIRE!! SIRE!! SIRE!!
PLEASE... NO MORE!! I CAN'T TAKE ANY MORE OF THIS HEAVENLY BLISS!! MY HEART WILL BURST IN ECSTASY!!

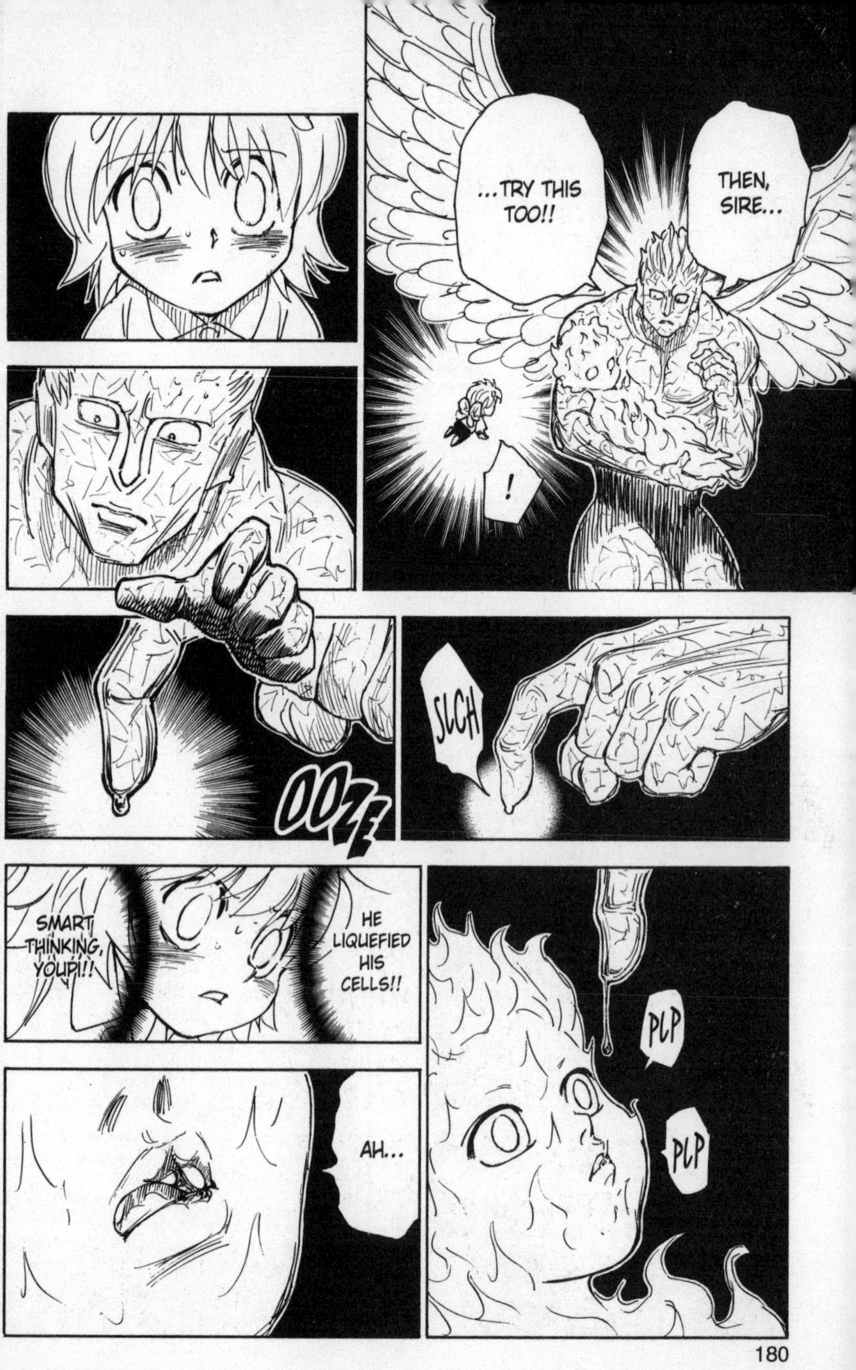
THEN, SIRE...
...TRY THIS TOO!!
!
SLCH
OOZE
PLP
PLP
HE LIQUEFIED HIS CELLS!!
SMART THINKING, YOUPI!!
AH...

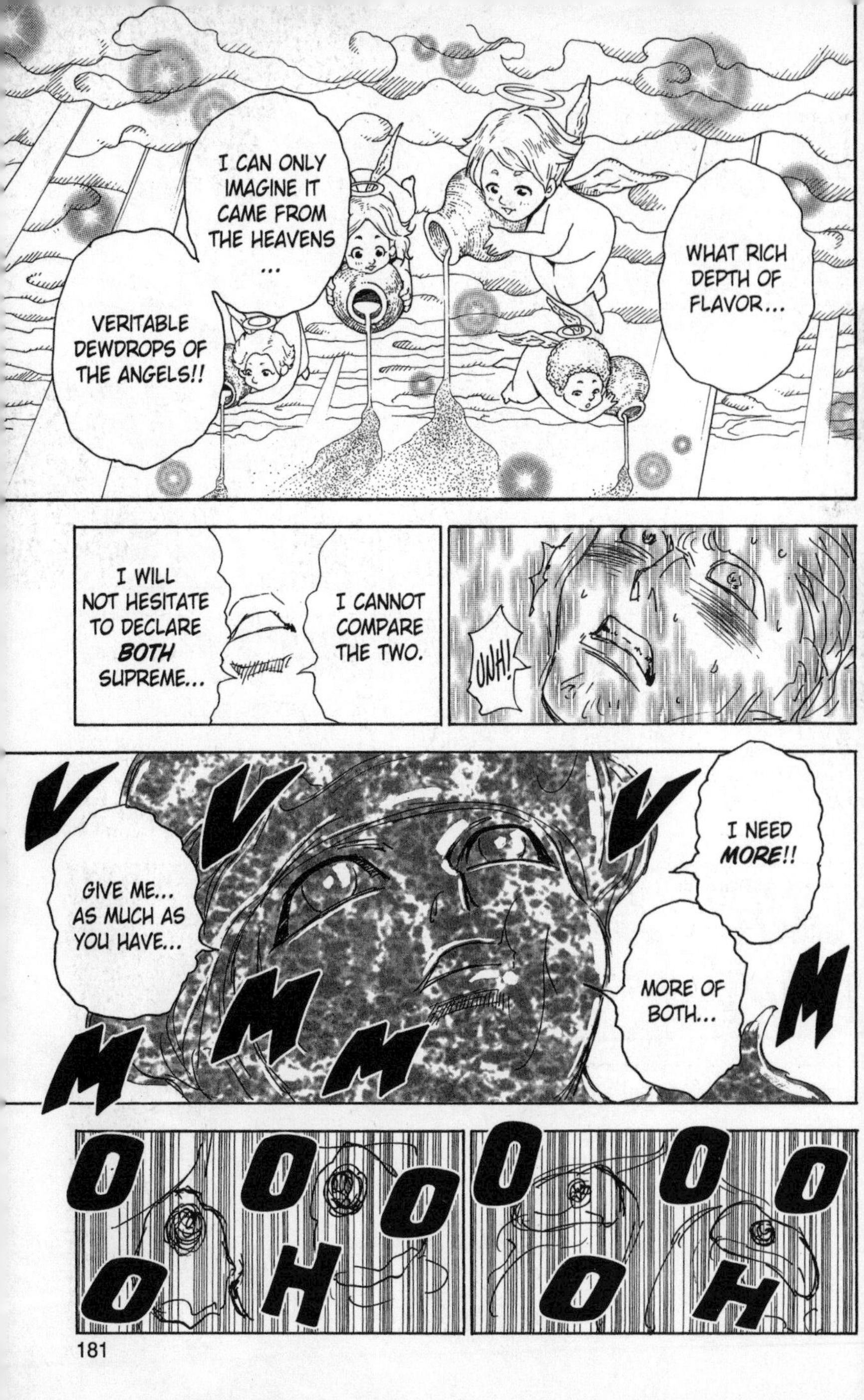
WHAT RICH DEPTH OF FLAVOR...
I CAN ONLY IMAGINE IT CAME FROM THE HEAVENS ...
VERITABLE DEWDROPS OF THE ANGELS!!
UNH!
I CANNOT COMPARE THE TWO.
I WILL NOT HESITATE TO DECLARE BOTH SUPREME...
VVV
I NEED MORE!!
MORE OF BOTH...
GIVE ME... AS MUCH AS YOU HAVE...
MMMMM
OOOOOH
OOOOH

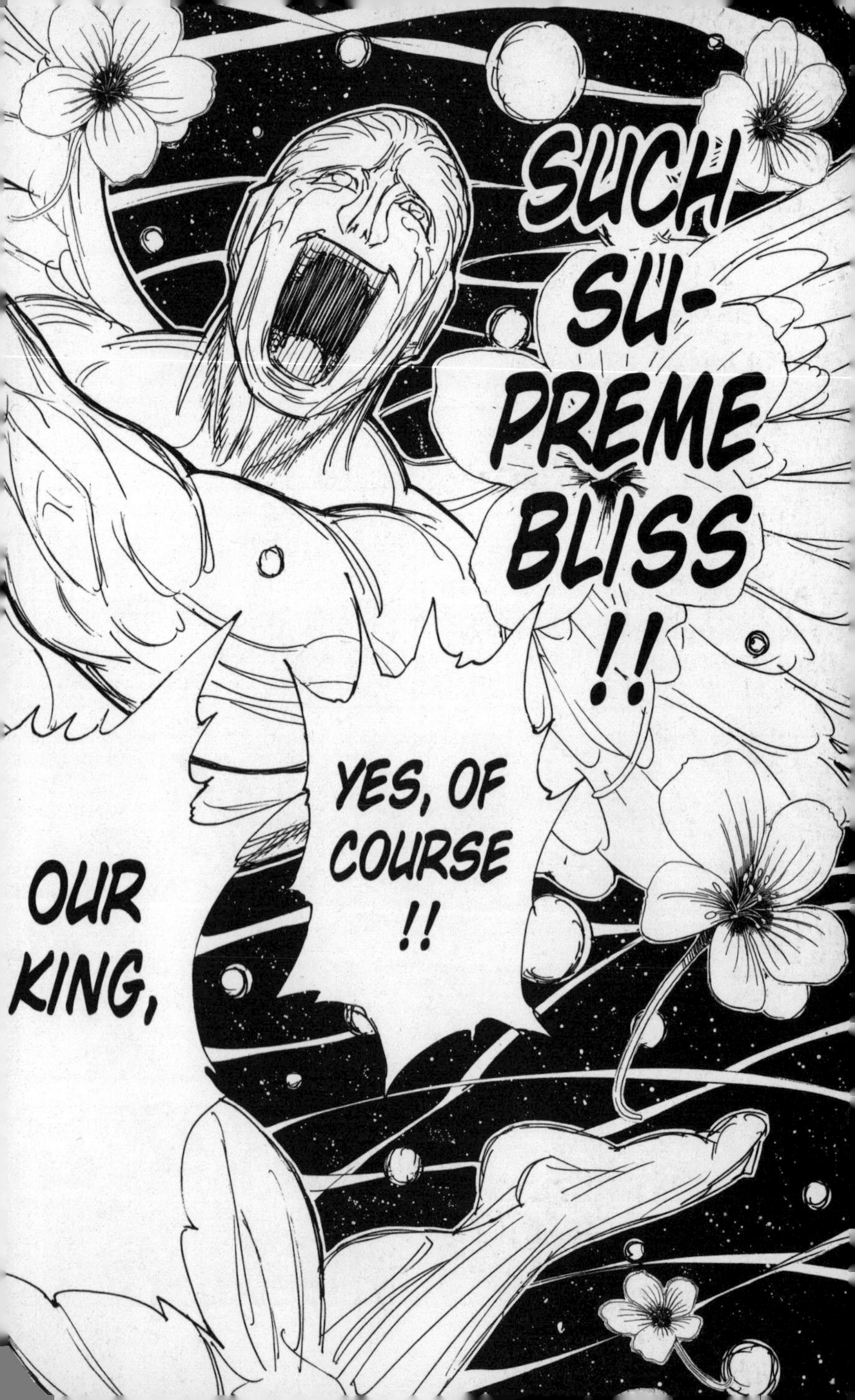
SUCH SU-PREME BLISS!!
YES, OF COURSE!!
OUR KING,

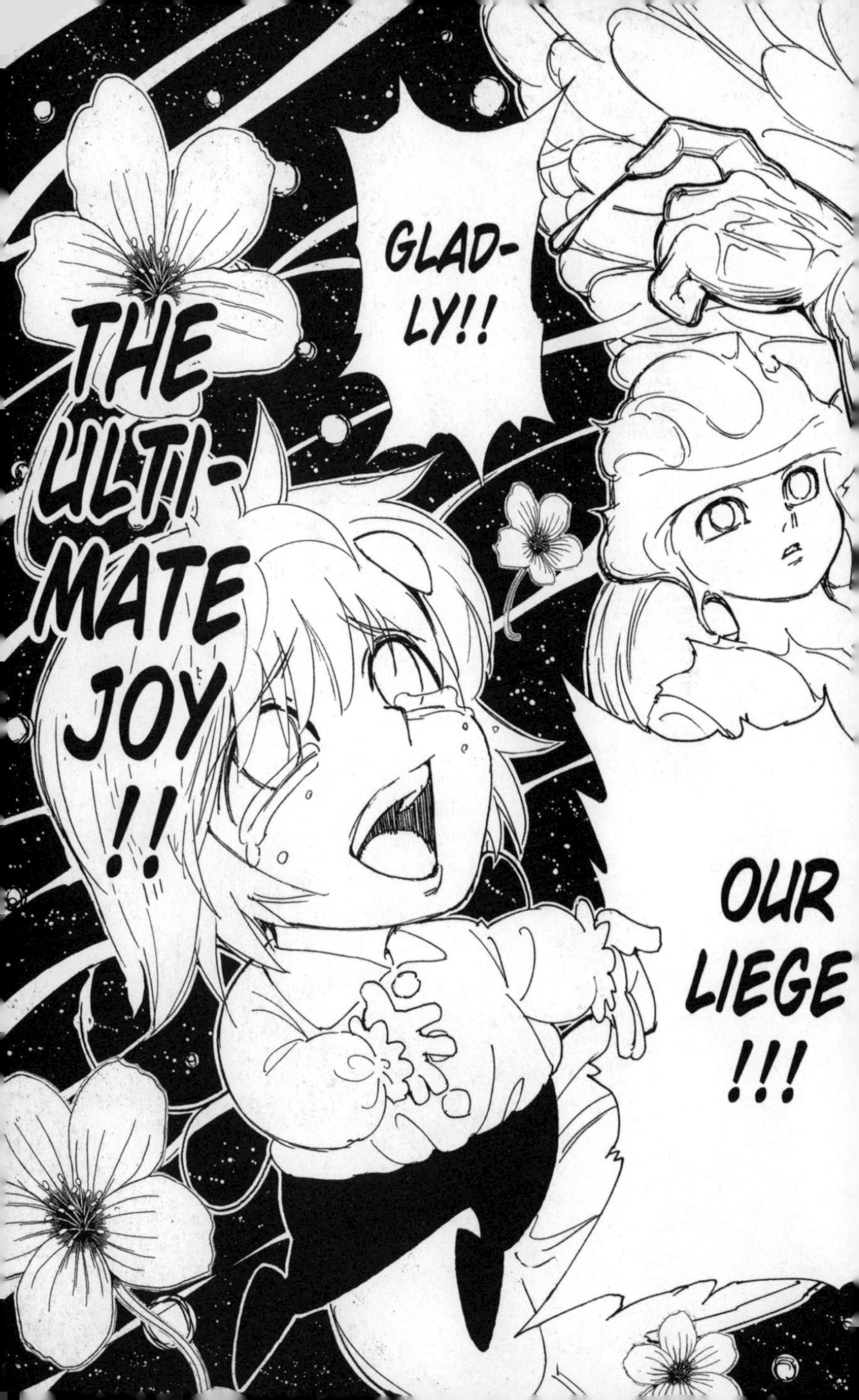
GLAD-LY!!
OUR LIEGE!!!
THE ULTI-MATE JOY!!

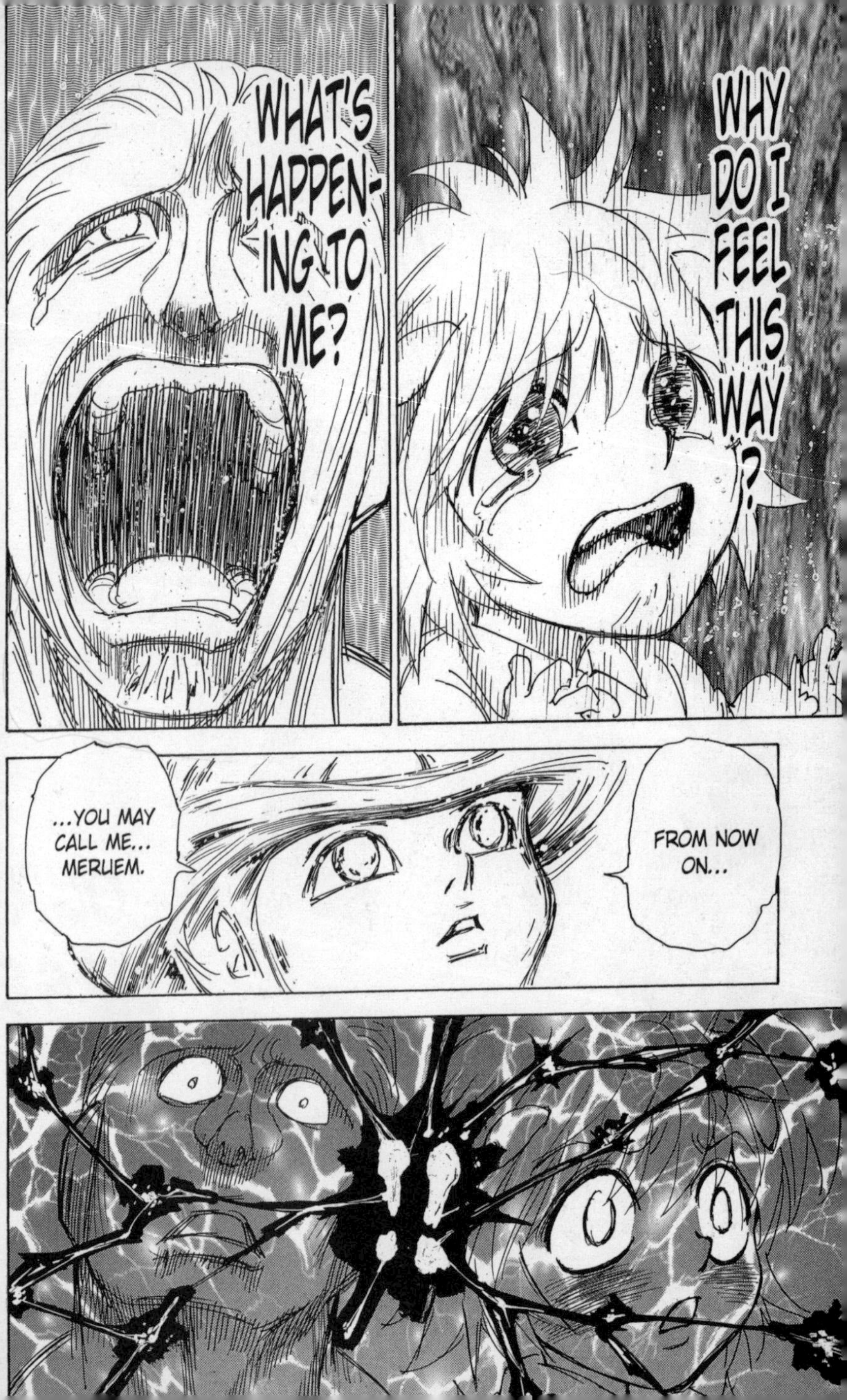
WHY DO I FEEL THIS WAY?
WHAT'S HAPPEN-ING TO ME?
FROM NOW ON...
...YOU MAY CALL ME... MERUEM.

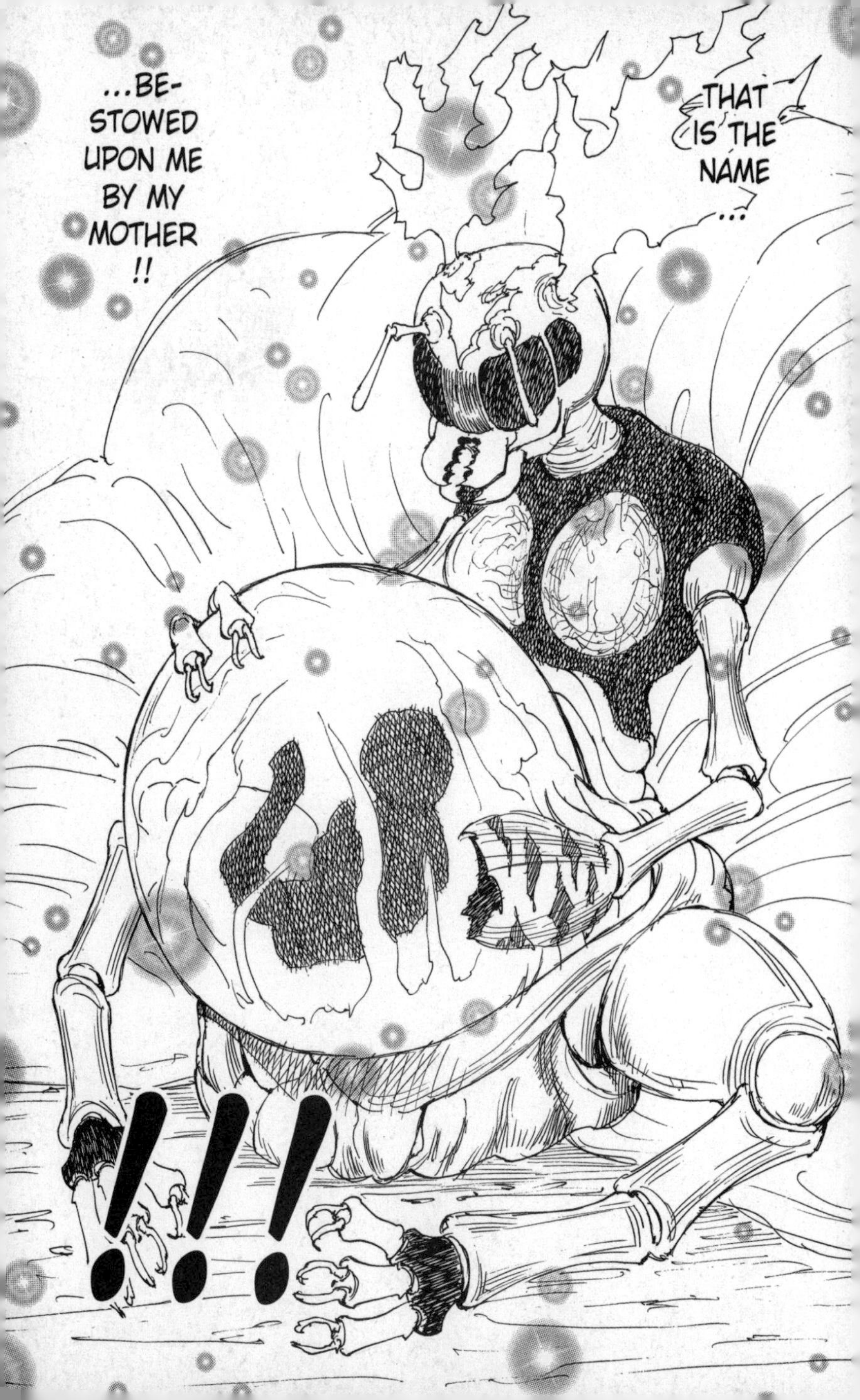
THAT IS THE NAME...
...BE-STOWED UPON ME BY MY MOTHER!!
!!!

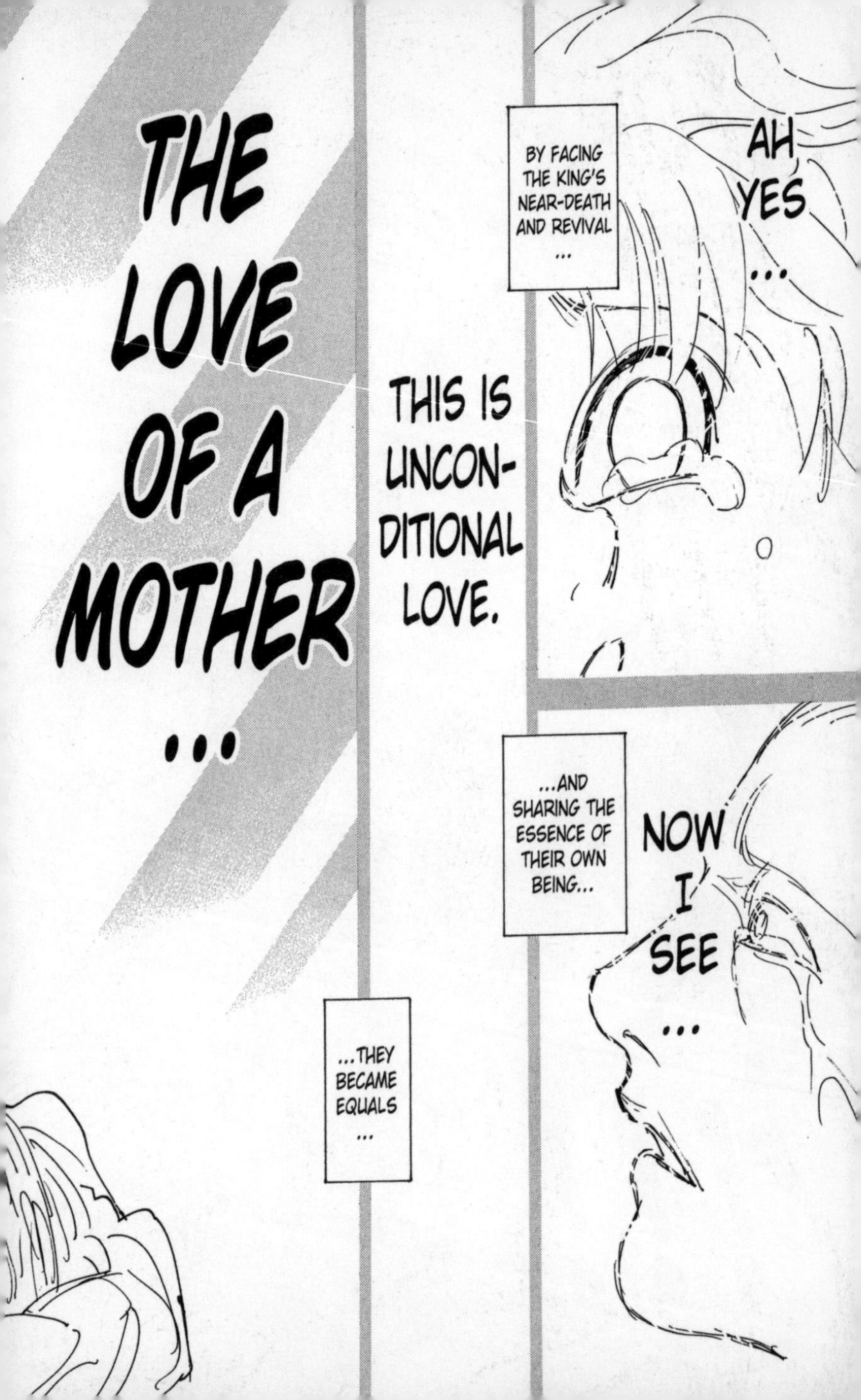
AH YES...
BY FACING THE KING'S NEAR-DEATH AND REVIVAL...
NOW I SEE...
...AND SHARING THE ESSENCE OF THEIR OWN BEING...
THIS IS UNCON-DITIONAL LOVE.
...THEY BECAME EQUALS...
THE LOVE OF A MOTHER...

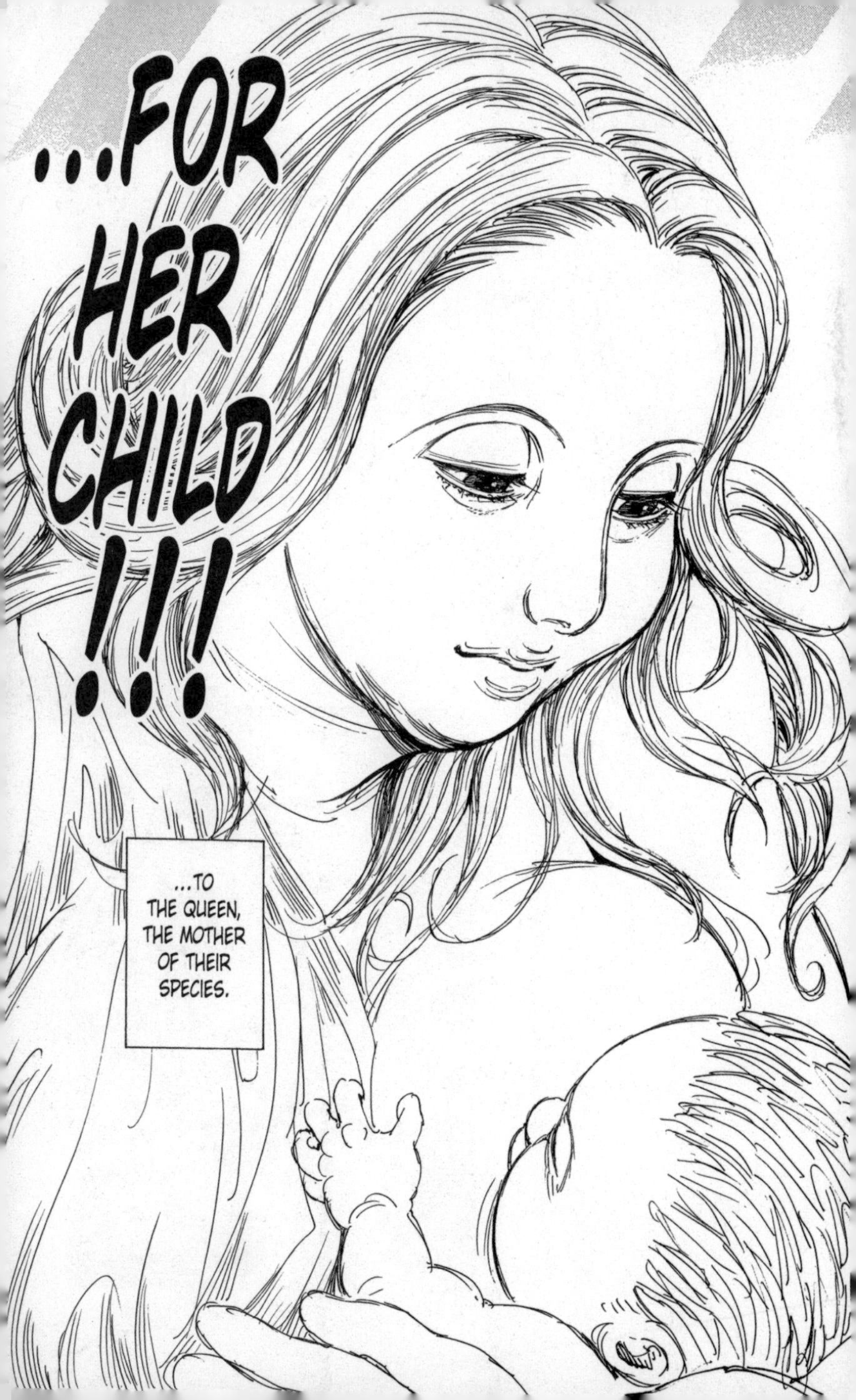
...FOR HER CHILD!!!
...TO THE QUEEN, THE MOTHER OF THEIR SPECIES.

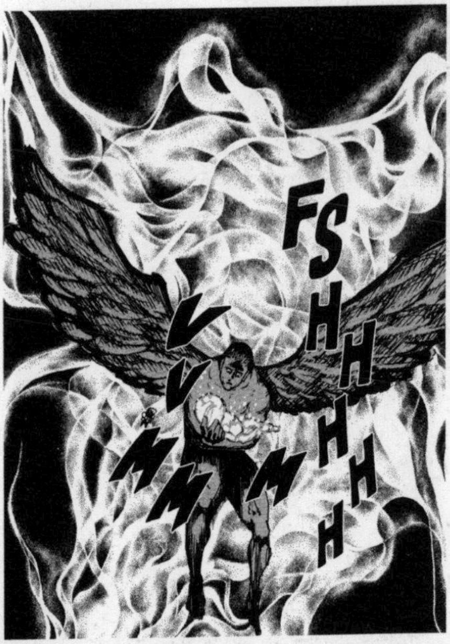
FSHHHHHH
VVMMMM

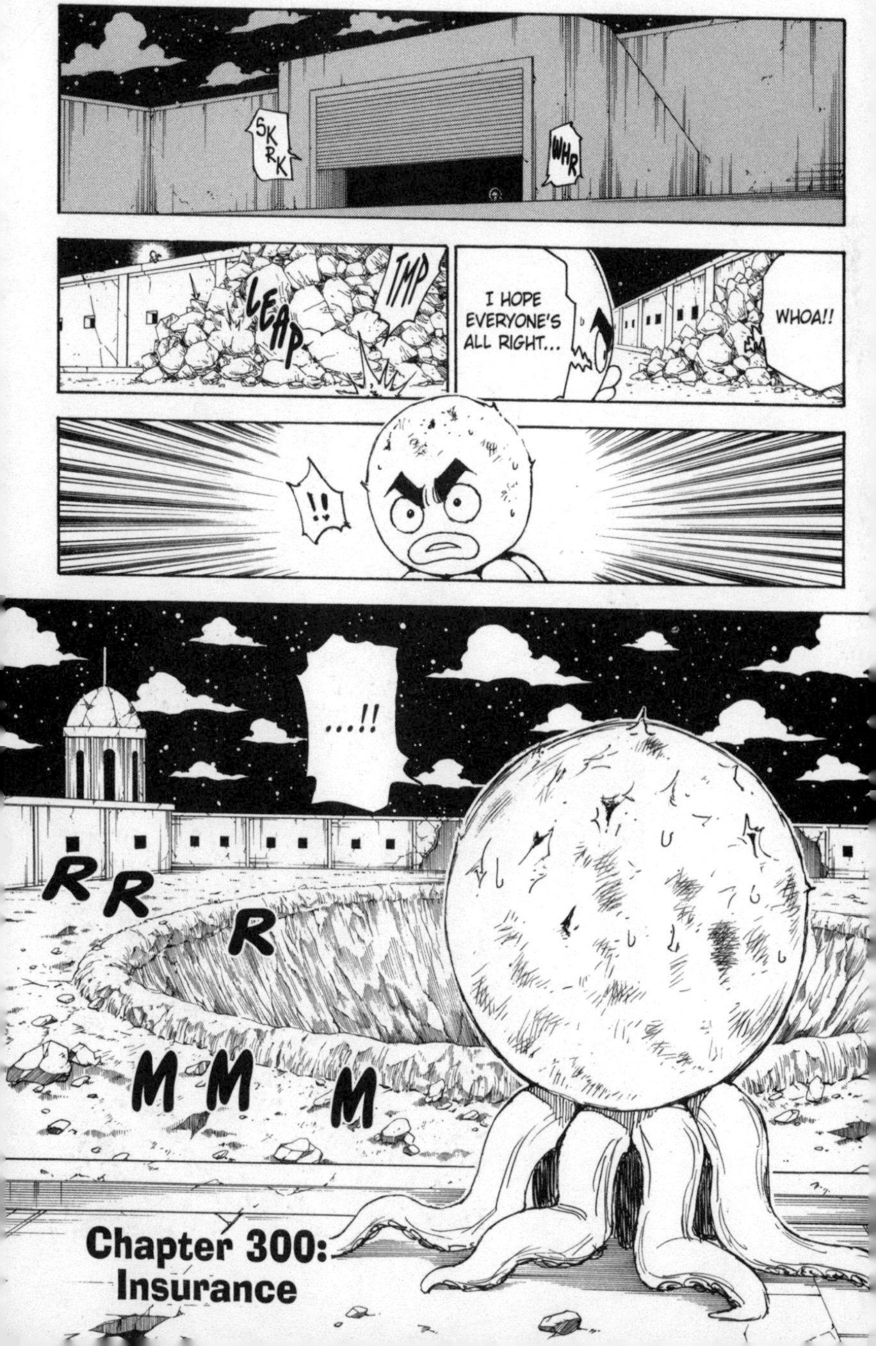
WHR
SKRK
WHOA!!
I HOPE EVERYONE'S ALL RIGHT...
TMP
LEAP
!!
...!!
RRR
MMM

Chapter 300: Insurance

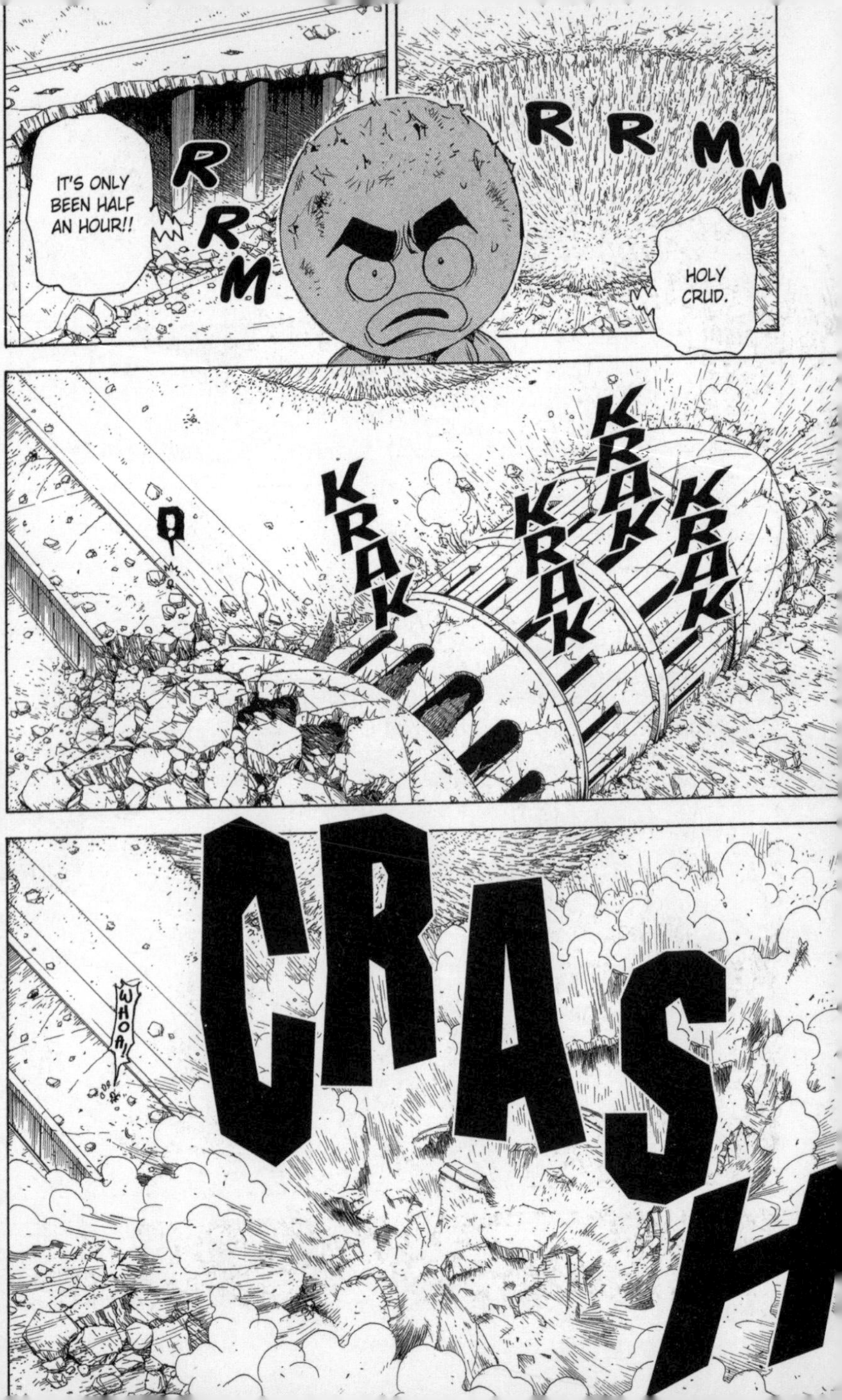
RRRRMMM
HOLY CRUD.
RRM
IT'S ONLY BEEN HALF AN HOUR!!
KRAK KRAK KRAK KRAK
CRASH
WHOA!

READ THIS WAY

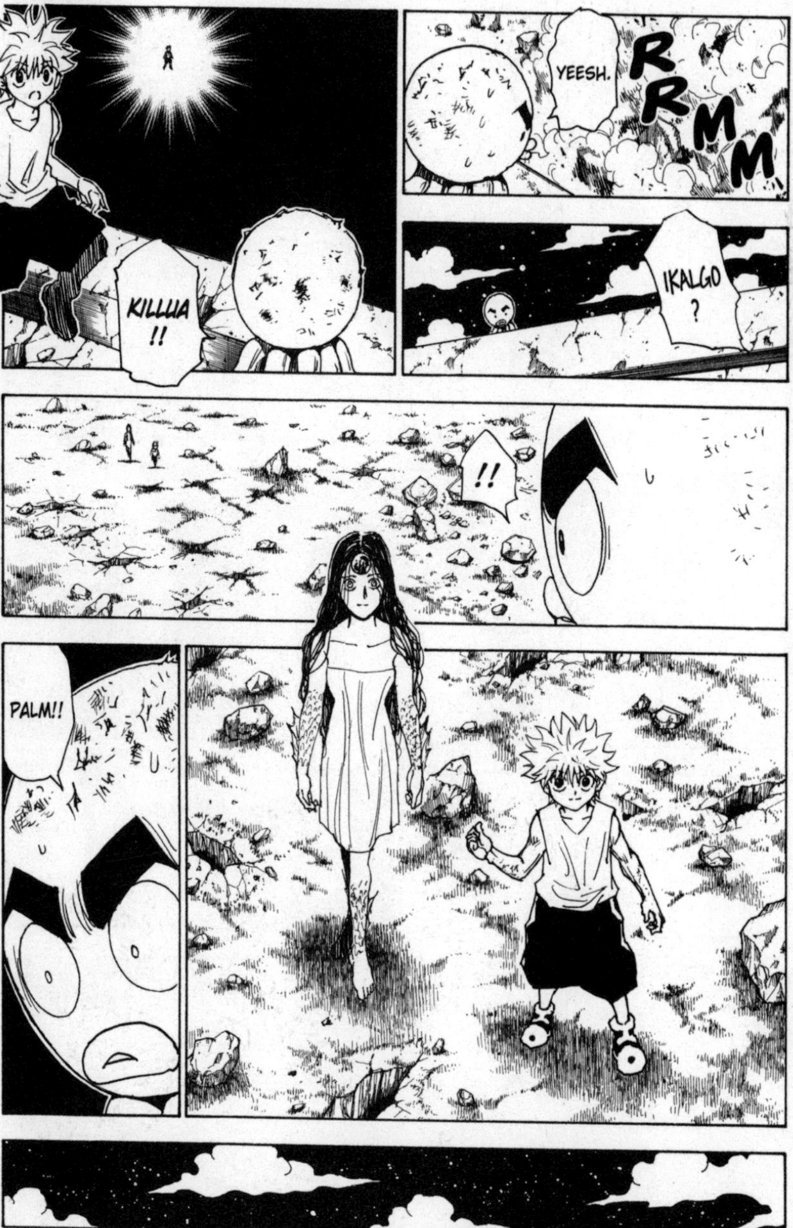
YEESH.
RRMM
IKALGO ?
KILLUA !!
!!
PALM!!

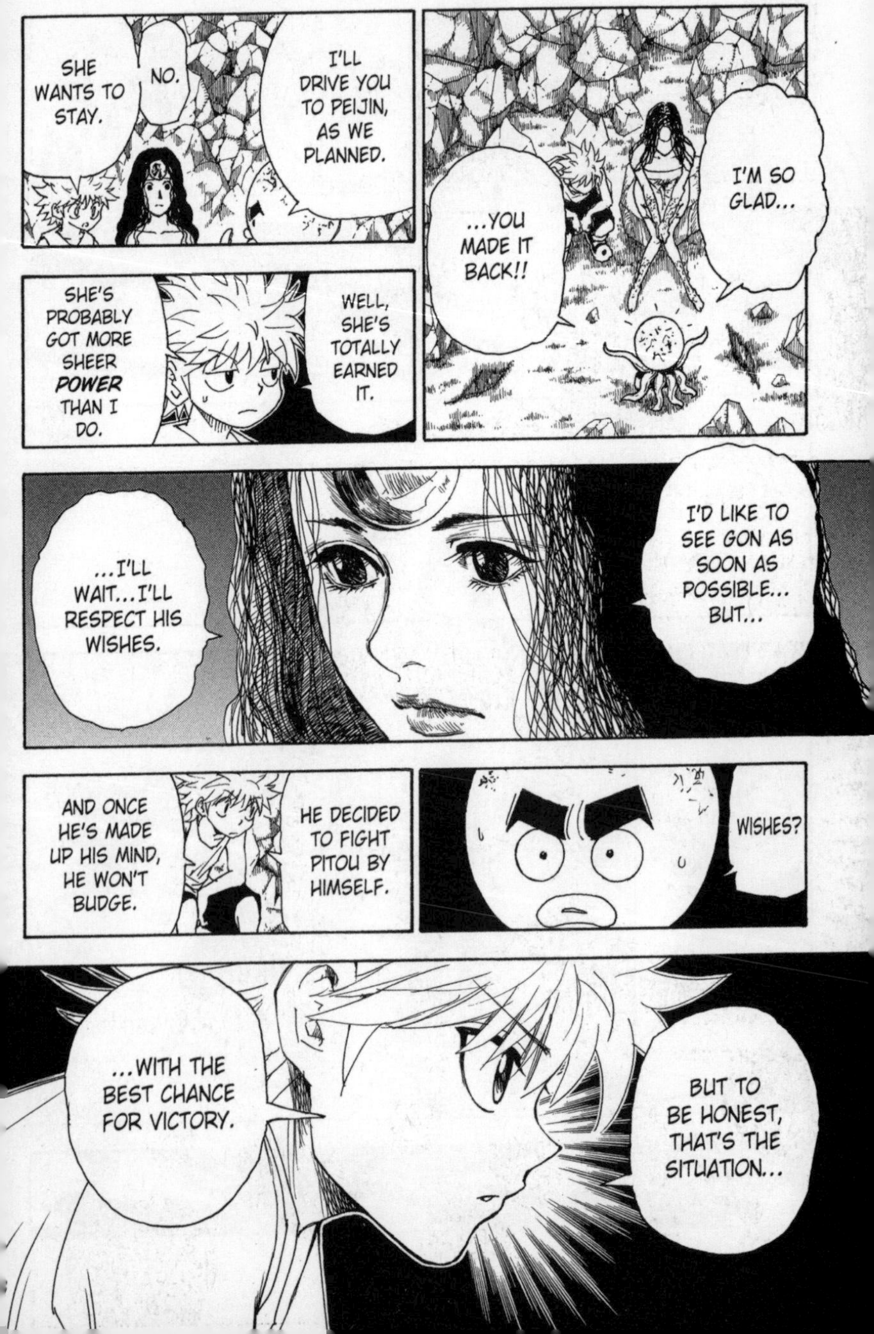
I'M SO GLAD...
...YOU MADE IT BACK!!
I'LL DRIVE YOU TO PEIJIN, AS WE PLANNED.
NO.
SHE WANTS TO STAY.
WELL, SHE'S TOTALLY EARNED IT.
SHE'S PROBABLY GOT MORE SHEER ***POWER*** THAN I DO.
I'D LIKE TO SEE GON AS SOON AS POSSIBLE... BUT...
...I'LL WAIT...I'LL RESPECT HIS WISHES.
WISHES?
HE DECIDED TO FIGHT PITOU BY HIMSELF.
AND ONCE HE'S MADE UP HIS MIND, HE WON'T BUDGE.
BUT TO BE HONEST, THAT'S THE SITUATION...
...WITH THE BEST CHANCE FOR VICTORY.

READ THIS WAY

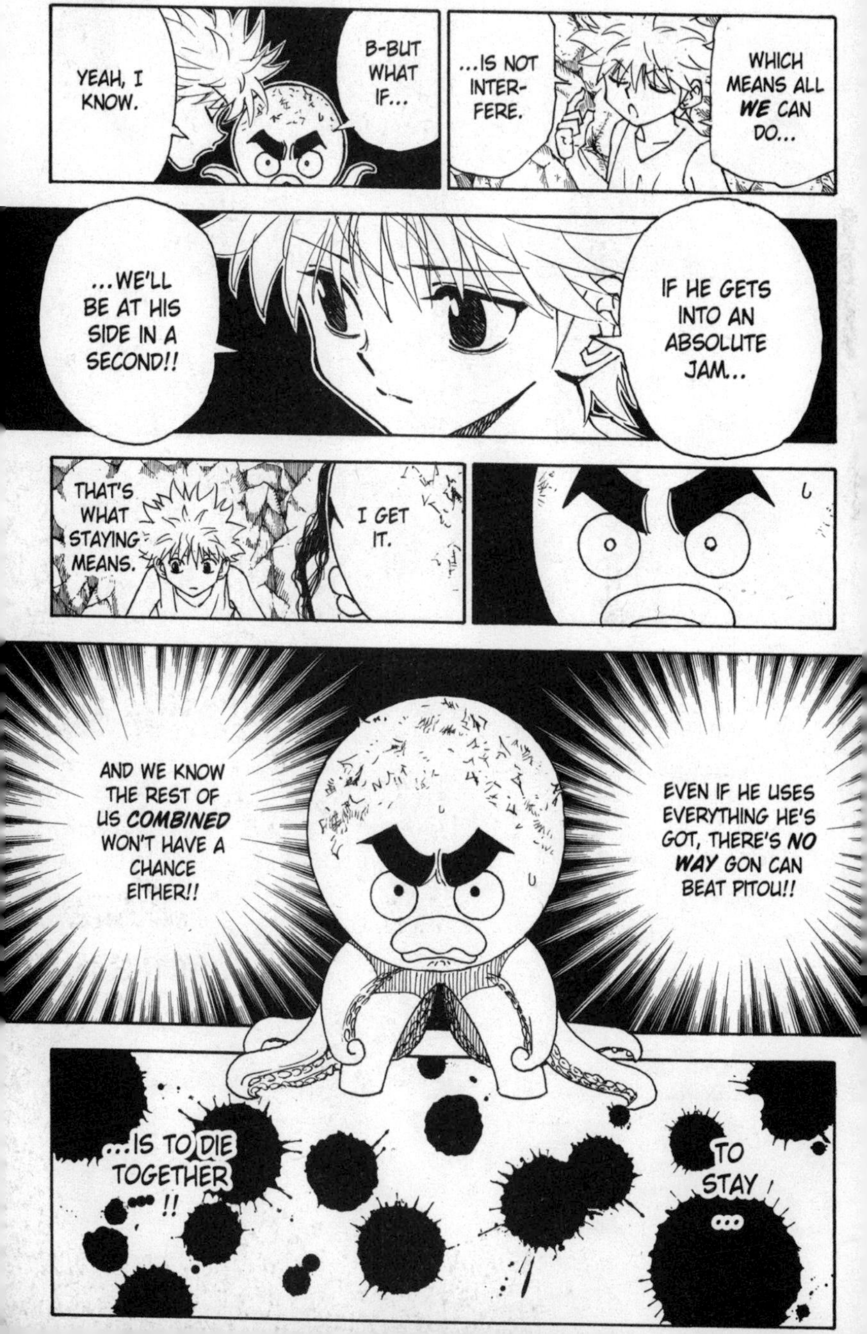

WHICH MEANS ALL WE CAN DO...
...IS NOT INTER-FERE.
B-BUT WHAT IF...
YEAH, I KNOW.
IF HE GETS INTO AN ABSOLUTE JAM...
...WE'LL BE AT HIS SIDE IN A SECOND!!
I GET IT.
THAT'S WHAT STAYING MEANS.
EVEN IF HE USES EVERYTHING HE'S GOT, THERE'S NO WAY GON CAN BEAT PITOU!!
AND WE KNOW THE REST OF US COMBINED WON'T HAVE A CHANCE EITHER!!
TO STAY...
...IS TO DIE TOGETHER...!!

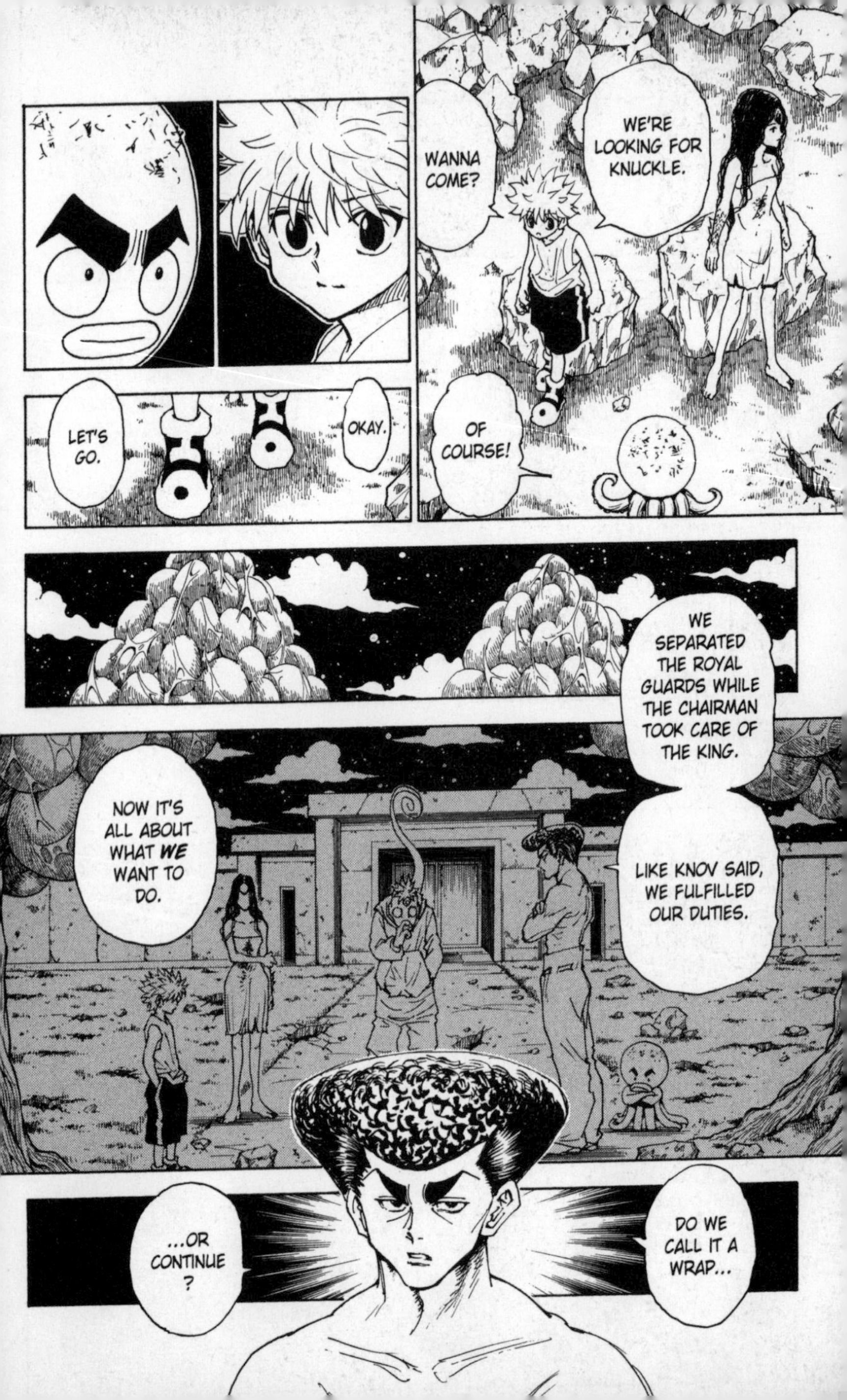
WE'RE LOOKING FOR KNUCKLE.
WANNA COME?
OF COURSE!
OKAY.
LET'S GO.
WE SEPARATED THE ROYAL GUARDS WHILE THE CHAIRMAN TOOK CARE OF THE KING.
LIKE KNOV SAID, WE FULFILLED OUR DUTIES.
NOW IT'S ALL ABOUT WHAT ***WE*** WANT TO DO.
DO WE CALL IT A WRAP...
...OR CONTINUE ?

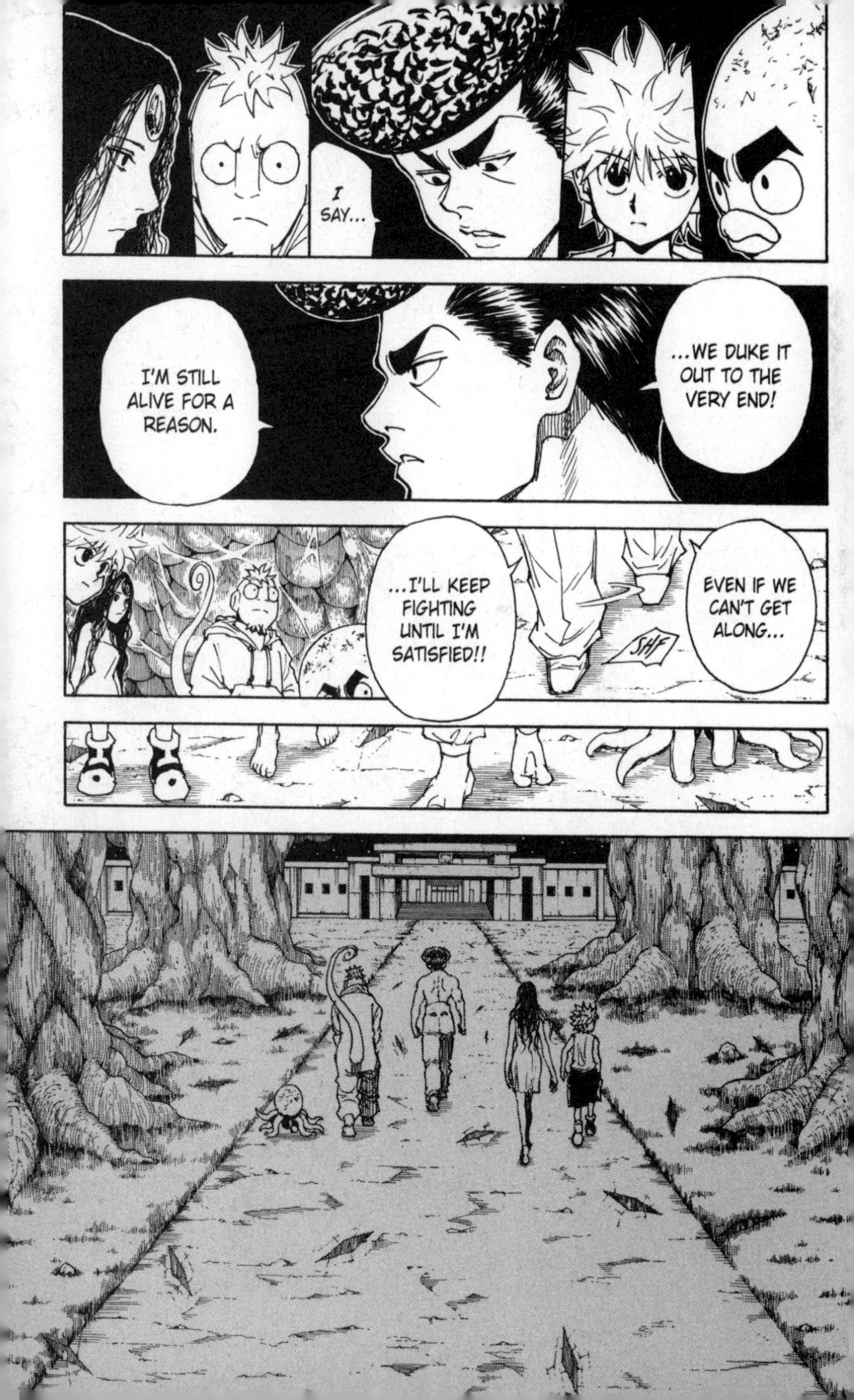
I SAY...
...WE DUKE IT OUT TO THE VERY END!
I'M STILL ALIVE FOR A REASON.
EVEN IF WE CAN'T GET ALONG...
SHF
...I'LL KEEP FIGHTING UNTIL I'M SATISFIED!!

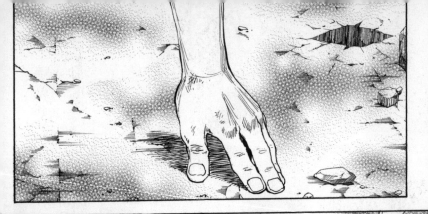

YOU'RE DONE.

SHf

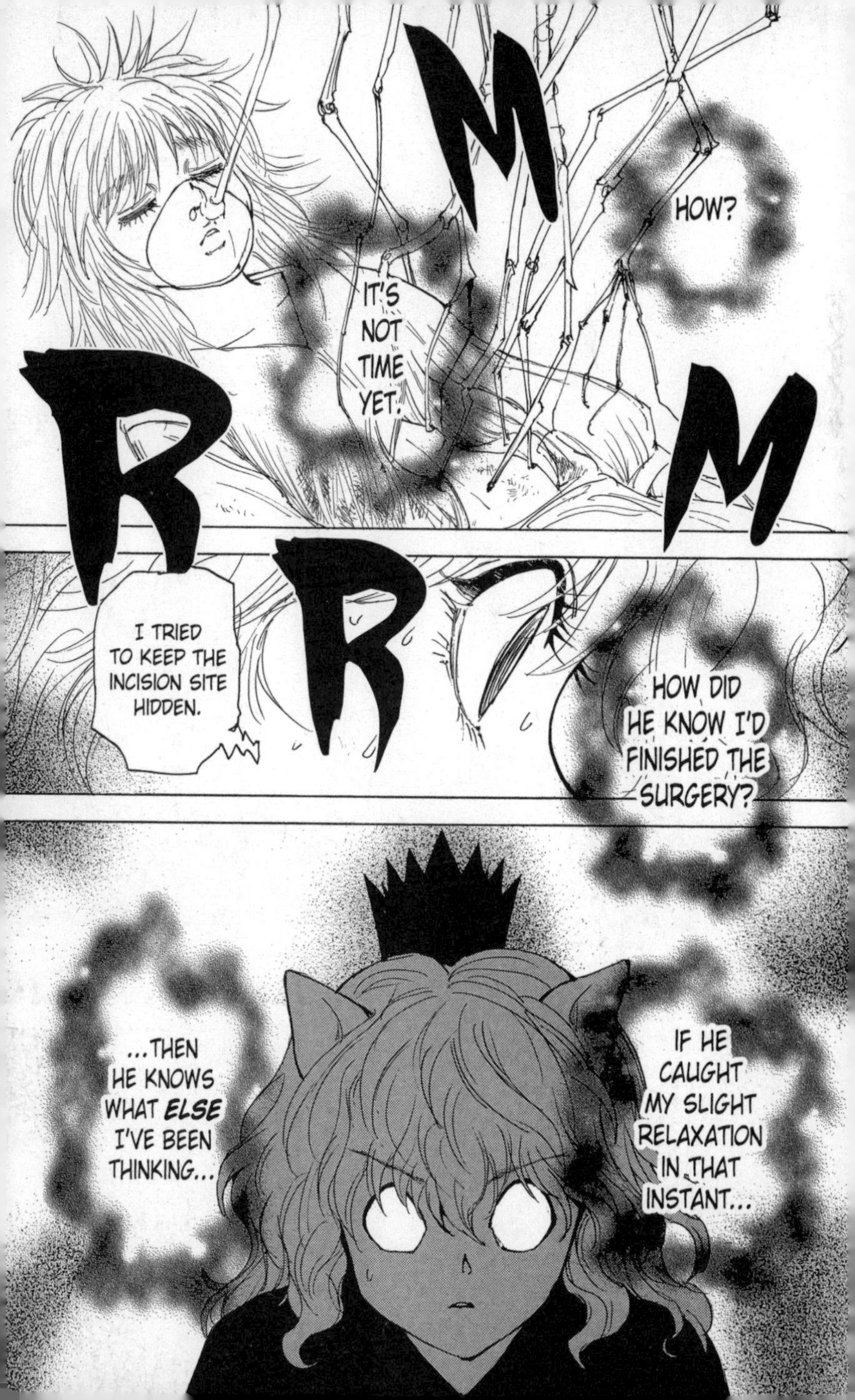

HOW?
IT'S NOT TIME YET.
RRMM
RR
HOW DID HE KNOW I'D FINISHED THE SURGERY?
I TRIED TO KEEP THE INCISION SITE HIDDEN.
IF HE CAUGHT MY SLIGHT RELAXATION IN THAT INSTANT...
...THEN HE KNOWS WHAT *ELSE* I'VE BEEN THINKING...

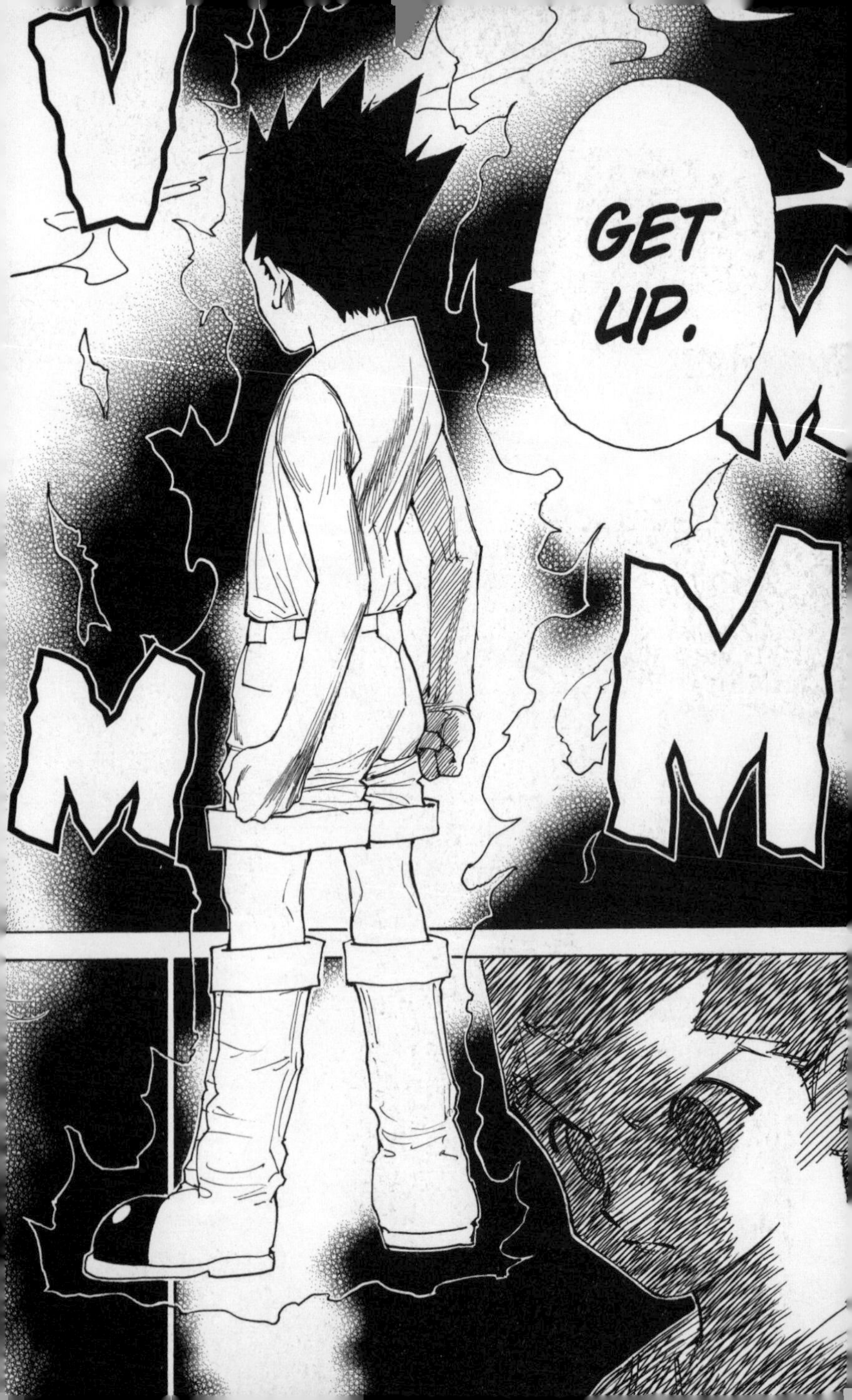
GET UP.

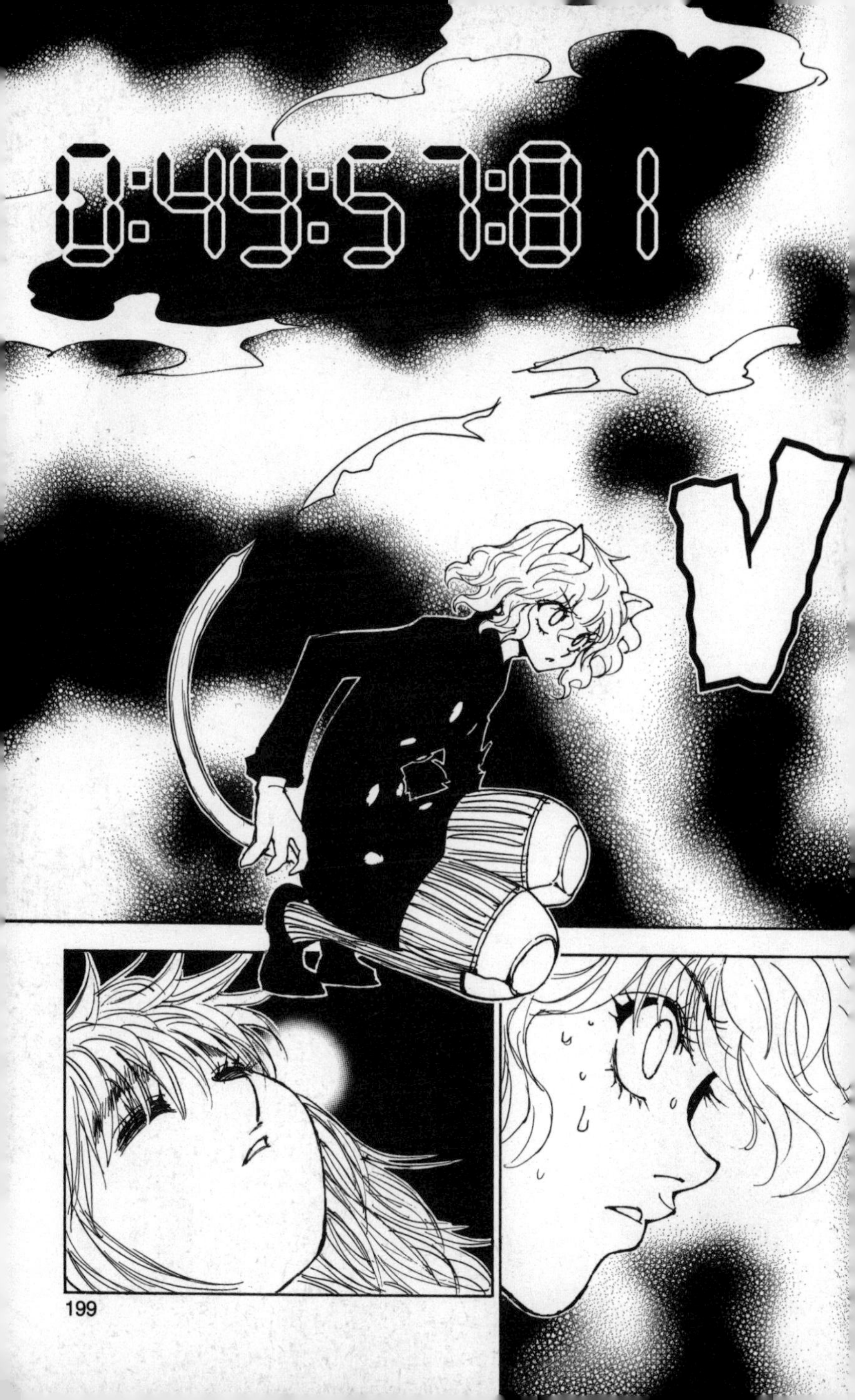
0:49:57:81
V

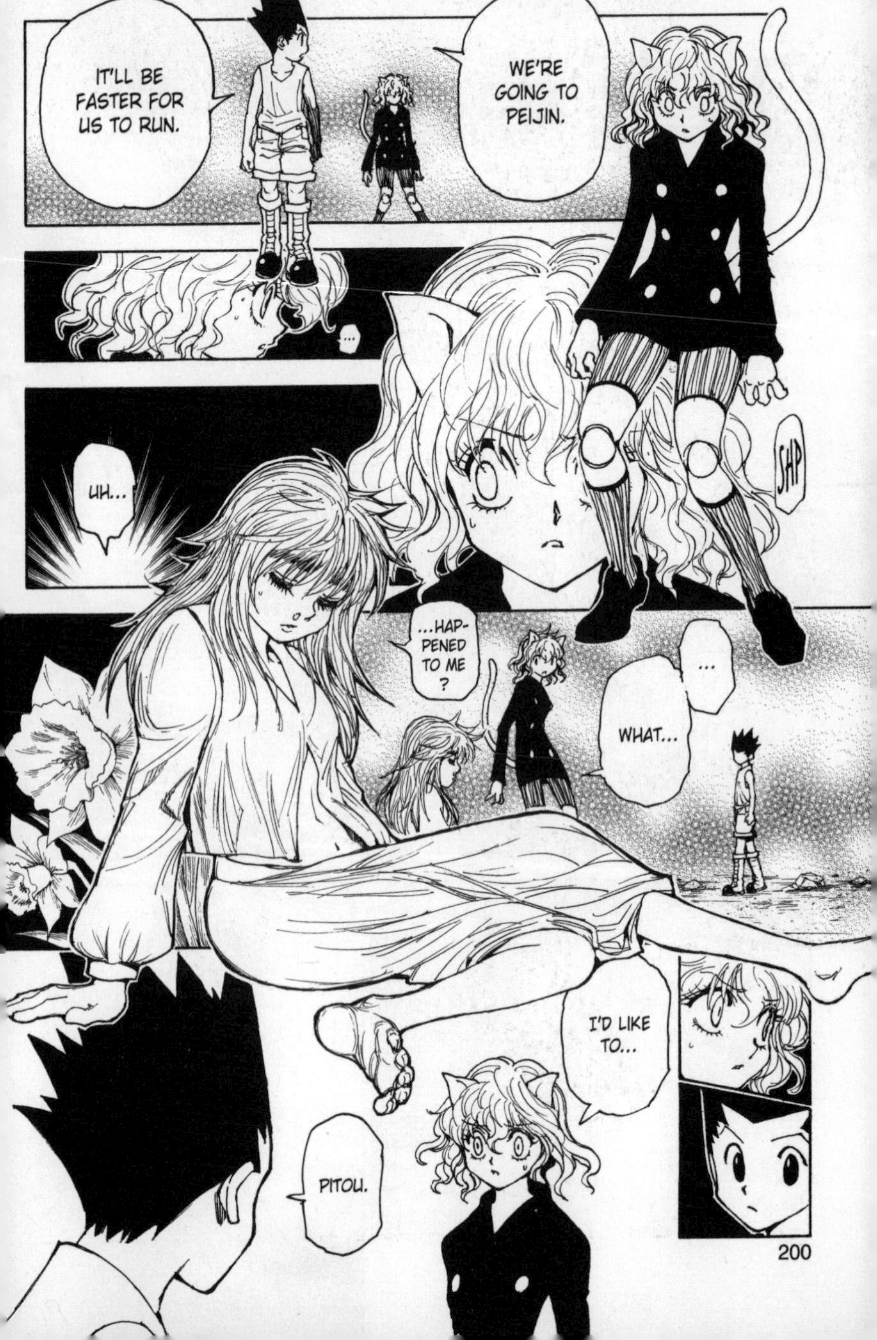

WE'RE GOING TO PEIJIN.
IT'LL BE FASTER FOR US TO RUN.
...
SHP
UH...
...
WHAT...
...HAP-PENED TO ME ?
I'D LIKE TO...
PITOU.

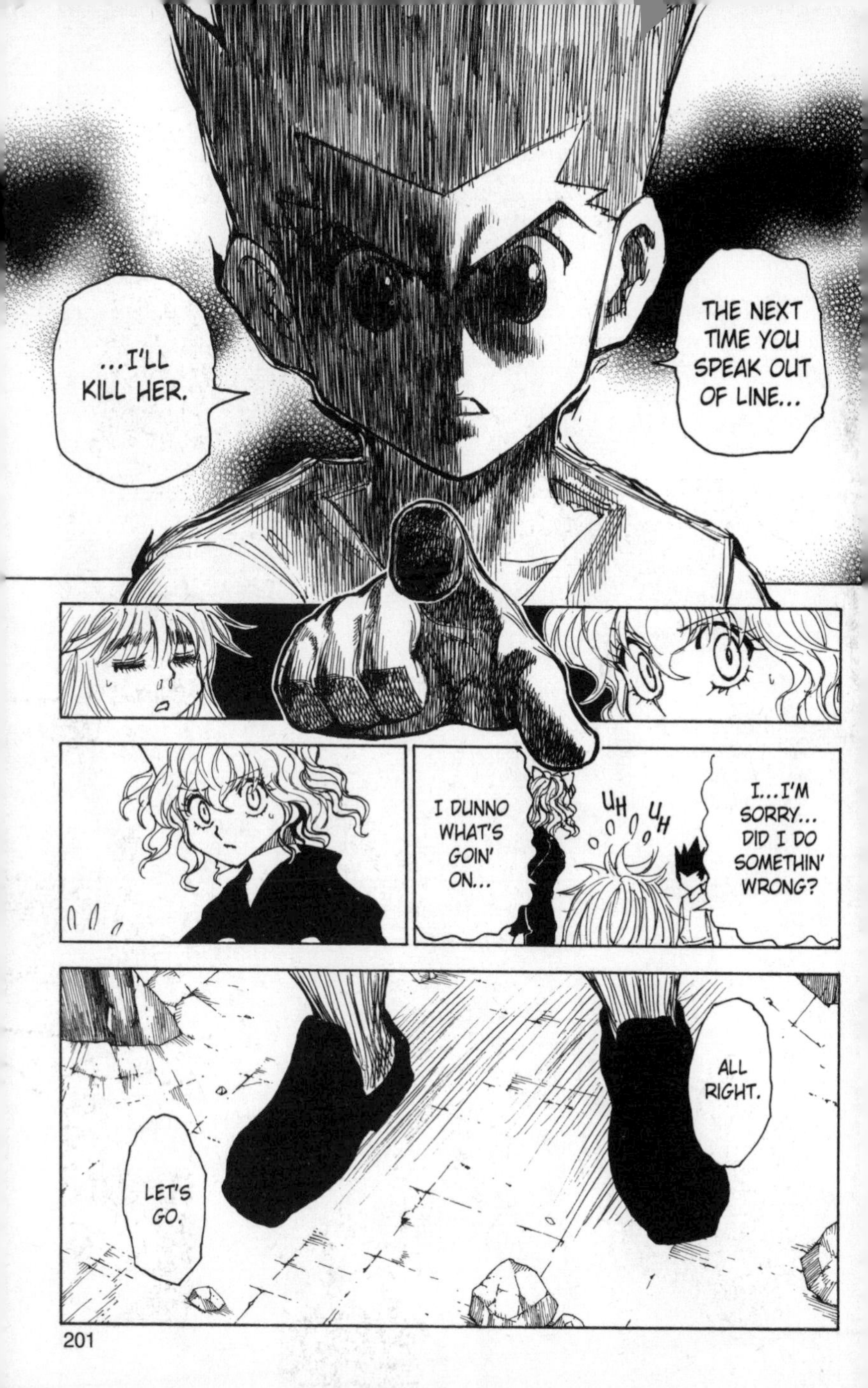
THE NEXT TIME YOU SPEAK OUT OF LINE...
...I'LL KILL HER.
I...I'M SORRY... DID I DO SOMETHIN' WRONG?
UH UH
I DUNNO WHAT'S GOIN' ON...
ALL RIGHT.
LET'S GO.

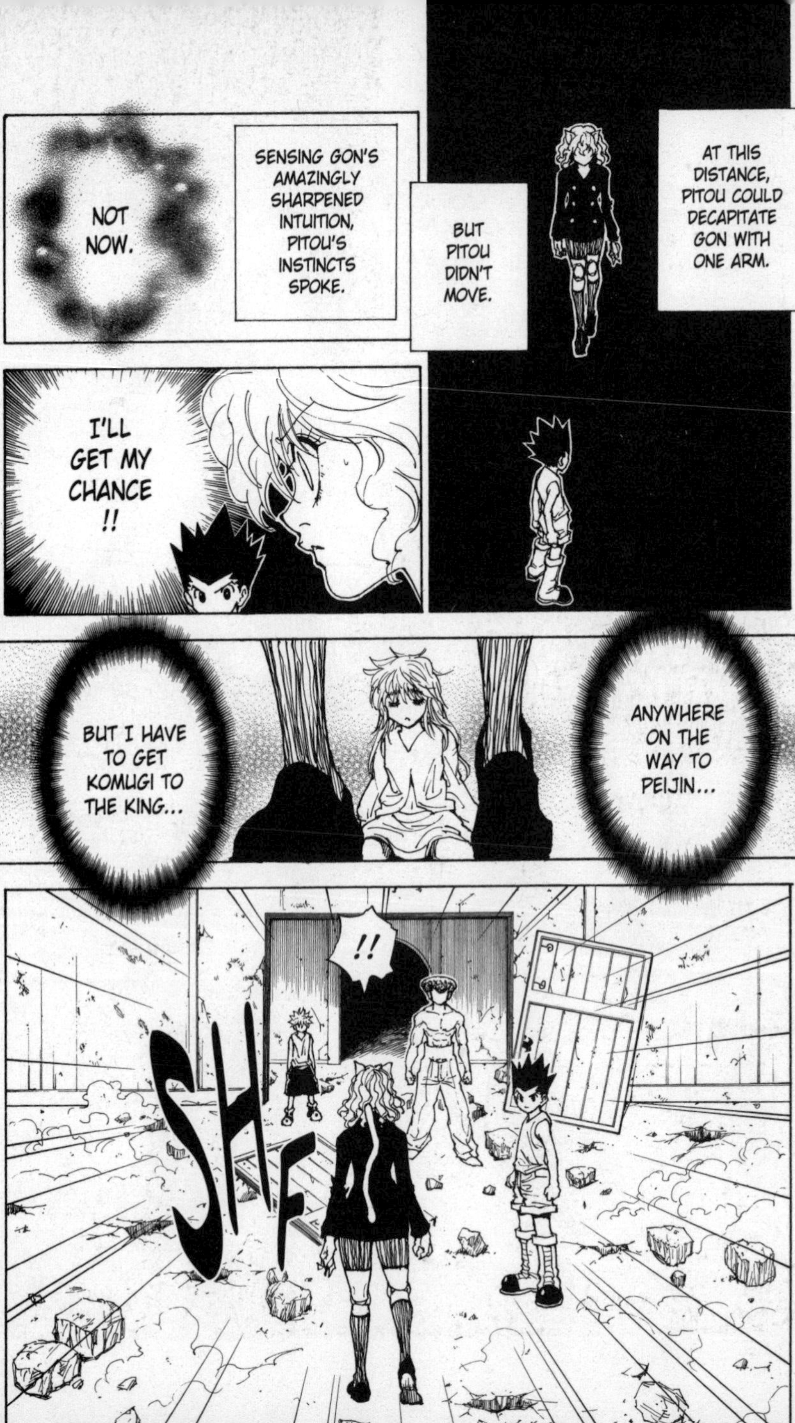
AT THIS DISTANCE, PITOU COULD DECAPITATE GON WITH ONE ARM.
BUT PITOU DIDN'T MOVE.
SENSING GON'S AMAZINGLY SHARPENED INTUITION, PITOU'S INSTINCTS SPOKE.
NOT NOW.
I'LL GET MY CHANCE !!
ANYWHERE ON THE WAY TO PEIJIN...
BUT I HAVE TO GET KOMUGI TO THE KING...
!!
SHF

READ THIS WAY

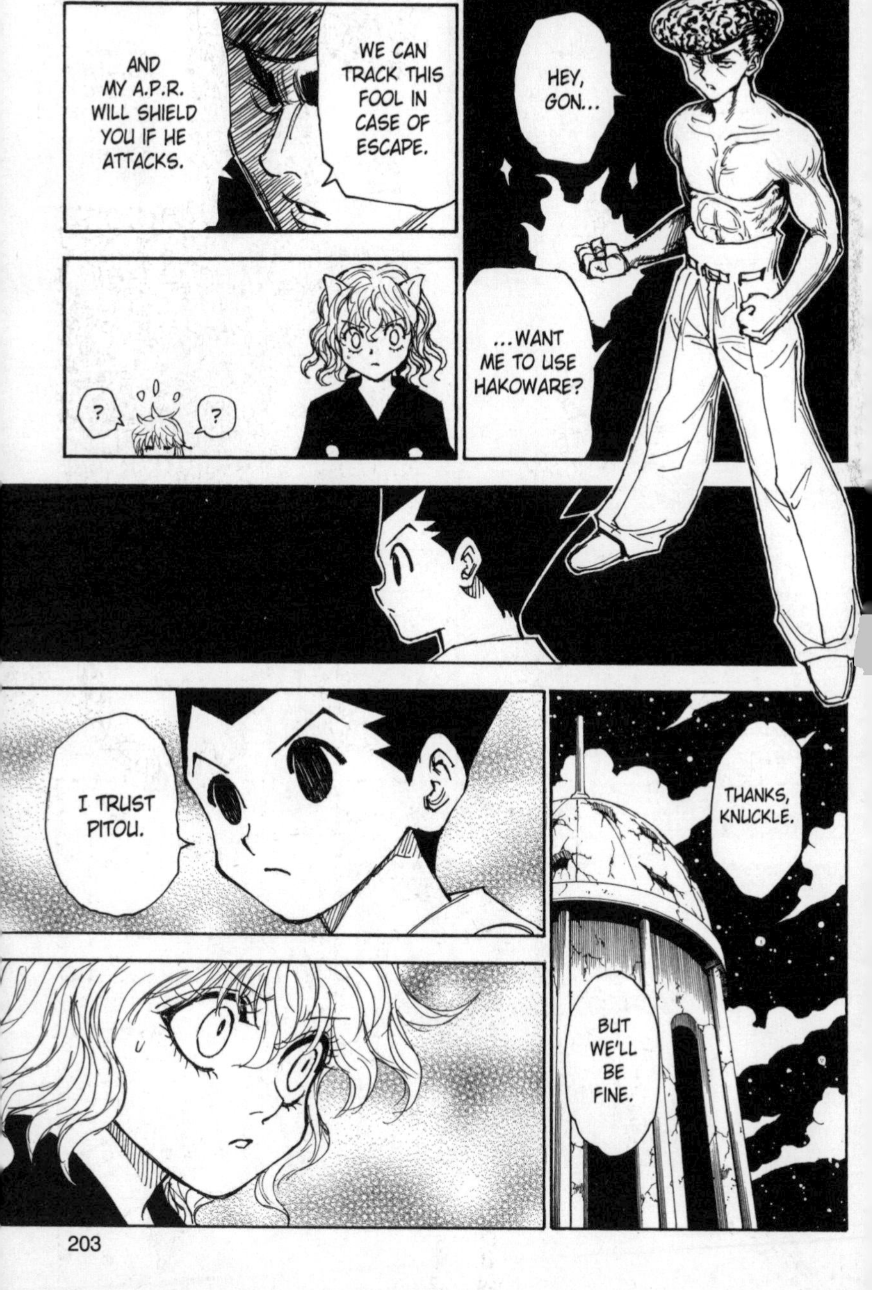

HEY, GON...
...WANT ME TO USE HAKOWARE?
WE CAN TRACK THIS FOOL IN CASE OF ESCAPE.
AND MY A.P.R. WILL SHIELD YOU IF HE ATTACKS.
?
?
THANKS, KNUCKLE.
BUT WE'LL BE FINE.
I TRUST PITOU.

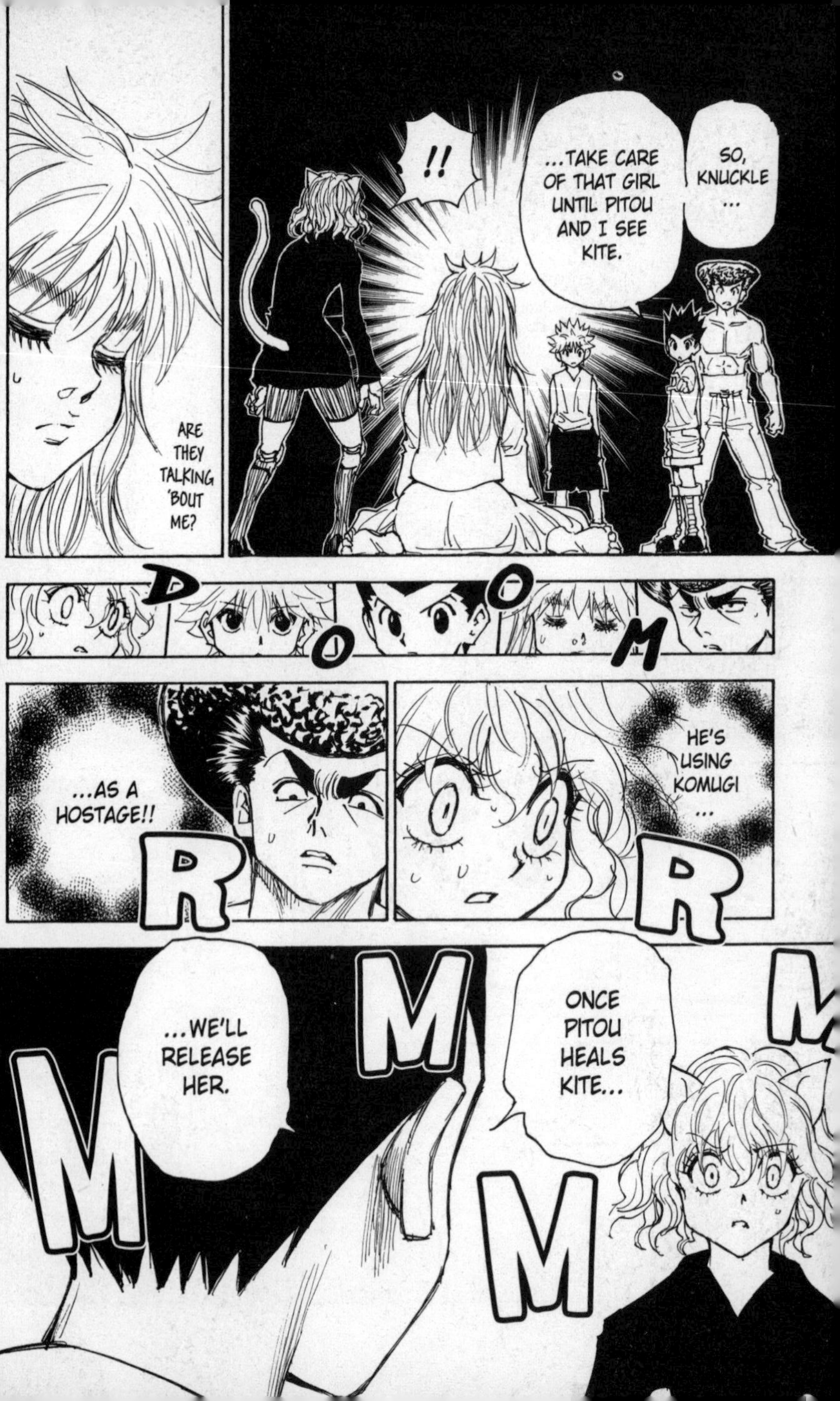
SO, KNUCKLE ...
...TAKE CARE OF THAT GIRL UNTIL PITOU AND I SEE KITE.
!!
ARE THEY TALKING 'BOUT ME?
DOOM
HE'S USING KOMUGI ...
...AS A HOSTAGE!!
RR
MMMMM
ONCE PITOU HEALS KITE...
...WE'LL RELEASE HER.

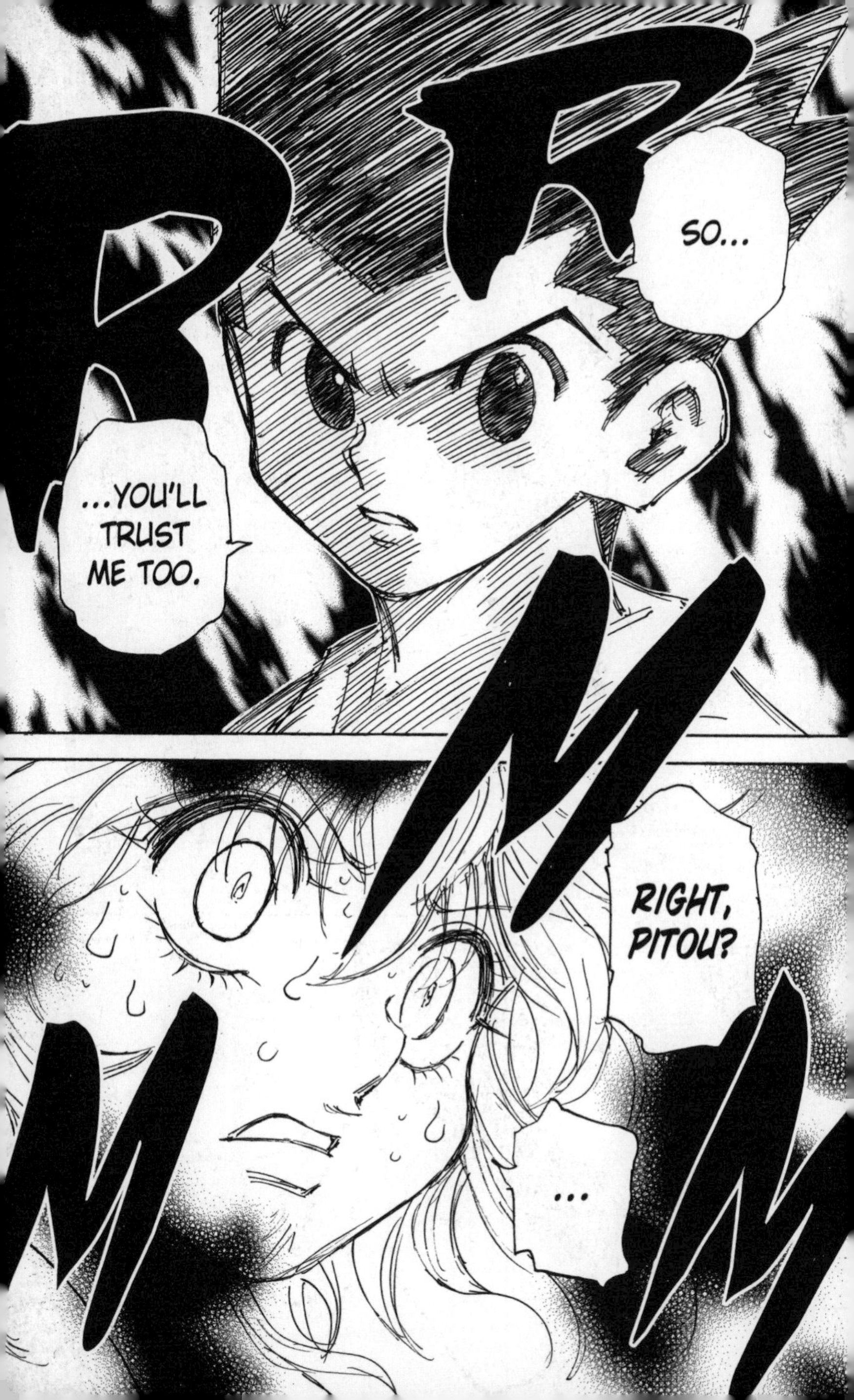
SO...
...YOU'LL TRUST ME TOO.
RIGHT, PITOU?
...

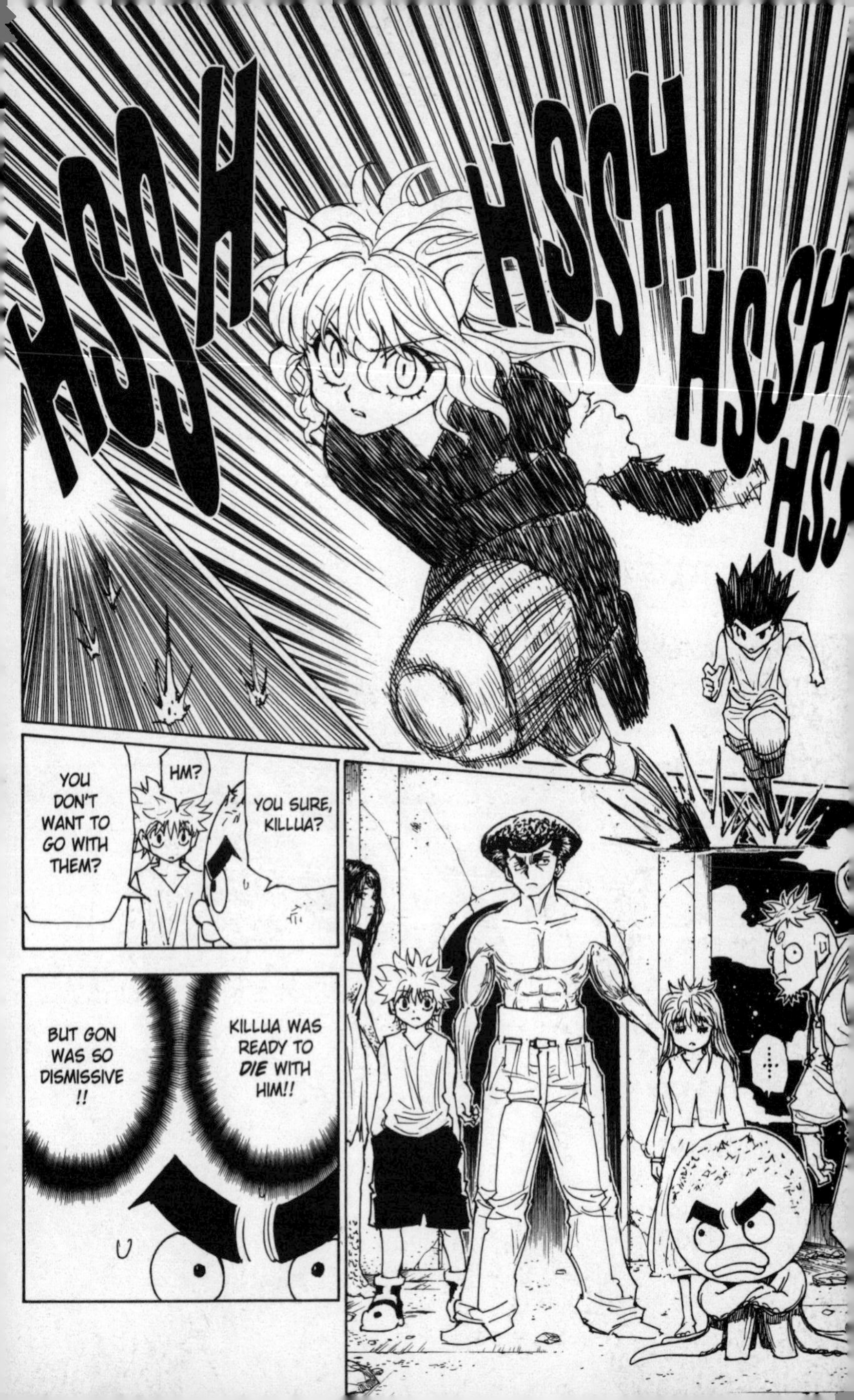

HSSH
HSSH
HSSH
HSS
…
YOU SURE, KILLUA?
HM?
YOU DON'T WANT TO GO WITH THEM?
KILLUA WAS READY TO *DIE* WITH HIM!!
BUT GON WAS SO DISMISSIVE!!

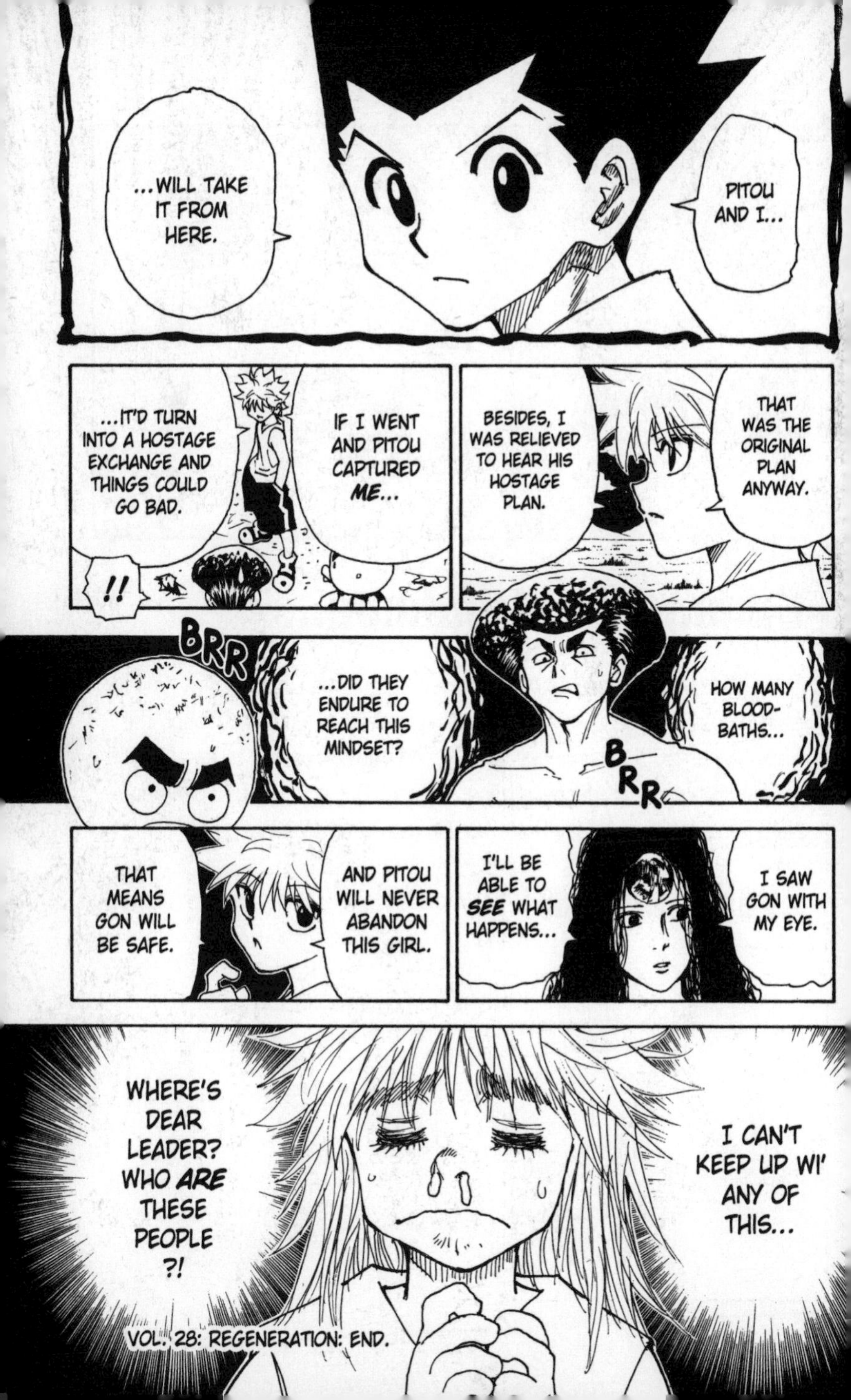
PITOU AND I...
...WILL TAKE IT FROM HERE.
THAT WAS THE ORIGINAL PLAN ANYWAY.
BESIDES, I WAS RELIEVED TO HEAR HIS HOSTAGE PLAN.
IF I WENT AND PITOU CAPTURED *ME*...
...IT'D TURN INTO A HOSTAGE EXCHANGE AND THINGS COULD GO BAD.
!!
HOW MANY BLOOD-BATHS...
BRR
...DID THEY ENDURE TO REACH THIS MINDSET?
BRR
I SAW GON WITH MY EYE.
I'LL BE ABLE TO *SEE* WHAT HAPPENS...
AND PITOU WILL NEVER ABANDON THIS GIRL.
THAT MEANS GON WILL BE SAFE.
I CAN'T KEEP UP WI' ANY OF THIS...
WHERE'S DEAR LEADER? WHO *ARE* THESE PEOPLE ?!
VOL. 28: REGENERATION: END.

Coming Next Volume...

Gon and his friends are on their last legs…but the Chimera Ant King is more powerful than ever! With the King revived by Pouf and Youpi, the Ants gather for their final assault. Gon has no choice but to gamble all his Nen on one final, desperate last chance. But how will he spend his Nen—and will it be enough to stop the return of the King?

Available now!

Seraph of the End
VAMPIRE REIGN

STORY BY Takaya Kagami ART BY Yamato Yamamoto
STORYBOARDS BY Daisuke Furuya

Vampires reign— humans revolt!

Seraph of the End
VAMPIRE REIGN
1
STORY BY Takaya Kagami
ART BY Yamato Yamamoto

Yuichiro's dream of killing every vampire is near-impossible, given that vampires are seven times stronger than humans, and the only way to kill them is by mastering Cursed Gear, advanced demon-possessed weaponry. Not to mention that humanity's most elite Vampire Extermination Unit, the Moon Demon Company, wants nothing to do with Yuichiro unless he can prove he's willing to work in a team—which is the last thing he wants!

THE LATEST CHAPTERS SERIALIZED IN WEEKLY SHONEN JUMP

RATED T+ FOR OLDER TEEN ratings.viz.com

SHONEN JUMP ADVANCED www.shonenjump.com

VIZ media www.viz.com

A KILLER COMEDY FROM *WEEKLY SHONEN JUMP*

A S S A S S I N A T I O N
CLASSROOM

STORY AND ART BY
YUSEI MATSUI

Ever caught yourself screaming, "I could just kill that teacher"?
What would it take to justify such antisocial behavior
and weeks of detention? Especially if he's the best
teacher you've ever had? Giving you an "F" on a quiz?
Mispronouncing your name during roll call...*again*? How about
blowing up the moon and threatening to do the same to
Mother Earth—unless you take him out first?! Plus a reward
of a cool 100 million from the Ministry of Defense!

Okay, now that you're committed... How are you going to
pull this off? What does your pathetic class of misfits have
in their arsenal to combat Teach's alien technology, bizarre
powers and...*tentacles*?!

ANSATSU KYOSHITSU © 2012 by Yusei Matsui/SHUEISHA Inc.

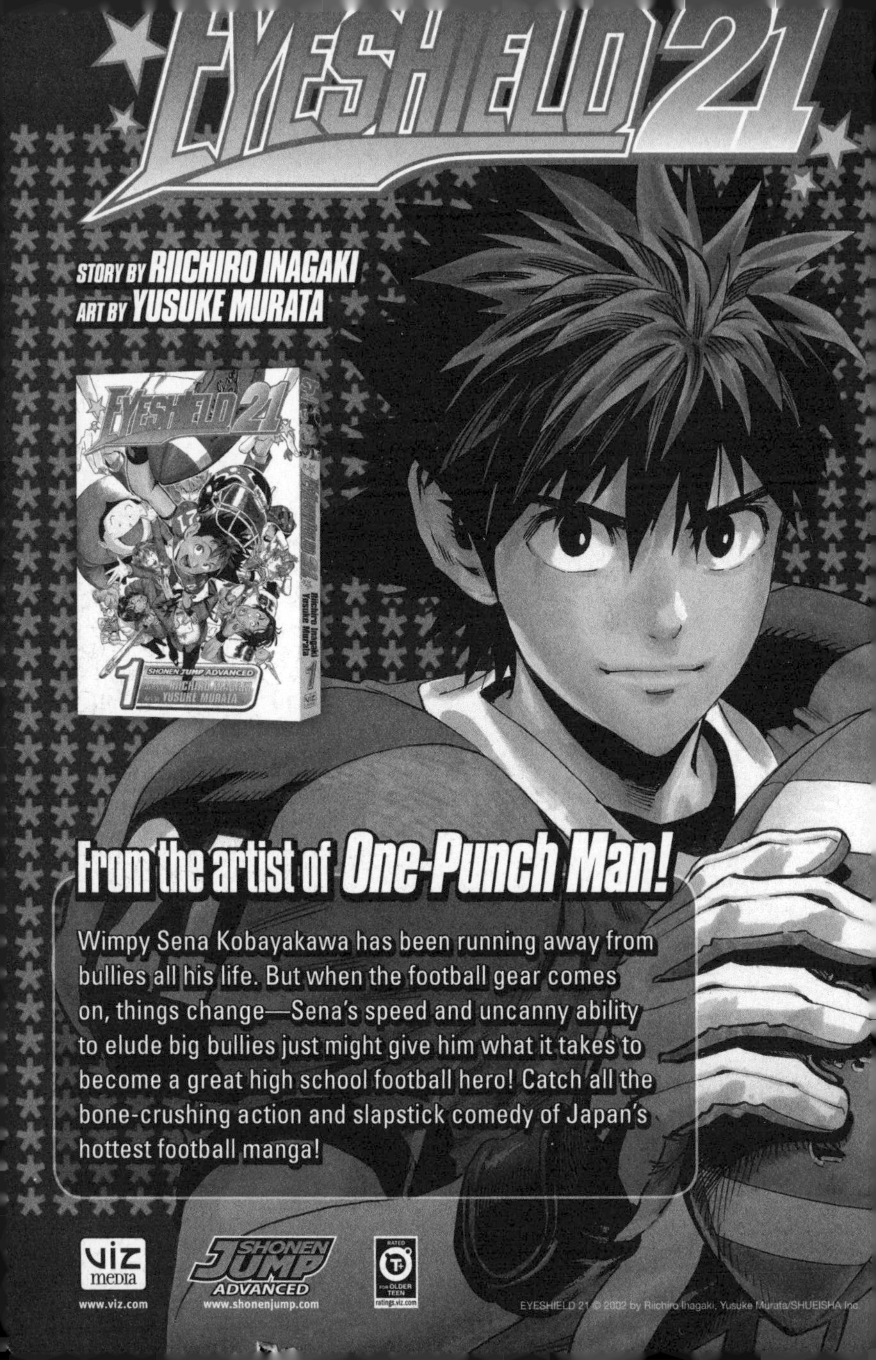
EYESHIELD 21
STORY BY RIICHIRO INAGAKI
ART BY YUSUKE MURATA
From the artist of One-Punch Man!
Wimpy Sena Kobayakawa has been running away from bullies all his life. But when the football gear comes on, things change—Sena's speed and uncanny ability to elude big bullies just might give him what it takes to become a great high school football hero! Catch all the bone-crushing action and slapstick comedy of Japan's hottest football manga!
viz media
www.viz.com
SHONEN JUMP ADVANCED
www.shonenjump.com
RATED T+ FOR OLDER TEEN
ratings.viz.com
EYESHIELD 21 © 2002 by Riichiro Inagaki, Yusuke Murata/SHUEISHA Inc.

THE BEST SELLING MANGA SERIES IN THE WORLD!

ONE PIECE

Story & Art by **EIICHIRO ODA**

As a child, **Monkey D. Luffy** was inspired to become a pirate by listening to the tales of the buccaneer "Red-Haired" Shanks. But Luffy's life changed when he accidentally ate the Gum-Gum Devil Fruit and gained the power to stretch like rubber...at the cost of never being able to swim again! Years later, still vowing to become the king of the pirates, Luffy sets out on his adventure in search of the legendary "One Piece," said to be the greatest treasure in the world...

www.shonenjump.com   www.viz.com

ONE PIECE © 1997 by Eiichiro Oda/SHUEISHA Inc.

A PREMIUM BOX SET OF THE FIRST TWO STORY ARCS OF ONE PIECE!

A PIRATE'S TREASURE FOR ANY MANGA FAN!

STORY AND ART BY EIICHIRO ODA

Comes with
EXCLUSIVE
POSTER
and the
ROMANCE
DAWN
mini-comic!

As a child, Monkey D. Luffy dreamed of becoming King of the Pirates.
But his life changed when he accidentally gained the power to stretch like
rubber...at the cost of never being able to swim again! Years later, Luffy sets off
in search of the "One Piece," said to be the greatest treasure in the world...

**This box set includes VOLUMES 1-23, which comprise
the EAST BLUE and BAROQUE WORKS story arcs.**

EXCLUSIVE PREMIUMS and GREAT SAVINGS
over buying the individual volumes!

WWW.SHONENJUMP.COM

ONE PIECE © 1997 by Eiichiro Oda/SHUEISHA Inc.

RATED
T
FOR
TEEN
ratings.viz.com

VIZ
MEDIA
www.viz.com

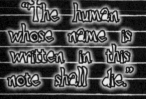

SHONEN JUMP
DEATH NOTE
デスノート

"The human whose name is written in this note shall die."

READ WHERE IT ALL BEGAN IN THE MANGA—ALL 12 VOLUMES AVAILABLE NOW

AN ORIGINAL NOVEL BASED ON THE CHARACTERS AND CONCEPTS FROM THE POPULAR MANGA SERIES

A GUIDE TO THE MANGA SERIES, COMPLETE WITH CHARACTER BIOS, STORYLINE SUMMARIES, INTERVIEWS WITH CREATORS TSUGUMI OHBA AND TAKESHI OBATA, PRODUCTION NOTES AND COMMENTARIES, AND BONUS MANGA PAGES

www.shonenjump.com

AVAILABLE AT YOUR LOCAL BOOKSTORE AND COMIC STORE.

RATED
T+
FOR OLDER
TEEN
ratings.viz.com

VIZ
media
www.viz.com

DEATH NOTE © 2003 by Tsugumi Ohba, Takeshi Obata/SHUEISHA Inc.
DEATH NOTE - ANOTHER NOTE LOS ANGELES BB RENZOKU SATSUJIN JIKEN - © 2006 by NISIO ISIN, Tsugumi Ohba, Takeshi Obata/SHUEISHA Inc.
DEATH NOTE HOW TO READ 13 © 2006 by Tsugumi Ohba, Takeshi Obata/SHUEISHA Inc.

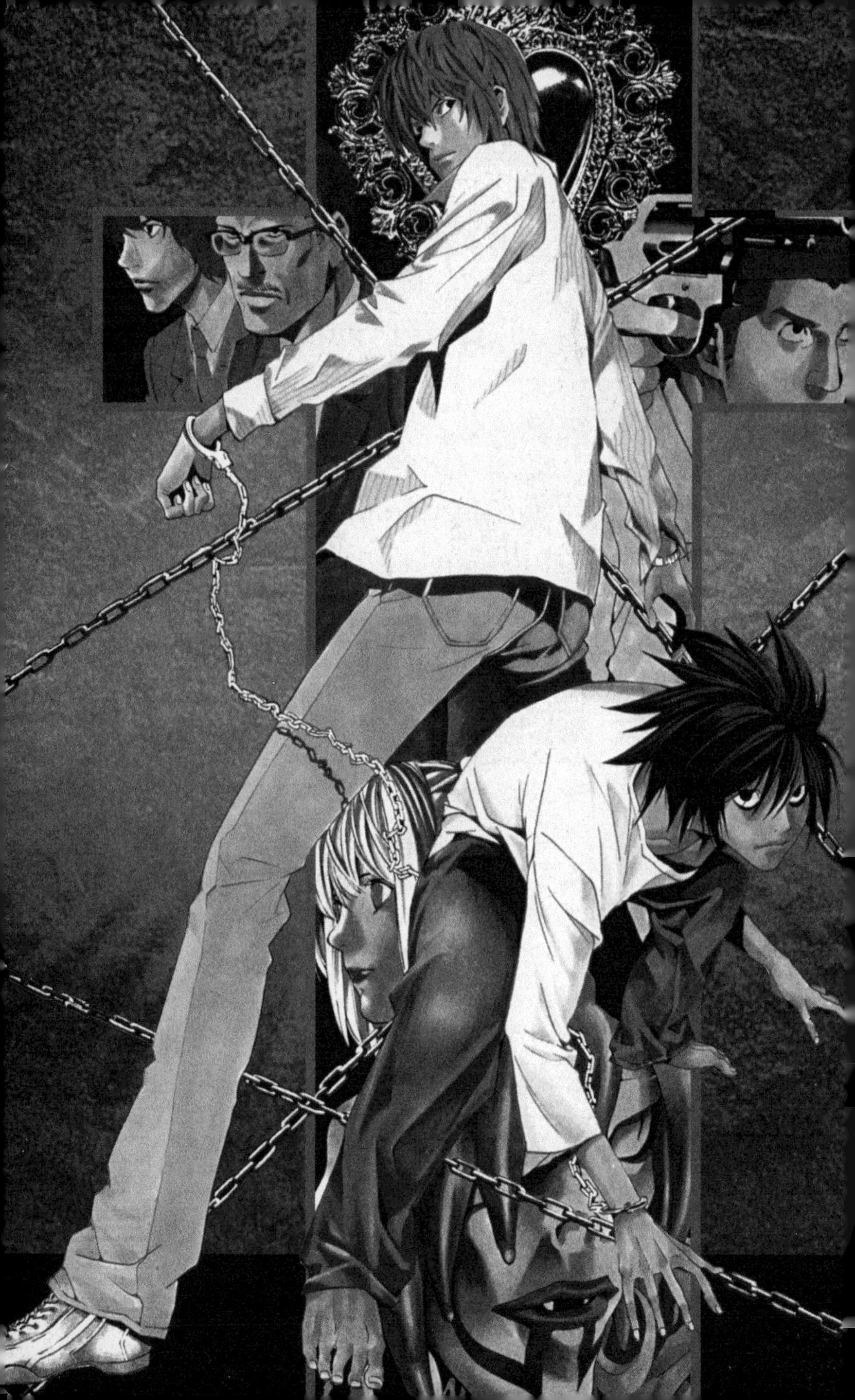

You're Reading in the Wrong Direction!!

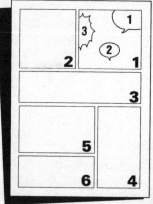

Whoops! Guess what? You're starting at the wrong end of the comic!

…It's true! In keeping with the original Japanese format, **Hunter x Hunter** is meant to be read from right to left, starting in the upper-right corner.

Unlike English, which is read from left to right, Japanese is read from right to left, meaning that action, sound effects and word-balloon order are completely reversed… something which can make readers unfamiliar with Japanese feel pretty backwards themselves. For this reason, manga or Japanese comics published in the U.S. in English have sometimes been published "flopped"— that is, printed in exact reverse order, as though seen from the other side of a mirror.

By flopping pages, U.S. publishers can avoid confusing readers, but the compromise is not without its downside. For one thing, a character in a flopped manga series who once wore in the original Japanese version a T-shirt emblazoned with "M A Y" (as in "the merry month of") now wears one which reads "Y A M"! Additionally, many manga creators in Japan are themselves unhappy with the process, as some feel the mirror-imaging of their art skews their original intentions.

We are proud to bring you Yoshihiro Togashi's **Hunter x Hunter** in the original unflopped format. For now, though, turn to the other side of the book and let the adventure begin…!

—Editor